❧ Narrating the Nation ❧

MAKING SENSE OF HISTORY

Studies in Historical Cultures
General Editors: Jörn Rüsen, Allan Megill and Alon Confino
in Association with Angelika Wülff

NARRATING THE NATION

Representations in History, Media and the Arts

Edited by
Stefan Berger, Linas Eriksonas and Andrew Mycock

Berghahn Books
NEW YORK · OXFORD

Published in 2008 by

Berghahn Books

www.berghahnbooks.com

EUROPEAN
SCIENCE
FOUNDATION
SETTING SCIENCE AGENDAS FOR EUROPE

Library of Congress Cataloguing-in-Publication Data

Narrating the nation : representations in history, media, and the arts / edited
by Stefan Berger, Linas Eriksonas, and Andrew Mycock.
 p. cm. -- (Making sense of history)
Includes bibliographical references and index.
ISBN 978-1-84545-424-1
1. Nationalism and the arts--Europe. 2. Arts, European. 3. Nationalism
and historiography--Europe. I. Berger, Stefan. II. Eriksonas, Linas. III.
Mycock, Andrew.

NX180.N38N37 2008
940.072--dc22

2008026632085

British Library Cataloguing in Publication Data

A catalogue record for this book is available from the British Library.

Printed in the United States on acid-free paper.

ISBN 978-1-84545-424-1 (hardback)

*To Neil Edmunds (1966–2008), fellow historian
and dedicated sportsman – in memory of
so many Friday afternoons*

Contents

Part III: Narrating the Nation as Film

Part IV: Narrating the Nation as Art and Music

Part V: Non-European Perspectives on Nation and Narration

List of Illustrations

Acknowledgements

I am grateful to the European Science Foundation, which is funding the programme 'Representations of the Past: The Writing of National Histories in 19th and 20th Century Europe' (NHIST, 2003–2008). This volume is the result of the first cross-team conference of the programme, which took place at the University of Glamorgan between 20 and 22 May 2004. Most of the contributions to this volume were presented as papers to the conference and thereafter comprehensively revised for publication. I am grateful to Dr Hugo Frey and Prof. Philip Bohlman for drafting additional chapters to this volume. They have both filled important gaps in the genres covered by this book. I would also like to thank four subsequent programme co-ordinators: Dr Linas Eriksonas, Dr Jonathan Hensher, Dr Andrew Mycock and Sven de Roode for all their hard work on the manuscript, which needed considerable editorial work, as many of the contributions are penned by authors whose first language is not English. Dr Eriksonas, as co-editor, has been closely involved in planning the conference and putting together the manuscript. I am particularly indebted to Dr Mycock, my other co-editor, for finalising the manuscript swiftly and with great professionalism.

NHIST has been a wonderful intellectual journey. On the way, I have met many fascinating colleagues and made many new friends. I would like to thank in particular my co-chairs, Prof. Guy Marchal and Prof. Christoph Conrad, for sharing many of the burdens and pleasures of directing a programme involving more than one hundred scholars from 30 European countries. The team leaders of the four teams have been doing splendid work in keeping their teams under control and alert, and the chairs of the programme would have been lost long ago without the wonderful work done by Professors Ilaria Porciani, Chris Lorenz, Matthias Middell, Lluis Roura, Tibor Frank and Frank Hadler. At the European Science Foundation, Dr Monique van Donzel and Ms Madelise Blumenroeder have been extremely supportive of the programme and very patient with answering queries and making the (near) impossible possible. Last, but not least a very special thanks to Dr Maurice Bric from the ESF's Standing

Committee for the Humanities who has given so generously of his time and valuable advice to help the programme achieve its goals.

Finally, I would also like to thank my colleagues at the University of Glamorgan, where the conference, which gave birth to this volume, took place. They had the courage to appoint me to a chair in history when I was just 35 years old and they welcomed me to the South Wales valleys very warmly. I had the privilege of spending five very good years with them, between 2000 and 2005. They were intellectually stimulating years and I feel that I can honestly say: 'Ich habe noch einen Koffer in Südwales'.

Stefan Berger
The University of Manchester

Narrating the Nation:
Historiography and Other Genres

STEFAN BERGER

Nation is narration.[1] The stories we tell each other about our national belonging and being constitute the nation. These stories change over time and place and are always contested, often violently so. Few paradigms in the realm of cultural sense-production have been as powerful as the national one, and the prominence of nationalism as an ideology and social movement in the world of today testifies to its continued and global appeal. The need for a better understanding of national narratives and how they have functioned from the early nineteenth century to the present day led the European Science Foundation to fund a five-year programme entitled 'Representations of the Past: The Writing of National Histories in Nineteenth and Twentieth Century Europe' (NHIST), which ran between 2003 and 2008.[2]

Under this programme, four teams co-operated closely to investigate the institutions, networks and communities that produced national histories and were themselves influenced by the idea of national history. They explored the construction, erosion and reconstruction of national histories in their relationship with other master narratives structuring diverse forms of historical writing (such as class, race, religion and gender). They discussed the interrelationship between national histories and regional, European and world histories. Moreover, they investigated the impact of borderlands and overlapping national histories on the spatial construction of national narratives. The programme focused on a systematic and comprehensive comparison of national historiographies in Europe that took into account the processes of cultural transfer between these historiographies. However, the programme directors and team leaders were not blind to the need to explore the importance of other genres to the evolution and shaping of national narratives, which is why they organised a conference on this topic at the University of Glamorgan in May 2004.[3] This book is largely the result of that conference. It begins with three chapters on the relationship between scientific history writing and the promotion of national narratives, followed by explorations of national narratives in other genres. The second part deals with literary representations of the national past, while the third part discusses film, and the fourth part analyses the relationship between national identity, architecture, the fine arts and music. A final section introduces some non-European perspectives on narrations of the nation.

For more than ten years now the topic of nation and narration has been a major theme in arts and humanities research. In particular, the recent turn towards research on memory has deepened the interest in the diverse ways in which collective identities (such as national identities) have been constructed.[4] Although one still encounters regularly the use of memory as synonymous with history, many writers have pointed out that the two need to be kept apart. One does not have to go as far as Pierre Nora in arguing that history and memory are incompatible. In fact, as many of the contributions to this volume suggest, history has contributed to the shaping of collective memories just as the latter have impacted on the writing of histories. This introduction will relate the arguments of the contributions in this volume to the wider research project of NHIST and point out in which ways they shed new light on our understanding of how stories of the national past have been and are being told.[5]

In part one Alan Megill's thoughts on the relationship between scientific enquiry (*Wissenschaft*) and national history start from a detailed critique of the programme proposal underlying the NHIST project. He is especially mistrustful of what he perceives as the political commitment of the programme, namely to help denationalise European history. Instead, he pleads for a form of history writing which is committed only to the search for truthfulness. The more the historians are able to distance the national past from the present, he argues, the more they are likely to fulfil what should be their major aim: to debunk mythical and untruthful speaking about the national past. He draws on a wide range of thinkers about history, from Ranke, Marx and Nietzsche to Febvre, to provide a powerful critique of presentism, where the past only functions as confirmation of present prejudices.

Megill also draws attention to the dangers inherent in conflating memory and history.[6] Where the former is rooted in personal experience and opinion, the latter, he argues, has to go beyond it, if it wants to fulfil its scientific ambitions, i.e. if it wants to be truthful. Megill posits the decline of both grand narrative and master narratives that, in his view, allows for the creation of many parallel stories that are based on different, sometimes even mutually incompatible memories.[7] The result may well be, he argues, a severe lack of societal cohesion. Megill ends with an extended reflection on the relationship between history and identity. Although he acknowledges the constructed nature of identities, he points out that those identities are also 'found' by individuals.[8] They have the power to appear 'natural'. To construct nations on identities rooted in history is unwise precisely because they tend to essentialise particular ways of belonging to the nation and exclude others. Megill ends by pleading for more self-reflective ways of determining belonging to a nation. He argues that allegiances should be based on answers to questions such as: what do we want to be loyal to? Moreover, what can serve as a basis for solidarities below the level of identity? Overall Megill provides us with a compelling critique of an identity politics rooted in history and championed by (professional) historians.

I find myself very much in sympathy with this critique. However, where I need to contradict Megill is in his particular reading of the NHIST proposal. Here he is, I argue, in danger of misunderstanding the basic underlying assumptions of the programme. I am grateful to him for engaging so directly with the aims and objectives of NHIST and will use part of the introduction to this volume to try lay to rest his fears regarding NHIST's rationale.

For a start, the NHIST project does not seek to analyse histories from a 'would-be universal perspective'. Rather, it is specifically European in its focus and asks how modern national histories have worked in nineteenth- and twentieth-century Europe. Neither does NHIST seek to contribute to the political project of debunking national histories and identities in order to strengthen Europeanness. Given the rather dubious balance sheet of nation-building processes in nineteenth- and twentieth-century Europe, it makes no sense to attempt nation-building at the European level. However, it does seem reasonable to want to contribute to a Europeanisation of history writing that starts from specific themes that are relevant to many European societies and pursues those themes in a comparative and transnational fashion. Furthermore, like Megill, NHIST starts from the assumption of the perspectival nature of all knowledge and it has laid out its own perspective as clearly as possible.

Unlike Megill, I do not believe that national master narratives are currently outdated and beleaguered. They may well be in particular European situations and locations, but not in others. As much of Eastern Europe has been emerging from the Soviet Union's ideological grip in the 1990s, national master narratives have enjoyed a strong revival, often actively and ably supported by national historiographies. Equally, in Western Europe, national master narratives have not only been challenging multi-national states such as Spain and Britain, but they have also enjoyed something of a revival in the face of fears over the creation of a European super-state transcending the nation-states.[9]

If national master narratives are continually being constructed and reconstructed in contemporary Europe, then historians, following Megill's own invocation of Febvre, have the task of drawing attention to the ways in which those narratives have been constructed in the past. In my view it is entirely legitimate to draw the questions which guide our historical writing from contemporary concerns. With Febvre, NHIST is very much seeking to draw the agenda of historical research from the present in order to liberate us from the burdens of the past. This is why NHIST seeks to relate contemporary construction processes of the nation to the construction of national histories over the past two centuries. Both continuities and discontinuities with past construction processes should be highlighted by such analyses precisely in order to prevent historians from discursively constructing national histories which have already demonstrated their problematic potential in the past.

By demonstrating the problematic aspects of constructions of national histories, the programme does not seek to promote alternative forms of history writing. By foregrounding the ways in which national histories contributed to rooting state allegiances in national identities, the programme does not seek to suggest alternative forms of fostering solidarity among large groups of people who often have precious little in common. However, if the results of our research make others promote alternative forms of history writing and question the traditional (national) basis for providing allegiance to a state, then all the better. In so many ways Megill's response to the programme proposal is already one such reaction to a research programme focussing on the inner workings of the construction processes of national narratives in history writing. Where Megill is mistaken is in his assumption that the programme will help to create alternative historical identities to those provided by national histories. Rather, and ironically entirely in line with Megill's own conclusion, it will restrict itself to analysing and criticising national identity claims based on historical writing. It is precisely because these historical constructions of national identity appear so easily as natural and eternal that NHIST insists on the constructed nature of such historical identity creation and highlights changes in the construction processes over time. By doing this it seeks to open a space where self-reflective allegiances, which tolerate difference and 'otherness', can replace essentialised (national) identities as the basis for solidaristic behaviour in larger communities. These allegiances may well still be national ones. After all, as Geoff Eley and Ronald Grigor Suny have written: 'Being national is the condition of our times ...' Whether they are correct in their optimistic assessment that 'belonging to a nation may be the kind of "cultural recovery" that could potentially lead – not to a politics of blood – but to acceptance, even celebration, of differences' remains to be seen.[10]

Of course, researchers seeking to understand the national conundrum from a variety of different perspectives are, themselves, not outside the discursive construction of the past but are participating in this process. Thus, they cannot adopt a universal perspective but are necessarily participating in the ongoing struggle over capturing the interpretative high ground and establishing stories about the past that are accepted by large parts of the people. What Megill takes as an explicit denial that historical opinion can go beyond personal opinion is not the deliberate conflation of memory and history. Rather, it is meant as explicit acknowledgment that historians cannot set themselves up as existing outside the continuous public discourse on the meaning of the past. They participate in it and cannot stand above it. Their specific training and expertise makes them authoritative voices in this discourse, but they have no exclusive or prior access to the truth. Historians cannot set themselves up as purveyors of truth and truthful 'science' against peddlers in and purveyors of myths. They need to recognise that they themselves are part and parcel of a wider public discourse over which meaning to give to the past. A democratic and pluralistic conception of debates about the past does not deny the importance of historical knowledge and of professional historians' role in providing and interpreting it. However, it does insist on the historians seeing themselves as an inclusive part of an ongoing process of reinterpretation. They are neither seeking nor establishing truths outside interpretation.[11]

This point is explicated in a powerful way in Chris Lorenz's paper that challenges the traditional juxtaposition between history as science and history as myth. Instead, he argues that myths, in particular religious myths, were built into the conception of scientific history right from its beginnings. Discussing the work of Leopold von Ranke and Wilhelm von Humboldt in particular, Lorenz demonstrates that the founding fathers of 'scientific' history were anything but hard-boiled empiricists. They adhered to the notion that ideas found expression in historical events and actors. It needed the historian's act of interpretation to extract these ideas from the mere facts of history. Yet, as Lorenz argues, it was through this act of interpretation that historians introduced new myths, the biggest of which was the invention of the nation and the subsequent writing of national history. The recent dominance of the constructivist school in nationalism studies has heightened our awareness of the roles historians played in the construction of the myths of the nations.[12] Through national history, they created a specific form of historical representation that accompanied the formation of the nation-state or sought to influence the existing self-definitions of a national consciousness. They shaped a variety of national master narratives that were situated within and were themselves part of cultural and political power relationships. Lorenz concludes that the terms of the debate have been set up in the wrong way. Rather than juxtaposing 'scientific' history and myths (as in William McNeill's idea of 'mythistory', which forms the starting point of Lorenz's reflections), Lorenz urges us to acknowledge that 'scientific' history always already was mythistory. The demarcation lines between myths and history have collapsed for good. This also has been one of the fundamental preconditions of the NHIST programme, in which Lorenz is heavily involved as team leader of a team investigating the narrative constructions of national master narratives vis-à-vis their non-spatial 'others', especially religion, class, ethnicity and gender.

Mark Bevir's search for a possible way of narrating the nation at the beginning of the twenty-first century starts from his unease with both social science history and what he calls 'developmental historicism'.[13] Social science history, he argues, neglected meanings, beliefs, desires and the whole range of human behaviour in a futile attempt to determine objective social factors by seeking to establish regularities, classifications and quantitative correlations. The growing recognition that people's choices determine actions and processes led to a return to narrative from the 1970s onwards. National histories since then have again been primarily concerned with narrating national characters and traditions. The danger he identifies in such an undertaking lies in the production of a cultural memory that constructs nations as organic units constituted by traditions. Therefore, Bevir suggests moving from 'developmental historicism' to 'radical historicism'. 'Radical historicism', in Bevir's understanding, would not give way to the relativism of the postmodernist stance of a 'free for all' in terms of the construction of national identity. Instead, it still seeks 'justified knowledge' about national identity, and does so on the basis of shared normative practices and rules. However, 'radical historicism' would also not lead us down the path of essentialising national histories. Rather, it insists on denaturalising the nation by stressing fragmentation, interruption and dispersion.

Together with Lorenz's chapter, Bevir's is making explicit some of the fundamental assumptions on which the NHIST project is based. In line with Bevir's 'radical historicism' NHIST highlights the importance of constructions of porous national borders. It underlines the existence of a plurality of contested national traditions and customs. It draws our attention to the transformations of national identities over time. And, last but not least, it uncovers the transnational flow of ideas which make all national identities hybrids. Hybridity has been a crucial concept in discussions of national identity for a number of years now. Scholars have been exploring the various discursive formations and flows of transfers between different cultures in order to show how sets of ideas around the nation were adopted and adapted in different spatial and social settings in order to serve a great variety of different purposes and powers. Pointing to the hybridity of the diverse constructions of the nation has allowed them to emphasise the provisional, relational and elusive character of constructions of national identity.[14] A self-reflective 'radical historicism', as practised by the NHIST programme, already takes into account that every critique of the nation and every description of it is shaped by the theoretical commitments and concepts of the narrator. Such 'radical historicism' moves beyond narrations of the nation towards narrations of the histories of networks of peoples and their agency.

Overall, the first part of the book has helped to clarify and outline some of the basic presumptions of the NHIST programme. If, at the beginning of the twenty-first century, there must be serious question marks behind the scientificity of scholarly historical writing,[15] the borders between 'scientific' representations of the national past and other such representations has become increasingly porous. History writing has never been the sole guardian of national narratives, and today histories and historians play only a limited role in the process of continuous reinterpretation of the national pasts. A range of other media and genres play a much more important role in shaping national discourses.

Traditionally, literature was one of the strongest competitors of history in its claim to narrate the nation to the widest possible audience. In part two of the book Ann Rigney points to the popularity of the historical novel and argues that the impact of fiction on national narratives was greater, particularly during the nineteenth and early twentieth centuries, even if historiography has enjoyed more 'cultural authority'. Literature became a major device for creating cultural memory precisely because it had greater possibilities of imagining the past and fitting it into a coherent plot structure. Fiction, Rigney argues, travelled more easily and spoke to a greater number of people than history. It also often had a longer shelf life than history.

John Neubauer, in his contribution, highlights the proximity of nineteenth-century historians and literary scholars, who both invested an enormous amount of energy into narrating the nation. The institutionalisation of historiographies and the rise of national histories was paralleled by the institutionalisation of literary scholarship and the nationalisation of a literary canon across Europe. The idea of a national literature forming the core of a national culture was particularly prominent in areas of Europe, where national identities were strongly contested, such as Germany and East-Central Europe.[16] National literature often had at its core a strong emphasis on folklore – in various sanitised and aestheticised versions.

Arguably, no novelist was as influential in using folklore to establish national founding epics as Walter Scott. As Linas Eriksonas argues, Scott's interest in national history was aroused following a visit to the battlefield of Waterloo. Subsequently, battles and military heroes became crucial ingredients in his constructions of Scottishness, which set an important model for 'national novelists' across Europe and the wider world. Scott linked his heroic battlefield narratives to the tales popular among the common people, thereby trying to ensure the widest possible appeal of his own narratives. However, his ambition went beyond popular success. He was keen to merge the multiple stories into an authoritative, uniform and homogeneous national narrative. Post-Waterloo, Eriksonas demonstrates, Scott was not alone in linking nations tightly to battlefield narratives. Military heroes and great battles came to dominate the national imagination across Europe.

The power of literature in framing and shaping national narratives is also brought out clearly in Sigrid Weigel's exploration of the importance of the concept of generation for national narratives. She finds that generational discourses are often strongly related to identity politics. Narrative sense making seems to rely heavily on the desire to relate personal experience to the experiences of an entire age cohort. Appeals to generational experience sometimes carried nationalist overtones, as was the case in the National Socialists' exploitation of the idea of the soldiers of the First World War (*Frontkämpfergeneration*). But, of course, war-time experiences were also instrumentalised to underline a pacifist message and the need to transgress national egotisms and move towards common European institutions and frameworks. The same generational experiences could service very different versions of identity politics.[17]

Arguably, if literature had the most powerful hold over national narratives throughout much of the nineteenth century, then film, the subject of part three of this book, has had the most powerful impact since the second half of the twentieth century.[18] After 1945, films about the holocaust have contributed widely to the problematisation of national identity discourses across Europe, as Wulf Kansteiner's contribution to this volume emphasises. Early representations of the holocaust in film were indeed often more concerned with national identity and national suffering than with genocide. With the exception of early Czech cinema, which succeeded in developing a new visual language in which some of the most honest representations of the holocaust were conveyed, most national cinemas in Europe only began to discover the holocaust as a major theme in the 1970s. Kansteiner proceeds to relate the representations of the holocaust in film during the 1980s to a variety of national identity debates in different nation-states. At the same time, however, he also highlights an increasing transnationalisation of holocaust memory in film, which found one of its most remarkable examples in the global reception of Claude Lanzman's 'Shoah'.

The many uses of film as vehicle for nationalism and as a means of transnational dialogue and understanding are also brought to the fore by Hugo Frey's chapter on the Cannes film festival. The festival itself was designed as a showcase for French cultural nationalism. Yet it propagated internationalism and took its message of international reconciliation seriously. Films accused of offending other nations were frequently withdrawn from the programme. Nevertheless, as Frey demonstrates, the contributions to the festival were frequently carrying a nationalist message throughout the 1950s. At Cannes national cinemas competed for international glory and recognition. By the end of the 1970s, Frey argues, nationalism's erstwhile strong connections to film were weakened considerably. Films shown at Cannes were now more often problematising and critically engaging with the national past. They were frequently discussing questions of national guilt and reflecting self-critically on the nation's history. However, film was not abandoning the national theme altogether. From the 1980s onwards, the trend was moving in the opposite direction – with neo-nationalism gaining ground in the cinemas across Europe once again.

Collective national memory has been influenced not only by history, literature and film. Public monuments, the fine arts and music have all been hugely influential in putting forward and emphasising national narratives. They are discussed in part four of this volume. Monuments to national heroes and events of national significance litter the European landscape. While the patterns, motifs and models of narrating the nation through monuments are limited and therefore invite transnational comparisons,[19] we also have the case of transnational events being widely commemorated in monuments. The Napoleonic wars, the revolutions of 1848, the First and the Second World Wars are examples of such truly European events that produced a monument culture across the continent. Historians played an active role in these cultures of commemoration across Europe, and the NHIST programme will provide specific answers as to how the European historiographies influenced these memorial cultures.

Heidemarie Uhl's chapter reviews the interplay between monument construction and the development of a holocaust memory in Austria since the 1980s. After 1945, the Soviet liberation monument in Vienna was brought into line with the theory of Austria as first victim of National Socialist aggression – an interpretation that became the crucial foundational narrative of the second Austrian republic. The victim theory allowed the Austrian state to honour the resistance to National Socialism (excluding, under the conditions of the Cold War, the Communist resistance) and, at the same time, to honour the Austrian soldier who allegedly did only his duty to the fatherland. When a more critical attitude to Austria's Nazi past surfaced in the context of the 1960s it still brought no effective challenge to the victim theory, but only underlined the importance of highlighting the Austrian resistance to Nazism (now beginning to incorporate the Communist resistance as well). Only following the Waldheim debate in 1986 was there a rediscovery of Austria's involvement in National Socialist crimes including the holocaust. Since then two crucial monuments in Vienna have been dedicated to the memory of the holocaust, making it an official part of Austria's commemoration culture and linking the Austrian holocaust discourse to international developments.

National and transnational memorial cultures were also intricately connected in the fine arts, as Michael Wintle demonstrates. Thus, tensions between national and European representations of the past were an important theme in nineteenth-century works of art.[20] Before the nineteenth century, representations of Europe were more prominent than representations of individual nations. They tended to stress the supremacy of Europe over the other continents. Such discourses of supremacy were easily adapted by visual images of the nation, when they became more prominent in the course of the nineteenth century. Attributes that were previously given to Europe were now transferred to the nation, but equally, Europe continued to be prominently represented as a family of nations, albeit one which looked increasingly cantankerous. Wintle's chapter powerfully underlines the fact that narrations of nation and narrations of Europe were by no means mutually exclusive. They often went hand in hand, with one narrative re-enforcing the other and vice versa.

Monuments and the fine arts provide powerful visual representations of the nation. Music, by contrast, is, as Philip Bohlman shows, fundamentally non-representational. And yet, the relationship between music and nationalism has been a very powerful one. Music gave voice to a wide variety of national struggles. National musical canons strengthened national allegiances, as musical styles were interpreted as giving expression to national characters. A variety of different musical genres interacted in diverse ways with narratives of the nation – often producing highly ambiguous and unstable messages. The specific performativity and narrativity of music requires agencies and subjectivities to shape and interpret the national meanings contained in music. Music's narratives about the nation, like those of other genres, were not so much about the past as about the understanding of the past in the present.

How then, one might ask, do these individual articles impact on our understanding of the construction of national narratives in Europe? What links are there between these different genres and their diverse ways of narrating the nation? By creating virtual communities, including national communities, literature played an influential role in shaping the cultural memory of nations. National 'awakenings' often started with language revivals. Once a national language was recovered, it had to be given a prominent place both in everyday life and in literature. Language societies and national academies played a crucial role in developing a national canon in literature and across a variety of different genres in the arts and in music. These canons tended to stress mono-lingualism and mono-culturalism, thus contributing to the destruction of the dense network of multi-lingual and multi-cultural communities across Europe. They also made extensive use of histories everywhere. The attractiveness of history for other genres becomes most obvious when considering an iconic novelist, such as Scott, for whom it was evidently not enough to achieve unparalleled success as a writer of fiction. He ultimately wanted to make his mark as a popular historian. Given the huge importance of interlinkages between the different genres and their practioners, both historians and scholars of literature, music, film and the arts need to study fictional, artistic, musical, visual and historiographical representations of the national pasts alongside each other.[21] Ultimately, therefore, the book becomes a plea to integrate further our studies of different genres and bring together in a truly interdisciplinary manner research on history, literature, film, the arts and music.[22]

Furthermore, the contributions to this volume raise a range of interesting questions regarding the relationship between memory and history writing, which will also have to be considered by the NHIST project more generally. Weigel's emphasis on the importance of the category of generation for discursive constructions of the past has implications both for collective memory and for history writing. Strategies of distancing oneself from the past or of bringing the past closer to the present often have their origins in desires either to wriggle out of one's responsibility for that past or emphasise precisely that responsibility.

However, research on historical constructions of the past should also take note of Weigel's concept of 'transgenerational traumatisation', where the memory of one event in the nation's past becomes central to the identity of generations which have no direct personal memory of that event. National Socialism and contemporary German identity is her chosen example, but one could equally point to the centrality of the Republic of Salo to contemporary Italian identity debates or to the Vichy complex in France.[23] In fact, one might ask whether the more recent construction of negative national pasts through a variety of different genres has not contributed to a European-wide culture of atonement of past national crimes which is based on the idea of 'transgenerational traumatisation'. If the national past is the major source of contemporary trauma, the search for non-national futures becomes all the more urgent.

As several commentators have pointed out over recent years, holocaust memory as cosmopolitanised memory has led to the universal proliferation of global human rights discourses.[24] Critical memory discourses focused on traumatic events such as the holocaust thus might serve as a way of fostering more self-reflective collective memories. However, we should be aware that memory discourses retain a great affinity to nostalgic identity discourses keen to construct borders between an 'us' and a 'them'. And in many parts of Europe, let alone the wider world, critical memory discourses are deeply unpopular. As Kansteiner reminds us in this volume, the absence of a holocaust discourse in Russia would thus explain the disregard of Russia for that human rights discourse.

However, Kansteiner also points out that in the cases of the United States and Israel, adherence to such a human rights discourse encourages self-righteousness and legitimates war and violence in Iraq and Palestine. Here the holocaust memory is used for the ruthless pursuit of national interests under transnational guises. Thus, transnational memories have their own problematic and cannot necessarily be read as unproblematic alternatives to outdated national memories. Such a message is underlined by the ambiguity of international film festivals, such as Cannes, which clearly fostered transnationalism as well as nationalism. Equally, Wintle's chapter on the fine arts underlines how nationalists keen to portray the nation easily adapted transnational European images. NHIST should take note of the complex interrelationship between different spatial identities in film and the fine arts and ask how spatial identities were related in regional, national, European and global histories throughout the nineteenth and twentieth centuries.

If Kansteiner is able to point out for the genre of film that the holocaust has been received increasingly as a transnational subject since the 1980s, it begs the question whether the NHIST project will be able to identify similar developments in the area of historiography. It will be of the utmost importance to differentiate between diverse national receptions and interpretations of key historical works, such as Raul Hilberg's classic on the destruction of European Jewry.[25] At the same time we will have to ask to what extent the Europeanisation of historiographies has tended to undermine distinct national traditions and produced complex interrelationships between local, national and transnational representations of the holocaust through historical writing. Other key events in modern European history need to be identified and we must ask whether a transnational European consciousness has been developing around such key events as the Napoleonic occupation of much of Europe in the early nineteenth century, the struggle for European constitutions in the half-century after 1815, the experience of the First and the Second World Wars, the Armenian genocide and the Gulag.

The last part of the book provides some much-needed non-European perspectives on the theme of nation and narration.[26] Peter Seixas compares the representations of national history in schoolbooks and on TV in Canada and the United States. TV history in both countries tends to be largely biographical and oriented towards major events in national history – with the theme of inner national unity central to the programme makers' choice of topics. Seixas finds Canadian TV less historiographically aware than its American counterpart. School history has witnessed a conservative backlash in the 1990s in both Canada and the United States. There are then, according to Seixas, clear indications that North America is returning to more traditional forms of narrating national history and turning its back on the attempt to move beyond national history, which was associated with the heydays of oppositional 'people's history' in the 1970s. The historiographical clocks in North America thus seem to chime to the same tune as the historiographical clocks throughout much of Europe, where the 1990s also witnessed attempts to return to national narratives.[27] The NHIST programme must be attentive to these chronological caesuras, whilst asking at the same time, for the realm of historiography, whether what seems at first a cyclical development might not at second glance indicate an important discursive shift. The recent German discourse on the German victims of the Second World War is a good example of this. On the surface, German public discourse seems to return to a trope already prevalent in the 1950s. However, what is returning has gone through three decades of intense working through the National Socialist past and is thus reappearing in an entirely different context to the one of the 1950s.[28]

Inventions of the modern nation originated in North America and Europe, but colonialism exported the narrative strategies and hierarchies of European national narratives across the globe. As colonial nations frequently sought to emulate what was presented to them as a distinct European path to modernity, their elites were left with a paradox. On the one hand, their own attempts to narrate the nation could only be a reflection of the 'hegemonic mirror' of the Europeans, but on the other hand, they could never hope to be able to construct histories that would equal those of the Europeans. The colonial nations found themselves trapped in the '"waiting-room" version of history', in which the '"first in Europe, then elsewhere" structure of global historical time' condemned them to an eternal 'not yet'.[29] Hence, the characteristic framing of national histories in the colonised world was one of backwardness and attempts to overcome backwardness in the hope of approaching the European model. Even following the rupture with colonialism, the narrative strategies and techniques remained heavily indebted to European models. Therefore, national histories outside of Europe (and North America) almost inevitably became 'discursive prisoners' of Eurocentrism. Jie-Hyun Lim traces the emergence of Japanese national history, which was first written exclusively for Western readers at the end of the nineteenth century. Japanese national historians attempted to escape the Orientalist paradigm by inventing their own Orient in the form of China and Korea. The construction of 'Japanese exceptionalism' became a means with which to establish Japan as Europe's equal.

From a global perspective, historians of historiography will have to ask in future, what precise role Western historiographical models of constructing national histories played in the non-Western world. If we take China, for example, Chinese historians argued that it was necessary to construct a Chinese equivalent of the European Renaissance and the Enlightenment. This could be done thorough a renewal of indigenous cultural traditions. Hence, at least in China, an imported sense of the national merged in complex ways with an insistence of local authenticity.[30] After all, in China as in India forms of narrating the nation existed for considerably longer than in Europe.[31] What was the relationship between those non-European national histories to the evolving idea of 'scientificity' in nineteenth-century Europe? Did European Romanticism or positivism in historical writing have equivalents in the non-European world? What impact did the global advances of Marxism in the second half of the twentieth century have on the merger between European and non-European perspectives? How much does the strong interrelationship between different spatial identities in the European context find a parallel in non-European histories? In other words, is the concept of *Heimat* useful also outside of Europe? Similarly, can we talk about transnational 'meso-regions' also outside of Europe? What tensions were produced by the growing internationalisation of historical networks and associations and the parallel growth of 'scientific nationalism'? Which significant 'others' emerged to rival the narrative dominance of the nation outside of Europe? What role did Islam in particular play in this respect? Were there similar 'history wars' ravaging the historical profession and the wider national public sphere outside Europe? Were the 'official' and the 'unofficial' histories of colonialism both inside and outside of Europe produced as a result of first imperialism and then decolonisation? Future research into the global history of national history writing will have to seek to provide answers to these questions, which are all touched upon by the contributions of Seixas and Lim in this current collection.

All of the contributions to this present volume problematise the narration of the nation in different genres and thus contribute to more self-reflective approaches to national histories. They point towards the need to explore the links between different genres more closely and to question clear-cut boundaries between national and transnational constructions of the past. As Maurice Samuels has recently shown, the visual and the textual came together in the early nineteenth century to produce a 'new spectacular mode of historical representation'.[32] Panoramas, dioramas and museums were early places where the visualisation of the past satisfied the wishes of the people to experience history as reality. Images became instruments with which to produce and strengthen collective identities, and textual representations of the past increasingly invoked spectacles of the past – especially battles and battlefields. Of course, this book cannot treat its subject matter in any exhaustive manner. Whole genres that have been important for the construction of national narratives are absent here. Newspapers,[33] the heritage industry,[34] radio[35] and the theatre[36] come to mind, as do other academic disciplines than history, especially linguistics, geography, theology, anthropology and archaeology. Historical narratives were often enthused with a specific sense of geography. The forces of geography and landscape determined the shape of the nation. Particular landscapes became symbols for the nation. Frontiers played a crucial role in national narratives in the United States and Australia. The Alps were as crucial to Swiss national history as the Amazon rainforest was to constructions of Brazil. As specific climates became connected to distinct national characters, environmental and natural history became important for the narration of the nation. How national pasts were represented in and through a variety of different genres needs many more comparative and transcultural explorations. This volume is just one small step to a deeper understanding of how national narratives contributed to cultural sense-production in the modern world.

Notes

1. H. Bhaba, ed., *Nation and Narration*, London, 1990. The literature on the constructed nature of the nation is legion. A.D. Smith, *The Nation in History: Historiographical*

Debates about Ethnicity and Nationalism, Cambridge, 2000, is a good introduction to the many strands of the constructivist school and its opponents.

2. For details see http://www.uni-leipzig.de/zhsesf/ and http://www.esf.org/nhist, including an overview of a planned six-volume 'Writing the Nation' book series to be published with Palgrave MacMillan between 2008 and 2010 and many stand-alone volumes of the NHIST programme.

3. U. Jensen and K. Naumann, 'Tagungsbericht: Representations of the Past: The Writing of National Histories in Europe. Forms of Representation and Representational Techniques: Narratives, Genres, Media, University of Glamorgan, 20–22 May 2004', in H-Soz-u-Kult, http://hsozkult.geschichte.hu-berlin.de/tagungsberichte/id=525

4. Kerwin Lee Klein, 'On the Emergence of Memory in Historical Discouse', *Representations* 69, 2000: 127–50; Alon Confino, 'Introduction', in Alon Confino, ed., *Histories and Memories of Twentieth-century Germany*, special issue of *History and Memory* 17, 1/2, 2005: 5–14. Here the reader will also find a wealth of further references on publications on memory which have looked specifically at the constructedness of national pasts.

5. For more details on the NHIST's interpretative arguments, see the mid-term reports of all four teams in Stefan Berger and Andrew Mycock, eds, *Europe and its National Histories*, special issue of *Storia della Storiografia* 50: 4, 2006. The NHIST's programme proposal and its conceptual framework are also laid down in the NHIST programme brochure (Stasbourg, 2004) and the two newsletters produced by NHIST in the autumn of 2004 and the autumn of 2006.

6. On the issue of history, memory and forgetting, there is, of course, a huge literature. See especially P. Ricoeur, *Memory, History, Forgetting*, Chicago, 2004; also inspirational on this topic are the many publications of Aleida and Jan Assmann.

7. For an excellent attempt to delineate the diverse conceptions of grand and master narratives in the philosophy of history, see K. Thijs, 'Master Narratives in the National Historical Cultures of Europe. Reflections on the Concept of "Narrative Hierarchy"', in Stefan Berger and Chris Lorenz, eds, *The Contested Nation: Ethnicity, Class, Religion and Gender in National Histories*, Houndmills, 2008.

8. On identity construction and history, see H. Friese, ed., *Identities: Time, Difference and Boundaries*, Oxford, 2002; also A. Assmann and H. Friese, eds, *Identitäten. Erinnerung, Geschichte, Identität 3*, 2nd ed., Frankfurt am Main, 1999.

9. On the paradox of the resilience of nationalism in an age where the nation-state is declining in importance, see B. Jenkins and S.A. Sofos, *Nation and Identity in Contemporary Europe*, London, 1996.

10. G. Eley and R. Grigor Suny, 'Introduction', in G. Eley and R. Grigor Suny, eds, *Becoming National: A Reader*, Oxford, 1996: 32.

11. On all of these issues see also the wonderfully perceptive introduction to historical theory by C. Lorenz, *Konstruktion der Vergangenheit. Eine Einführung in die Geschichtstheorie*, Cologne, 1997.

12. S. Berger, M. Donovan and K. Passmore, eds, *Writing National Histories: Western Europe since 1800*, London, 1999; going well beyond historiography and including in particular the genre of art are M. Flacke, ed., *Mythen der Nationen. Ein europäisches Panorama*, Munich, 1998, and M. Flacke, ed., *Mythen der Nationen. 1945: Arena der Erinnerungen*, 2 vols, Mainz, 2004.

13. I would still prefer the term 'historism'. As I first outlined in an article in *Past and Present* in 1995, 'historism' (German, *Historismus*) is an evolutionary, reformist concept which understands all political order as historically developed and grown. It is often connected with the works by Leopold von Ranke who is sometimes regarded as a founding figure of historism. 'Historicism' (German, *Historizismus*) is based on the notion that history develops according to predetermined laws towards particular ends. Such a notion of history has been defined and powerfully critiqued by Karl Popper, *The Poverty of Historicism*, London, 1957.

14. P. Werbner and T. Modood, eds, *Debating Cultural Hybridity*, London, 1997.

15. H. Feldner, 'The New Scientificity in Historical Writing around 1800', in S. Berger, H. Feldner and K. Passmore, eds, *Writing History: Theory and Practice*, London, 2003: 3–22.

16. See also M. Cornis-Pope and J. Neubauer, eds, *History of Literary Cultures of East-Central Europe: Junctures and Disjunctures in the 19th and 20th Centuries*, Amsterdam, 2004.

17. J. Reulecke and E. Müller-Luckner, eds, *Generationalität und Lebensgeschichte im 20. Jahrhundert*, Munich, 2003.

18. A. Williams, ed., *Film and Nationalism*, New Jersey, 2002.

19. See, for example, C. Tacke, *Denkmal im sozialen Raum: Nationale Symbole in Deutschland und Frankreich im 19. Jahrhundert*, Göttingen, 1995.

20. On the representation of history in the fine arts see also the classic F. Haskell, *History and its Images*, New Haven, 1993, as well as S. Bann, *The Clothing of Clio*, Cambridge, 1984.

21. See, for example, the interesting interdisciplinary contributions in M. Einfalt, J. Jurt, D. Mollenhauer and E. Pelzer, eds, *Konstrukte nationaler Identität: Deutschland, Frankreich und Großbritannien (19. und 20. Jahrhundert)*, Würzburg, 2002.

22. This is also the aim of the interdisciplinary Centre for the Study of Cultural Forms of Modern European Politics (Cultmep), based at the University of Manchester. See www.ahc.manchester.ac.uk/cidra/cultmep

23. On the trauma produced by war in the twentieth century and its aftermath, see also M. Evans and K. Lunn, *War and Memory in the Twentieth Century*, Oxford, 1997.

24. See, among others, the recent volume by Daniel Levy and Natan Sznaider, *The Holocaust and Memory in the Global Age*, Philadelphia, 2005.

25. Raul Hilberg, *Die Vernichtung der europäischen Juden*, 3 vols, Frankfurt am Main, 1990. The book was first published in English in 1961 and came out in a first German translation in 1982.

26. For an attempt to provide such a global contextualisation of constructions of national history writing, see S. Berger, ed., *Writing the Nation: A Global Perspective*, Houndmills, 2007.

27. S. Berger, 'A Return to the National Paradigm? National History Writing in Germany, Italy, France and Britain, 1945 to the Present', *The Journal of Modern History* 77:3, 2005: 629–678.

28. B. Niven, ed., *Germans as Victims: Remembering the Past in Contemporary Germany*, Houndmills, 2006.

29. D. Chakrabarty, *Provincialising Europe: Postcolonial Thought and Historical Difference*, Princeton, 2000: 6–9.

30. E.Q. Wang, 'China's Search for National History', in E.Q. Wang and G. Iggers, eds, *Turning Points in Historiography: A Cross-cultural Comparison*, Rochester, 2002: 185–208.

31. D. Woolf, 'Of Nations, Nationalism and National Identity: Reflections on the Historiographical Organisation of the Past', in E.Q. Wang, ed., *The Many Faces of Clio: Cross-cultural Approaches to Historiography. Festschrift for Georg G. Iggers*, Oxford, 2006: 71–103.

32. M. Samuels, *The Spectacular Past: Popular History and the Novel in Nineteenth-century France*, New York, 2004.

33. On the modern media, see J.H. Brinks, E. Timms and S. Rock, eds, *Nationalist Myths and the Modern Media: Cultural Identity in the Age of Globalisation*, London, 2005.

34. On the heritage industry see the theoretically intriguing, though largely British-centred comments by R. Samuel, *Theatres of Memory*, London, 1994; see also S. MacDonald and G. Fyfe, *Theorising Museums: Representing Identity and Diversity in a Changing World*, Oxford, 1996.

35. I. Marßolek and A. von Saldern, eds, *Radiozeiten: Herrschaft, Alltag, Gesellschaft (1924–1960)*, Potsdam, 1999.

36. K. Gounarridou, ed., *Theatre and Nationalism*, New York, 2004; S.E. Wilmer, ed., *Writing and Rewriting National Theatre Histories*, Iowa City, 2004.

PART I

SCIENTIFIC APPROACHES TO NATIONAL NARRATIVES

Chapter 1

Historical Representation, Identity, Allegiance

ALLAN MEGILL

There is a tension in the 'National Histories in Europe' project that became clear at the first session of the Glamorgan conference from which this volume is derived. The tension – and it is a legitimate tension – is between, on the one hand, history as offering a disinterested, 'scientific' account of historical reality that makes a claim, however attenuated, to objectivity and, on the other, particular human solidarities as objects not just of study but of commitment.[1]

The disinterested, scientific side of the project is manifested throughout the detailed research proposal that the 'National Histories in Europe' research network submitted to the European Science Foundation in January 2002 in its successful bid to obtain funding. However, more generally accessible is an eight-page brochure describing the project that was put on the Web in February 2004. Consider the following account of the proposed activities of 'Team Two' (deeply involved in the Glamorgan conference), which was charged with the task of investigating the topic, 'Narrating National Histories'. 'National "master" narratives', we are told,

> always stand in close relationship with narratives, such as those based on gender, ethnicity, class and/or religion. In what ways have such social cleavages mattered to national history writing? This team will investigate the links and interdependencies between histories written from a national perspective and those written from a perspective of class, gender, race, ethnicity, and religion.[2]

The brochure goes on to identify five areas on which research will focus: origins and foundational myths of national histories; main actors and heroes in national narratives; the claims to uniqueness or to special missions in national histories; conceptions of decline, renewal and rupture in national histories; and the inclusion or exclusion of 'non-spatial Others' in national master narratives.

Everything that the brochure says here suggests that the researchers are engaged in an objective process of scholarly investigation. Of course, the histories on which they propose to focus were written 'from a national perspective', as the brochure notes. However, there is no suggestion that the Team Two researchers will be writing from any such partial perspective. On the contrary, everything in the above statement suggests that they plan to be rigorously disinterested in their work. They want to show, as clearly and accurately as possible, how national histories relate to histories written from other perspectives. The researchers' perspective is a would-be universal perspective: the perspective of those who desire to know how things really were and are.

On the other hand, the 'National Histories in Europe' project also proposes to contribute to European solidarity and mutual understanding. The following statement in the brochure exemplifies this aspect of the enterprise:

> National history is central to national identity. A sustained and systematic study of the construction, erosion and reconstruction of national histories across a wide variety of European states is a highly topical and extremely relevant exercise for two reasons: firstly, because of the long and successful history of the national paradigm in history-writing; and, secondly, because of its re-emergence as a powerful political tool in the 1990s in the context of the accelerating processes of Europeanisation and globalisation. National histories form an important part of the collective memory of the peoples of Europe. National bonds have been, and continue to be, among the strongest bonds of loyalty. A genuinely trans-national and comparative investigation into the structures and workings of national histories will play an important part [...] in preparing the way for further dialogue and understanding among European nation-states.[3]

I cannot object to the aspirations embedded in this statement. Further, the weighty research proposal of 2002 reveals the high degree of co-ordinated intelligence that has gone into the project, which is based, as the brochure says, on 'the collaboration of more than 60 leading scholars from more than 20 countries'.[4] There is much to be learned from the programme of research that the project organisers have laid out. Nor do I object to the presence of the project's 'committed' side *as such*. For example, I do not claim that it is some sort of logical contradiction that a project should involve a commitment to both truth and social solidarity. On the contrary, a 'double orientation' or 'unresolving dialectic' is essential to the project of (scientific) historical research and writing.[5] My comments have to do rather with refining certain aspects of the analysis and with pointing out some of its underjustified assumptions.

How much of a role can historical research and writing play in the attempt to move forward to a free, united, peace-loving and benevolent Europe? My general sense of the matter is that history has a relatively limited and specialised role to play in such developments. In fact, I think it rather dangerous when history gets committed to 'the good cause', whatever that cause may be. Rather, history's basic commitment ought to be to speaking both interestingly and truthfully about matters of the past. History should seek to offer, in Paul Veyne's words, a *récit véridique* – a 'truthful narrative'.[6] Admittedly, a 'truthful narrative' may turn out not to be a *true* narrative, as we learn when we see the errors and blind spots of one generation of historians being corrected by later generations. Historical knowledge always has a provisional aspect to it. Yet the historian's *distinctive* duty is to speak truthfully about the past. The historian ought to criticise forthrightly erroneous or unjustified claims about the past, no matter how worthy and good-hearted are the commitments of those who make these claims. In this sense, historians have the task of maintaining a certain detachment between the past on the one hand and the present and the presumed future on the other.[7]

I am more favourably impressed by certain observations of Ranke, Marx and Nietzsche concerning the relation between history and current aspirations and desires than I am by the very positive view of this relation adopted by some recent historians. Famously, in 1824 the young Leopold Ranke remarked that 'history has been assigned the office of judging the past, of instructing the present for the benefit of future ages'. Ranke took issue with this view. *His* work, he tells his readers, 'wants only to show what actually happened'.[8] Ranke was reacting here against a long tradition of thinking that gave to history the task of being a preceptor of life, offering general rules by which we might guide our actions. He was surely justified in rejecting the morally and pragmatically oriented approaches to history that he found in earlier writers. First, such histories could only produce distorted representations of the past. Second, the claim to offer lessons in ethics and prudence was fraudulent, for such-and-such actions in the past were judged exemplary on the basis of pre-existing views held by the authors in question, which they then found 'confirmation' for in the past. The resulting history was thus an exercise in false confirmation, giving back to the present the present's own prejudices dressed up in the garb of antiquity.

Ranke was mainly interested in how a pragmatic conception of history was likely to distort our apprehension of the past. With Marx it is different. I am thinking, of course, of the beginning of *The Eighteenth Brumaire of Louis Bonaparte* (1852), where Marx regrets the harmful impact that representations of past events can have on action in the present. His words are famous but still worth quoting: Hegel, Marx mistakenly claims,

> remarks somewhere that all great events and characters of world history occur, so to speak, twice. He forgot to add: the first time as tragedy, the second as farce:

rèCaussidi (PE) in place of Danton, Louis Blanc in place of Robespierre, the Montagne of 1848–51 in place of the Montagne of 1793–95, the Nephew in place of the Uncle.[9]

In short, Marx sees representations of the past as impairing historical actors' grasp of the present. Although in other respects their positions are dramatically different, Ranke and Marx are here making complementary points: the one holding that presentist concerns distort our representations of the past, the other holding that representations of the past impair our understanding of the present.

As for Nietzsche, his best-known discussion of historical matters is his *Untimely Meditation* of 1874, 'On the Uses and Disadvantages of History for Life'. Although his conceptualisation in this essay is unclear, Nietzsche's argument appears to be that the right orientation to the past involves some sort of fluid shifting among a 'monumental' attitude, which deifies figures in the past; an 'antiquarian' attitude, which engages in a kind of local reverence towards the past; and a 'critical' attitude, which subjects the past to condemnation. Nietzsche also suggests that there are competing 'historical', 'unhistorical' and 'supra-historical' approaches to the past, but what he had in mind here is even less clear.[10] However, in *On the Genealogy of Morality* (1887), Nietzsche articulated a position very different from that offered in the 1874 essay.[11] In *On the Genealogy of Morality* Nietzsche writes that we ought to cultivate an attitude of 'active forgetfulness' with regard to the past.[12] In this later work Nietzsche seems to be saying that we need to *get over* the past – not forgetting it, exactly, but certainly rejecting the notion that it has any sort of *a priori* claim over us.

What is common to these bits of Ranke, Marx and Nietzsche is a wish to distance the past from the present and future. In Ranke, the distancing is aimed at 'saving' the past, whereas in Marx and Nietzsche it is aimed at saving the present and especially the future. Something like such an attitude of distancing, I contend, ought to be normative for historians now.

In fact, I think that it *is* normative among those historians who have thought seriously about the matter. Consider Lucien Febvre, the great co-founder of the *Annales* school. In a 1949 essay entitled 'Vers une autre histoire' that memorialises his murdered colleague Marc Bloch, Febvre envisages a 'problem-oriented' history, by which he meant a history that approaches the past with the aim of solving problems relevant to the present. As part of this project, Febvre wished to get away from what he saw as the burdening and distorting weight of the past. He criticised 'traditional' societies for 'produc[ing] an image of their present life, of its collective aims and of the virtues required to achieve those aims', and then projecting a 'sort of prefiguration of the same reality' on the past.[13] In contrast to the traditional view, Febvre judged that history is a liberation from the past: 'history is a way of organizing the past so that it does not weigh too heavily on the shoulders of men'.[14] This liberation, Febvre explicitly states, involves a kind of forgetting. In Febvre's view,

> it is essential for human groups and societies to forget if they wish to survive. We have to live. We cannot allow ourselves to be crushed under the tremendous, cruel, accumulated weight of all that we inherit.[15]

Febvre's view as expressed here seems to me to be quite different from the emphasis in the 'National Histories in Europe' brochure on national history as 'central to national identity', on national histories as forming 'an important part of the collective memory of the peoples of Europe', and on the 'national bonds' that 'have been, and continue to be, among the strongest bonds of loyalty' among Europeans.[16] I do not mean to suggest that there is *radical* opposition here, for it seems clear that the 'National Histories in Europe' project potentially leaves room for other ways of conceptualising bonds of unity among people. However, those other ways are not stated, and the limits of an approach focussed on 'memory' are decidedly not made clear.

In the research proposal of January 2002, the authors, referring to the national historiographies of the nineteenth and twentieth centuries, allude to 'the pretences of national history as an objective science working within the boundaries of a rational discourse'. They find in this tradition of history writing 'a plethora of mythopoetic concepts' that 'structured very diverse historical interpretations'.[17] The authors and animators of the 'National Histories in Europe' project are surely correct to suggest a connection between national histories and 'mythopoetics', and one looks forward to the further research that will help us understand in a more exact way how it was so. (One example of such a study is Linas Eriksonas's *National Heroes and National Identities: Scotland, Norway and Lithuania*[18]). What I find inadequate in the proposal – in the midst of many other things that I admire – is an apparently too quick setting aside of any claim that 'objectivity' in some sense might make upon us, and the absence of a discussion of alternatives to mythopoetics (or to the recently fashionable notion of 'mythistory'[19]) as a unifying device for the nation or other large human groupings. The project rightly envisages going beyond a merely national grounding of the social order, but it does not envisage a different kind of grounding than the kind that it attributes to an earlier, and 'pretentious', national history.

It is obvious that notions of memory play an important role in the project. As the 'National Histories in Europe' brochure puts it, 'National histories form an important part of the collective memory of the peoples of Europe'.[20] The 2002 research proposal also seems to suggest – in a *prise de position* closely connected with the widespread tendency these days to run together history and memory – that it is a mistake to think that 'historical science' is able to go beyond 'personal opinion'. To cite the proposal at greater length:

The claim that historical science could go beyond personal opinion frames the problem in such a way as to allow only for inadequate answers. It [namely, framing the problem as being a matter of going beyond personal opinion] distracts from asking how the personal is inscribed *on all levels* [my emphasis] of the historical work, e.g., on the questions that historians ask, their choice of topic, their methodologies, units of investigation, measure of comparison, and use of master narratives. In that sense, Pierre Nora's famous distinction between 'history' and 'memory' seems to fall prey to the myth of 'scientific' history and its alleged adherence to detached and objective analysis.[21]

To be sure, it will not do to attempt to apply to history old notions of 'absolute' objectivity that purport to underpin a single, coherent, unified and authoritative account of human history.[22] There are compelling reasons for denying that there can be a pure, absolutely objective description of anything in history. On the contrary, all historical objects are inevitably viewed *partially*, from the perspective of the particular historian-observer: indeed, to some extent historical objects are actually the creation of the historian. For example, when Petrarch (allegedly) climbed Mount Ventoux, he did not know, and could not have known, that he was 'opening the Renaissance' because the concept 'Renaissance' did not yet exist. But it is in principle entirely legitimate for the historian to see Petrarch as 'opening the Renaissance' in climbing Mount Ventoux, even in the absence of any intention on Petrach's part to do so, if the historian can show that Petrarch's (alleged) climbing of Mount Ventoux was a paradigmatic event that somehow exemplified or put into motion the larger set of events to which 'the Renaissance' applies.[23] Similarly, people in August 1914 did not know that they were beginning what would become the First World War, nor did people in 1618 know that they were fighting the Thirty Years' War – but these, too, are in principle legitimate descriptions of events that were already underway in 1618 and 1914.

However, acknowledging the irreducibly perspectival aspect of history does not entail holding that history cannot go beyond mere 'personal opinion'. Even less does such an acknowledgement entail identifying 'history' with 'memory'. I use the word *memory* here in a broad sense, as I think the authors also do. In the present context, I understand 'memory' as designating not only people's memories of their own experiences but also such related realities as tradition and commemoration. Of course, over roughly the last twenty-five years the nexus 'memory–tradition–commemoration' has acquired much greater weight within the historical profession than it had in earlier dispensations. (For example, there was no room for 'memory' in Ranke's conception of historiography: he mistrusted memoirs, and looked instead for state documents and for accounts written contemporaneously with the events being described.)

One can connect historians' growing acceptance, lately, of what one might think of as 'memory extended' to the decline in persuasiveness of previously widely accepted notions of 'grand' and 'master' narratives in history. The discipline of history as it emerged in the nineteenth century was closely connected with the extension of the power of the European nation-state. In Germany, France, England and the United States, the newly professionalised discipline of history tended to serve as an ideological support for the state. Historians laboured in support of the Prussian state and its extension; in support of the secularly-based French republic, with its *mission civilisatrice*, that emerged after France's defeat by Prussia in 1871; in support of England and its Empire; and for the national and then imperial pretensions of the United States. In each case a 'master narrative' was seen as running through the nation's history – a master narrative of the nation's movement from its early beginnings, through the rise of national self-consciousness, to its current struggle for recognition and success. Behind such master narratives there lay a larger 'grand narrative' that had emerged in the eighteenth century out of a secularisation of the Christian redemption story. In its essential core, the 'grand narrative' told a story of growing freedom and advancing culture within the framework of a system of nation-states.[24]

Although further research needs to be done on the subject, it seems clear that the relative solidity of these master and grand narratives gave to historical writing a particular shape and feel. In general, commitment to such narratives tended to generate a history that was authoritative in tone and that was focussed on the actions and institutions of the state. The substructure of such histories was provided by the idea of an increasing actualisation of freedom. Although the differences were usually only a matter of degree, sometimes the story was told in a liberal register, with emphasis placed on the increasing freedom of the individual to pursue his private interests and to have a voice in the running of the state, and sometimes it was told in a conservative or authoritarian register, with emphasis placed on cultural cultivation (*Bildung*) and on the freedom and power of the state itself.

Today these variant master narratives, and the grand narrative that underpins them, are lacking in essential authority. They have been lacking in essential authority since roughly the time that people began to see the war that began in 1914 as a slaughterhouse. Admittedly, it cannot be said that *nobody* believes in the old grand and master narratives any more. For example, I am often struck by the extent to which many US undergraduates – and not *only* undergraduates – still believe in the American master narrative of the 'city on the hill' standing as the 'last best hope of mankind'– the 'hope of the world', as President Nixon once put it.[25] Nevertheless, for most people who think about such matters – and even for many people who do not – neither the old national master narratives nor the grand narrative of freedom and *Bildung* is persuasive any more. Instead, there prevails, in the apt phrase of Jean-François Lyotard, an 'incredulity' towards such overarching narratives.[26]

If history is not the purveyor of some sort of authoritative narrative of human advance, what then does it offer? Today, in popular culture and to some extent even among professional historians, 'history' frequently offers something that is more akin to 'memory' in its various senses. When history no longer looks forward to constructing either an objective 'grand narrative' of history as a whole or a more limited but still objective 'master narrative' of some segment of the past, one response is to focus on what is personal and immediately striking. The decline of grand and master narrative also seems likely to heighten the sense that the historian should be the spokesperson for some particular group in the present – whether one variety or another of the downtrodden, or a supposedly elite group whose elite character has not been adequately recognised. Such commitments to the particular are not necessarily benign. In fact, the opposite has often been the case, with 'histories' giving a kind of fake legitimacy to present-day arrangements or aspirations of a deeply oppressive or conflict-directed sort. It stands to reason that a historiography that sees its task as speaking for some particular group in the present will necessarily be under a constant temptation to subordinate the past to the supposed needs of that group in the present.

I think that it would be quite a mistake for historians to allow themselves to become cheerleaders for the good European cause. The distinctive task of historians is not to promote morality, solidarity and good policy in the present, although it is possible that, as a by-product of their work, they might sometimes succeed in doing so. However, I do not believe that achieving such good effects should at all be the focus of their attention. I believe that professional historiography has an important public role to play, but I find that its public role is largely a matter of countering fantasies about the past that arise in people's minds as pseudo-justifications for agendas and ways of life that they wish to promote in the present.

The first thing that we need to attend to – it is an obvious point, and it is certainly recognised in the 'National Histories in Europe' project – is that people relate to their pasts in other ways than through the work of professional historians. This becomes particularly clear when one looks at the way people have responded to genocide and other large-scale crimes, at least when they have had some reason to identify with the victims of these crimes. Such crimes are of concern not only to historians but also to (other) social scientists, as well as to jurists, philosophers, theologians, novelists, poets and artists, and to people generally, beyond the above-noted professions and ways of seeing. People have responded to such events in at least four different ways: by investigating and reconstructing what actually happened; by the cultivation of memory, commemoration and tradition; by the creation of aesthetic forms; and by ethical, philosophical and religious or theological reflection.[27] And of course people also 'respond' by denying what happened, or by completely ignoring the events in question.

The Shoah, which occurred in the relatively recent past on European territory, involved the murder of millions of people, and has had an impact on millions of other persons, is a good test case for thinking about the various non- or extra-historiographical ways by which people orient themselves towards the past. (One could pick other examples. My choice of this example reflects my own participation in European culture in an extended sense of the term.) Much of people's orientation towards the Shoah has to do with memory, commemoration and tradition. When the sole survivor of a killing pit at Pinsk, Rivka Yoselewska, testified at the Eichmann trial in Jerusalem in 1961, her testimony had an impact and power of a kind that a historian cannot normally expect to achieve.[28] Something of the same impact can be discovered in certain works of art – in painting, literature and film, as well as in museums and in other buildings commemorating the Shoah and the culture that was destroyed in it. One thinks, for example, of Claude Lanzmann's monumental 9½-hour film *Shoah* (1985). Finally, there are works whose main emphasis is on investigation and reconstruction – the 'works' of jurists, as well as those of journalists (characteristically writing about the very recent past) and, of course, of historians.

In sum, historians are not the only group of persons who seek to come to grips with the past. When we think about national (and other) kinds of histories, we need to bear in mind the existence of different ways of coming to grips with the past. This is especially necessary, of course, because some of these other historical or history-related representations and presentations are likely to have a far wider impact than written history, especially written history of an academic sort. We need to understand the functions that other forms of addressing the past serve. We also need to understand their limitations.

Consider, for example, Ken and Ric Burns's nine-episode television series, *The Civil War*, which may well be the best film documentary on the history of the United States ever made. Generally known as 'Ken Burns's *Civil War*', the series faced the considerable challenge of dealing with a conflict that long preceded the invention of moving pictures. Nonetheless, by an innovative use of thousands of still photographs of civil war soldiers, politicians, agitators, cities, landscapes, battles and ruins, as well as by an attentiveness to the character of the voices reading the hundreds of texts that we hear over the course of the series, the film-makers gave to their creation an immediacy and directness that one would not have expected in advance. It is also necessary to note that the series is historically and pedagogically 'responsible'. The film-makers do not make claims that contradict the historical evidence. In working on the series, they consulted many historians who had expertise in the US civil war and related matters, and it is evident that they benefited from some of this advice. In addition, a number of historians appear on screen as 'talking heads': they have the function of explicating events, situating them in a wider context and offering interpretations as to their historical significance. If one's wish is to inform young Americans about certain facts concerning the bloodiest conflict in American history, Ken Burns's *The Civil War* is a good place at which to begin. It can also be recommended to non-Americans who wish to gain, with a relatively short investment of time, some insight into the history and character of the United States.

The question that arises in the present context is: what can a work like *The Civil War* tell us about the relation between history and national-identity – or supra-national-identity – building? It is a relevant question, for if historically oriented identity building is going to occur in the present age, it is surely much more likely to take place by means of popular presentations that have something of the character of Ken Burns's *Civil War* than through the writings of professional historians. Further, Burns's work is 'good to think with' in the context of this question precisely because it is such a good example of the attempt to convey a certain 'knowledge' and 'experience' of history in a popular medium.

What *The Civil War* most clearly reveals, I believe, are the dangers inherent in the attempt to link history to an identity that one then wishes to serve as the foundation of a present political order. There is no doubt that *The Civil War* offers, to use a cliché that seems apt in the present context, a 'compelling emotional experience' to those who sit down and watch it. The photographs of battlefields, of bodies and (especially) of soon-to-die young men tug at the heartstrings. So does the larger picture that *The Civil War* offers – its picture of a country torn apart and then forcibly brought back together again, at the cost of over 600,000 dead (and many more wounded) in what had been a country of 30,000,000 people. There is no doubt that all of this is connected to issues of American identity. Three million men fought in the war, often hundreds of miles from home, at a time when many people travelled no further than ten or twenty miles from their place of birth. The entire country followed, and was affected by, the war's course and outcome. One of the 'talking heads' in the series, the popular historian Shelby Foote, asserts that 'Before the war it was said "The United States are" – and after the war it was always "The United States is". That sums up what the war accomplished. It made us an is.'[29] There could be no better summation of the identity-creating force that the civil war exerted, and continues to exert, on the people of the United States.

How useful and good is it to ground a state on such historical foundations as this? (After all, that is what one is doing, if identity is central to politics.) Without in any way calling into question the considerable achievement of the Burns brothers in constructing their account of the civil war, one can nonetheless discern some highly questionable implications for politics and for the state system in their work. A crucial point, of course, is that the American identity (as distinguished from Massachusetts, Connecticut, New York,

Pennsylvania and Virginia, etc., identities) was forged in a *war*, and not in some other set of events. This is a historical fact: it cannot be gotten round. Very often, other national identities were forged in war also: for example, it is a cliché, but apparently, a true cliché, that Australian identity was created on the battlefield at Gallipoli in 1915.[30]

The problem here is that rooting a political identity in a particular set of historical events brings with it biases that may not be noticed in the absence of a serious critical effort. The presence of such biases is such a pervasive and unavoidable part of historical narrative that one needs to question whether polities ought to be grounded in historical narratives *at all*. To be sure, one can engage in the critique of the historical narratives in question. This is clearly a large part of what the participants in the 'National Histories in Europe' project propose to do. However, any such critical approach is unlikely to find the same popular favour that appeals to identity will have. Narrative, after all, has an inherent persuasive force of its own. We are encouraged to go with the flow, and not question what is being said.

Consider the following statement by the historian Barbara Fields, spoken on screen in the Burns civil war documentary (and possibly chosen by the film-makers out of many other things that Professor Fields also said, but that sounded less dramatic):

> [The Founders] adopted a constitution that *required* a war to be sorted out, and therefore *required* a war to make real a nation out of what was a theoretical nation as it was defined at the Constitutional Convention [my emphases].[31]

Fields's reference, here, is to the contradiction, in the United States Constitution, between its commitment to the principles of freedom and its recognition of the institution of slavery. The question that needs to be asked is: how does Fields know that the abolition of slavery required a war for its ending? The short answer is that she has no grounds for knowing this. Yet she says it. She converts the fact that the civil war did happen into a claim that it had to happen (for the desired end to be achieved). Slavery was ended in many other polities without recourse to war; nor do there seem to be any really persuasive grounds for holding that, as a result of the civil war, the United States was speedier in according equal rights to African-Americans than would otherwise have been the case. After all, the American civil rights movement only began to enjoy some significant success roughly a century after the civil war ended.

Consider, further, the words of another talking head from the final episode of *The Civil War*, the historian Stephen B. Oates, who tells us all that

> The civil war is not only the central event of American history but it's a central event in large ways for the world itself. If we believe today, and surely we must, that popular government is the way to go, it is the way to the emancipation of the

human spirit, then the civil war established the fact that a popular government can survive ... So the war becomes, in essence, [...] a testament for the liberation of the human spirit for all time.[32]

It is a quite stunning series of propositions that Professor Oates advances in the course of a twenty-second sound bite. (Perhaps he would be more nuanced in written discourse, or perhaps not.) What is being presented to millions of viewers – without supporting argument – is, first, the claim that 'popular government' is *the* good form of government, the form of government to which all peoples should direct their aspirations. (Since no other popular form of government is presented in *The Civil War* than the American form, one assumes that it is the American form of popular government that is here intended.) Second, the implicit claim of Fields's and Oates's observations taken together is that freedom, equality and popular government are legitimately attained, and may legitimately be spread, by military means.

Can one much wonder at the direction of American policy with regard to Iraq in 2002–2004 when American identity is supplied with this kind of myth-historical foundation? As I write these words, in December 2004, the justifying argument for that military adventure has become America's mission to spread democracy. I open the local newspaper and see, starting on the front page, an account of the funeral of a local twenty-year-old Marine corporal, who died in Fallujah, Iraq, on 19 November. According to the article, his friends and family said that his purpose 'was to fight for democracy and freedom, and to live according to God's will'.[33] Moreover, when I observe the mythic apprehension of American history in American popular media and consciousness more generally, I am led to wonder whether polities ought to be based on history at all. Since identity is in significant measure the product of historical experience, this is as much as to wonder whether polities ought to be based on identity at all. This is the subject of another paper, but I can say a few words about the matter here.

Of course, Frenchmen are Frenchmen, Dutchmen are Dutchmen, Germans are Germans, and so on, in rather the way that, two hundred years ago, Virginians were Virginians and New Englanders were New Englanders. Particular identities are one of the delights of life, but this does not mean that they ought to be taken as the foundation for states or for international confederations. It seems to me that it is profitable here to make a distinction between *identities* and *allegiances*. It is a mistake, I wish to suggest, to think about the general problem of the relationship between history writing and human beings' relations to each other in and between large groups without keeping in mind these two forms of human solidarity – which are related, but also clearly different.

I take an *identity* to be a form of human solidarity that, once it is put into place, functions in a *quasi-natural* way. That is to say, an identity is something that, once it is in place, is seen as no longer a matter of *choice*. Note that I am not saying that identities are natural *tout court*, but only that they appear natural once they have emerged or have been adopted. The ideal typical form of identity is the type that arises over time without any conscious attempt to create it. This is the kind of sense of self that individual human beings normally acquire over the course of their childhoods, without knowing that they are doing so. Collective identity-formation is often much the same: people take it in in a largely non-reflective, unintentional way, as the by-product of living of their lives. But of course, as we well know, collective identities are also *formed*, as a result of deliberate effort, most obviously as a result of teaching carried out in schools. For example, religious identity is deliberately inculcated in Sunday schools, and 'national' identity is often inculcated with something like the same deliberateness in elementary and secondary schools.

The formation of both individual and collective identity surely exists on a continuum between the unintentional and the intentional. In the most recent generation, from the late 1970s onward, there has been much talk of the 'inventing' or 'imagining' of collective identities as a more or less intentional process – one thinks of Hobsbawm and Ranger, of Benedict Anderson, and of the French *lieux de mémoire* project directed by Pierre Nora, among other examples.[34] However, although the recent focus has been on how collective identities can be intentionally made, it seems obvious that they also emerge more or less 'naturally' from things that happen. Identity seems to be one of those things that is both invented and found. The relative balance between the two cannot be discussed at a theoretical level, but can only be dealt with in relation to specific historical instances. What seems evident is that, once it has been invented, identity gives the impression of being *there*, existing as a reality and not as a choice to be made.

I dwell on this point because of the distinction I want to make between solidarities of *identity* and solidarities of *allegiance*. Identities are conceptions as to who we *are*. Allegiances, on the other hand, are conceptions as to what we *wish* to be loyal to. An allegiance can indeed be a matter of choosing to be loyal to a particular collective identity. This was certainly the basic underlying idea of the nation-state, to which much national history seems to have been intended to contribute. However, we need to uncouple identity and allegiance. Not all allegiance is tied to identity, let alone national identity. It seems clear that if a polity is to function well, it must indeed rely on solidarities that go beyond the closer solidarities of family and neighbourhood, of congregation and village. In this sense, the basic idea behind the notion of the national state is correct. However, it is possible, and in a multicultural world probably desirable, to attempt more and more to foster solidarities that are not identities.

One thinks, for example, of the solidarity that Churchill tapped into, and perhaps also in part created, from May 1940 until the end of the Second World

War – a solidarity that somehow managed to override, obviously without eliminating, the sharp class divisions, rooted in all sorts of injustices, petty and grand, that permeated British society at the time. More negatively, one thinks of the failure of the French in the period up to May 1940 to arrive at a comparable solidarity and sense of unified action. One also cannot help but wonder whether the fate of European Jewry in that period would have been less terrible had European Jews not been so fragmented by cross-cutting allegiances, of greater or less intensity, to French, Czech, Italian or other forms of national solidarity, by the fragmentation within Jewry as between different types of religious commitment, and between religious commitment and a rejection of that commitment. All of this should be considered within the context of national states that for the most part were insufficiently committed to solidarities of allegiance that might have better hindered the Nazi policy of isolation and deportation than did solidarities (or lack thereof) arising from identity.

Identities are rooted in past historical experience and in the continuation of that experience in collective memory. Allegiances can just as well be rooted in a present-day willed commitment to a constitutional polity and to behaviour that is congruent with that polity. One thinks, for example, of India, a multi-ethnic, indeed multi-national, country if there ever was one. It would be fatal to attempt to root such a polity in national identity. Nevertheless, the rooting of such a polity in allegiance to norms of public and political behaviour that we can think of as constitutional norms is more than conceivable. Identity *continues* (or *seeks* to continue) the past. Constitution, on the other hand, seeks to constitute anew, and then to follow what has been constituted. Such constituting norms, which in a Nietzschean sense might be considered 'unhistorical' or even 'supra-historical', have a deeply ambiguous relation to historically created identities. Accordingly, perhaps we should think of history writing, not as something that engages in the building of national identities, but rather as something that critiques all historical identity-claims, and in doing so, as a by-product, opens a space for constitutional allegiances and behavioural norms that stand at a remove from what is *simply* given to us by the past.

Notes

1. S. Berger, C. Conrad and G.P. Marchal, '"Representations of the Past: National Histories in Europe": Proposal for a New Scientific Programme in the Humanities', unpublished ESF project proposal, dated January 2002; in author's possession.
2. European Science Foundation (ESF), *Representations of the Past: National Histories in Europe (NHIST): An ESF Scientific Programme*, Strasbourg, 2004: 5. http://www.esf.org/publication/171/NHIST.pdf
3. Ibid., 1.
4. Ibid., 4.

5. A. Megill, 'Some Aspects of the Ethics of History-Writing: Reflections on Edith Wyschogrod's An Ethics of Remembering', in D. Carr, T.R. Flynn and R.A. Makkreel, eds, *The Ethics of History*, Evanston, IL, 2004: 47, 71 n. 5.
6. P. Veyne, *Comment on écrit l'histoire, suivi de Foucault révolutionne l'histoire*, Paris, 1978: 13.
7. As I was revising this paper, I found that Jonathan Gorman makes a similar point as to the relation between historical representation and present political hope, and does so in response to precisely the paragraph of the ESF brochure that I quoted just above. Completely independently of this paper or of the talk out of which it grew, he also quotes it *in toto*. See J. Gorman, 'Historians and Their Duties', *History and Theory* 43, 4, 2004: 113; also personal communication from Gorman.
8. L. Ranke, *Histories of the Latin and Germanic Nations from 1494–1514* (1824), 'Preface', in F. Stern, ed., *The Varieties of History: From Voltaire to the Present*, 2nd ed., New York, 1972: 53.
9. K. Marx, 'The Eighteenth Brumaire of Louis Bonaparte' (1852), trans. B. Fowkes, in K. Marx, *Surveys from Exile, Political Writings*, vol. 2, ed. D. Fernbach, New York, 1973: 146.
10. F. Nietzsche, 'On the Uses and Disadvantages of History for Life', in F. Nietzsche, *Untimely Meditations*, trans. R.J. Hollingdale, 1874, Cambridge, 1983: 60–77.
11. As Thomas H. Brobjer demonstrates, after 1875/76 Nietzsche 'almost completely ignored' his *Untimely Meditation* on history, and 'a few times he outright rejected its argument and content'; T.H. Brobjer, 'Nietzsche's View of the Value of Historical Studies and Methods', *Journal of the History of Ideas* 65, 2, 2004: 301. Although a lot of attention has been lavished on Nietzsche's 1874 essay, it is not at all representative of his thinking about history.
12. F. Nietzsche, *On the Genealogy of Morality: A Polemic*, trans., with notes, M. Clark and A.J. Swensen, 1887, Indianapolis, Ind., 1998: 35–36.
13. L. Febvre, 'A New Kind of History', in his *A New Kind of History and Other Essays*, trans. K Folca, ed. P. Burke, New York, 1973: 27–43.
14. Ibid., 41.
15. Ibid., 40.
16. ESF, *Representations of the Past*, 1.
17. Berger et al., 'Proposal', 8.
18. L. Eriksonas, *National Heroes and National Identities: Scotland, Norway and Lithuania*, Brussels, 2004.
19. J. Mali, *Mythistory: The Making of a Modern Historiography*, Chicago, 2003.
20. ESF, *Representations of the Past*, 4.
21. Ibid.
22. For a discussion of four types of objectivity – absolute, disciplinary, procedural and dialectical – see A. Megill, 'Introduction: Four Senses of Objectivity', in his edited *Rethinking Objectivity*, Durham, NC, 1994: 1–20; expanded version in A. Megill, *Historical Knowledge, Historical Error: A Contemporary Guide to Practice*, Chicago, 2007, 107–24.
23. A.C. Danto, *Narration and Knowledge*, New York, 1985: 143–81; see esp. p. 169. The book includes the integral text of *Analytical Philosophy of History*, 1965.
24. On the grounding of the nineteenth-century historical profession in an ultimately Christian grand narrative, see A. Megill, '"Grand Narrative" and the Discipline of History', in F.R. Ankersmit and H. Kellner, eds, *A New Philosophy of History*, Chicago, 1995: 151–73, 263–71; repr. in A. Megill, *Historical Knowledge, Historical Error*, 165–87.
25. R.M. Nixon, 'Address to the Nation about the Watergate Investigations', 30 Apr. 1973, http://www.watergate.info/nixon/73-04-30watergate-speech.shtml
26. J-F. Lyotard, *The Post-Modern Condition: A Report on Knowledge*, trans. G. Bennington and B. Massumi, Minneapolis, Minn., 1984: xxiii.

27. A. Megill, 'Historiography as a Written Form', in D.L. Shelton, ed., *Encyclopedia of Genocide and Crimes against Humanity*, vol. 1, New York, 2004: 448–51.

28. L. Douglas, *The Memory of Judgment: Making Law and History in the Trials of the Holocaust*, New Haven, Conn., 2001: 170–71.

29. K. Burns and R. Burns, producers, *The Civil War* [television series], 1990: episode 9.

30. On 30 November, 2004, a Google search of 'Gallipoli' and 'Australian identity' yielded 657 hits.

31. Burns and Burns, *Civil War*, episode 9.

32. Ibid.

33. K. Andrews, 'Hundreds Attend Marine's Memorial', *The Daily Progress*, Charlottesville, Va., Nov. 28, 2004: A1, A12.

34. E. Hobsbawm and T. Ranger, *The Invention of Tradition*, Cambridge, 1983; B. Anderson, *Imagined Communities: Reflections on the Origin and Spread of Nationalism*, 1983, London, 1991; P. Nora, *Les Lieux de mémoire*, 7 vols, Paris, 1984–92.

Chapter 2

Drawing the Line: 'Scientific' History between Myth-making and Myth-breaking

CHRIS LORENZ

In December 1985 William McNeill presented a paper to the American Historical Association's annual meeting. At the time McNeill, who had earned his fame with widely acknowledged books such as *The Rise of the West* and *Plagues and People*, was president of the AHA and one of the pioneers of a kind of history which has since become known as 'global history' or 'world history'. The title of his paper was as original as it was enigmatic: 'Mythistory, or Truth, Myth, History, and Historians'. Published in the same year as a chapter in a volume entitled *Mythistory and Other Essays*, it was original inasmuch as 'mythistory' was a newly coined term, and enigmatic because history and myth had traditionally been considered by professional historians to be polar opposites. The dividing line between history and myth had only recently been questioned by hard-line postmodernists – and McNeill was not known for his postmodern predilections.[1] On the contrary, McNeill was a serious craftsman if there ever was one, possessing a fine sense for innovation and for what was going on within the profession. It is hardly surprising, then, that his prediction that the term 'mythistory' would not catch on with his colleagues turned out to be correct.

Here I will take his article as a point of departure in order to analyse the fundamental tensions between the two central epistemological and practical claims made by 'scientific' historians for their subject since its beginnings as an academic discipline in Europe. The epistemological claim related to the status of history writing as a *Wissenschaft*, that is, a methodical truth-seeking discipline: academic history, above all else, claimed to do away with all myths about the past and to replace them with The Truth – or, at least, some truths. Accordingly, academic history had become characterised by its *Wissenschaftsanspruch*, its claim to scientificity, although this claim could be based on a wide variety of methodological positions, ranging from Comtean positivism to Rankean historicism.

Next to this epistemological claim, however, academic history always claimed to fulfil a practical function, namely, to provide a certain degree of guidance in practical life, and this constituted its *Orientierungsanspruch*, its claim to practical orientation.[2] For most professional historians over much of the nineteenth and twentieth centuries this practical orientation was about creating some kind of identification with the state, most often the nation-state. This was no accident since the professionalisation of academic history was very much a state affair; most professional historians were literally fed by the state. Not without justification, then, have historians been called 'priests of the state'.

In the following article I shall analyse McNeill's argument in order to show the fundamental and unresolved opposition between its epistemological and its practical claims. I shall argue that the practical claims undermine the epistemological claims in a manner that is characteristic of scientific history from the early nineteenth century onwards. The stronger its epistemological claims, the weaker its practical claims – and vice versa.

I shall start by arguing that McNeill tries to bridge the opposition between his epistemological and practical claims in two ways. On the one hand, he projects the practical aims onto the process of history itself and thus 'objectifies' them. This strategy of 'hardening' the practical goals by 'objectifying' has characterised scientific history since its foundation. The other strategy used by McNeill to bridge the opposition between history's epistemological and practical aims, however, consists of 'softening up' the epistemological claims of scientific history by integrating its practical goals into the 'soft' and 'subjective' aspects of historical epistemology. In this respect scientific history has seen the notions of 'narrative', 'meaning' and 'interpretation' turn into the loci within which practical 'meaning' is situated. Hayden White's attempt in *Metahistory* to connect specific types of ideological content to specific narrative forms is the logical endpoint of this train of thought (although it should be noted that McNeill's notion of 'mythistory' is not indebted to White). Nevertheless, the question of whether narrative history can claim to represent truth is as fundamental for McNeill's 'mythistory' as it is for White's *Metahistory*.[3]

After having reconstructed the birth of 'mythistory', I shall go on to analyse the notion of myth itself in order to establish its relationship to the concept of history. This will lead us to an examination of the anthropological debate regarding myth and its functions, including myths of the nation. Thirdly, I shall raise the question of whether the nation itself can be seen as a myth. This question is fundamental for the historical credentials of 'scientific' history, because 'scientific' historians have been the prime academic constructors of nations. Finally, I shall go back to the writings of Ranke and Von Humboldt in order to locate the origins of 'scientific' history's epistemological difficulties. Paradoxically, it will turn out that McNeill's problem of drawing the line between 'scientific' history and myth was already embedded in the project of 'scientific' history itself.

From 'Scientific' History to 'Mythistory'

> Myth and history are close kin inasmuch as both explain how things got to be the way they are by telling some sort of story. But our common parlance reckons myth to be false while history is, or aspires to be, true. Accordingly, a historian who rejects someone else's conclusions calls them mythical, while claiming that his own views are true. However, what seems true to one historian will seem false to another, so one historian's truth becomes another's myth, even at the moment of utterance.[4]

With these intriguing sentences McNeill opens his article, and the rest of it he devotes to answering the delicate question of how scientific history got into its current predicament, with scientific historians regarding each others' histories as 'mythical' and truth increasingly being 'privatised' rather than becoming universal.

This situation is all the more puzzling because the original rationale of scientific history was to replace myths about the past with true stories. Almost all of the treatises about 'scientific' history produced by nineteenth-century historians abound in statements about exchanging mythical, fraudulent, 'amateur' and/or 'artistic' efforts for true reconstructions.[5] Almost all histories of historiography also argue that 'myth' is something scientific history left behind long ago, usually locating the break somewhere between the seventeenth and the nineteenth century (with Herodotus and Thucydides being habitually cited as its Greek precursors).[6] Take Collingwood for instance, who characterises myth in contrast to history, which deals with human actions localised in time and space, as follows:

> Myth [...] is not concerned with human actions at all. The human element has been completely purged away and the characters of the story are simply gods. And the divine actions that are recorded are not dated events in the past: they are conceived of as having occurred in the past, indeed, but in a dateless past which is so remote that nobody knows when it was. It is outside all our time reckoning and called 'the beginning of things'. Hence, when a myth is couched in what seems a temporal shape, because it relates events one of which follows another in a temporal shape, the shape is not strictly speaking temporal, it is quasi-temporal.[7]

According to Collingwood, history is only concerned with temporally dated human actions and is thus the opposite of myth, which deals with gods acting in times beyond temporal markers.

What had happened to the project of 'scientific' history since it first took flight, full of self-confidence? McNeill, who initially shared the traditional historians' aversion to methodology, formulates the following answer: although scientific history had made great progress since the beginning of the nineteenth century by transcending pre-existing divisions, such as those resulting from religious controversies, it had failed in generating a consensus comparable to that found in the natural sciences.[8] He offers two explanations for this state of affairs. Firstly, although many individual facts in history can be established beyond reasonable doubt, history cannot be reduced to individual facts: 'To become a history, facts have to be put together into a pattern that is understandable and credible [...]. In order to make facts "understandable", the historian imputes "meaning" to them, and in order to make them credible the historian has to take account of the expectations of the audience he or she is addressing'.[9] So McNeill explains the absence of an epistemological consensus among historians by the fact that historians connect historical facts in meaningful patterns – alias narratives – and that these meaningful patterns have no general epistemic validity, because their credibility is restricted to specific audiences (as was the case in the rhetorical tradition).

Secondly, McNeill presents the reflexivity of these (symbolically structured) meaning patterns as an explanation for the absence of consensus in history. His argument is as follows:

> The great and obvious difference between natural scientists and historians is the greater complexity of the behavior historians seek to understand. The principal source of historical complexity lies in the fact that human beings react both to the natural world and to one another chiefly through the mediation of symbols. This means, among other things, that any theory about human life, if widely believed, will actually alter actual behavior, usually by inducing people to act as if the theory were true. Ideas and ideals thus become self-validating within remarkably elastic limits [...]. The price of this achievement is the elastic, inexact character of truth, and especially of truths about human conduct.[10]

Therefore, McNeill's second explanation for the absence of consensus in history is the reflexivity of 'theories about human life', because this type of 'theory' alters human conduct itself. McNeill thus makes no fundamental distinction between the ('first order') 'theories about human life' of historical actors themselves and those ('second order') theories developed by historians *ex post facto*. His argument seems to be that both kinds of 'theory' may turn into self-fulfilling prophecies (he may have been thinking of theories like nationalism or racism, although he does not mention them).

According to McNeill, 'shared truths' are necessary in order for groups and cultures to survive, because they create in-group solidarity and function as a group's 'social cement'. Sects, religions, tribes and states from the Sumer to modern times have all based their identity and cohesion on 'shared truths' in the form of shared beliefs, ideals and traditions. Here McNeill seems to lump together any collective belief system under the heading of 'shared truths', including all kinds of belief about the past. 'Yet to outsiders, truths of this kind are likely to seem myths [...] because different groups usually have different versions of the truth about themselves and in all likelihood this sort of social and ideological fragmentation will continue indefinitely'.[11]

Is there any uncontested place for *historical* truth in this fragmented world? It is clear that McNeill, who refers to the 'truth' of 'meaning patterns' or narratives produced by historians and not the truth of historical factual statements, answers this question in the negative, because the idea that 'scientific method' would create a consensus among 'professional' historians has turned out to be just 'a recent example of such a belief system': 'Choice is everywhere; dissent turns into cacophonous confusion; my truth dissolves into your myth even before I can put words on paper'.[12]

However, he then, quite surprisingly given the logic of his argument, states that he is 'not ready to abandon' his liberal faith that in the free marketplace of ideas 'truth will eventually prevail', notwithstanding the present confusion.[13] Still, the same logic forces him to qualify his own appeal to the 'liberal' idea of truth as just another 'faith', so in the end the regulative idea of truth for him is subject to a 'take it or leave it' approach, rather than forming a constitutive principle of 'scientific' history as such. In this respect McNeill's standpoint can be likened to that of a postmodernist *manqué*, who in the end recoils from the conclusion of his own argument.

At this point in his argument McNeill constructs a bridge in his analysis between the 'fragmented' epistemological universe in which it is hard, if not impossible, to draw a line between myth and truth, and a 'fragmented' normative universe. Large numbers of people, ranging from Iranian Moslems to American sectarians (religious and otherwise), 'exhibit symptoms of acute distress in the face of moral uncertainties, generated by exposure to competing myths'. The result of these worldwide moral uncertainties is 'an intensified personal attachment, first to national, and then to sub-national groups, each with its distinct ideals and practices'. This moral fragmentation also pertains to historians because 'the historical profession faithfully reflected and helped to forward these shifts of sentiment'. Women's, black and postcolonial history have been booming ever since.[14]

Like any postmodernist worth his salt, McNeill does not buy into the professional ideology according to which 'professionalisation equals objectivity', and neither does he have a fundamental problem with disciplinary fragmentation.[15] Given the history of 'scientific' history, he regards the moral and practical allegiances of historians to specific groups as only natural: 'Such activity confronted our traditional professional role of helping to define collective identities in ambiguous situations. Consciousness of a common past, after all, is a powerful supplement to other ways of defining who "we" are.'[16]

Historians have in fact always been active in defining boundaries between an 'Us' and a 'Them'.[17] National historiography is the best known genre in point, Herodotus providing the model with his emphasis on the supreme value of political freedom within a territorially defined state. Because all human groups like to be flattered rather than criticised, historians are 'under perpetual pressure to conform to expectations by portraying the people they write about in a positive light; and a mingling of truth and falsehood, blending history with ideology, results'.[18] Most national and group history is of this nature, according to McNeill, although the precise mixture of detachment and emotional involvement varies with every historian; 'truth, persuasiveness, intelligibility rest far more on this level of the historian's art than on source criticism'.[19]

McNeill's distinction between source criticism and the 'art' of putting the facts together in credible 'meaning patterns' or narratives goes back to Ranke, as we shall see, although the exact relationship between both activities has received very little attention either from historians or philosophers of history. Yet the identity-constructing and identity-enhancing aspects of history writing are essential to the whole enterprise, because 'myths' of this sort are self-validating and enhance the chances of the 'survival' of groups, especially during conflicts. Therefore, the historian has no choice but to choose: 'Where to fix one's loyalties is the supreme question of human life, and is especially acute in a cosmopolitan age like ours when choices abound.'[20]

What McNeill presents here is what we could call an *observational theory* characteristic of a historian. He presents the theory as a description of 'how it actually is': according to him, the world just *is* both cosmopolitan and fundamentally fragmented – and so is the discipline of history.[21] His next move is to connect his *cognitive* observational theory to a *normative* theory of the practical function of history. In true Kantian spirit McNeill concludes that in our cosmopolitan age the only realistic and morally acceptable option for the historian is to pledge his loyalty to humanity as a whole:

> Instead of enhancing conflicts, as parochial historiography inevitably does, an intelligible world history might be expected to diminish the lethality of group encounters by cultivating a sense of individual identification with the triumphs and tribulations of humanity as a whole. This, indeed, strikes me as the moral duty of the historical profession in our time. We need to develop an ecumenical history, with plenty of room for human diversity in all its complexity.[22]

This transition from the cognitive to the normative level is a typical methodological move for a historian, and dates back to the origins of 'scientific' history. The basic mechanism supporting the transition is the projection of the normatively preferred process onto the 'factual' process of history itself, which leads to the 'objectification' of these processes. In this way, the historians of the nation-state simply identified history itself with the genesis and development of nation-states, just as the historians of class struggle simply identified history itself with the genesis and development of class struggles. Remarkably, even historians who advocate 'the postmodern condition' have actually identified history itself with the genesis and development of this 'condition'.[23] Taking a normative position, such as furthering the cause of the nation, furthering the cause of one class in the class struggle, or furthering the 'postmodern condition', is then represented as being a more or less cognitive step, simply a matter of 'reading the sign of the times' or 'riding the waves of history'.

McNeill is aware that world history is still a suspicious genre for most historians because they think that truth only resides in the documents. World history, with its reliance on literature rather than archival sources, is therefore often regarded as necessarily vague or even 'unhistorical'. According to McNeill, this is mere prejudice, but fortunately the historian's practice is often better than his epistemology. With a more reflective epistemology it is not hard to attain 'a better historiographical balance between Truth, truths and myth'.[24]

Since Eternal Truth is not the stuff of human affairs, Truth with a capital T can be discarded. However, McNeill argues that

> Truths with a small t are what historians achieve when they bend their minds as critically and carefully as they can to the task of making their account of public affairs credible as well as intelligible to an audience that shares enough of their particular outlook and assumptions to accept what they say. The result may be called mythistory [...].[25]

For McNeill, then, truths in history depend for their status on their plausibility for a particular audience, and are not universal. Therefore, truths in history are multiple, although this does not mean that one mythistory is as good as another: 'Some clearly are more adequate to the facts than others'[26] in terms of temporal and spatial scope, range and accuracy. As we have seen, historiography has, by and large, made progress in this respect according to McNeill's liberal conviction, so that 'to be a truth-seeking mythographer is [...] a high and serious calling'.[27] So in the end, and quite remarkably, McNeill still appeals to (Popperian) epistemic criteria when it comes to evaluating different species of 'mythistory', probably because he knows that in any 'scientific' discourse overtly normative arguments tend to blow up in one's face. So, at the very end of his argument, McNeill once again turns back at the sight of its logical consequences, preferring to sail his boat into a reassuringly safe 'scientific' harbour. How the epistemic criteria of scope and accuracy are supposed to function in a fundamentally 'fragmented' scientific universe remains unclear, alas. His decision to prevent his postmodern flirt with the notion of myth from developing into a full-blown relationship at the *moment suprême* thus comes at a price – the price of his argument's consistency.

All in all, with the notion of 'mythistory' the traditional rationale of 'scientific' history remains at stake, because the demarcation between scientific, methodical truth and myth constituted the very rationale of 'scientific' history in the first place. By blurring the line between scientific history and myth, it is no longer clear whether there is any distinction, and if so, what this distinction is. What is now called for, then, is a clarification of the notion of myth.

What is Myth? Myth from the Ancient Greeks to the Present

In her overview of the notion of myth the anthropologist Joanna Overing immediately identifies the problem McNeill has raised in his concept of 'mythistory':

> The first relevant question in the study of myth is: how do we know that something falls within the genre of myth? How do we categorise this, but not that, as myth? Why, for instance, should we decide to use the term 'myth' and not 'history' in describing a particular piece of discourse? Whether in the context of Amazonia or Eastern Europe, the boundaries between myth and history are not clear, and one reason for this is that the category of myth is not easily defined. We might perhaps say that the use of the term 'myth' is more a judgmental than a definitional or propositional procedure: its attribution requires a judgment having to do with standards of knowledge and its organisation.[28]

Myth, according to Overing, owes its bad reputation to Greek philosophy, in which it was identified with a category of fictional discourse at some point between the eighth and the fourth century BC 'Myth or *mythos* became understood as a form of speech opposed to reasoned discourse or *logos*. As such myth became defined as opposed to both truth (myth is fiction) and to the rational (myth is absurd).'[29] Both the historian Thucydides and the philosopher Plato identified myth with 'old wives' tales, the fabulous and the marvellous – the opposite of truthful discourse.

Earlier on, myth had possessed a more positive ring, with a capacity both to express the fundamental truths of existence and a capacity to give pleasure and to involve the emotional participation of an audience. These qualities ensured myth's power to captivate an audience and to be effective. McNeill attributed these same characteristics to 'mythistory'. So, in short, all the major oppositions associated with the notion of myth today go back to the rationalist oppositions of Greek antiquity: the opposition between *mythos* and *logos*, between the contextual and the universal, between the absurd and the logical, the emotional and the rational.[30] These oppositions were all reproduced by nineteenth-century anthropology, which turned myths into its object of inquiry: *mythos* was taken to be evidence of barbarian, primitive cultures, while *logos* was exclusively attributed to Western civilisation.

While anthropologists took primitive cultures as their object of enquiry, they studied other people's myths – people's fictive constructions of reality or 'phantom realities', to use the phrase of Overing. Thus, like the ancient Greeks, nineteenth-century anthropologists, and their successors well into the twentieth century, continued to view mythology as fictive, consisting of fabulous, untrue stories about unreal gods and heroes that erroneously explained a people's past to them.[31] Anthropology acknowledged the rationality of the 'savage mind', but it did not acknowledge the truth claims embedded in the savage 'worldviews'. It could not, for instance, accommodate such 'primitive' ideas as the concept of rain being caused by urinating gods, within the rational Newtonian universe.

The classical demarcation between the mythical 'reality of the really made-up' of 'primitive' people and our 'real', scientifically known reality, however, has recently been questioned by anthropologists (just as McNeill did for history). Marshall Sahlins argued in his *Islands of History* (1985) that in Polynesian culture the distinction between (fictitious) myth and (real) history does not hold water: myths in Polynesian culture are the key to its cosmology and its conception of history. Overing makes the very same point with regard to the Piaroa-tribe in Amazonia: their mythical gods are part of their narratives about their history; and their mythical time does not belong to a closed past, but rather remains omnipresent. Furthermore, she argues that the Piaroa live within an evaluative universe, quite unlike the Western one, in which 'nature' is not a separate domain to be subjugated and controlled by humans: 'All postulates about reality in an evaluative universe, including those about physical reality, are tied explicitly to a moral universe.'[32] Therefore, Overing refers to the 'truth of myths' in this cosmological sense – very much in the sense in which McNeill was referring to the 'shared truths' essential for every culture: 'Myths simply express and deal with a people's reality postulates about the world, and mythic truths pertain more to a moral universe of meaning than to a "natural" one (in the sense of the physical unitary world of the scientist). For those educated within a Western tradition, myth is a strange place indeed to discover "truth"'[33] – although not for McNeill, as we have observed.

Next to the nebulous dividing line between myth and history, there is a second issue raised by Overing that is pertinent to McNeill's argument about identity-construction by history. This is what one could call the performative function of myths in making the distinction between identity and difference, between an 'Us' and a 'Them'. Myths contain heroic stories about the origins and fate of specific communities and as such express images of selfhood by stating sets of identity criteria for a community. In this way myths help constitute communities' distinctness from others by creating boundaries.[34] Often these images of selfhood are simultaneously based on images of threatening and despised others as their 'alien' *Doppelgänger*, as Schöpflin argues. So myths create communities by demonising others, although the degree of this demonisation can vary.[35] McNeill proposed an identical thesis with regard to history.

The third and final aspect of myth pertinent to McNeill's argument is the solidarity function of myth connected to the performative function just mentioned. Next to boundary creation, the role of myth in *solidarity creation*, through rituals, liturgies and symbols, is essential: 'The outcome of participation in ritual and, therefore, of accepting that one's relationship to the community is structured by myth, is the strengthening of both the collectivity and the individual's role in it [...] The common participation in ritual produces bonds of solidarity without demanding uniformity of belief. People can act together without consensus.'[36] Myth thus works on a *pre-rational* and *emotional* level that is crucial to its functioning. However, in order to fulfill this function myth must somehow resonate in 'collective memories', and therefore cannot be 'imagined' or 'invented' at will. Remarkably, McNeill made the very same points for history: he argued that histories are necessary for the solidarity and 'survival' of communities, and are dependent on their acceptance by a particular audience, which is in turn dependent on the compatibility of their presuppositions with their organising concepts.[37]

So, comparing Overing's and Schöpflin's analysis of myth with McNeill's analysis of history – which resulted in the introduction of the paradoxical notion of 'mythistory' – we have to draw the conclusion that on first inspection the dividing line between myth and history does not seem to hold or is, at best, imperceptibly thin. This would imply that we have to face the possibility that 'scientific' history is not only engaged in 'myth-breaking', but also in 'myth-making' – a conclusion already drawn by postmodernists. And, of course, the image of 'scientific' history would only get worse with the deconstruction of the privileged object of 'scientific' history since the latter half of the nineteenth-century itself – the nation – as a myth. This is exactly the predicament historians have found themselves in over the last decade or so.[38]

Is the Nation a Myth?

The importance of the question of whether the nation is also a myth – a 'self-validating' myth in McNeill's terms – can hardly be overestimated because since the nineteenth century 'scientific' historians have been among the prime architects of nations and of nation-states. If the answer is yes, there are even more compelling grounds to categorise 'scientific' history as 'mythistory' than those McNeill adduced, because he did not specifically address national history. 'Myth-making' – *horribile dictu* – may even have formed a greater part of the activity of scientific historians than 'myth breaking'.[39]

In the literature on nationalism, the dominant constructivist positions *à la* Benedict Anderson and Eric Hobsbawm definitely seem to back up the thesis that national historians have been 'mythmakers' *par excellence*. The notion that nations are 'imagined communities' (Anderson) which again are dependent on 'invented traditions' (Hobsbawm/Ranger), essentially identifies national historians as the main protagonists in the processes of 'imagining' and 'inventing'. By the same token, all essentialist notions of the nation developed from the early nineteenth century onwards can be deconstructed as the cognitive strategies of 'scientific' historians to cover up their own 'imagining' and 'inventing' practices. Anti-constructivist positions like that of Anthony D. Smith nowadays appear to be no more than footnotes to their constructivist counterparts, in the sense that they only emphasise that nations cannot be 'imagined' and 'invented' *at will* (because 'imagined' nations are only effective if they 'resonate' with something 'real').[40]

Also important in this context is the fact that constructivist authors have emphasised that the nation is not only an 'imagined', but also an 'emotional' community, that is 'produced' and 'staged' using the same cultural mechanisms, metaphors and practices as religion.[41] Therefore, nationalism is directly linked to the Christian religion, and there are good reasons to interpret nationalism as the 'nationalisation' of Christianity (and this will take us to the very origins of 'scientific' history in Ranke and Von Humboldt, as we shall see in the next section). Like religion, the nation is produced through rituals, cults and myths.[42] Religion's central values, love, sacrifice and death, are also those of the nation. Moreover, love is easily transformed into hatred towards those outside the community, while fallen soldiers are often represented as the 'incarnation of the nation'.[43] Both religious and national cults are centred on a sacred dogma and a sacred object – God and The Nation. Both have sacred symbols and both have a fixed calendar and fixed places for their cult-rituals – churches and national monuments. The international academic boom of *lieux de mémoire* projects derives its impetus from this analogy.

Both cults also worship special persons, who are regarded as 'mediators' between the world of the sacred and the world of the profane – in religious cults these special persons are saints and martyrs, and in national cults they are national heroes, especially those who founded The Nation and those who sacrificed their lives for it. In both cults, violent death in defence of the Sacred Cause is represented as worthy and meaningful – as a sacrifice – because it helps the community in question to continue its existence. In both cults, we therefore usually encounter a cult of the dead. Both cults essentially define *moral* communities that define the borders of human solidarity, using similar vocabularies (with central notions like 'cult', 'sacrifice', 'eternity', 'incarnation', 'salvation', 'martyrdom', 'communion' and 'resurrection').[44] It is no accident, therefore, that Schöpflin in his taxonomy of myths also emphasised the Christian semantic structure of the national myths of redemption and suffering, the national myths of election and the civilising mission, the national myths of rebirth and renewal, and the national myth of a shared descent.[45]

One could argue on the basis of these overwhelming similarities that the case for 'mythistory' in national history is very convincing. Etienne Francois and Hagen Schulze recently summarised the general verdict on nineteenth-century 'scientific' national history as follows:

> Was the nineteenth century not a period in which everyone – historians, politicians and public opinion – was convinced that historical science had to be pursued with the aim of making it an objective science as opposed to the myths which it would destroy by bringing the whole truth about the past out into the daylight? [...] The result was that too often national myths have been dressed up as scientific truth.[46]

The diagnosis only gets worse when one realises that much twentieth-century national history was no better than its nineteenth-century counterpart. So, all in all, 'scientific' history has never known where to draw the line between myth-making and myth-breaking, and 'scientific' national historians have themselves been very active in helping to construct the myth of the nation while simultaneously deriving their 'scientific' legitimacy from a discourse of 'myth-breaking'. The very marginality of the history of historiography within the historical discipline – implying a very limited interest on the part of 'scientific' historians in their own history – may plausibly be interpreted as a professional mechanism in order to repress this threatening past. 'Don't look back' still seems the safest strategy for *everybody* with an unsettling past – including 'scientific' historians.[47]

The Source of the Troubles: Troubles at the Source

The foregoing discussion, then, has given 'scientific' history something of a pounding, as McNeill's proposal to rename 'history' as 'mythistory' has gone pretty much unchallenged (even if it contains some internal inconsistencies that need to be resolved). Our short investigation into the history of the concept of myth seems to support McNeill's diagnosis, as myth and history were found to be fulfilling essentially the same function, and anthropologists are no longer either able or willing to draw a fundamental line between history and myth.

Our inquiry into the debate about nations and nationalism pointed in precisely the same direction: national histories constructed by 'scientific' historians in the nineteenth-century have been deconstructed in recent decades as thoroughly mythical. The emotional function of national history, emphasised by the constructivists' contribution to this debate, only added extra force to the thesis that it is impossible to draw a firm line between national history and national mythology. The same could be said about the observation that striking similarities exist between discursive structures and practices relating to the nation and religion.[48] The recent debate about the Europe-wide phenomenon of *Volksgeschichte* in the twentieth century clearly suggests that the problem did not disappear in 1900, or after 1945.[49] The nation, in short, appears to be a prime example of the 'self-validating' type of myth revealed by McNeill's analysis, and in this capacity it may still be with us today.

The question that now needs to be addressed in this last section, then, is where the crisis of 'scientific' history comes from and whether there is any reason to hope that it will go away. There are two answers to this question: one reassuring and one rather alarming. The reassuring answer is that all debate and insecurity about the 'scientific' status of history is due to the fashionable and temporarily unsettling influences of postmodernism, feminism and multiculturalism.[50] This answer has, for obvious reasons, been the most popular one among 'scientific' historians.[51] Moreover, as historians know very well, there is always a 'post-' to every 'post-', and it is just a matter of time until 'post-postmodernism' will solve the crisis of 'scientific' history.

The more alarming answer, however, is that the crisis of 'scientific' history is *not* just a temporary phenomenon, but is built into the foundations of scientific history itself. Here I will argue for this second answer and I will do so by showing that the problem of 'mythistory' is already traceable in the writings of two of the 'fathers' of 'scientific' history, Leopold von Ranke and Wilhelm von Humboldt.

For those who are used to identifying Ranke with the critical method and the critical method with empiricism in history, the idea of looking for the origins of the 'myth problem' in Ranke would probably seem a strange idea. In the US the 'empiricist' reading of Ranke is most common, but it is certainly not restricted to that country alone. In their introduction to an English edition of Ranke's selected writings, Georg Iggers and Konrad von Moltke have flagged up this problem. Ranke's famous dictum that historians should write 'wie es eigentlich gewesen', based on the application of the critical method, has usually been misinterpreted as an advocacy of hardboiled 'empiricism', implying a restriction of scientific history to 'the facts'. This interpretation, however, is completely wrongheaded because it misses what Ranke meant by 'eigentlich': 'It is not factuality, but the emphasis on the essential that makes an account historical.'[52] And what Ranke regarded as essential in history was not established by the critical method, but only by his *Ideenlehre* – his idealistic theory of history, which functioned as his interpretative framework or observational theory.

According to this (Neoplatonic) theory, history was a process in which specific immanent ideas were present, realising themselves in the form of forces. States, religions and languages were such ideas, and Ranke saw each particular state, religion and language as a manifestation of such an idea, in the process of realising itself in a struggle against others – especially through the actions of 'great men', who were able to grasp the ideas of their time, the *Zeitgeist*.[53] The capacity to intuitively 'grasp' ('Ahnen', 'Divination') the ideas immanent in history was at least as essential for scientific history as the mastery of the critical method, because the factual establishment of events does not as yet constitute history for Ranke and von Humboldt. Only by connecting established facts to their immanent ideas, and thus by creating their meaningful unity – their *geistige Einheit* or their essential *Zusammenhang* – 'scientific' history was born.

Now both von Ranke and the other founders of the German Historical School of *Historismus* emphasised the 'theoretical', *non*-empirical aspect of scientific history as one of its *two* defining characteristics. Characteristically, the opening sentences of Ranke's early treatise *On the Character of Historical Science* read: 'History is distinguished from all other sciences in that it is also an art. History is a science in collecting, finding, penetrating; it is an art because it recreates and portrays that which it has found and recognised. Other sciences are satisfied simply with recording what has been found; history requires the ability to recreate.'[54]

Humboldt's equally famous treatise *On the Historian's Task* (1821) emphasises the 'theoretical', non-empirical aspect of scientific history even more clearly than Ranke: 'The historian's task is to present what actually happened. [...] An event, however, is only partially visible in the world of the senses; the rest has to be added by intuition, inference, and guesswork.'[55] The facts are just the 'raw material, but not history itself. [...] The truth of any event is predicated on the addition – mentioned above – of that invisible part of every fact, and it is this part, therefore, which the historian has to add. Regarded in this way, he does become active, even creative [...].'[56]

So both von Ranke and von Humboldt emphasised that interpretative activity, based on the *Ideenlehre*, was as essential for 'scientific' history as the critical method itself and that to ignore this aspect of the historian's activity 'is to miss the essence of truth itself'.[57] No wonder that Johan-Gustav Droysen, whose *Historik* is the first book-length treatise on historical method in the tradition of *Historismus*, also presented source criticism as merely a first step towards establishing the facts, the 'interpretation of ideas' being the real interpretative accomplishment of scientific history.[58]

I have gone back to the very origins of 'scientific' history in Germany because here we find the origins of the problems McNeill is raising. This holds both for the problem of history's scientific status and for history's practical status. First, for Ranke and Von Humboldt 'scientific' history consisted both in the application of the critical method in order to establish 'true' facts *and* in the 'creative' or 'artistic' interpretation of the facts on the basis of their *Ideenlehre* in order to connect them and bring out their actual 'meaning'. Ranke and von Humboldt actually regarded these ideas as active forces (*Kräfte*) immanent in history *itself*, and therefore by projecting their (Neoplatonic) theory onto reality, they treated it as if it were no different from historical reality.[59] What is remarkable, though, from our present point of view, is that their awareness of the 'theoretical' nature of history writing was *not* matched by an awareness of a plurality of possible theories. Therefore, all the epistemological problems of 'scientific' historians who realise that reality can be approached and interpreted through *different* theories *not* universally shared, are simply absent from the writings of Ranke and Von Humboldt. Of course, the explanation for their 'blindness' in this respect is that their *Ideenlehre* was not just a 'theory' for them, but their Christian worldview. Religious 'myth', therefore, was built into the foundations of 'scientific' history itself, and therefore it is small wonder that their ideas were 'reduced' by an empiricist reading later on.

So, although Ranke and Von Humboldt – contrary to most of their twentieth-century scions – were conscious of the fact that 'scientific' history was based not only on a (critical) *method*, but also on a *theory*, they simply failed to consider the possibility of other theories than the *Ideenlehre* and the epistemological problems resulting from the presence of *several* theories. What an epistemologically conscious 'scientific' history would have needed from its beginning, therefore, was a reflection on how to compare different theories and narratives with each other, and a reflection on how to evaluate their different epistemological and practical qualities.

This 'omission' at the very origin of 'scientific' history has had serious consequences for its later development, because those historians, who would later recognise the plurality of theories and narratives, lacked the theoretical tools and the theoretical justification to compare and evaluate them rationally. As a consequence of this theoretical *Leerstelle* the reflection on the preferences for and the evaluation of theories in history became 'subjectivised' and was conceived of in terms of the individual 'historical imagination' or of 'an act of faith'.[60] Historical theory, if recognised at all, was thus positioned outside the domain of rational, epistemological discourse. Seen in this light we can conclude – perhaps a little maliciously – that the 'scientific' history of Ranke and Von Humboldt was 'mythical' from its inception. 'Mythistory' finally turns out to be not a specific *Geburtsfehler* (failure at birth), but the birth of 'scientific' history itself.[61]

Unlike Ranke and Von Humboldt, McNeill expressly identifies scientific history with establishing facts by the critical method, and he thus exemplifies the 'empiricist' reduction of Ranke which Iggers and Von Moltke have commented upon. Owing to this 'empiricist' interpretation, McNeill only encounters the problems which will lead him to formulate the notion of 'mythistory' when he observes that history requires *more* from historians than just establishing the facts: these problems typically arise when he introduces the notion of 'meaning' (or 'interpretation'), which was still part and parcel of Ranke's conception of *Geschichtswissenschaft.*[62]

The scope of the notion of *Wissenschaft* had of course narrowed substantially between 1820 and 1985, resulting among other things in the 'expulsion' of the act of interpretation from the ground it had held during the reign of empiricism – only to make a triumphant return following the demise of empiricism as the dominant philosophy of science in the 1960s. Still under the spell of empiricism, however, McNeill equates science with consensus, and a science which is at the same time an art, as history was for Ranke, is no longer a life option for McNeill.[63] Therefore, his insight that 'interpretation' is just as essential for 'scientific' history as a critical method, constitutes a *problem* for McNeill, while it was still something of a *truism* for Ranke and Von Humboldt. Therefore, McNeill's acknowledgement that 'scientific' history, as a consequence of subjective 'interpretation', is characterised by an obvious *absence* of consensus leads him to the conclusion that history must be something *less* than a 'science' – and for this 'hybrid' he coins the term 'mythistory'. Small wonder, then, that Ranke's well-known ideas about the 'impartiality' and 'objectivity' of the historian are not even mentioned by McNeill.[64] 'Mythistory', an apparent *contradictio in adjecto* within the framework of 'scientific' history, is the logical end station of this train of argument.

McNeill's second reason for re-labelling history as 'mythistory' is related to its practical, reflexive function: all histories, being 'theories of human behaviour', influence human action and may even turn into self-fulfilling prophecies – the 'myth of the nation' included. This argument has no corollary in Ranke and Humboldt, because according to their theory the course of history ultimately is not so much determined by the intentions of human actors, but by God. Therefore, self-fulfilling prophecies do not fit into their framework and are not subjected to scrutiny. Yet Ranke and Humboldt nevertheless justify history's practical function through their observational theory.

According to Humboldt,

> the historian, in order to perform the task of his profession, has to compose the narrative of events in such a way that the reader's emotions will be stirred by it as if by reality itself. It is in this way that history is related to active life. History does not primarily serve us by showing us through specific examples, often misleading and rarely enlightening, what to do and what to avoid. History's true and immeasurable usefulness lies rather in its power to enliven and refine our sense of acting on reality, and this occurs more though the form attached to events than through the events themselves [...] [T]here is no successful intervention in the flow of events except by clearly recognising the truth of the predominating trend of ideas at a given time and by adhering to this truth with determination.[65]

In short, history's practical function is guaranteed for Ranke and Humboldt by the fact that historians, by showing the 'actual' reality of events – their 'essence', so to speak, stripped of what is merely 'accidental' – enable readers to see the 'trend' and to act accordingly. In their view historians could only show their readers tidal movements and waves of history, and the only practical choice human beings had was either to ride the waves or be swept away by them. Given this view, they could not foresee that 'scientific' history itself might ever be among the victims.

Notes

1. I have analysed the postmodern arguments of Michel Foucault, Michel de Certeau and Keith Jenkins for the 'mythical' character of history in '"You Got Your History, I Got Mine": Some Reflections on the Possibility of Truth and Objectivity in History', *Österreichische Zeitschrift für Geschichtswissenschaften* 10, 4, 1999: 563–84.
2. See G. Scholz, *Zwischen Wissenschaftsanspruch und Orientierungsbedürfnis. Zu Grundlage und Wandel der Geisteswissenschaften*, Frankfurt am Main, 1991: 38; 'Die Geisteswissenschaften aber, so wurde oft gesagt, verlieren an Bedeutung, an Bedeutsamkeit das, was sie an strenger Wissenschaftlichkeit gewinnen und vice versa. Sie haben das Ziel, Wissenschaft zu sein; sie haben aber auch andere Ziele: Sie wollen z.B. Orientierungen für das private und öffentliche Leben geben. Und dies beides geht nicht immer leicht zusammen.'
3. For an analysis of White's approach to the notion of truth, see my 'Can Histories Be True? Narrativism, Positivism and the "Metaphorical Turn"', *History and Theory* 37, 3, 1998: 309–29.
4. W. McNeill, 'Mythistory, or Truth, Myth, History, and Historians', in *Mythistory and Other Essays*, Chicago, 1985: 3.
5. See Moses Finley, 'Myth, Memory, and History', *History and Theory* 4, 3, 1965: 281–302; P. Heehs, 'Myth, History and Theory', *History and Theory* 33, 1, 1994: 1–19; G. Iggers, 'Historiography between Scholarship and Poetry: Reflections on Hayden White's Approach to Historiography', *Rethinking History* 4, 3, 2000: 373–90; J. Mali, *Mythistory: The Making of a Modern Historiography*, Chicago, 2003; R. Collins, 'Concealing the Poverty of Traditional Historiography: Myth as Mystification in Historical Discourse', *Rethinking History* 7, 3, 2003: 341–65; Jerry Bentley, 'Myths, Wagers, and Some Moral Implications of World History', *Journal of World History* 16, 1, 2005: 51–82. For a historiographical overview, see F. Stern, ed., *The Varieties of History: from Voltaire to the Present*, 2nd ed., New York, 1972.
6. See, for example, A. Momigliano, *The Classical Foundations of Modern Historiography*, Berkeley, 1990; and A. Grafton, *The Footnote: A Curious History*, Harvard, 1997.
7. R.G. Collingwood, *The Idea of History*, Oxford, 1976: 15.
8. McNeill, *Mythistory*, vii: 'As a young man, I thought methodology was a waste of time'.
9. Ibid., 5.
10. Ibid., 6–7.
11. Ibid., 7–8.
12. Ibid., 8–9.
13. Ibid., 9.
14. Ibid., 9–10.
15. See A. Megill, 'Fragmentation and the Future of Historiography', *American Historical Review* 96, 3, 1991: 693–98.
16. McNeill, *Mythistory*, 11. Cf. Scholz, *Orientierungsanspruch*, 26: 'But history writing in the humanistic tradition serves not only individual education but also the education of the nation, its national and cultural identity'.

17. Cf. Lorenz, 'Towards a Theoretical Framework for Comparing Historiographies: Some Preliminary Considerations', in P. Seixas, ed., *Theorizing Historical Consciousness*, Toronto, 2004: 25–49, esp. 29–32.
18. McNeill, *Mythistory*, 12.
19. Ibid., 13.
20. Ibid., 15–16, 19.
21. Elsewhere I have elaborated this position as 'internal realism': 'Historical Knowledge and Historical Reality: A Plea for "Internal Realism"', *History and Theory* 33, 3, 1994: 297–327.
22. McNeill, *Mythistory*, 16–17. See also 'The Care and Repair of Public Myth', *Mythistory*, 23–42.
23. For example, see K. Jenkins, 'Introduction' to his edited *The Postmodern History Reader*, London, 1997: 3; '[For] postmodernity is not an ideology or position we can choose to subscribe to or not, postmodernity is precisely our condition: it is our historical fate to be living now.'
24. McNeil, *Mythistory*, 17–19.
25. Ibid., 19.
26. Ibid., 19.
27. Ibid., 19–22.
28. J. Overing, 'The Role of Myth: An Anthropological Perspective, or: "The Reality of the Really Made-up"', in G. Hosking and G. Schöpflin, eds, *Myths and Nationhood*, London, 1997: 1. See also M. Dehli, 'Mythos', in S. Jordan, ed., *Lexikon Geschichtswissenschaft. 100 Grundbegriffe*, Stuttgart, 2002: 223: 'In jedem Fall muss dabei neu definiert werden, was konkret als Mythos verstanden wird, da es eine umfassende und verbindliche Definition der Begriffe Mythos und Mythologie nicht gibt. Allgemein läßt sich nur sagen, dass mit Mythos eine Sprachform bezeichnet wird, die nicht rational überzeugen, sondern symbolisch-emotional wirken will.' See also Daniel Woolf, 'Myth and history', in D. Woolf, ed., *A Global Encyclopedia of Historical Writing*, vol. 2, New York and London, 1998: 642. He defines the relationship between myth and history as the relationship between the mythical or legendary past and the documentable past as studied by historians: 'Myth is in some ways the mother of history, but the child's relationship to the parent has been both nurturing and at times quarrelsome.'
29. Overing, 2
30. Ibid., 3.
31. Ibid., 4.
32. Ibid., 13
33. Ibid., 12. G. Schöpflin, 'The Functions of Myth and a Taxonomy of Myths', in G. Hosking and G. Schöpflin, eds, *Myths and Nationhood*, London, 1997: 19, also equates myth with worldview: 'Myth is one of the ways in which collectivities – in this context especially nations – establish and determine the foundations of their own being, their own systems of morality and values [...] Centrally, myth is about perceptions rather than historically validated truths (insofar as these exist at all), about the ways in which communities regard certain propositions as normal and natural and others as perverse and alien'.
34. See also Schöpflin, 'Function of Myths', 22.
35. Overing, 17. It is remarkable that in the colonial encounter images of 'The Other' are often phrased in terms of sexual and culinary excess – next to the cannibalistic Wild Man there is the sexually profligate Wild Woman - while simultaneously a mechanism of inversion is at work: 'While for the indigenous discourse sexual excess speaks of a superfluity of power, in the logic of conquest sexual excess becomes the sign of degeneracy, and therefore of impotence'. On the role of 'aliens' in Russian histories, see J. Wertsch, 'Specific narratives and schematic narrative templates', in Seixas, ed., *Theorizing Historical Consciousness*, 49–63.
36. Schöpflin, 'Function of myths', 21.

37. Schöpflin, 'Function of Myths', 26; McNeill, *Mythistory*, 19.

38. Some historians have been questioning the scientific credentials of national history from the First World War onwards, because in many of the belligerent states the dividing line between national history and political propaganda got blurred beyond recognition. The founding myth of 'scientific' history that professionalisation equals 'objectivity' did not survive this war unscathed. The pleas after this war for making history more 'scientific' by ignoring or relativising state-related 'events' and 'politics', as for instance by historians Henri Pirenne and Marc Bloch, owed much to the loss of credentials of 'scientific' national history during and after this war. See also L. Raphael, *Geschichtswissenschaft im Zeitalter der Extreme*, Munich, 2003.

39. For the German example, see S. Berger, *Inventing the Nation: Germany*, London, 2004: 111–65.

40. See A.D. Smith, 'The "Golden Age" and National Renewal', in Hosking and Schöpflin, *Myths and Nationhood*, 36–60; and A.D. Smith, 'The Origins of Nations', in G. Eley and R. Grigor Suny, eds, *Becoming National: A Reader*, Oxford, 1996: 106–32, esp. 124; '[...] the nation that emerges in the modern era must be regarded as both construct and a real process, and that in a dual sense'. This point of view, however, is not fundamentally different from Hobsbawm's, who also emphasises the importance of 'real' 'proto-nationalism' for the later formation of nationalism. See E. Hobsbawm, *Nations and Nationalism since 1780: Programme, Myth, Reality*, Cambridge, 1990: 46–80.

41. See E. Francois, H. Siegrist and J. Vogel, 'Die Nation. Vorstellungen, Inszenierungen, Emotionen', in their edited, *Nation und Emotion: Deutschland und Frankreich im Vergleich 19. und 20. Jahrhundert*, Göttingen, 1995: 24–25. See also E. Francois and H. Schulze, 'Das emotionale Fundament der Nationen', in M. Flacke, ed., *Mythen der Nationen: ein Europäisches Panorama*, Munich/Berlin, 1998: 17–33. Anderson himself also raises the question of the 'profound emotional legitimacy' of the nation in his introductory chapter, but does not really address it in the rest of the book. See B. Anderson, *Imagined Communities*, rev. ed., London, 1991: 4.

42. Benedict Anderson is the exception to the rule, emphasising the census, the map and the museum as the institutions for nation-creation. See Anderson, *Imagined Communities*, 163–87. For his neglect of the role of religion Anthony D. Smith has criticised him as 'neo-Marxist'.

43. See also H.K. Bhabba, 'DissemiNation: Time, Narrative, and the Margins of the Modern Nation', in his edited, *Nation and Narration*, London, 1990: 300, who emphasises the direct connection between love and hate, quoting Freud on the 'Narcissism of Minor Differences': 'It is always possible to bind together a considerable number of people in love, so long as there are other people left to receive the manifestation of their aggressiveness'. Agression will be projected onto the Other or the Outside, according to Bhabba.

44. See Francois, Siegrist and Vogel, 'Die Nation', 25–27. Bhabba rightly stresses the necessity of forgetting previous fissures and struggles in the process of nation constructing. See Bhabba, 'DissemiNation', 311: 'To be obliged to forget – in the construction of the national present – is not a question of historical memory; it is the construction of a discourse on society that *performs* the problematic totalisation of the national will [...] Being obliged to forget becomes the basis for remembering the nation, peopling it anew, imagining the possibility of other contending and liberating forms of cultural identification.' On the relationship between history and forgetting see further: Paul Ricoeur, *History, Memory, Forgetting*, Chicago, 2004.

45. Schöpflin, 'Function of Myths', 28–34.

46. '"Ist das 19. Jahrhundert nicht die Epoche, in der jedermann, Historiker, Politiker und Öffentlichkeit davon überzeugt ist, dass die Geschichtswissenschaft insbesondere deswegen gefördert werden müsse, weil sie eine objektive Wissenschaft sei und weil sie, im Gegensatz zu den Mythen, die sie zerstöre, die ganze Wahrheit des Vergangenen ans

Tagelicht fördere" [...] Das Ergebnis war nur allzu oft der nationale Mythos, als wissenschaftliche Wahrheit verkleidet.' Francois and Schulze, 'Das emotionale Fundament der Nationen', 18 (author's translation). See also P. Geary, *The Myth of Nations: The Medieval Origins of Europe*, Princeton, NJ, 2002.

47. For the case of the German historians, see P. Schöttler, ed., *Geschichtsschreibung als Legitimationswissenschaft 1918–1945*, Frankfurt am Main, 1997.
48. See in particular M. Flacke, ed., *Mythen der Nationen*.
49. See M. Hettling, ed., *Volksgeschichten im Europa der Zwischenkriegszeit*, Göttingen, 2003; and Schöttler, ed., *Geschichtsschreibung als Legitimationswissenschaft*.
50. For diagnoses of the situation in the US, see P. Novick, *That Noble Dream: The 'Objectivity Question' and the American Historical Profession*, Cambridge, 1988; and J. Scott, 'History in Crisis? The Other Side of History', *American Historical Review* 94, 1989: 680–92.
51. See Lorenz, 'You Got Your History, I Got Mine'.
52. L. von Ranke, *The Theory and Practice of History*, eds G. Iggers and K. von Moltke, Indianapolis and New York, 1973: xx. See also R. Vierhaus, 'Rankes Begriff der historischen Objektivität', in R. Koselleck et al., eds, *Objektivität und Parteilichkeit in der Geschichtswissenschaft*, Munich, 1977: 63–77; and D. Fulda, *Wissenschaft aus Kunst. Die Entstehung der modernen deutschen Geschichtsschreibung 1760–1860*, Berlin and New York, 1996.
53. Ranke dealt with European rather than with national history, which for him was basically a history of the European state-system. Nations tended to become states according to him, but they never coincided. See Ranke, *Theory and Practice*, 61–131.
54. Ibid., 33. It is beyond the scope and aim of this chapter to discuss Ranke's view on other sciences.
55. W. von Humboldt, 'On the Historian's Task', in Ranke, *Theory and Practice*, 5.
56. Ibid., 6.
57. Ibid., 7. See also page 23: 'The historian must, therefore, not exclude the power of the idea from his presentation by seeking everything exclusively in his material sources; he must at least leave room for the activities of the idea'.
58. J.-G. Droysen, *Historik*, ed. P. Leyh, 1857, Stuttgart, 1977, 166; 'Mit dieser Interpretation der Ideen ist das historische Verständnis vollendet'.
59. Humboldt, 'Historian's Task', 14: 'It is, of course, self-evident that these ideas emerge from the mass of events themselves, or, to be more precise, originate in the mind through contemplation of these events undertaken in a truly historical spirit: the ideas are not borrowed by history like an alien addition, a mistake so easily made by so-called philosophical history.' Ranke's and Humboldt's theory of ideas therefore has been aptly characterised as Protestant *Geschichtstheologie* and as 'a highly speculative philosophy' which in 2006 one might easily qualify as 'mythical'. Few 'scientific' historians today would state that God is present throughout history and that states are 'ideas of God'. See also Iggers and von Moltke, 'Introduction', xlvii–lv, especially lxix: 'What Ranke considered to be the objective forces operating in history was to an extent the projection of his own value views into history.'
60. See, for instance, Collingwood, *Idea of History*, 231–49, and C. Becker, 'What Are Historical Facts' and C. Beard, 'Written History as an Act of Faith' – both in H. Meyerhoff, ed., *The Philosophy of History in Our Time*, New York, 1959: 120–40, 140–53.
61. See also Harold Mah, 'German Historical Thought in the Age of Herder, Kant, and Hegel', in L. Kramer and S. Maza, eds, *A Companion to Western Historical Thought*, Oxford, 2002, 148: 'But what should be noticed is that historicist histories were guilty of their own ways of historical myth-making'.
62. Here we can suspect the direct influence of both Carl Becker and Arnold Toynbee on McNeill. See his chapters on both historians in *Mythistory*, 147–74 and 174–99.

63. Whether science presupposes consensus is another question, of course. Paul Feyerabend and Nelson Goodman have convincingly argued against this view. See C. Lorenz, 'Historical Knowledge and Historical Reality'.
64. See also Iggers and von Moltke, 'Introduction', liv: 'There are no rational criteria by which the objectivity of such historical knowledge can be judged other than a subjective sense of certainty on the part of the historian'.
65. Humboldt, 'Historian's Task', 9–10.

Chapter 3

National Histories:
Prospects for Critique and Narrative

MARK BEVIR

A classic national history narrates the formation and progress of a nation-state as a reflection of principles such as a national character, liberty, progress and statehood. Such histories present the state as both reflecting and moulding a national identity or consciousness. What are the prospects for national history today?

Several recent books carry an aura of nostalgia for national histories. Stefan Collini, Peter Mandler, and Julia Stapleton have all written wistfully about classic national histories, their role in national life, and even the nation itself. Of course, their nostalgia has different tones. Stapleton adopts a belligerent tone; she seeks to champion the work of intellectuals who wrote in and of the nation even as national histories went into decline during the twentieth century; she asserts the importance of local and concrete affiliations as opposed to multiculturalism and universalism.[1] Mandler has a more upbeat and revisionist tone; he argues that popular history flourishes today but he distinguishes this popular history from academic history, and he suggests that the latter is more marginal than it once was; he renounces the myths of national destiny even as his narrative suggests that such myths gave academic history a glorious but perhaps irretrievable position in national life.[2] Collini adopts an aloof tone of ironic and even scornful detachment; he is dismissive of the alternatives to national histories and yet also of the viability of the classic national history. He defends the public voice of the historian while arguing that this voice needs be more essayistic and selective and while hinting that the result will be a better, less mythical and more cultivated understanding of the national character and its history.[3]

Why, one might ask, do accounts of the decline of national histories give off an aura of nostalgia for just such histories? The nostalgia arises partly because the authors offer external social and historical explanations for the decline of national histories: national histories have waned less because of their own failings than because of changes in society.[4] The nostalgia arises in addition because the relevant changes in society are one's about which the authors are at best ambivalent: national histories have waned, it seems, because society has gone to the dogs. Once we thus dissect the aura of nostalgia, we are better able to appreciate how seductive it can be. Personally I find it easy to brush-off Stapleton's opposition to a more multicultural Britain, but I have some emotional sympathy for Mandler and Collini's ambivalence towards intellectual populism, the professionalisation of historical studies, social science, mass media and dumbing-down.

The seductive nature of nostalgia should not obscure the fact that we are not being given valid arguments for the revival of classic national histories. Empirical accounts of the decline of national histories and even nations rarely will have philosophical or normative implications for the validity and desirability of national histories and nations. The fact that we do not like an X that has replaced Y cannot of itself give us a reason to revive Y. We would have a reason to revive Y only if we thought Y itself was good, intellectually valid or at the very least better than X, in a situation where it and X are the only two alternatives available to us. It is unlikely, of course, that Collini, Mandler, or even Stapleton intended to offer anything like a formal, philosophical defence of classic national histories. To the contrary, they are typically rather evasive about the intellectual validity of such histories. It is rather more likely, however, that this evasiveness is connected to the nostalgia in their work and so to the impression that they sympathise with such histories. On the one hand, Collini, Mandler and Stapleton share an almost Whiggish distrust of abstract principles and so formal assessments of the validity of different approaches to history. Yet, on the other hand, the impression that they are loosely sympathetic to classic national histories only gains additional credence from the ways in which their views thus echo the very Whiggism that pervades so many classic national histories and the vision implicit therein of the role of history in national life.[5]

So, it is one thing to debate whether or not historical conditions have altered so as to leave little space for the production and consumption of classic national histories, and it is quite another thing to offer a philosophical analysis of the intellectual validity of such histories. Let us focus, in what follows, on the question of the reasonableness of the idea of a national history.

What does philosophy tell us about the validity of national histories? I want to approach this question in a way that will continue to engage the nostalgia of Collini, Mandler and Stapleton. This nostalgia owes much to their ambivalence about not only populism and the mass media but also social science and technocracy. To begin, I will reinforce this ambivalence by offering a philosophical analysis of the failings of social science history. Yet, as I have suggested, ambivalence towards what has replaced the classic national histories does not validate such histories. To the contrary, I will argue that a philosophical analysis of the failings of social science history should lead us to recover narrative as a form of explanation, but not to tie narratives to apparently given principles of character, nation or liberty; instead our narratives should make use of a pragmatic concept of tradition. Thereafter I will go on to consider the implications of rejecting both social science history and the developmental historicism that characterises the classic national histories. I will suggest that we are left with a radical historicism that lends itself to perspectival critique and decentred narratives.

****

There is a fairly common narrative of the fate of national histories. This narrative begins by emphasising the extent to which national histories arose as a tool for nation-building. It thereby highlights the extent to which the master narratives found in so many national histories of the nineteenth century embodied grand principles of nation, liberty and progress. It goes on to suggest that these master narratives fell out of favour during the twentieth century for various reasons. One reason might be that the academic discipline of history became increasingly professional: historians demanded greater rigour, and adopted narrower temporal and topical foci. Another reason might be that the wider public lost interest in the past, at least as a guide to identity or action: the elite turned to the social sciences for guidance, while the masses turned to new forms of popular entertainment – history itself, it might even be said, became entertainment to be consumed as heritage, computer game, family genealogy or commemorative celebration.[6]

Historical arguments appeal to various causes to account for the apparent decline in national histories. Many of these causes are independent of the reasonableness of the idea of a national history: the epistemic reasonableness of a historical narrative does not vary, for example, according to whether or not consumers would want to read it. Yet one of the causes invoked does raise epistemic issues. Historians point to the replacement of history by the social sciences as the inspiration for our attempts to understand social life, and also to direct it through public policy.[7] We might add here that the social sciences had a dramatic impact upon history itself: they inspired new ideas of historical evidence, sources of evidence, methods of analysing evidence, and theories with which to account for evidence. Arguably their impact extended from practices that were self-consciously labelled 'social science history' to the rise of social history as an alternative focus to elder political and diplomatic histories. Anyway, the point is that the rise of social science history raises epistemic issues for the classic national history. It seems that an argument showing the validity of social science history would imply that national histories declined because the social sciences offer us superior forms of knowledge. Alternatively, the suggestion that social science history is invalid would give us reason to reconsider the merits of national histories even if not to be nostalgic for such histories.[8]

We need to be careful here how we characterise social science history. Scientific aspirations arose before the purported decline in national histories. In Britain, David Hume's *History of England* was itself an attempt to instantiate a sceptical and scientific approach to history in accord with the ideas of the Enlightenment and in opposition to notions of the ancient constitution, contract and resistance.[9] Nonetheless, the modern social sciences can perhaps be associated with the later rise of a modernist empiricist epistemology in the late nineteenth and the early twentieth centuries. Although many Enlightenment thinkers associated a scientific spirit with a search for generalisations across societies, typically they prescribed a historical method as that by which to reach generalisations; they sought to provide scientific accounts of the historical development of human societies. In contrast, modernist empiricists later adopted more atomistic and analytic modes of inquiry. Modernist empiricists increasingly took an atomistic stance to particular institutions and practices, separating them out from their national context, and then analysing them in comparison with similar units from other nations, so as, finally, to generate correlations and classifications that were thought to explain them. Social science history can refer, at least for our purposes, then, to approaches to history that draw more or less heavily upon techniques of analysis and concepts of explanation derived from modernist empiricist or even positivist styles of social science.

Social science history prompts distinctive approaches to both the study of earlier national histories and the crafting of new ones. The emphasis falls in both cases on the importance of cross-national and perhaps trans-historical regularities and classifications, ideally supported by quantitative correlations. Consider the study of earlier national histories. Social science history might encourage attempts to develop systematic accounts of the construction of national histories across a number of states. These accounts might correlate the number of such histories produced or some of their allegedly key features with, say, the genre of representation, the year in which statehood was established or the level of economic development. Perhaps social science historians might explain the production of master narratives by reference to their correlation with specific institutional conditions. Perhaps they might explain the demise of such narratives by means of a correlation with the rise of professional associations of historians or the entry of women into the profession. Similarly, social science history might encourage attempts to craft new national histories based on comparative forms of analysis. These analyses might explain the rise and development of nations by reference to correlations and typologies that provide macro-historical contexts for diverse cases. Perhaps the rise of the nation-state might be explained, for example, by means of a correlation with the increasingly capitally intensive nature of warfare.[10]

The epistemic validity of social science history depends, then, on the implicit notion that correlations and classifications constitute valid forms of explanation within the human sciences. Typically, the relevant correlations and classifications are ones that rely on social categories such as class, economic interest or institutional position. Hence, social science history depends, to be more precise, on the assumption that we can explain human behaviour by reference to allegedly objective social facts. This assumption allows social science historians to postulate explanations that more or less bypass the meanings or beliefs embedded in action. It allows them to reduce beliefs to intervening variables to which they do not need to appeal directly. Therefore, instead of explaining why people wrote master narratives by reference to their beliefs and the traditions informing them, social science historians might do so by pointing to the functional dictates of nation-building. Or instead of explaining why people forged nation sates by reference to their beliefs and desires, social science historians might do so by saying that the nation-state was better able to generate the capital needed for warfare. No doubt, few social science historians want to claim that class, economic interests or institutional norms really generate actions without passing through human consciousness. Rather, they want to imply only that the statistical correlations between, say, the capital costs of warfare and the rise of nation-states, or the rise of master narratives and the consolidation of states, allows us to bypass beliefs and desires. They want to suggest that belonging to a class or fulfilling a role gives one a set of beliefs and desires such that one will act in a given way. In this view, to be a state actor is to have an interest in securing the capital needed for warfare so as to be able to expand that state and protect it from the expansion of others.

Social science history assumes that we can reduce beliefs and desires to mere intervening variables. Yet this assumption has been decisively undermined by the many philosophical challenges to positivism that have flourished since the 1960s.[11] Many of these challenges derive from the rejection of the possibility of pure experience. A range of philosophical arguments have emphasised that propositions or beliefs do not have a one-to-one correspondence to the world, but rather refer to the world only within actual contexts, where these contexts might be language games, paradigms, webs of belief, or discourses. All these arguments suggest that experiences always embody prior theories. Experiences always involve something like categorisation; individuals identify objects or events as instances of a category that is defined in relation to other concepts. Even our everyday accounts of our experiences embody numerous realist assumptions such as that objects exist independently of us, persist through time, and act causally upon one another. The impossibility of pure experience implies, contrary to social science history, that we cannot reduce beliefs and desires to mere intervening variables. When we say someone X in a position Y has given interests Z, we necessarily bring our particular theories to bear in order to derive their interests from their position and even to identify their position. Someone with a different set of theories might believe that someone in position Y has different interests or even that X is not in position Y. The important point here is that the way the people we study saw their position and their interests must depend on their theories, which might differ significantly from ours. X might have possessed theories that led her to see her position as A, not Y, and her interests as B, not Z. For example, some state actors might believe that they should promote global peace and justice even at the expense of securing the capital resources needed to sustain warfare.

Social science history appears to presuppose a flawed concept of historical explanation. It seeks to bypass the contingent beliefs and meanings that inform actions so as to find correlations between social facts or to model social facts on the basis of assumptions about rationality. More generally still, it often appears to assume that the concept of necessary causation found in the natural sciences also fits human actions and so history. The modelling of history on a scientific concept of causation seems to have two main attractions. Sometimes it represents an attempt to claim for a favoured approach to history the prestige of natural science: talk of explaining nations, actions and the like by causal laws can sound impressively rigorous when compared to less formal approaches. At other times it springs from lax thinking: its proponents rightly recognise that there is a universal feature of explanation such that to explain something is to relate it to other things, and this leads them wrongly to assume that the relationship between *explanans* and *explanandum* also must be universal, where the prestige of natural science ensures they then identify this universal relationship with the scientific concept of causation. The main attractions of social science history seem to derive, therefore, from the prestige of the natural sciences. Surely, however, we should not take the success of natural science to preclude other forms of explanation?

The scientific concept of causation is inappropriate for history since, as we have found, we cannot reduce beliefs and desires to intervening variables. We can explain actions and practices properly only if we appeal to those beliefs and desires that inform them. When we explain actions as products of reasons, we imply that the actors concerned in some sense could have reasoned differently, and if they had done so, they would not have acted as they did. Because actions and practices depend on the reasoned choices of people, they are the products of decisions, rather than the determined outcomes of laws or processes; after all, choices would not be choices if causal laws fixed their content. Hence, history instantiates a concept of rationality that precludes our explaining actions and practices in ways that embody the concept of causation that operates in natural science. Historians have to allow for the inherent contingency of the objects they study, including nations and their histories.

****

The nostalgia of much recent writing on national histories derives in part from ambivalence about social science history. If the rise of social science and technocratic policy-making were wrong-turnings, then perhaps – if we only could – we should turn back and recreate a lost era of public intellectuals and national histories. Again, if we cannot properly elucidate the rise and changing nature of nations by means of comparisons, correlations and classifications, perhaps we should do so through narratives of their development. Yet the emphases here should fall on the 'perhaps'. When we question the validity or desirability of some Y that has replaced an X, we might give ourselves reason to reconsider X, but we do not give ourselves reason to champion X. Nostalgia for classic national history is justified, in other words, only if it is philosophically valid. The classic national histories instantiated a developmental historicism: they told narratives framed by principles of nation, liberty and progress. I want briefly to describe such developmental historicism before then suggesting that although narrative is a valid form of explanation, we should not frame narratives by reference to such principles.

Developmental historicism inspires distinctive approaches not only to the crafting of national histories but also to the study of earlier national histories. The emphasis fell in both cases on fidelity to the inherited, and arguably inherent, characters and traditions of particular nationalities. In this view, a nation embodies a specific and typically unique character or spirit that manifests itself in particular traditions and customs. The British, or at least the English, nation often is portrayed, for example, as restrained, tolerant, pragmatic and more social than political. Hence, developmental historicists did not attempt to reduce any given national history to a broader generalisation based on cross-national correlations or classificatory systems. To the contrary, they relied on a narrative form of explanation; more particularly, they told narratives that explored national histories in terms of the local characters and traditions of the relevant nations.

Equally, developmental historicism might encourage accounts of previous national histories as themselves being expressions of the character and tradition of a nation. In this view, the master narratives of old were written by historians who drew sustenance from the very identities that informed their histories; these historians mined the local character and traditions of their nation so as to find wisdom therein, and they thereby acted as the guardians of the national spirit. In the case of Britain, developmental historicists might argue, for example, that the grand historians of the nineteenth century – A.V. Dicey, Leslie Stephen, J.R. Seeley, and others – shared an affinity for the very British identity they reproduced in their writings; they shared the strong moral sense, the love of liberty and the respect for justice and fair play that they found exhibited in British history. Developmental historicists might add that even in the twentieth century, historians such as Arthur Bryant, G.M. Trevelyan, and A.L. Rowse captured in their work similar ideas of an English or British character, ideas that proved important in fostering the national spirit exhibited in the Second World War.[12] In this view, national histories participate, at least when they are well conceived and well written, in the cultural foundations of the nations whose histories they tell. Hence, developmental historicists might conclude that a proper narrative explanation of these national histories should refer to just those identities and traditions that they themselves evoke as the guiding principles of the nation.

When we consider the epistemic reasonableness of developmental historicism, it is important to distinguish a general commitment to narrative as a form of explanation from a specific commitment to narratives based on appeals to national principles, characters or traditions. It is arguable, for example, that the failings of social science history establish that a proper grasp of human actions requires something akin to narrative, but that does not imply that narratives should be framed by appeals to certain principles. Let us turn first, then, to a general analysis of narrative as a form of explanation.

One common way of distinguishing history from natural science is to define natural science in terms of causal explanation and history in terms of understanding or empathy.[13] These definitions suggest that historians try to reconstruct objects, but not then to explain them. In contrast, historians often conceive of their narratives as explanations that point to the causes of actions. Indeed scholars from all sorts of disciplines use the word 'cause' to describe the explanatory relationship between the entities or events they study. When they do so, they use the word 'cause' to point to connections of the sort characteristic of explanation in their discipline without thereby conveying a philosophical analysis of the connection. To reject social science history is to imply that history relies on narrative conceived as a form of explanation that evokes connections different in kind from those of the natural sciences. What are those connections? How do they explain actions?

Narrative explanations typically relate actions to the beliefs and desires that inform them.[14] Their abstract form is: an action X was done because the agent held beliefs Y according to which doing X would fulfil a desire Z. These narrative explanations postulate two types of connections. The first relates actions, beliefs and desires to one another so as to show they fit together. We might call these conditional connections. Conditional connections typically relate agents' beliefs to one another, including their beliefs about the effects of their actions, so as to make sense of the fact that they thought the actions would fulfil one or more of their desires. The second type of connection embodied in narrative explanations is that which relates desires to the actions that they motivate. We might call these volitional connections. Volitional connections enable us to make sense of the fact that agents moved from having desires to intending to perform actions and then to acting as they did. Crucially, conditional and volitional connections are neither necessary nor arbitrary. It is because they are not necessary that history differs from the natural sciences. It is because they are not arbitrary that we nonetheless can use them to explain actions.

Conditional connections relate agents' beliefs and desires to one another so as to make sense of the fact that they thought an action would fulfil one or more of their desires. Conditional connections exist when the nature of one object draws on that of some other. The latter conditions the former so they do not have an arbitrary relationship to one another, but equally the former need not follow from the latter so they do not have a necessary relationship to one another. More particularly, conditional connections exist when beliefs and desires reflect, develop or modify themes that occur in others. A theme is an idea suggested by the specific character of several beliefs and desires. Any belief or desire gives us intimations of associated ideas that might or might not have been picked up by the person involved. When they are picked up, they become themes that link the relevant beliefs and desires. Because conditional connections are not arbitrary, themes must be immanent in the objects they bring together. Similarly, because conditional connections are not necessary, themes must be given immediately by the content of the beliefs and desires they connect. Historians do not identify a theme as an instance of a general law defining a fixed relationship between the objects they are considering. Rather, they describe a theme solely in terms of the content of the particular objects it relates to one another. When people cannot see the conditional connection between two objects, we can bring them to do so only by describing other beliefs and desires that fill it out, not by reference to a covering law.

Volitional connections enable us to make sense of the fact that agents moved from having desires to intending to perform actions and then doing so. They exist when a will decides to act on a desire and then does so. Our beliefs and desires typically give us all sorts of grounds for doing all sorts of things. The will then selects the particular actions we are to perform from among the alternatives thus presented to us. It forms an intention to act by deciding which action we should perform out of the many we have grounds for performing. It is necessary to postulate the will here because of the space that separates desires from intentions. This space suggests that we should conceive of the will reaching a decision in an unrestricted process in which previously formulated intentions, current preferences and future possibilities interact with one another. The decisions the will then makes give us our intentions. Although our decisions give us intentions, we can act on such intentions only because of the ability of the will to command us so to do. Once we have decided to do something, we still have to command ourselves to do it. The will has to instigate a movement of the body, a calling to mind of a particular memory, or some such thing. Volitional connections come into being when the will operates so as to transform one's stance towards a given proposition first from being favourable to it to a decision to act on it and then to a command so to do. Typically, however, historians do not speculate on psychological questions about how the will operates, but rather take volitional connections for granted. Narrative explanations thus consist largely of implicit or explicit accounts of the themes that link all kinds of actions, beliefs and desires to one another; that is to say, they locate beliefs, actions and practices in their particular historical contexts.

****

Today we confront the philosophical collapse of the positivism that informs social science history with its attempts to explain historical particulars by reference to mid-level or even universal generalities. This collapse requires us to return to a historicism in which particulars are explicated by being placed in appropriate contexts composed of yet other particulars. However, while we thereby return to a narrative form of explanation, we need not return to the developmental historicism of the classic national histories; we need not centre our narratives on apparently given principles, characters, traditions or nations.

Developmental historicists relied on apparently given principles to guide their narratives. Typically they conceived of nations as organic units constituted by common traditions associated with ethical, functional and linguistic ties as well as a shared past. They then implied that these traditions embodied principles that provided a basis for continuity as well as for gradual evolution in the history of a nation. While some of them postulated a racial or biological basis to national traditions, others saw these traditions as products of geographical and other contexts that were supposed to have provided favourable settings for the emergence of particular character traits and social practices.[15] The history of England was often narrated, for example, in terms of a national character that was supposed to encompass individualism and self-reliance, a passion for liberty, a willingness to pursue enterprise and trade, and a no-nonsense pragmatism, all of which in their turn were sometimes traced back to Teutonic roots among the tribes and village communities of Northern Europe. In addition, developmental historicists often framed the unfolding of national characters, traditions and principles using organic metaphors or evolutionary theories.[16] At times, they even postulated a more general process of evolution such that they were able to locate different nations or civilisations at various stages of the process. They implied that all civilisations followed a broadly similar path of development, but that different contextual factors had given rise to varied characters and traditions such that some were currently further along this path than others. Hence, one fashionable reason for comparing different nations was precisely to clarify the nature of this general path of development.

It is worth emphasising that the collapse of positivism requires us to deploy a concept akin to that of tradition to capture the importance of contexts in explanations of beliefs, actions and practices. Of course, there have been philosophers who believed that the individual was wholly autonomous; they argued that people are able to come to hold beliefs and so act independently of specific contexts. Yet the concept of autonomy has been made implausible by the powerful arguments against positivism and the idea of pure experience. No doubt people come to believe the things they do only in the context of their own lives. Nonetheless, because people cannot have pure experiences, they must construe their experiences in terms of prior theories. Because they cannot arrive at beliefs through experiences unless they already have a prior set of beliefs, their experiences can lead them to beliefs only because they already have access to tradition.

A tradition constitutes the necessary background to the beliefs people adopt and the actions they seek to perform. Nonetheless, we need not adopt the particular concept of tradition that typically informs developmental historicism.[17] To begin, we might offer a counter-factual argument against the very idea that traditions define limits to the beliefs people later might go on to adopt. Imagine counter-factually that we could identify limits imposed by traditions on the beliefs individuals could adopt. Because traditions would impose these limits, they could not be natural limits transcending all contexts. Moreover, because we could identify these limits, we could describe them to those individuals who inherited the relevant traditions. Therefore, assuming they could understand us, they could come to recognise these limits, and thereby understand the beliefs they allegedly could not adopt. However, because they could understand the sorts of beliefs these limits preclude, and because there could not be any natural restriction preventing them from holding these beliefs, they could adopt these beliefs, so these beliefs could not be beliefs they could not come to hold. Perhaps one aspect of this counter-factual argument might still appear to need justifying, namely, the assumption that the individual affected by a limit could understand our account of it. Surely though we have no reason to assume that people cannot translate between sets of beliefs no matter how different they might be. When the individuals concerned first approached our account of the limit, they might not have the requisite concepts to understand us, but surely they would share some concepts, perceptions, practices or needs with us, and surely they could use these as a point of entry into our worldview so as eventually to understand us.

The foregoing counter-factual argument establishes that traditions only ever influence, as opposed to deciding or restricting, the beliefs that people adopt and the actions that they attempt to perform. This means that traditions must be products of the undetermined agency of individuals. Perhaps this insistence on the fact of agency will seem incompatible with a rejection of autonomy and an insistence on the unavoidable nature of tradition. However, our reasons for evoking tradition allow for individuals modifying the beliefs and practices they inherit. Just because individuals start out from an inherited tradition does not imply that they cannot go on to adjust it. Surely, the ability to develop traditions is an essential part of our being in the world? We are always confronting slightly novel circumstances that require us to apply tradition anew, and a tradition cannot fix the nature of its application. When we confront an unfamiliar situation, we have to extend or modify our inheritance to encompass it, and as we do so, we thereby develop this inheritance. Every time we apply a tradition, we reflect on it, we try to understand it afresh in the light of the relevant circumstances, and we thus open it to innovation. Change occurs even when people think they are adhering to a tradition they regard as sacrosanct.

Although tradition is unavoidable, it is so only as a starting point, not as something that determines or limits later performances. We should be wary, therefore, of representing tradition as an inevitable presence in all that the individual ever does in case we thereby leave too slight a role for agency. In particular, we should not imply that tradition is in anyway constitutive of the beliefs people later come to hold or the actions they later seek to perform. Although individuals must set out against the background of a tradition, they later can extend or modify it in a way that might make it anything but constitutive of their later beliefs and actions. Hence, we should conceive of tradition primarily as an initial influence on people; the content of the tradition will appear in their later performances only insofar as their agency has not led them to change it, where every part of it is in principle open to change.

This analysis of tradition as a starting point but not a destination undercuts the fixity, even the essentialism, which typically characterises the principles evoked by developmental historicists. Often developmental historicists equate traditions with fixed cores to which they then ascribe temporal variations or even a progressive unfolding. No doubt, there are occasions when we legitimately can point to the persistence through time of an idea. Equally, however, we might choose to concentrate on a tradition in which no idea persists over time. We might identify a tradition with a group of ideas widely shared by a number of individuals even though no one idea was common to all of them. Alternatively, we might identify a tradition with a group of ideas that passed from generation to generation, changing a little each time, so that no single idea persisted from start to finish. Indeed, we usually will encounter difficulties if we try to define a tradition by reference to some fixed core. We will do so both because individuals are agents who play an active role in the learning process and because we cannot identify limits to the changes that individuals can introduce to the beliefs they inherit. Because people often want to improve their heritage by making it more coherent, more accurate and more relevant to contemporary issues, they often respond selectively to it; they accept some parts of it, modify others and reject others.

Once we accept that traditions do not have fixed cores, we undermine many attempts to narrate national histories in terms of apparently given character traits or principles. We can no longer appeal to fixed principles to define the past and relate it to the present in a continuous process of development. National characters, national traditions, and even nations no longer appear as the outer expressions of given traits. Rather, the principles associated with them now appear as the contingent consequences of the various ways in which people have adopted, modified and rejected their varied inheritances. Nations do not embody fixed principles that determine their nature or the ways in which they develop. They are instead the constantly changing products of a human agency that is in its turn indeterminate.

****

We are at a critical juncture in the study and production of national histories. Neither social science history nor developmental historicism retains epistemic legitimacy. Our faith in them has dwindled along with our beliefs in pure experience and ineluctable progress. Social science history has fallen before a revived historicism: the beliefs and actions people adopt are saturated with their particular prior theories, so we can explain them properly only by relating them to their specific contexts, not by appeals to trans-historical correlations and classifications. Developmental historicism has fallen before a growing sense of contingency: human agency is indeterminate, so we can narrate shifts in contexts properly only if we depict them as open-ended, not as determined by allegedly given principles. We require ways of studying earlier national histories and crafting new ones that allow appropriately for both historicism and contingency – we require a radical historicism.[18]

Let us start with the prospects for studies of earlier national histories. As we have seen, social science history suggests we might seek to correlate the production of national histories with other alleged social facts such as the level of economic development, while developmental historicism suggests we might understand the content of earlier national histories as themselves being a reflection of the character or tradition of the relevant nation. Both suggest that their own perspective is neutral, whether as science or the expression of a shared tradition. In contrast, radical historicism might prompt us to offer perspectival critiques of many national histories. It might lead us to debunk earlier national histories by narrating them as contingent products of specific historical contexts. Of course, social science history and developmental historicism can inspire criticisms of earlier national histories: perhaps a social science historian might argue that an institution which national historians represent as a product of the national character is in fact explained by a transnational correlation covering similar institutions in other nation-states; and perhaps a developmental historicist might argue that a national historian has misinterpreted the character or tradition at the heart of their nation, maybe seeing tolerance where there is really class prejudice. However, even if social science history and developmental historicism can inspire such criticisms, we might contrast their type of criticism, conceived as a kind of audit, with the perspectival critique prompted by a radical historicism. In this contrast, an audit embodies a concern to identify the strengths and weaknesses of a national history with respect to specific facts or judgements. While an audit can be a perfectly acceptable mode of evaluation – notably if it is aware of its own historicity and contingency – it still limits criticism to what we might describe as fault-finding. The critic lists one or more faults, big or small, in a national history so as to pass judgement on its merits from a perspective that at least gestures at a given set of facts or judgements from which that history departs.

Radical historicism supplements fault-finding with perspectival critique. It finds fault, of course. It typically suggests that many of the histories told by social science historians fail adequately to elucidate people's motivations since these historians assume that motivations can be read off from correlations. It suggests that the master narratives of developmental historicism fail properly to acknowledge the diversity of the characters, identities, customs and traditions found in a nation. Nonetheless, radical historicism takes historicism and contingency seriously in a way that situates such fault-finding in a perspectival critique. Consider the implications of the particularity of our own perspectives as critics of any given national history. Once we allow that our criticisms are not based on given facts, but rather infused with our own theoretical assumptions, we might well become somewhat hesitant to find fault; we might be wary of treating our particular theoretical perspective as a valid one from which to judge others. This hesitation might give rise to self-reflexive moments in our presentations of our studies of earlier national histories, and these moments might suggest that our criticisms arise against the background of theoretical commitments and concepts that others might not share. It might lead us to be reflexive about the source of our authority, for while we can not avoid taking a stance in a way that commits us to the epistemic authority of some set of beliefs, we might at least recognise that this authority is provisional and justified within a contingent set of concepts, and we might even recognise that we are offering a narrative that is just one among a field of possible narratives. In this way, we would move from fault-finding to critique. Instead of evaluating others in terms of apparently given facts, judgements or concepts, we would find ourselves either juxtaposing rival narratives or asking what should follow from a set of concepts that we happen to share with those with whom we are engaging.

Consider now the implications of the particularity of any given national history as the object of our critique. All too often national histories present themselves as based on given or neutral narratives based, in turn, on secure empirical facts or scientific theories. Critique consists less of an audit of its object than in the act of unmasking its object as contingent, partial, or both. It might unmask the contingency of its object by showing it to be just one among a field of possible narratives. It might unmask the partiality of its object by showing how it arises against the background of an inherited tradition that is held by a particular group within society and perhaps even serves the interests of just that group. We might also add here that critique almost always overlaps with some of the faults we find, for by unmasking the contingency and partiality of national histories, it typically portrays them, even if only tacitly, as being mistaken about their own nature or even as eliding their own nature in the interests of a group or class.

Critique privileges unmasking over evaluation. Unmasking typically occurs through either philosophical or historical analysis. Critique can deploy philosophical analysis to unpack the conceptual presuppositions of a national history and to highlight elisions, contradictions and gaps within these presuppositions. Much of this essay has been an attempt to sketch just such a philosophical critique of positivism in social science history and essentialism in developmental historicism. However, critique also can deploy historical analysis to unpack the roots of these presuppositions and other related ideas in particular traditions, debates or other contexts. When national histories attempt to ground their correlations or narratives in allegedly given facts about social or national life, they efface the contingency not only of the practices of which they tell but also of themselves as particular modes of knowing. Critique can show how these modes of knowing – developmental historicism and social science history – are themselves historically contingent. It can show how representations of the nation that present themselves as neutral or scientific are in fact temporally and culturally circumscribed. We move from fault-finding to critique; in other words, we shift our attention from an audit of a national history in terms of a given set of facts or judgements to the use of philosophical and historical analyses to bring into view the concepts and theories that inform it. Arguably, such critiques already appear in various studies of the production of national identities in the heritage industry, the history of historiography, national imaginaries and popular culture.

It is worth emphasising that perspectival critique does not imply a pernicious relativism. Although the idea that all narratives embody particular perspectives or assumptions does undermine the ideal of absolute certainty, we can relinquish this ideal and still avoid a pernicious relativism. Even if we have to give up epistemologies such as verificationism and falsificationism, we still might defend an account of justified knowledge that refers to the comparison of rival narratives; we still might defend the reasonableness of some narratives, and not others, by reference to shared normative rules and practices by which to compare rival accounts of agreed propositions – as opposed to given facts. Perhaps this account of justified knowledge will appear problematic as a guide to how to deal with the relatively high levels of incommensurability that exist between widely different approaches to history, such as, say, social science history, developmental historicism and radical historicism. If we disagree about the relative merits of narratives, we might try to draw back from the point of disagreement until we find a common platform – consisting of ways of reasoning, standards of evidence and agreed propositions – from which to compare the narratives. The worry is, of course, that different approaches to history might give rise to rival forms of explanation and varied standards of evidence. Perhaps the nature of justified knowledge might be part of what is at issue. Yet, even if historians disagreed about the nature of explanation and justified knowledge, however, they still can engage with one another. Because approaches to history seek to explain human beliefs, actions and practices, they presumably include the claim, at least implicitly, that they might be applied successfully to explain the beliefs, actions and practices of earlier historians. Each approach might provide an account of the experience and fate of the others. The reasonableness of an approach could consist in its ability to provide a better account of developments, problems and stumbling blocks of other approaches than can those others themselves. Hence, perspectival critique, far from leading to a pernicious relativism, can be seen as a way of overcoming relatively high levels of incommensurability by offering historiographical narratives of rival approaches to the radical historicism upon which it typically relies.

****

To argue that perspectival critique does not entail relativism is forcefully to raise the question of what alternative national histories radical historicists might craft today. This question gains further importance from two related considerations. First, critique typically lacks purchase unless it is combined, at least tacitly, with an appeal to a better alternative: since we have to act, we have to hold a web of beliefs on which to act, so we cannot forsake our current beliefs unless a better one is available. Secondly, as we have seen, radical historicist critiques of earlier national histories typically make the claim that these earlier histories failed to capture all of the varied identities and practices adopted by peoples, and this claim, in its turn, relies at least implicitly on the evocation of narratives revealing more of the plurality of these identities and practices.

Radical historicists will return to narrative forms of explanation akin to those of developmental historicists, but their narratives will eschew the old appeals to apparently given principles, characters and customs; they will replace overly essentialist concepts of tradition with more pragmatic ones. What difference might this make for the national histories they craft? One difference arises over what it means to conceive of identities, traditions or nations as concrete, social realities. Although racial historicists might allow that traditions are embedded in practices – which are, of course, part of concrete social reality – they will not concede that particular identities, traditions or nations are natural kinds, with definite boundaries by which we might individuate them. There are no natural or given limits to particular nations by which we might separate them out from the general flux of human life. The border of a nation does not clearly appear with those who are descended from some group, who live within some territory, who are citizens of some state, who speak some language, or anything else of the sort. The problems of individuating nations are most clear when we distinguish them from states: nations can aspire to a statehood they do not possess, and states can cover only part of a nation or be multinational. National identities are typically based on ethnicities, symbols, memories, myths and other constructions whose salience crosses geographical borders. Yet radical historicism suggests that we cannot treat as natural kinds even those nation-states with fairly clear-cut territorial domains, such as Britain with its maritime boundary. Of course, states have borders associated especially with the limits to its sovereign authority over a population and its commercial and other activities. Nonetheless, we need to learn to conceive of a state's borders as porous and vague. Even populations and commerce constantly escape any one political authority as in weak states or states with multi-level governance, and as with much migration and trade.

Where we locate the border of a nation, and so how we conceive of it, is a pragmatic decision that we can justify only by reference to the purposes of our so doing. It is we who postulate borders so as to demarcate the domain of our historical inquiries or to draw attention to those features of the flux of human life that we believe best explain one or more object or event. Hence, when radical historicists craft national histories, they are likely to pay special attention to the production and crossing of borders. Boundaries appear as constructed not natural, and as porous not fixed. Radical historicists highlight, first, the constructed nature of borders. Their national histories might include accounts of the processes by which national identities have been constructed in concrete historical contexts. Perspectival critiques are, in this respect, a contribution to alternative national histories that narrate the ways in which peoples construct nations through the production of a historiography and also historical images and myths in other media, such as novels and films.[19] Radical historicists highlight, secondly, the porous nature of borders. Their national histories might include accounts of transnational flows, including diasporas and exiles. The history of the British state can be told as that of at least four nations, to which we might add the exchanges associated especially with Europe and Empire.[20]

Another difference between radical historicism, with its pragmatic concept of tradition, and developmental historicism, with its more essentialist one, appears in their characteristic analyses of the conventions, shared understandings or interactions that are found within traditions, practices or nations. No doubt, practices exhibit conventions and nations often have relatively stable customs. Yet, we can conceive of these conventions and customs as emergent entities, rather than as constituting or structuring the relevant practices or nations. Therefore, we might accept that participants in a practice or members of a nation often seek to conform to the relevant conventions or customs, but we also might point out, first, that they do not always do so, and, second, that even when they do, they still might misunderstand the conventions and customs. Hence, we should not take conventions and customs as having a constitutive relationship to practices or nations. To the contrary, we have seen that individuals are agents who are capable of modifying – and who necessarily interpret – the beliefs that they inherit, and so, by implication, the actions that are appropriate to any practice in which they participate. This argument does not imply that everyone is a Napoleon who, as an individual, has a significant effect on the historical direction a nation takes. It implies only that people are agents who are capable of modifying their inheritance and so acting in novel ways. When they do so, they are highly unlikely to have a significant effect on a nation unless other people make similar modifications, and even then the changes in the nation would be unlikely to correspond to any that they might intend. Nations rarely, if ever, depend directly on the actions of any given individual. They do consist solely of the changing actions of a range of individuals.

All dominant national characters and traditions are constantly open to contestation and change. They do not constitute the nation. To the contrary, they arise as contingent products of processes of contestation and change. Hence, when radical historicists craft national histories, they are likely to pay special attention to these processes. National characters and traditions appear as diverse and discontinuous. Therefore, radical historicists highlight not just the production and crossing of borders, but also, thirdly, the plurality of the identities and customs found within any nation. When historians invoke collective categories – the principles, characters and traditions of developmental historicists, as well as the correlations and classifications of social science historians – these categories are liable to hide, wilfully or otherwise, the diverse beliefs and desires that motivated individuals. Peoples include racial and gender differences, and differences within races and genders, that are neglected if we lump them together as a more unified nation.[21] So, radical historicists might explore the ways in which dominant identities elide, and even define themselves against, others. The rise of some British identities can be told, for example, in terms of an overt opposition to a Catholicism associated with the French.[22] Radical historicists highlight, fourthly, discontinuity as identities are transformed over time. Shifts in the British nation appear, for instance, to involve novel projections back onto the past, rather than a continuous development of core themes. The national identity changed dramatically from a sense of Englishness forged during Tudor times, through the Britishness that arose during the wars against France, on to the invention of an Imperial mission, the elegiac invocation of the shires, and, we might now add, New Labour's vision of 'Cool Britannia'.[23]

When radical historicists represent the nation as constructed, transnational, differentiated and discontinuous, perhaps they might describe the result as a history beyond, or even without, the nation. Their narratives of social construction denaturalise the nation, showing it to be the imagined product of specific historical processes. Their narratives of transnational flows disperse the nation, highlighting the movement of ideas, customs and norms across borders. Their narratives of difference fragment the nation, exhibiting some of the plural groups within it. Their narratives of discontinuity interrupt the nation, revealing ruptures and transformations through time. Is a denaturalised, dispersed, fragmented and interrupted nation even remotely close to what is normally meant by a nation? Far from being nostalgic for national histories, perhaps it is time we started to tell the histories of networks of peoples. Perhaps we should craft histories of all sorts of overlapping groups, only some of whom attempted, more or less successfully, to construct national imaginaries and to impose those imaginaries on others.

Notes

1. J. Stapleton, *Political Intellectuals and Public Identities in Britain since 1850*, Manchester, 2001. Also see now J. Stapleton, *Sir Arthur Bryant and National History in Twentieth Century Britain*, Lanham, MD, 2005.
2. P. Mandler, *History and National Life*, London, 2002. Also see now the even more revisionist P. Mandler, *The English National Character: The History of an Idea from Edmund Burke to Tony Blair*, New Haven, 2006.
3. S. Collini, *English Pasts: Essays in History and Culture*, Oxford, 1999.
4. I have attempted to chart some of the changing ways in which nations have been represented in M. Bevir, 'Political Studies as Narrative and Science, 1880–2000', *Political Studies* 54, 2006: 583–606.

5. It is perhaps relevant here that Mandler's first book was a sympathetic appreciation of Whiggism: see P. Mandler, *Aristocratic Government in the Age of Reform: Whigs and Liberals, 1830–1852*, Oxford, 1990. Stapleton's was, similarly, a sympathetic appreciation of the political thought of a late Whig: see J. Stapleton, *Englishness and the Study of Politics: The Social and Political Thought of Ernest Barker*, Cambridge, 1994. Collini's co-authored second book, likewise, conveys sympathy for a Whig approach to the study of politics: see S. Collini, D. Winch and J. Burrow, *That Noble Science of Politics*, Cambridge, 1983.

6. Mandler is fairly welcoming to the popular consumption of history as entertainment: see Mandler, *History and National Life*. Collini is less respectful and even rather surprised by such 'public fuss': Collini, *English Pasts*, 2.

7. Mandler, *History and National Life*.

8. It is perhaps relevant that Collini's first books were on an early British sociologist and nineteenth-century notions of a political science, and that they suggested there was something amiss with the ambition to explain social life in terms set by a modernist science. See S. Collini, *Liberalism and Sociology: L.T. Hobhouse and Political Argument in England, 1880–1914*, Cambridge, 1979; and Collini, Winch and Burrow, *That Noble Science of Politics*. It is perhaps relevant too that Stapleton's first book, which began as a doctoral thesis supervised by Collini, exhibits a clear sympathy for Ernest Barker's attempt to defend a Whiggish and historical approach to the study of politics in the face of the rise of such modernist science. See Stapleton, *Englishness and the Study of Politics*.

9. D. Forbes, *Hume's Philosophical Politics*, Cambridge, 1975: 125–92.

10. C. Tilly, *Coercion, Capital, and European States, 990–1990*, Cambridge, MA, 1992.

11. Useful overviews include R. Bernstein, *The Restructuring of Social and Political Theory*, Philadelphia, 1976; and B. Fay, *Contemporary Philosophy of Social Science*, Oxford, 1996.

12. See Stapleton, *Political Intellectuals*.

13. Thus, the well-known debate over whether or not narrative is explanatory revolved around the issue of whether or not narrative could be assimilated to a strictly causal or a covering-law form of explanation associated with the natural sciences. See, in particular, the classic argument that narrative is a sketchy or partial version of the nomological-deductive form of explanation, as found in C. Hempel, 'The Function of General Laws in History', *Journal of Philosophy* 39, 1942: 35–48. For a general account of the debate, see M. Murphy, 'Explanation, Causes, and Covering Laws', *History and Theory* 25, 1986, 43–57.

14. Recent discussions of narrative include M. Bevir, 'Historical Explanation, Folk Psychology, and Narrative', *Philosophical Explorations* 3, 2000: 152–68; J. Bruner, 'Narrative and Metanarrative in the Construction of the Self', in M. Ferrari and R. Sternberg, eds, *Self-awareness: Its Nature and Development*, New York, 1998: 308–31; A. Juarrero, *Dynamics in Action: Intentional Behaviour as a Complex System*, Cambridge, MA, 1990; and P. Roth, 'Narrative Explanation: The Case of History', *History and Theory* 27, 1988: 1–13.

15. See, for Britain, P. Mandler, '"Race" and "Nation" in Mid-Victorian Thought', in S. Collini, R. Whatmore and B. Young, eds, *History, Religion, and Culture: British Intellectual History, 1750–1950*, Cambridge, 2000: 224–44.

16. On evolutionary narratives in the nineteenth century, see especially J. Burrow, *Evolution and Society: A Study in Victorian Social Theory*, Cambridge, 1966. For their resonance in Whig historiography, see J. Burrow, *Whigs and Liberals: Continuity and Change in English Political Thought*, Oxford, 1988.

17. For an example of the divide between relevant concepts of traditions, see M. Bevir, 'On Tradition', *Humanitas* 13, 2000: 28–53; and B. Frohnen, 'Tradition, Habit, and Social Interaction: A Response to Mark Bevir', *Humanitas* 14, 2001: 108–16.

18. I hope that the content of 'radical historicism' will be clear from what has gone before and what follows. For a philosophical defense of some of its leading themes, see M. Bevir, *The Logic of the History of Ideas*, Cambridge, 1999.

19. Cf. R. Hewison, *The Heritage Industry: Britain in a Climate of Decline*, London, 1987; E. Jones, *The English Nation: The Great Myth*, Stroud, UK, 1998; J. Garrity, *Step-daughters of England: British Women Novelists and the National Imaginary*, Manchester, 2003; and J. Richards, *Films and British National Identity*, Manchester, 1997.

20. Cf. R. Samuel, 'Four Nations History', *Theatres of Memory*, vol. 2: *Island Stories: Unraveling Britain*, London, 1999: 21–40; N. Davies, *The Isles*, Oxford, 1999; and P. Gilroy, *The Black Atlantic: Modernity and Double Consciousness*, London, 1993.

21. Cf. P. Gilroy, *There Ain't No Black in the Union Jack: The Cultural Politics of Race and Nation*, Chicago, 1991.

22. L. Colley, *Britons: Forging the Nation 1707–1837*, New Haven, 1992.

23. Cf. Jones, *The English Nation*; Colley, *Britons*; P. Rich, *Race and Empire in British Politics*, Cambridge, 1986; and R. Samuel, ed., *Patriotism: The Making and Unmaking of British National Identity*, vol. 1: *History and Politics*, London, 1989.

PART II

NARRATING THE NATION AS LITERATURE

Chapter 4

Fiction as a Mediator
in National Remembrance

ANN RIGNEY

Remembrance as Cultural Practice

Recent years have seen considerable advances in our understanding of the ways in which societies recollect their past. Where earlier discussions were often derived from psychological models, there has been a growing realisation in various fields that collective memory should be studied in the first instance as a cultural phenomenon: as the product of the historically variable cultural practices that bring images of the past into circulation. After all, communication in some form or other, even if this is only between parent and child, is a prerequisite for transferring recollections and making them social. The past can only be invested with meaning for groups of people through observable acts of remembrance in the form of stories, rituals, monuments, images, poems, epitaphs, and so on.[1]

This 'cultural turn' in social memory studies, exemplified in the work of Jan and Aleida Assmann among others, has allowed us to move beyond the fruitless opposition between 'history' and 'memory' that for too long bedevilled debates. It offers a conceptual framework within which particular memory practices can be studied in an integrated way, calling upon expertise from various disciplines. Historiography, historical films, museums, literary canons, theatre, commemorations: all of these represent cultural forms of remembrance, although they are neither equivalent nor interchangeable. They use different media and protocols; they function in different circumstances and involve different groups;

and, last but not least, they exercise different types of cultural and epistemological power. Thus, modern historiography, as the scholarly and institutionalised investigation of the past, wins hands down when it comes to cultural authority and impact on the educational system. In contrast, films, novels or plays enjoy less authority, but are generally more popular and thus arguably more influential. In the swings and roundabouts of cultural practice, what one form of remembrance wins on authority, the other may win on allure.

Identifying and classifying the different mnemonic practices in use at any given time, and studying their long-term evolution, is itself a worthwhile endeavour. Even more interesting, however, is to consider the interactions between these historically variable practices, as they reinforce, mimic or criticise each other, and as they circulate among different social groups. For collective remembrance is not just dependent on a single medium, nor is it a once-off affair: stories circulate across different media and different forms of remembrance, and in the process they acquire or lose popularity and prestige. An account of a particular event may thus migrate from oral storytelling in the private sphere, to historiography, to a film, to a public monument or museum and, from there, back again to an oral retelling. In this way, different forms of remembrance reinforce, echo and modify each other, helping to spread familiarity with certain events and figures across different groups. At some points, a version of events becomes accepted by the relevant institutions as an official account of the common past.

Is there a key to these dynamics? As the title of his *Les cadres sociaux de la mémoire* (1925) famously suggested, Maurice Halbwachs saw an interdependence between the 'social frames' within which people remember and what they find relevant to recall.[2] Whether we are dealing with the family, the nation, or the ethnic or religious group, it is still generally agreed that the 'social frame' helps define the relevance of certain topics and draws up a dividing line between what is forgettable and what is valuable for those doing the remembering. In other words, what is recollected is closely linked to whose experiences are being remembered, what Eviatar Zerubavel calls the 'mnemonic community'.[3] As different groups emerge and look for a common past, so too does the relevance of certain topics shift. The basic point can be illustrated by Augustin Thierry's manifesto for a new 'national' history in the 1820s, in which he announced his desire to get away from the histories of kings and to write what was truly relevant, the history of the nation as exemplified in the 'experiences of men like ourselves'.[4]

Memorability derives from shifting patterns of relevance, then. But it is also a matter of packaging, of being able to represent the past in an evocative way. Jan Assmann has shown the importance of finding 'figures of memory' (*Erinnerungsfiguren*) in public recollections.[5] This means finding ways to evoke the past in a form (be this a narrative, a monument or a commemorative ritual) that gives a focus and shape to remembrance and makes it imaginable for third parties. In the case of figurative monuments in the heroic mode, for example (think of the monument to the Hungarian land-taking in Budapest, erected in 1896), immense swathes of experience involving many individual actors are summed up in an eye-catching set of figures. Cultural remembrance is thus shaped in practice by the different 'languages' or models we have for talking about events, and these are closely tied to contemporary aesthetics and to representational practices in other fields. As the recent Holocaust monument in the centre of Berlin illustrates, for example, the heroic and highly figurative mode of nineteenth-century monuments has generally been replaced by abstract forms of expression which are more consonant with modern art, where the dominant mode is reflective rather than celebratory.

Behind such trends lies the fundamental, familiar and yet intriguing fact that different monuments, stories or ceremonies, dealing with unique events relevant to particular mnemonic communities, are nevertheless based on common models that are not specific to the group. A striking illustration can be offered from the field of recent historiography where Pierre Nora's *Lieux de mémoire* (1984–92) provided a basic model which was followed and, in the process, adapted in many other countries across Europe. While each national case is *sui generis* and involves unique material, the model for shaping that material is an international migrant that is adapted to local conditions. The general principle of 'shareware' is illustrated in striking detail in Joep Leerssen's recent study of comparative nineteenth-century nationalisms, which shows many common patterns of nation-building right across Europe.[6]

Taking these various factors into account, it can be shown that 'memorability' is dependent on a combination of shifting social frames, relevance and our ability to devise appropriate cultural forms for 'figuring' certain topics in a public way.[7] As I have argued at length elsewhere, the emergence of newly relevant topics into public remembrance goes hand in glove with finding new ways to talk about them in an evocative way that makes them 'stick'.[8]

This brings me to the main concern of this paper. What is the role of fictional storytelling in these dynamics? More specifically, what role has it played alongside other media in cultural remembrance within a national framework? The dynamic and interactive model outlined above allows us to approach this question without having to fall back into the familiar groove of seeing literature as merely a corrupted form of history or as another world entirely. In what follows, I will analyse the role of fictional storytelling instead as one mode of remembrance alongside others, yet one that may do distinctive things.

Historical Fiction

Specialists in the field of literary studies have long abandoned static notions of genre, which pit a monolithic entity like 'fiction' or 'literature' over against 'historiography'. Instead, as my opening remarks suggest, the models of culture that currently inform the discipline are dynamic ones.[9] They presuppose that cultural practices are continuously evolving as a result of the exchanges between them and the circulation of ideas across different media. From this perspective, borders between artistic and popular literature, between visual and verbal media, between art and scholarship, are recognisable and at times extremely important; at the same time they are also permeable and shifting. So, while generic labels are necessary for analysing trends and the emergence of common models, they have to be used with caution, historicised, and their mutability taken into account.

It is against the background of this caveat that I use 'fiction' here, as a general umbrella term to designate cultural practices that are governed by the principle of 'poetic licence': the freedom in principle to deviate from what is accepted as factual for the purposes of producing artistic works.[10] This principle affects both works of 'high' art with philosophical ambitions and popular works primarily concerned with entertainment. Fiction in this very general sense is usually taken to be a defining feature of the arts in the modern period as it operates in many different media – literature, theatre, film, just to name the most obvious. In practice 'fiction' largely coincides with the practice of 'mimetic fiction', that is, with invented stories in which characters and situations are 'brought to life' and the audience, viewers or readers invited to participate virtually in their lives. While recognising the importance of theatre (especially in earlier periods) and of film (especially in the twentieth century) as media of mimetic fiction, my focus here will be on fictional writing, specifically on the genre known as the 'historical novel' – a genre whose emergence as a cultural model at the beginning of the nineteenth century coincided with the growing interest across Europe in national histories.[11]

What I call here for convenience 'the historical novel' represents a literary practice that, like any other genre, changes as certain procedures become formulaic or superseded by new ones, or as fusions take place with other forms (the memoir, the realist novel, autobiography, romance, philosophical tale, historiography, metafiction, soap operas, comic books, and so on). This means that recent variations on the basic model bear as much if not more resemblance to other contemporary works of literature than they do to their counterparts in the early nineteenth century. Yet scholars are generally agreed that there is an evolutionary connection between works from the two periods that justifies considering them together. Thus, Amy Elias' recent study of late twentieth-century experiments in historical fiction traces their genealogy back to the model of Scott's novels: they are relatives, albeit distant ones.[12] This is not the place to give a full historical account of the evolution of the historical novel as a genre in European literature, but some indication of its cultural importance and its chequered career are in place.

Walter Scott's groundbreaking *Waverley* appeared in 1814 and, though it was not without precedents, was nevertheless seen at the time as representing a new option alongside narrative poetry, historical drama and historiography as an appropriate literary form for representing the past.[13] What is generally called the 'Scott model' is characterised by the focus on private individuals (usually imaginary) caught up in moments of social turmoil (mainly historical), written in a highly vivid style with lots of local colour allowing the reader to recreate imaginatively the events portrayed and what it was like to be part of them. As Ina Ferris has shown in her excellent study of its literary contexts, the success of Scott's model lay in its fusion of gothic romance and antiquarian study, of the 'female' romance and high-status history, which ensured that it succeeded in having a broad appeal, reaching groups who would not normally have read novels or, alternately, historiography.[14]

Thanks too to some canny marketing tactics, Scott's novels became international bestsellers of hitherto unknown proportions and were translated throughout post-Napoleonic Europe. Moreover, they 'migrated' to other countries, both in the original and in translation, in such a way as to inspire others to write about events located in their own country, but using the Waverley novels as models.[15] Thus, Hendrik Conscience's *Leeuw van Vlaanderen* (*The Lion of Flanders*, 1838) on the struggle between the Flemish and the French in the Middle Ages was largely inspired by *Ivanhoe* (1819). Like Scott's story of the struggles between the Saxons and the Normans (itself another version of his earlier works dealing with the Highlanders and Lowlanders in Scotland), Conscience's novel is not only organised around the struggle between the indigenous population and the intruders, but it opens with the scene of a group of horsemen entering into new territory. Alternatively, to take another example, Alexander Pushkin's *Captain's Daughter* (*Kapitanskaja docka*, 1836) deals with the Pugachev rebellion in eighteenth-century Russia but does so using a combination of figures gleaned from several of Scott's works: the naïve hero who is sent to the periphery of the state and becomes embroiled in rebellion and whose experience provides the perspective on historical events (*Waverley*, *Old Mortality*, 1816), and the woman who goes to the sovereign to plead for someone's life (*Heart of Midlothian*, 1818).

In this way, the narrative patterns of Scott's historical novels dealing with Scottish history can be said to have helped pave the way for stories written by people working within different social frames and other literary traditions. A fuller list of works in other languages inspired by Scott's work would include Alessandro Manzoni's *The Betrothed* (*I promessi sposi*, 1825), Victor Hugo's *Notre-Dame de Paris* (1831), and many lesser-well known novels in Portuguese, German, Hungarian and Czech. A systematic study of the spread and mutation of the Scott-style historical novel throughout Europe and an analysis of its role within nationalist cultures has long been a desideratum. The recently published *Reception of Sir Walter Scott in Europe* (2006) has been a welcome step in this direction and confirms the popularity of the novel as a medium for 'cultivating' the national past, as Leerssen puts it.[16]

Within the literary culture as such, the historical novel became *the* dominant genre within European literature in the period up to 1840–1850. After that it fell victim to its own success and, becoming formulaic, effectively died out as an inspirational model and 'descended' to the realm of juvenile or popular fiction. There are later exceptions, of course, most notably Tolstoy's *War and Peace* (*Vojna i mir*, 1869) and Hugo's *Les misérables* (1862), and a continuous stream of novels (and later films) with a historical character might also be cited throughout the twentieth century.[17] However, in general, the creative energies of prominent literary artists in the Modernist period were redirected to the representation of contemporary society or the future rather than the past as such. In the last 30 years or so, however, the genre has really come into its own again, being generally seen as a dominant form in postmodernism and within the contemporary literary scene across the continent. Thus, authors like José Saramago, W.G. Sebald, Amin Maalouf, Imre Kertész, Günter Grass, Ivo Andrić, Orhan Pamuk, amongst many others, have all applied their literary art to writing fiction with a historical dimension, very often bearing on the traumatic historical events of the twentieth century or on historical versions of intercultural conflict.[18] This second blossoming of the historical novel has sometimes been explained by factors internal to literary traditions (recycling a once popular, but now marginalised genre is a recognised mechanism in the dynamics of literary history).[19] Nevertheless, as Amy Elias has recently argued, the timing in both cases may also have something to do with the particular functionality of this genre in dealing with the experience of rupture (the Napoleonic era in the one case, the post-Second World War in the other case).

However great the diversity within this very large body of literary materials, all the works mentioned so far are crossbreeds, hybrids. They enjoy the freedom to invent at the same time as they claim in some way to give an image of how things were or, at the very least, address through storytelling our understanding of particular historical events or particular periods. Historical fiction thus perennially muddies any clear distinction between 'pure' literature and 'pure' history, or between 'factual writing' and 'imaginative writing' and this 'neither fish nor fowl' status has until recently proved an obstacle to its scholarly treatment. Within the broader framework offered by the concept of cultural remembrance, however, and against the background of advances in our understanding of how representation works in different types of discourse and circulates between them, it has become possible to think in new ways about historical fiction.

In what follows, then, I put the case that the (infamous) hybridity of the historical novel is not just some unfortunate deviation which turns it into opium for people who should know better, but precisely the source of its functionality as a central junction in the circulation of cultural memory through different memorial practices. I put forward three related arguments to support my case: the first relates to the novel's role in making events representable; the second has to do with its role in showing the relevance of 'forgotten' parts of the past; the third relates to its role as mediator between mnemonic communities. Given the confines of this paper, I can do no more than sketch the theoretical outlines for more detailed case studies in the future.

Making Memorable: Turning Events Into a Story

As studies of the novel since Mikhail Bakhtin have emphasised, a novel represents a non-specialist and 'non-disciplined' discourse that, in telling stories about people in recognisable worlds, picks up on all sorts of other more specialist discourses and cultural practices.[20] Following what was said earlier about the circulation of stories across different media, novels can be seen as having a role to play as a meeting point where various other forms of remembrance are picked up and reworked. Most obvious in the case of the historical novel is its reworking of documentary sources – as in the case of Scott who added footnotes to his later editions or, more recently, Pat Barker who includes a bibliography in her *Regeneration* trilogy on the First World War (1991–95). Less obvious perhaps is the way in which novelists build on non-textual forms of remembrance or evoke other sorts of monuments in their work. The story of Hugo's *Notre-Dame de Paris* is grafted onto the discussions taking place in his own time regarding the cathedral as a site of memory, and represents thus a way of bringing verbal representations of the site into circulation.[21] More recently, W.G. Sebald has gone so far as to include actual photos in his novels along with maps of particular memory sites: his novel *Austerlitz* (2001), for example, includes photos and diagrams of a fortress outside of Antwerp that also plays a part in the story. In this way, novels play a role alongside other forms of remembrance in circulating ideas about the past.

However, novelists are not only into the business of passing on images. For better or for worse, they also *add* something with the help of imagination and literary skills: a story and the possibility of virtually participating in the past experiences of particular individuals using whatever techniques are available.[22] Since the pioneering work of Hayden White, we know that presenting events in an emplotted form (with beginning, middle and end) answers to people's desire to believe in the underlying coherence of history (he calls this the 'value of narrativity in the representation of reality').[23] However, how does one turn events into a story if they do not naturally have a story form and do not necessarily even lend themselves to narrativisation? Especially if, like historians, you are bound to the rules of evidence? From the perspective of these questions, poetic license takes on a different complexion:

the freedom to invent enjoyed by novelists may be simply a help in shaping events into a story. The downside is that while poetic license makes it easier to narrativise events, it inevitably reduces the writer's claim to be giving a believable account of history or to be contributing to discussions of history. But this downside may in practice be of secondary importance in relation to the initial – and sometimes lasting – appeal of a 'memorable' story to the public at large.

Pushkin's treatment of the Pugachev rebellion illustrates this point. The fictional *Captain's Daughter* was actually preceded by Pushkin's non-fictional account of the same topic that, despite the considerable amount of original research that had gone into its making, had been criticised as a 'still-born' child when it appeared in 1833.[24] In recycling much of his information in the novel and adapting the Scott model to his material, Pushkin could introduce a strong storyline focussed on the main character whose transformation from naïve young man to slightly wiser married man through his involvement in the rebellion provides the main narrative frame into which the history of Pugachev is embedded. The cultural longevity of Pushkin's novel, the fact that his story has stuck in what A. Assmann calls the 'working memory' of society,[25] is testimony to its success in making the rebellion memorable even if the latter has been transformed with regard to the historical record.[26] This does not mean that novelists get the last word. Research has shown that a striking, but fictional narrative dealing with historical topics may give rise to rewritings and corrected versions on the part of historians (this is what happened, for example, in the case of Scott's *Old Mortality*) although these corrective histories do not necessarily replace the original fiction entirely as a common point of reference.[27] In many cases, such fictions have not only been reread in new editions, but have also enjoyed a new life as opera, film or television series.

While the element of plot is an important element in stories – certainly in more traditional narratives like those of Scott and Pushkin – it does not account fully for the value of narrativity as White claimed it did. The possibility of identifying and 'living along' with individuals as they experience events would seem to be as important a feature of stories as their coherence as such. This is certainly the case with more recent historical novels, where plot is a less dominant feature or only present in a rudimentary form, but where we as readers are still invited to become virtually involved in somebody else's experience. (In a novel like Kadare's *Chronicle in Stone* [*Kronike në gur*, 1971], for example, the key to the story lies in the characters and the various things that happen to them rather than in any main set of events leading to a denouement and closure.) Partly in response to such changes in literary practice, but partly also as a result of the realisation that plot and coherence was not the whole story, recent post-structuralist narratology has located the essence of storytelling in the virtual experience of another time and place that it offers.[28] Those who enjoy 'poetic license' often use their freedom to invent to give us, with the help of literary techniques and literary skills, the illusion of access to other people's minds as they experience and recall events. Although she comes from another set of discussions, Alison Landsberg's idea that media can offer a form of 'prosthetic memory' through which we experience events vicariously fits in with this shift to the experiential in recent narratology. As a medium of prosthetic memory, storytelling helps mediate across temporal and cultural boundaries by presenting individual experience to third parties in a vivid and highly imaginable way.[29] This experiential dimension was already an important feature of the classical historical novel, but it has become a dominant feature in more recent works, which often abandon the more epic style of the earlier novels to focus on a central consciousness through whom events are perceived. Thus, Graham Swift's novel *Waterland* (1983) offers a wide-ranging tapestry involving the history of the landscape, local history, family history and personal history, but ties these various fragmented stories to the consciousness of one central character who is trying to sort out his own life.

The fact that access to other people's minds is based on a fiction does not necessarily take from its role as heuristic tool in opening up other worlds to contemporary readers and enabling them to imagine themselves in unfamiliar social frames. Obviously the more literary skills the writer can bring into play the more successful this 'experiential' and heuristic dimension can become. Moreover, the same literary skills may be used, not only to get a reader engrossed in the world of the story, but also to draw attention to the activity of story-telling and the options chosen (or not) by the narrator. In this regard, it is significant that Scott's highly emplotted novels were already prefaced by an elaborate and highly self-conscious play with imaginary narrators that package the stories in a reflective layer. In this sense, they were far from naïve attempts to reconstruct the past or an unreflective 'indulgence' in the easy-way-out of fiction. This self-reflexive dimension provides another point of similarity to more recent works, like Swift's *Waterland* or Sebald's *Austerlitz*, that are both as much meditations on memory as they are accounts of particular events. It would seem that literature, in providing a space for experimenting with ways of representing the world, also gravitates towards engaging us in critical reflection on the nature of remembrance itself.

Making Memorable What Has Been Forgotten

In one of the earliest essays on Scott's *Old Mortality* (1816), written in the *Archives philosophiques*, the anonymous reviewer praised the relevance of the subject matter:

Les aventures d'un soldat, dans le courant d'une campagne, peuvent fournir la matière d'un roman où l'histoire se représentera fidèlement dans des scènes d'imagination: mais, pour que cette représentation soit fidèle, il ne faut pas y faire entrer les aventures d'un général.[30]

[The adventures of a soldier in the middle of a campaign can provide materials for a novel in which history is represented faithfully in imaginary scenes; but for this representation to be faithful, the adventures of generals should not enter into it.]

The syntax is complicated, but the message is clear: better a fictional account of unimportant soldiers than a factual account of well-known generals. Indeed to focus on a general would no longer be representative of what the reviewer clearly considers to be where history is 'at' – i.e., with the experiences of the people rather than with the strategies of their leaders. Behind this comment is a clear political preference with the nation taken as a social frame for looking at the past, but behind the comment is apparently also gratitude for the fact that historical fiction had succeeded in bringing into circulation the memory of certain experiences, hitherto left out of official histories. With the help of the novel, the lives of the ordinary soldier had been figured, albeit with the help of fictional scenes, and thus retrieved from oblivion.

Time and again in the reception of Scott's work and that of other novelists we see this balancing out of relevance against veracity: some freedoms with literal truth could be a price well paid if it allowed more relevant topics to be represented for the first time – figured, articulated, brought into the public arena. The duty to remember certain groups who are identified as belonging within the social frame of the mnemonic community can apparently weigh heavier in certain circumstances than the commitment to literal truth regarding things that are not so relevant. This is what I have elsewhere called the *faute-de-mieux* principle: the idea that 'relevant' novels, despite their obvious shortcomings with regard to historiographical norms, may acquire a greater value than works of history on 'irrelevant' subjects if they succeed in recalling the actions or experiences of those with whom those doing the remembering can identify.[31]

Following the dynamic and interactive model of culture briefly sketched at the beginning of this paper, it is possible to read the history of the historical novel as an ongoing exploration of what has 'been beyond the grasp' of historians. Repeated statements on the part of writers and their readers have linked novelistic practice to a constantly renewed desire to get to the other side of official accounts, to experiences that had been written out of the picture. Typical of this tradition was a story written in 1983 by Danilo Kiš in which he evoked an imaginary 'encyclopedia of the dead' that was characterised precisely by the explicit 'absence of famous people', with the only condition for inclusion being 'that no one whose name is recorded here may appear in any other encyclopedia'.[32]

Exploring the other side of what has appeared elsewhere could be a matter of shifting attention to a particular set of topics: everyday life and mores, for example, which was described by Balzac as the 'history forgotten by historians' and the one which he considered to be his vocation to write.[33] Writing the 'other side' of historiographical memory could also be a matter of focussing on the history of excluded social groups, the victims and the subalterns, women and the disenfranchised – or, in Victor Hugo's words, the experience of 'people who labour [...] of oppressed women, and suffering children – all those who suffer in obscurity'.[34] In Hugo's case, the exploration of domains purportedly 'forgotten' by historians clearly involved expanding the social frame within which public remembrance was conceived, expanding the imagined community of the nation inwards, as it were, to include women, children and other unfortunates. We have already seen this emphasis on those 'left out of history' in Kiš' work; but it also recurs in Elsa Morante's *History: A Novel* (*La storia*, 1974) and in Ismail Kadare's *Chronicle in Stone*: both these novels narrate events from the Second World War from the perspective of the politically and socially dispossessed. Since focussing on different groups often involves different aspects of experience, expanding the social frame goes hand in glove with expanding the range of what might be considered 'memorable' events. In this regard, it is interesting to note a tendency in recent historical fiction to foreground the *family* and its secrets, rather than the nation, as the privileged frame for remembrance. One could think here, for example, along with Swift's *Waterland* and Kiš' *Encyclopedia of the Dead*, of Jean Rouaud's *Fields of Glory* (*Les champs d'honneur*, 1990) and Günter Grass' *Crabwalk* (*Im Krebsgang*, 2002).

If novelists have positioned themselves in their difference from historians, so too have many historians defined their agendas in their difference from novelists: both parties evolve by virtue of mutual criticism and by trying to pull away from each other. This is illustrated by Macaulay's famous comments to the effect that Scott had picked up the gleanings left over by historians and turned them into a scintillating story, but that historians would now take over from there and 'do the same thing' without the use of invention and according to the rules of their own trade. That it took more than a century for cultural history to blossom is indicative of the fact that 'taking over from novelists' was easier said than done.[35] Nevertheless, it is worth considering the evolution of historiography as partly a response, be this in the form of correction or emulation, to what the makers of fiction were up to. From this perspective, for example, Jean Renoir's film *La Marseillaise* (1936) or Sasha Guitry's film *Si Versailles m'était conté* (1953) could even be read as first drafts of Pierre Nora's *Lieux de mémoire* in that they use a symbolic site or actual location, rather than a particular set of events, as the focal point of their representation of national history.

Since historiography, like novel writing, continues to evolve as a cultural practice, the nature of what lies beyond its reach keeps changing as well. Balzac's belief that historians had neglected the history of manners obviously no longer holds water in an age when cultural history has assumed such a prominent place within the discipline. This does not mean that historians now do the work of novelists, however, but that contemporary novelists have shifted ground and are now exploring other 'forgotten' parts of public remembrance. For example, the representation of suffering as a result of war, political violence and displacement, and their impact on the lives of individuals caught between two cultures (as in Amin Maalouf's *Les échelles du levant* [1996] and Sebastian Faulks' *Birdsong* [1993]), to name just a couple of examples).

Someone like Scott made 'memorable' certain types of experience by incorporating them into a highly plotted narrative modelled on popular romances of the eighteenth century. His successors in the twentieth century have experimented with other sorts of forms. However, in all these cases, novelists could be said to provide a figurative form for recalling particular types of experience that for one reason or another have been left out of official forms of remembrance. This is because they were simply considered insignificant or, as importantly, simply because people could not find an appropriate form for talking about them in the public arena and in a memorable way that would engage the public's understanding and empathy. Creative writers have continued to play a role in adjusting the social frames within which the past is interpreted publicly, and expanded the repertoire of forms and modalities we can use in such cultural remembrance. Indeed, there are grounds for arguing that historical fiction (first as novel and, later as film) has had a structural role to play in the modern period as a platform for remembrance on the part of subaltern communities or marginalised groups not represented within official histories. It has also been an important medium for dealing with issues that have hitherto not been articulated. This has led Geoffrey Hartman among others to argue recently that literature is a cultural force that works against rigidity and stagnation in collective remembrance, by keeping open as it were the frames within which we conceive of the past.[36] Experimentation with different ways of representing the past, from Scott to Sebald, has also helped in 'keeping open' the view of the past and our relation to it.

Part of the perpetual 'tug-of-war' between creative writers and historians has to do with different visions of the nature of public remembrance itself. It has already been pointed out that novelists not only practise different ways of dealing with the past (using personable narrators and emphasising individual experience), but also often engage in self-conscious reflection on remembrance itself. There is a consensus among literary critics that this self-reflexive element has become a dominant feature of what is loosely called 'postmodern' writing. In this regard, Linda Hutcheon has proposed the term 'historiographic metafiction' to describe what she sees as characteristic of many recent examples of historical fiction, specifically in the literary medium. By 'historiographic metafiction' she means a type of writing, often with fantastic elements, that is simultaneously a medium of storytelling about the past and a critical reflection on the way societies can and should deal with history. Often this critical reflection finds expression in radical reworkings – what Astrid Erll calls 're-visioning' – of canonical narratives which have influenced the common understanding of certain periods in history. Thus, J.M. Coetzee famously rewrote the story of Robinson Crusoe in his work *Foe* (1986), which invites the reader to think about what was left out of the usual accounts of European expansionism.[37] Clearly, such novels are no substitute for historiography (nor are they meant to be), but the case exemplifies the fact that collective remembrance is multifaceted and complex: that there are different modes of remembrance in society that hit off and reinforce each other. Indeed, a survey of the role played by creative writers in 'narrating the nation' would surely not be complete without at least passing mention of the help they have given from the sidelines in desacralising and undermining national myths through parody and various other forms of comic relief.

Circulating Across Borders

That Scott's works were international bestsellers has already been mentioned. So too has the fact that fictional narratives help in shifting the social horizons in which people think about the past. In this final part of my argument, I want to take off from these points to say something more about the ways in which literature (along with all the other arts, including film) not only helps redraw mental borders, but actually circulates across linguistic and national frontiers.

Most readers will be familiar with Benedict Anderson's argument about the role of the media in creating 'imagined communities' like the nation. They will also remember that he singled out novels as having had a particular role to play in this process since they have traditionally evoked a social reality in which individuals are shown to share a world even when they do not actually ever meet face to face. As such, the novel was a sort of imaginative gymnasium that created the mental fitness for people to take on board an abstract community called the nation (as presumably television plays a similar role on a larger, more global scale nowadays).[38] Although it obviously needs historical nuancing, there is certainly something to be said for this view of the novel. Anderson's argument can be extended to include the specific role of historical novels in creating a mental space where present-day readers can become involved in the lives of people in the past, and hence in creating that 'communality of the dead and the living' which Michelet once described as the ultimate aim of the historian.[39]

Anderson's frame of reference was firmly a national one; however, there is no reason why novels' power to produce 'imagined communities' should always be applied in the service of a specifically national social frame rather than a regional or class-based one. Moreover, surely one of the most striking things about literary works, especially novels, is that they travel across borders with relative ease, both in translation and in the original.[40] Pushkin's *Captain's Daughter* illustrates the principle.

Up to a point, of course, the same can be said of works of historiography since, like all other texts, they have the capacity to circulate across linguistic and national borders. This does happen, of course, as is borne out by the influence of Nora's *Lieux de mémoire* mentioned earlier. Yet, going by the number of translations and the size of the editions, fiction seems to migrate more easily and to reach a broader public, travelling across linguistic and social borders and, in the form of new editions or filmic adaptations, across generational divides. Fiction can travel with such ease, I would argue, thanks to the experiential and reflective dimensions discussed earlier that ensure that they have a value in themselves for the reader that is independent of their initial relevance. In other words, a reader does not have to have a prior stake in the history of Bosnia or Turkey to read the novels of Ivo Andrić or Orhan Pamuk, since the promise of a narrative experience and the aesthetic pleasure in the narration itself may be enough to get one going. However, having once started, readers may become imaginatively involved and their interest in a particular historical arena be aroused. In this way, the historical novel as a medium helps promote an imaginative link to other groups, creating prosthetic memory in Landsberg's sense. Thus, the Nobel prize-winning Ivo Andrić's *The Bridge over the Drina* (*Na Drini cuprija*, 1945) was described in the TLS as opening up new social perspectives: 'Andrić possesses the rare gift [...] of creating a period-piece, full of local colour, and at the same time characters who might have been living today'.[41] A bridge is located in one particular place, but a novel about that bridge reaches us here.

Most thinking about national identity and national remembrance has been from the inside out as it were, supposing a 'national' community whose members have a prior interest in the common past and even a duty to know it. When it comes to fiction, however, the interest does not necessarily precede the reading of the story, but can be aroused by it or 'cultivated' by it, to use Leerssen's term: Scott turned the history of Scotland into the focus of sustained attention – not only for readers in Scotland, but also elsewhere in England and the continent. If we consider the role of fiction in national remembrance from a point of view which includes its reception and not just its production, then we are led to conclude that it has not only been a medium for shaping national remembrance, but also for building pontoons between mnemonic communities – both within the nation and across national borders. Alternatively, to put this another way: it is a stepping-stone medium for encouraging people to look beyond their present social frame of reference.

Conclusion and Perspectives

In 1850 Alessandro Manzoni, author of one of the most memorable of historical novels, *The Betrothed*, did an intellectual volte-face and wrote a long essay condemning the genre for its hybridity.[42] The genre was the literary equivalent of trying to mix oil with water, Manzoni complained, and always fell between two stools: it was neither pure literature nor pure historiography, and was therefore condemned perpetually to be nothing much at all. Manzoni's criticism was perhaps a reaction to the excessive popularity of the genre in the previous decades and an indication that the Scott model had played itself out for the nonce in more formulaic displays of local colour and predictable plots. However, it is also symptomatic of a structural uneasiness about historical fiction, whether in a literary or a cinematic form, which has continued to haunt this cultural crossbreed. What I have been doing in the preceding pages is, above all, retrieving historical fiction from its position as the 'other' of historiography by showing how it has had a constructive role to play within the dynamics of public remembrance. As we have seen, it plays this role by doing its own thing (telling stories using literary means); by working in conjunction with other media and mnemonic forms, including museums, movies and histories; but also by working critically against what regular historians do in the spaces beyond their ken – and perhaps outside their brief.

In emphasising the contributions of historical fiction to the formation and revision of national remembrance, the focus has been on what it can do and what it often does, rather than what it fails to do. I take it as a given that historical fiction fails to do many things, and that not every work in the genre attains the same level of complexity, nuance and insight into historical experience; and that not every work of historical fiction succeeds in opening up new horizons. Indeed some historical novels are predictable exercises in 'doing things with local colour'; while others give a view of the past that, by historiographical standards, is a gross distortion, the source of new myths, or a mere replay of clichés. That professional historians should be often outraged and suspicious is inevitable – but also fitting. As I have been arguing here, the collective remembrance of events has thrived as much by dissent as by convergence and imitation.

Studies of 'national histories in Europe' should therefore consider both fictional and historiographical remembrance in relation to each, specifically with regard to the constant recalibration of relevance, forms of representation and social frames that occur in the spaces between them. How have these different discourses operated as cultural media and how, in the process, have they both fixed and expanded the social frames within which we imagine our pasts?

Notes

1. J. Assmann (1992), *Das kulturelle Gedächtnis: Schrift, Erinnerung und politische Identität in frühen Hochkulturen*, Munich, 2000: 47; A. Assmann, *Erinnerungsräume: Formen und Wandlungen des kulturellen Gedächtnisses*, Munich, 1999. A. Erll, *Kollektives Gedächtnis und Erinnerungskulturen: Eine Einführung*, Stuttgart, 2005 provides a very useful overview of discussions regarding historically variable 'memory cultures'. For an excellent survey of recent English-language discussions that comes to similar conclusions, see J.K. Olick and J. Robbins, 'Social Memory Studies: From "Collective Memory" to the Historical Sociology of Mnemonic Practices', *Annual Review of Sociology* 24, 1998: 105–40.
2. On the relation between relevance and changing social frameworks, see also I. Irwin-Zarecka, *Frames of Remembrance: The Dynamics of Collective Memory*, New Brunswick, NJ, 1994.
3. E. Zerubavel, *Time Maps: Collective Memory and the Social Shape of the Past*, Chicago, 2003.
4. Letter to the *Courrier Français* (23 July 1820); quoted in R. Nephi Smithson, *Augustin Thierry: Social and Political Consciousness in the Evolution of a Historical Method*, Geneva, 1973: 82.
5. Assmann, *Das kulturelle Gedächtnis*, 37–42.
6. J. Leerssen, *National Thought in Europe: A Cultural History*, Amsterdam, 2006.
7. For more on the recycling of models of remembrance, see A. Rigney, 'Scarcity, Plenitude and the Circulation of Cultural Memory', *Journal of European Studies* 35, 1–2, 2005: 209–26.
8. For more on the relationship between the relevant and the representable, see A. Rigney, *Imperfect Histories: The Elusive Past and the Legacy of Romantic Historicism*, Ithaca, NY, 2001: 59–98; also Rigney, 'Scarcity, Plenitude and the Circulation of Cultural Memory', 221–23.
9. From within the field of literary studies this dynamic approach to culture, which sees literary writing in its interactions with other practices, has been most prominently formulated within the framework of New Historicism; for example, S. Greenblatt, 'Culture' in F. Lentricchia and T. McLaughlin, eds, *Critical Terms in Literary Study*, Chicago, 1995: 225–32.
10. I use here a pragmatic definition of fiction (as make-believe, as involving a 'suspension of disbelief' on the part of readers) rather than a definition based on the status (true or imaginary) of the things referred to. See also A. Rigney, 'Semantic Slides: History and the Concept of Fiction' in R. Torstendahl and I. Veit-Brause, eds, *History-making: The Intellectual and Social Formation of a Discipline*, Stockholm, 1996: 31–46.
11. For general surveys of the historical novel, see among others G. Lukács, (1936–37), *The Historical Novel*, trans. H. Mitchell and S. Mitchell, Harmondsworth, 1981; E. Wesseling, *Writing History as a Prophet: Postmodernist Innovations of the Historical Novel*, Amsterdam, 1991; A.J. Elias, *Sublime Desire: History and Post-1960s Fiction*, Baltimore, MD, 2001.
12. Elias, *Sublime Desire*.
13. The secondary literature on Scott is vast and continues to grow. A bibliographical survey of the earlier period is provided in J.C. Corson, *A Bibliography of Sir Walter Scott*, Edinburgh, 1943. Recent works that have informed this analysis include J. Millgate, *Walter Scott: The Making of the Novelist*, Toronto, 1984; Ina Ferris, *The Achievement of Literary Authority: Gender, History, and the Waverley Novels*, Ithaca, NY, 1991; Ian Duncan, *Modern Romance and Transformations of the Novel: The Gothic, Scott, Dickens*, Cambridge, 1992; F. Robertson, *Legitimate Histories: Scott, Gothic, and the Authorities of Fiction*, Oxford, 1994.

14. Ferris, *The Achievement of Literary Authority*; further elaborated in Robertson, *Legitimate Histories*.

15. The scale of the phenomenon is evidenced in the bibliography of Scottish literature in translation (BOSLIT), available online from the University of Edinburgh. A recent, remarkably detailed survey of publishing practices shows that Scott's novels (along with several of the poems he wrote before becoming a novelist) broke all records and continued to sell very well late into the century; W. St Clair, *The Reading Nation in the Romantic Period*, Cambridge, 2004.

16. M. Pittock, ed., *The Reception of Sir Walter Scott in Europe*, London, 2006. J. Leerssen has classified the different activities and cultural forms, from editing literary works to setting up monuments, used in the nineteenth century to 'cultivate' a sense of national identity; 'Nationalism and the Cultivation of Culture', *Nations and Nationalism* 12, 4, 2006: 559–78. His extensive international survey confirms the importance of the historical novel as one of these genres; for some of his findings see also www.hum.uva.nl/philology. The 'Projekt historischer Roman' at the University of Innsbruck provides an overview of historical novels written in German: http://histrom.literature.at/register.html.

17. A good survey of the changing fortunes of the historical novel is provided by E. Wesseling, *Writing History*, 5–58. On the nineteenth century as a post-war period, see Elias, *Sublime Desire*; also P. Fritzsche, *Stranded in the Present: Modern Time and the Melancholy of History*, Cambridge, MA, 2004.

18. Recent variations on the genre have been studied from a literary-historical perspective in: Wesseling, *Writing History as a Prophet*; A. Nünning, *Von historischer Fiktion zu historiographischer Metafiktion*, Trier, 1995; Elias, *Sublime Desire*.

19. As in the Formalist model proposed in: J. Tynjanov, (1927) 'On Literary Evolution', in L.Matejka and K. Pomorska, eds, *Readings in Russian Poetics*, Cambridge, MA, 1978: 66–77.

20. M.M. Bakhtin, 'Discourse in the Novel', in his *The Dialogic Imagination*, ed. M.Holquist, trans. C. Emerson and M. Holquist, Austin, 1981: 259–422.

21. S. Friedrich, 'Erinnerung als Auslöschung: Zum Verhältnis zwischen kulturellen Gedächtnisräumen und ihrer medialen Vermittlung in Victor Hugos *Notre-Dame de Paris* und *Les misérables*', *Arcadia: Zeitschrift für vergleichende Literaturwissenschaft* 40, 1, 2005: 61–78.

22. Assmann, *Erinnerungsräume*, 249–64; see also A. Rigney, 'Portable Monuments: Literature, Cultural Memory, and the Case of Jeanie Deans', *Poetics Today* 25, 2, 2004: 361–96.

23. H. White, *The Content of the Form: Narrative Discourse and Historical Representation*, Baltimore, MD, 1987: 1–25.

24. T. J. Binyon, *Pushkin: A Biography*, London, 2002: 478.

25. The distinction between 'archival' and 'working' memory is discussed in Assmann, *Erinnerungsräume*, 133–37.

26. For a more extensive discussion of this point, see Rigney, *Imperfect Histories*, 16–31.

27. Rigney, *Imperfect Histories*, 45–56.

28. M. Fludernik, *Towards a 'Natural' Narratology*, London, 1996; M-L. Ryan, *Narrative as Virtual Reality: Immersion and Interactivity in Literature and Electronic Media*, Baltimore, MD, 2001.

29. A. Landsberg, *Prosthetic Memory: The Transformation of American Remembrance in the Age of Mass Culture*, New York, 2004.

30. Trans. AR. *Archives philosophiques, politiques et littéraires* 2, 1817: 24–54 (26–27).

31. Rigney, *Imperfect Histories*, 53–58.

32. D. Kiš, (1983) *The Encyclopedia of the Dead*, trans. M.H. Heim, Evanston, IL, 1997, 43.

33. H. de Balzac, (1842) *La comédie humaine*, vol. 1, ed. P. Citron, Paris, 1965–66: 52.

34. Trans. AR. V. Hugo, (1862) *Les misérables*, vol. 3, Paris, n.d.: 282.

35. T.B. Macaulay, (1828) 'History' in his *Critical, Historical and Miscellaneous Essays*, vol.
     1, New York, n.d.: 270–309 (307–8); for an account of attempts to bring this project into
     practice, see Rigney, *Imperfect Histories*, 59–98.

36. G.H. Hartman, 'Public Memory and its Discontents', in *The Uses of Literary History*, ed.
     M. Brown, Durham, NC, 1995: 73–91; note that Hartman uses the word 'literature' here as
     synonymous with 'works of artistic merit' and not simply as synonym for fiction.

37. On the literary revisioning of canonical narratives, see A. Erll, 'Re-writing as Re-visioning:
     Modes of Representing the "Indian Mutiny" in British Novels, 1857 to 2000', *EJES:
     European Journal of English Studies* 10, 2, 2006: 163–85.

38. B. Anderson, (1983) *Imagined Communities: Reflections on the Origins and Spread of
     Nationalism*, London, 1991: 26; for a critical elaboration of this argument, see J. Culler,
     'Anderson and the Novel', *Diacritics* 29, 4, 1999: 20–39.

39. J. Michelet, (1872–74) *Histoire du dix-neuvième siècle*, ed. B Leuillot, Paris, 1982: 268.

40. This process is well illustrated in F. Moretti, *Atlas of the European Novel 1800–1900*,
     London, 1999.

41. Quoted on the back cover of I. Andrić, *The Bridge over the Drina*, trans. L.F. Edwards,
     New York, 1994.

42. A. Manzoni, (1850) *On the Historical Novel*, trans. S. Bermann, Lincoln, NB, 1983.

Chapter 5

The Institutionalisation and Nationalisation of Literature in Nineteenth-century Europe[1]

JOHN NEUBAUER

> Our profession emerges with the flow of the national idea;
> it is not a scholarly observer but part of it.[2]

Founding Literary History: The Schlegel Brothers and Coleridge

Textual criticism is very old, but modern philology, including literary scholarship was born in the decades either side of 1800. I shall argue that the institutionalisation of literary scholarship in the nineteenth century was deeply implicated in the formation and development of modern nationalism. How this Europe-wide process developed, how ideas about national literature crossed borders and assumed new meanings has not yet been explained in an overarching manner, though valuable contributions on individual national literatures have been made.

Friedrich Schlegel (1772–1829) first conceived of literary history as an evolving system of individual works and authors, a subsystem of cultural history. He began in 1794–96 with studies of ancient Greece and Rome in the hope of deriving from universal patterns those that would be applicable to the study of modern literature. However, by the time he published the first volume of his history of ancient literature (1798) Schlegel had come to realise that the study of the ancients alone would not provide the material he needed. He therefore turned his gaze to the Romantic Age, which for him (and subsequently for Hegel and others) included the Middle Ages from Dante onwards, as well as Cervantes, Shakespeare and all of modern European literature up to his own age. The first product of this new concept was the short 'Epochen der Dichtkunst' (The Epochs of Poetry) in his *Gespräch über die Poesie* (1799), which he published in *Athenaeum*, a journal he edited together with his brother August Wilhelm (1767–1845).[3] The corresponding theoretical formulation of a *Romantische Universalpoesie* is to be found most succinctly in Friedrich's famous Athenaeum Fragment number 116.[4]

The Schlegel brothers had conceptualised literary history according to the organic model of the emerging epigenetic biology of the time.[5] As Friedrich Schlegel noted in 'Epochen der Dichtkunst', 'In the Homeric plant we notice, as it were, the origin of all poetry; the roots are lost to our sight but the blossoms and branches of the plant emerge from the darkness of Antiquity in their incomparable splendour'.[6] These first enquiries into the history of European literature had been made before any professorships were established in the subject area. In 1789 the rather small University of Jena, surely the most hospitable at that time to literature, thanks mostly to Goethe's involvement in its administration, had appointed Friedrich Schiller – but to a chair in history. Schiller's inaugural lecture of 1789 was therefore appropriately entitled *Was heißt und zu welchem Ende studiert man Universalgeschichte?* (What is and for what Purpose does one Study Universal History?). With the support of Schiller, August Wilhelm Schlegel moved to Jena in May 1796 in the hope of securing a post at the university as a literary scholar and historian. Friedrich followed in 1799 and did a *Habilitation* to qualify for a professorship. Their hopes did not materialise, and the bitterly disappointed brothers left Jena in 1801. They moved to Berlin and subsequently to other cities, lecturing on the history of literature in rented halls outside the universities. Samuel Taylor Coleridge (1772–1834), the first great English literary critic and historian, did not fare much better. He also lectured on various aspects of European literary history in rented halls, and never received a university appointment.

In the years of peregrination after the Jena failure August Wilhelm was more successful than Friedrich. Between 1801 and 1804 he gave public lectures in Berlin (only published in full in 1884), and in 1808 in Vienna.[7] Friedrich moved to Paris and delivered lectures on German philosophy and literature (to audiences of between twenty and twenty-five listeners), and in 1803–1804 he held a *privatissimum* on the history of literature for Sulpiz and Melchior Boisserée. He repeated the course the following year in Cologne. In these lectures, as well as in the journal *Europa*, Friedrich wanted to reveal the cultural unity of Europe by outlining the development of literature in France, Italy, Spain, Portugal, England, Germany and the Nordic countries against the background of classical Greek literature.[8]

After delivering lectures in Cologne on German language and literature (1807), Friedrich converted to Catholicism in 1808 and moved to Vienna, hoping for support from his successful brother there. Due to the Napoleonic wars, he was unable to hold his own Vienna lectures, the *Geschichte der alten und neuen Literatur*, until 1812; their publication was delayed until 1815. By then, Friedrich's ideological orientation had radically changed. As Hans Eichner writes, 'the follower of Fichte had become a Catholic, the partisan of the French Revolution – its determined opponent and European Cosmopolitan – a German patriot and an admirer of the Holy Roman Empire of the German Nation.'[9] Schlegel dedicated his history to Metternich and, in return, the 'Iron Chancellor' ennobled the historian. Ironically, Schlegel's lectures, which lent strong support to the state and advocated the status quo, had come close to being suppressed. The university was of the opinion that such extra-mural lectures were unnecessary; the police had rejected his application and only the Emperor's intervention secured the permission, on the condition that a police observer was present at the lectures.[10] In the end, the lectures were held at the university from 27 February to 30 April 1812 and were a great success.

Schlegel's newly acquired Catholic, conservative and nationalist position is reflected in his dedication to Metternich. As the author explained, he wanted to bridge the deep gulf between the literary and intellectual world on the one hand and 'practical reality' on the other. His goal was to demonstrate 'how decisively a nation's spiritual culture (*Geistesbildung*) might often intervene even in the great global events and in the fate of nations'.[11] Literature was not mere entertainment or a copy of the 'real world' but also a political force.

In his opening lecture, Schlegel explained the message he aimed to convey to the political class of the day, namely that literature was the 'essence' (*Inbegriff*) of the nation's intellectual life.[12] At the same time he acknowledged that scholars and writers had traditionally been isolated from the world and the 'social culture' (*Bildung*) of the upper classes as well as from the rest of the nation.[13] Divisions within the artistic-intellectual culture and its separation from the people were, according to Schlegel, the greatest obstacles to the development of a general national culture.[14] However, as the author argued, the eighteenth century had, in Germany and the other European nations, heralded a revival of 'national spirit'.[15] In practice, what Schlegel meant was that from now on literature ought to serve the state and, more specifically, glorify the national past:

> From a historical perspective which compares people according to their value it is most important for the nation's further development, even for its whole spiritual existence, that the folk should retain those great national memories of its distant origins that usually vanish. Poetry's prime business is to preserve and to glorify them. Those national memories, which constitute the most splendid parts of its heritage, are possessed and represented by the folk, an advantage that nothing else could have. And if the folk finds itself ennobled, elevated in its self-esteem due to its great past and its memories of a primeval time, if it has, in a word, poetry, then it will also be raised to a higher level in our eyes and judgement.[16]

The primary concern of poetry was thus to preserve and glorify great national memories from the dim past of national history. This is why the *Nibelungenlied* was for Schlegel the 'latest version' of ancient, quasi-mythic memories, comparable to the Homeric epics.[17] It should be added that, notwithstanding his Catholicism and conservative nationalism, Friedrich Schlegel broadened the scope of his literary history in these lectures. While he had previously included only ancient Greece and the major West-European languages, he now dedicated his fifth lecture to Indian literature, a section of the eighth to Arabic and Persian poetry, and much of the tenth lecture to the literature of 'the most northern and the eastern people of Europe'.[18] Friedrich's Vienna lectures were pioneering both for their historical and cultural breadth, and for their narrowly national and religious approach. The latter, above all his national concept of literature, not only foreshadowed the future but actually furthered literature's nineteenth-century institutionalisation and nationalisation: literature and literary scholarship acquired a political justification, and social as well as academic prestige, by becoming as it were the keeper of the national soul. The emergence of a comparative, supra-national approach to literature, which Schlegel had earlier championed, became merely a secondary effect, a weak response to the primary trend of institutionalisation and nationalisation. As if echoing Friedrich, the great Czech historian, František Palacký, remarked in 1837 that nations that did not contribute to the gradual emergence of European and universal literature actually did not count.[19]

Vernacular literature and national philology were major forces in the forging of the modern European nations, especially in Eastern Europe, where poets and philologists were among the shapers of national identity, constructing *texts* on the one hand, and *institutions* on the other. We may categorise these activities according to the modes of text construction: (1) language revival, (2) vernacular translations, (3) writing vernacular lyric poetry, (4) collecting and publishing oral poetry, (5) editing and reissuing older texts, (6) writing new national epics, (7) writing historical fiction, (8) canonising national poets and (9) writing national literary histories. We may also categorise these activities' modes of institutionalisation: (1) founding vernacular journals and newspapers, (2) establishing publishing houses, (3) founding literary and cultural societies, (4) staging vernacular plays, (5) building national theatres and opera houses, (6) establishing national academies, (7) establishing national libraries, (8) establishing university chairs for vernacular language and literature and (9) introducing vernacular language and literature into the school curricula.

Since this article focuses on nineteenth-century national narratives, it will only touch upon the creation of institutions rather tangentially. However, while discussing the former one should not forget that literary texts had been occasioned and often made possible by the newly established institutions for literature and philology. Many of the Schlegel brothers' successors were able to write literary histories because of the relative comfort that academic jobs at universities, libraries and academies provided. Equally, national theatres and opera houses furthered the writing and performance of vernacular plays and operas.

National Awakening: General Considerations

One might have expected literature to have been institutionalised in the western part of Europe first and only later in its 'backward' eastern and southern parts. Yet the first chair for English literature at the University of London was established only in 1829; in Germany, August Wilhelm Schlegel assumed the first chair in literature (*Literatur und die schöne Wissenschaften*) at the University of Bonn in 1818. Eastern Europe's Cracow and Prague, two of the oldest universities of the Continent, were ahead in this respect: Cracow's chair for Polish literature was established in 1782, while František Martin Pelcl (1734–1801) assumed the newly established Chair for Czech Language and Literature at the Charles University of Prague in 1793. At the University of Pest, which moved across the Danube from Buda in 1784, András Frigyes Halitzky assumed a chair for German language and literature in 1792, and the distinguished linguist, Miklós Révai (1750–1807) started teaching Hungarian language and literature in 1802.

The institutionalisation of literature was a matter of national identity rather than economics. In England and France, which, as Europe's most industrially advanced nations, had a robust self-image, it progressed relatively slowly. In contrast, the problematic identities of Germany, Italy, some Scandinavian and most Eastern European cultures led to an early harnessing of literature and philology for national purposes, and these disciplines took on a key role in the struggle for a national language, a national culture and political independence. The rise of vernacular literature was often a prelude to state formation, if not a precondition for it; similarly, national literary histories were often written and national literary institutions established either in lieu of national independence, in preparation for it or with the purpose of strengthening it. Germany had a paradoxical role in this respect: key ideas about national literature originated with Herder and the German Romantics, but were then appropriated by the movements of national awakening in Poland, Bohemia, Slovakia, Hungary and other East-Central European countries to fight against the domination of German language and literature. Germany aggravated its identity problem by exporting it eastward.

However, this picture is perhaps too simple. Firstly, the national awakenings were not directed only against the hegemonic cultural powers of Germany, Russia and Turkey. For example, the Hungarian national awakening and its state-supported projects to strengthen Hungarian language and literature soon had to confront the national awakening of the country's Slovak, Romanian and Croat minorities. Secondly, while national awakenings went through similar phases, they were not simultaneous. Most national cultural revivals took place in the nineteenth century, but many of them continued well into the twentieth. Differing circumstances determined their greatly differing speed. A broad, supranational characterisation of the process must therefore face what Siegfried Kracauer has called the *'Gleichzeitigkeit des Ungleichzeitigen'* (simultaneity of the heterotemporal). Thirdly, capital cities assumed dual, conflicting roles. The institutionalisation of literature enhanced their national character, turning them into symbols of the nation. 'Every nation has a holy city of which it thinks with piety and pride', wrote Jókai in his novel *Kárpáthy Zoltán* when giving an account of the great flooding of Pest in 1838.[20] National revivals led to the building of national theatres, libraries, academies and other representative national institutions in the capital cities, turning them into true national cultural centres.

Yet these capitals of national pride were also cosmopolitan centres and magnets for foreign writers and intellectuals. Apart from German-language (and often also Yiddish) newspapers and theatres, all capital cities also harboured all kinds of associations, printing presses, publishers and other institutions catering for the country's minorities and for people from neighbouring countries. In short, capital cities were not only the fulcrum of the national literary culture but also sites of cultural dispersion and diversification. In reaction to this, European countries, especially in the central and eastern regions, witnessed populist movements that glorified the countryside and idealised the pristine origins of a national oral culture, vilifying the capital's cosmopolitan culture, its industrial gloom, its decadence and its immigrant Germans, Jews and other foreigners. The Romanian Octavian Goga (1891–1938) and the Hungarian Szabó, Dezső (1879–1945), populist writers leaning towards clashing modes of chauvinism, agreed that Budapest was a kind of modern Babylon. Even the young Béla Bartók could write:

> A real Hungarian music can originate only if there is a real *Hungarian* gentry. This is why the Budapest public is so absolutely hopeless. The place has attracted a haphazardly heterogeneous, rootless group of Germans and Jews; they make up the majority of Budapest's population. It is a waste of time trying to educate them in a national spirit. Much better to educate the [Hungarian] provinces.[21]

Language Revivals

All national awakenings started with language revivals, but these were all different in nature. In Germany, the turn towards the German language was in good measure directed against the use of French, still prevalent in the court of Frederick the Great. In Eastern Europe it was directed against the use of

German (heavy-handedly propagated under Joseph II), against Latin, and, among the South Slavic people, against Old Church Slavonic. In Hungary, the Parliament decreed in 1792 that Hungarian, not Latin, was the official language in public offices. In Prague, German replaced Latin as the language of instruction at the Charles University in 1784, but the government decreed in 1816 that Czech was the official language in secondary education.

The nineteenth-century European language revivals were furthered by the emergence of German philology, especially the work of the brothers Jacob (1785–1863) and Wilhelm Grimm (1786–1859), compilers of the great German dictionary that carries their name. Vienna was a crucial centre of transmission, especially for the Slavic countries and Hungary. It was here that the great Slovene philologist Jernej (Bartolomäus) Kopitar (1780–1844) worked as a Slavist, as an Imperial censor for Slavonic subjects (!), and later as a professor and Director of the Library at the University. Barely thirty, he published his *Grammatik der Slavischen Sprache in Krain, Kaernten, und Steyermark* (1809) and a *Slavische Sprachkunde* (1811). Later, in 1836, he published a study that claimed that the Slovene language was identical to the old church language of all Slavs.

When the young Vuk Štefanović Karadžić (1787–1864) fled from the Serbo-Turkish war to Vienna in November 1813, Kopitar encouraged him to engage in linguistic studies and the collection of folklore, drawing up an agenda of research that the only slightly younger Serb would carry on for the rest of his life, though with very different political aims. Karadžić rapidly published his *Pismenica serbskoga jezika po govoru prostoga naroda* (Orthography of the Serbian Language According to the Usage of the Common People) in 1814, as well as several collections on folklore, which I shall discuss later. Jacob Grimm published a German translation of Karadžić's short Serb grammar in 1824, but Karadžić's principle, 'write as you speak and read as is written' was violently opposed by the Orthodox Church, which insisted on retaining Old Slavonic.[22] Karadžić sympathised with the Croat 'Illyrian' movement, and he was a signatory of the 1850 Vienna *Književni dogovor* (Literary Agreement) on the two languages, but in the long run the Croats' agreement with Karadžić that mixing dialects to develop a standard was undesirable and that the South Serbian dialect was the best common standard proved ill-judged.

Similar problems dogged the revival of the Czech and Slovak languages. The 'patriarch' of Slavic philology, Czech Jesuit Josef Dobrovský (1753–1829), established the view that a single Slavic language had once existed. However, he believed that Czech literature, as a patriotic and popular matter, should not be confused with the science of linguistics, which made him unpopular with the Romantic generation that followed. Indeed, one of the leading figures of that generation, Josef Jakub Jungmann (1773–1847), was perhaps more of a literary figure than a linguist. He published his major linguistic achievement, the five-volume *Slownjk česko-némecky* (Czech–German Dictionary), only in 1835–39, after spending most of his life translating foreign literature into Czech, and compiling rudimentary Czech literary histories.

Dobrovský's idea of an original pan-Slav language was used by the following generation for ideological and political purposes, but it ran against particularist currents. Anton Bernolák (1762–1813), a Jesuit from Bratislava, had in 1787 set the norms for standard Slovak in order to make literature accessible to the common people. His codification of Slovak was disliked by opponents of a schism with Czech and the other Slavic languages, as well as those who resented the fact that the codification was based on the dialect of Western Slovakia (around Bratislava), which was Catholic. Ľudovít Štúr (1815–1856), the key figure of the next generation, established the Central-Slovak dialect as the standard. He and his Protestant followers wrote in Czech until the early 1840s, but managed to reach an agreement in 1843 with the Catholic Ján Hollý, a representative of Bernolák's generation, on standardising the Slovak language. The separation from Czech now became inevitable. In 1844, Josef Miloslav Hurban published the first book in Štúrist Slovak (vol. 2 of the almanac *Nitra*). In 1845, Štúr was permitted to start a new, Slovak-language journal, the *Slovenskje narodňje novini* (Slovak National News) and its literary supplement *Orol tatránski* (The Tatra Eagle), which became the platform for a group of Slovak Romantics. By using Slovak and portraying Czech as corrupted by German, Štúr hoped to make Slovak more palatable to the Hungarians.

The leading Czech historian, František Palacký (1798–1876) opposed Štúr's codified Slovak, and two Slovak expatriates joined him. Josef Šafařík (1795–1847), who lived in Prague and became Director of the University Library and extraordinary professor of Slavonic Studies, was worried about the disintegration of a unified Czech and Slovak language, whilst Jan Kollár (1793–1852), who was a Lutheran minister of the Slovak community in Pest, protested violently against the codification's destruction of what he called the 'reciprocity' between the Slavic languages and literatures.[23] Kollár declared that the schism was a 'sin against civilisation', and he abusively called Slovak the language of pigs, coachmen and cooks. Šafařík, Kollár and others published a pamphlet against Štúr's 'secession', but to no avail, as the 'corrected' version of Štúr's codification, adopted in 1851, won the day.[24]

Romanian and Hungarian linguists had no such quarrels since in both cases the language had no extant relatives in its locality, but the question of how these languages came about was equally divisive. For example, Samuil Micu-Klein and Gheorghe Şincai claimed in their first grammar of the Romanian language that Romanian descended from Latin, laying the ground for the politically explosive Daco-Romanian theory.[25]

Cultivating the Vernacular

The revived and codified vernacular languages had to be cultivated both in everyday life and in literature, for ultimately only practice could confirm or reject the neologisms and adaptations. Language reformers adopted a variety of principles when writing or translating poetry. At one extreme were those who insisted that the revival should make use only of native resources. Hoping to regain a native purity, they sought indigenous words and expressions for everything foreign. In his poem 'To Vitkovics' (1811) Ferenc Kazinczy (1759–1831) introduces a visitor who admires all those whose 'beautiful language is not mixed with others [...] who speak as they write – in a word who came from us, grew up with us, stayed with us.'[26] However, Kazinczy, leader of the Hungarian language renewal, in fact meant to ridicule this remark; he regarded as provincialism what would have suited Vuk Karadžić. Kazinczy preferred an internationally oriented renewal that relied on literal translations, adopting foreign formulations even at the cost of straining the vernacular.

Jungmann, whom we have already mentioned, held a similar view for Czech, although he based his translations and adaptations on Dobrovský's notion that the Slavic languages were originally one: by adopting many words from the other Slavic languages in his translations Jungmann hoped to lead the Czech literary idiom towards a reunification with them. His translations of Milton's *Paradise Lost*, Chateaubriand's *Atala*, Goethe's *Hermann und Dorothea*, various works by Schiller and many others sought to refine the vernacular. Most of his neologisms did indeed catch on. In his own, less successful poetry he experimented with various metrical systems. Like Šafařík and Palacký, Jungmann claimed that Czech prosody was quantitative and he thus came into conflict with the ageing Dobrovský, who insisted, rightly, that Czech prosody was accentual (syllabotonic).[27] In the Serb language, Branko Radičević (1824–1853) showed with his *Pjesme* (Poems), published in 1847, that the nativist conception of language advocated by Karadžić was suited to the writing of non-folkloric poetry.

Jan Kollár, the bitterest opponent of Štúr's separatist codification of the Slovak language, was a pan-Slavist despite spending most of his life in Pest. Like Šafařík, he studied at the University of Jena (1817–19), and it was there that he embraced pan-Slavism. Inspired by Herder's *Ideen* and the Wartburg Festival of the German youth (which he considered one of the greatest moments of his life), he discovered traces of a lost Slavic population around Jena and most of northern Germany.[28] His greatest poetic achievement, the *Slávy dcera* (Daughter of Sláva), was a collection of sonnets (645 of them in the final edition of 1852), in which the image of Mina Schmidt, daughter of a minister near Jena whom Kollár had thought dead but met again and married in 1835, merges with that of Sláva – symbol of the lost Slavic inhabitants of northern Germany whose fate Kollár's introductory song (*předzpěv*) to the collection bewails.[29]

Founding the National Canon

The formation of a national identity required that a set of national texts be collected, developed, cultivated and canonised as founding texts and symbols of the nation's essence. To begin with, each self-respecting nation had to recuperate, very much in the spirit of Friedrich Schlegel, the myths and legends of its pre-historic past, either in the form of founding epics or popular lyric poems. Cultivation of the distant past required: (1) the collection, reworking and publishing of national epics and other poems from the oral tradition, and (2) the writing of new national epics if there were gaps to fill. The first task was entrusted to the philologists, the second to the poets, though the line between them was blurred because the philologists often surreptitiously performed creative tasks by reshaping what they found or even forging 'documents of the past'. The philologists also contributed to the national programme by: (1) canonising national poets, (2) writing histories of national literatures, and (3) training the future teachers and scholars of vernacular language and literature. The main contributions of the creative writers themselves were: (1) their personal involvement in the national awakening, in politics as well as culture, (2) fiction and poetry on contemporary issues, and (3) historical novels and dramas.

Since, strictly speaking, historical novels and dramas were the only exclusively nineteenth-century literary forms to 'narrate the nation', and since Ann Rigney's article in the present volume provides an excellent analysis of the problematic relationship between nineteenth-century historical fiction and history writing, I shall limit myself to a few remarks about historical fiction and national awakening.[30] Historical novels and dramas have been attacked both for their subjective approach to history and for fuelling a harmful nationalism, even chauvinism. Both accusations are only partially justified. While history served merely as exotic costume in many historical romances, others were based on serious historical research, and their fictional elements only served to provide psychological realism, easy readability and a perspectival mode of representation. They were, indeed, 'subjective', but often no more so than studies by the new professional historians, who were often (perhaps unconsciously) equally guided by the national and social prejudices of their age, in spite of their claim to 'scholarly objectivity'. The spectrum was wide on both sides, as was the range in the relationship between historians and writers of historical fiction. While positivism was on the rise, many historians, from the Czech František Palacký (1798–1876) to the French Jules Michelet (1798–1874), were still writing in a powerful literary style and understood the power of literature. Thus, Palacký wrote in a letter to Karel Havliček in 1852: 'if we want to become a nation, it will not be sufficient to have a history, but we shall need representative men in the world of letters. At this point, a single Walter Scott would be more valuable to us than five Žižkas'. High praise indeed for Scott, considering that for Palacký the Hussite revolt of Žižka was the highpoint of Czech history. Indeed, we shall see that at crucial moments Palacký's patriotism could overrule his scholarly temper.

Folklore

The rise of nineteenth-century nationalism in the German lands had brought to light a submerged heritage of popular lore. This included *Des Knaben Wunderhorn* (1806–8), two volumes of folklore collected by Achim von Arnim (1781–1831), and Clemens Brentano (1778–1842), the medieval epic *Nibelungenlied*, which was based on an older oral tradition and generated interested in foundation myths and heroic epics and, last but not least, the publication of *Kinder und Hausmärchen* (1812–15), the *Deutsche Sagen* (1816–18), and *Deutsche Mythologie* (1835), by Jacob and Wilhelm Grimm.

The Grimm brothers had inspired the collection of folklore all over Europe. Their contact in the Slavic world was Kopitar, who maintained an extensive correspondence with German philologists and published several of his articles in Friedrich Schlegel's *Deutsches Museum*, and, moreover, had attracted a number of young scholars to Vienna and helped their careers. As has already been mentioned, he became Karadžić's mentor in matters of folklore collecting. Karadžić's first publications of folklore allowed Kopitar to introduce his protégé to Clemens Brentano, the Grimm brothers and later to Goethe.[31] Indeed, he translated Karadžić's *Pjesnarica* (Song Book) into German and sent it in 1815 with a dedication to Goethe (whom Karadžić would visit in 1823 and 1824), and it was thanks to his mediation that Jacob Grimm wrote a lengthy and highly positive review of the book in the same year.

Karadžić collected and published a great quantity and variety of folklore in subsequent years, and, with Kopitar's help, he worked hard to popularise Slav folklore abroad. In particular, his recovery of Serbian heroic epics had a most profound impact on both nineteenth-century folklore research and national movements in Eastern Europe, all of which suddenly endowed the Serbs with a glorious mythical past that became the envy of other ethnic groups and aspiring nations in making. Following Schlegel, the possession of poetic memories of ancient times raised the nation's reputation in the eyes of foreign observers. As Jacob Grimm wrote: 'Of all Slavonic races, the Serbs are by virtue of their language (so rich and suitable for poetry) the most blessed with poems, songs, and stories.'[32]

Indeed, a veritable wave of admiration for folk poetry swept over Europe. One of those who directly benefited from it was Prosper Mérimée (1803–1870). In 1827, he published the folklore collection *La Guzla* that purportedly contained translations of Illyrian and Morlach folk poems. He managed to fool a great many people, including Pushkin, before it became known that the book was a hoax. Collecting or, better, *constructing* heroic epics became a national sport, as each nation sought historical legitimation through founding myths and national epics. Many national epics in Eastern Europe emulated the Serbian example. When no such epic poem could be discovered, it was, as a rule, written by a representative national poet or simply forged.

Romanticism is usually credited, not without good reason, with the formulation of concepts of originality, genius and authenticity upon which, in turn, modern notions of authorship and intellectual property rest. But in the context of the Romantic 'discovery' of folk poetry these notions become compromised to such an extent that we may, with equal justification, regard Romanticism as the modern source of inauthenticity and forgery: collecting, editing and publishing folk poetry became inextricably linked with finding and constructing, authorship and editorship. Paradoxically, these fusions of originality with imitation were usually motivated by a desire to uncover buried ancient layers of 'genuine' folk poetry, usually inspired by an attempt to revive a lost ethnic consciousness.

The taint of inauthenticity had in fact already been present in the first famous collection of 'folk poetry', James Macpherson's *Fragments of Ancient Poetry Collected in the Scottish Highlands and Translated from the Gaelic or Ersic Tongue* (1760) and his subsequent publication of ancient poems by the 'ancient bard', Ossian. Ironically, Ossian became the voice of authenticity for one of the very first (pre-)Romantic heroes, Goethe's Werther.

The depth of desire for a national epic felt by movements of national awakening is best illustrated by the notorious case of the 'ancient manuscripts' forged by Václav Hanka (1791–1861) and his associates.[33] Hanka started out as a pupil and enthusiastic supporter of Dobrovský, went to Vienna in 1814, and became a follower of Kopitar. Upon his return to Prague, he 'discovered' on 16 September 1817 in Dvůr Králové a manuscript that became known as the *Rukopis Královédvorsky* (Královédvorsky Manuscript). Its first part consisted of six ballads, the second of eight shorter songs. The following year, an anonymous person sent Francis Count Kolowrat-Liebsteinsky, Lord High Castellan of the Prague Castle, two small parchments, the first containing a few lines entitled 'The Decree of Domestic Laws', the second a longer text with the title 'The Judgment of Libuše'. The texts were said to have been discovered in Zelená Hora, and subsequently became known as the 'Zelenohorský Manuscript'. Several other small documents emerged in the next decade, retrospectively recognised as attempts to substantiate the authenticity of the Královédvorsky and Zelenohorský manuscripts.

Throughout the nineteenth century, leading Czech intellectuals and artists, as well as the general public, believed (or wanted to believe) in the authenticity of the manuscripts on patriotic grounds. They seemed to put the Czechs on par with the Serbs, and expressed a strong anti-German sentiment that resonated with the Czech movement for independence. Palacký, though he had some doubts, wrote in his diary in 1819: 'With inexpressible joy I read the Královédvorsky manuscript for the first time early this summer, together with my dear Šafařík. How you have been transfigured in your glory, O Motherland! Once more you have held high your noble head, and nations look to you with admiration.'[34] As if echoing Schlegel, A.V. Svoboda wrote in the introduction to the second edition of the manuscripts that Czech writers who adopted the Czech language 'felt painfully the lack of ancient national songs, which, as all were aware, are the necessary origin and foundation of all national culture'.[35]

Yet Kopitar had his doubts, and Dobrovský, who had initially believed in the authenticity of the Královédvorsky manuscript, declared in 1823, after examining the 'Zelenohorský Manuscript' that it was the work of 'forgers driven by excessive patriotism and hatred for the Germans'.[36] He was subsequently denounced in vicious personal attacks as unpatriotic, and no one dared defend him. By 1840, Palacký had put his earlier doubts aside and convinced the more cautious Šafařík to write jointly *Die ältesten Denkmäler der böhmischen Sprache*, which defended the contested manuscripts and rejected Dobrovský's views.

The cultural authority and appeal of the Hanka manuscripts remained enormous throughout nineteenth-century Bohemia, and even beyond its borders. Attacks on their authenticity in the late 1850s by Austrian scholars were dismissed for their alleged political motivation; the fortieth anniversary of their 'discovery' was celebrated with a book by ten leading poets, among them Jan Neruda. Libuše's great national vision in Smetana's eponymous national opera was based on the 'Zelenohorský Manuscript'.[37] When the first Czech and Moravian critics raised some questions in the 1870s, they were slandered and silenced.

The final battle over the authenticity of the Hanka manuscripts took place in 1886–87, following Jan Gebauer's article published in T.G. Masaryk's journal *Athenaeum*.[38] Supporting Gebauer's case, Masaryk emotionally accused the leading writers and journalists who preferred a national myth to truth: 'what kind of a land is this, if people who mask their brutality and ignorance behind the banner of the nation can publicly slander anyone who is committed [...] to the truth out of what is surely the noblest patriotism? Should literary charlatans be the arbiters of national questions?'[39] Masaryk received responses such as 'Go to the devil, you repulsive traitor', and unfortunately even prominent writers like Jan Neruda and Eliška Krásnohorká joined the attack, though in a more civilised manner.[40]

The controversy surrounding the Hanka manuscripts shows how deeply literature and literary scholarship were implicated in the evolution of nationalism in the nineteenth century. The case was extreme but by no means unique. Between 1874 and 1881 in Bulgaria, for instance, Stefan Verković published a collection of songs that spoke about an ancient homeland in the East, the emigration of the Slavs from India, and ancient gods. Verković claimed that the songs, which came to be known as the Veda Slovena (Slavic Vedas), originated from prehistoric and pre-Christian times and were recorded 'from the Macedonian-Rhodopi Bulgarian Pomaks'.[41] By 1903, it became evident that what Verković had all too eagerly accepted as national mythology was the forgery of a school teacher.

Not all nineteenth-century national epics were forgeries. In the Nordic and Baltic countries, great national epics were constructed by means of collecting and creative editing. Witness the Finnish *Kalevala* (1849), collected and integrated by Elias Lönnrot (1802–1884) in the 1830s and 1840s; the Estonian *Kalevipoeg* (1857–61), collected and integrated by Friedrich Reinhold Kreutzwald (1803–1882) between 1836 and 1861; and the Latvian *Lāčplēsis* (1888) by Andrejs Pumpurs (1841–1901). When János Arany, the leading Hungarian poet received on 19 April 1857 a copy of the Hungarian translation of the Královédvorsky Manuscript (1856), he exclaimed in a letter three days later; 'Powerful remnants of a folk poetry from the distant dawn. Only we have nothing!! We must produce mythology, must produce ancient epics – otherwise empty spaces and deserts.'[42] The encounter with the forgeries occasioned Arany's 1860 essay 'Naïve eposzunk' (Our Folk Epos) on the troubling question of why such epics did not exist in Hungarian, and this was surely a major impulse for Arany's own epos, *Buda halála* (Buda's Death), which recounts how Attila assumed power by killing Buda, his older brother and the legitimate king.[43] *Buda halála* was to be the first part of a never completed vast epic cycle that would have narrated the rise and fall of Attila and its aftermath. This would link the narrative to the *Nibelungenlied* on the one hand, and to a mythic foundational story about the Székely prince Csaba on the other, thus legitimating the Hungarians' presence in their present home through their kinship with the Huns and the integration of their myth within the Germanic sagas.

Rhetorical uses of folk poetry in the nineteenth century involved not only conflicts with the 'Other' across the border, but also internal conflicts that were equally threatening to budding national identities and attempts to forge national unity. Folk poetry could only function properly as a unifying force within nineteenth-century national ideologies if it was linguistically standardised and exemplary in terms of morality and politics. Language reforms and folklore collections attempted to refine, standardise and codify the vernacular. The task was usually entrusted first to language societies and later to national academies. However, language revivals were fed by two conflicting impulses: on the one hand, the language had to be standardised and modern, on the other it had to be based as closely as possible on its rustic primeval shape. Both the archaic and modern aspirations rejected heterogeneity and dialects as threats to the norms of efficiency and purity. This conflict posed problems for folklore collectors: the desire for unity and cohesion, supported by a scientific belief in rational systems, collided with another scientific principle, namely empirical faithfulness to the language of the oral performers utilised in fieldwork and the desire for accuracy in recording. Recitals in dialect endangered the postulated linguistic unity by deviating from what was already codified and standardised.

Two examples may illustrate this problem. 'Back to the [sound and pristine] language of the folk' was a frequent slogan of language reformers, who fought either a dominating foreign language or culture (German, Russian, Turkish, or for that matter Hungarian, Polish or Czech) or an older form of the vernacular tradition. Advocating the principle 'write as you speak and read as is written', Karadžić originally went as far as recommending that modern writers use the dialect of their native region. However, practising this principle was not only impractical, it also endangered the very project of national unity (and the fight against foreign oppression) that the language reform was to serve.

The Hungarian János Kriza had to confront a similar problem when preparing his pioneering folk-song collection *Vadrózsák*.[44] His manuscript contained ample diacritical marks to record faithfully the actual Székely dialects, but when he sent the page proofs to the leading literary authority of the day, Pál Gyulai, the critic responded that Kriza's scholarly accuracy diminished the popular force and appeal of the texts. Kriza, no longer able to change the proofs, defensively admitted in his foreword that by seeking to find the finest nuances of dialect and intonation he had perhaps injured the 'expression' of 'true Székelyness'.[45] However, what did 'true Székelyness' mean? In retrospect, Kriza's inability to revise seems a blessing in disguise, for the conflict did not simply set linguistic scholarship against folklore, or nuance against overall expression, but represented a conflict between *langue*, standardised language, and *parole*, language as it is spoken. In yet another dichotomy, the uniform language of a hypothetical 'Székelyness' clashed here with a language concept of heterogeneity based on dialects and intonations. In the aftermath of the failed 1848–49 revolution, it was a politically loaded choice. As Kriza wrote in the foreword to his book, 'the reanimated soul of the nation descended deeper into itself' after the political tragedy in order to 'fortify and solidify the very roots of its own national essence against destructive dangers'.[46] Thus, Kriza considered his collection to be a contribution to his nation's search for identity. Yet his commitment to linguistic faithfulness to the variety of spoken Transylvanian dialects undermined the consistency of the material and the supposedly unified national creativity behind it, unintentionally suggesting both a Transylvanian heterogeneity and a difference with respect to Hungary proper.

Faithfulness to the oral tradition also became a problem when folklore was to be fitted into an appropriate national ideology in order to edify the nation by reflecting an 'unspoilt' national spirit. The male heroes of folk songs and epics were not exemplary: they were often drunk, barbaric and lewd as well as brutal to their wives. To make them serviceable within a Christian-national ideology they had to be sanitised and aestheticised, folklore had to be censored and partially repressed. Figures of the outlaw, which populate both the folklore and the 'high literature' of Eastern Europe, were particularly difficult to fit into these moral and national agendas. Both right-wing and communist regimes had to refashion figures like the Slovak Jánošík, the Hungarian Sándor Rózsa, the south-Slav Krali Marko, the Ukrainian Kossacks, or the multinational Hajduti (Hajduks) into East-European Robin Hoods (i.e. morally upright heroes that help the poor or fight for national liberty), for the real and imaginary outlaws were inherently ambiguous. Krali Marko in folklore is often a drunkard, a brigand, an unfaithful husband or a Turkish vassal; if one version of the 'kidnapped wife' motif narrates how Marko's wife is kidnapped, another shows how Marko kidnaps somebody else's wife and kills his mother. Marko's heroic battles in folklore are conducted not against enemy stereotypes but against individuals who may be allies in other versions (or episodes). In short, folklore often did not deliver what nineteenth-century nationalism required. As the famous Bulgarian Modernist Pencho Slaveikov wrote in 1904, 'the songs of these people are populated by various prehistoric animals but not by a single king; they recount events that had never happened, not a single one is glorified by official history'.[47] Indeed, Bulgarian scholars have found hardly anything in Bulgarian folklore about the country's nineteenth-century war of liberation.

National Literary Histories

The crowning achievements of nineteenth-century literary scholarship were national literary histories that integrated the recuperated oral vernacular literature and republished older texts, stories of language revival and the canonisation of national poets. The result was a single national literary narrative that claimed to embody, as it were, the fortunes of the national soul. According to Benedetto Croce, De Sanctis's *Storia della letteratura italiana* (1870–71) was 'a history, whose protagonist was precisely Italian literature, even Italy; the individual writers were presented only as phases in the general development'.[48] Indeed, De Sanctis had envisioned his work as a history of Italy.[49] Piotr Chmielowski wrote in his Polish literary history (1899) that although he could not reconstruct the soul of the whole nation, he would offer hints 'about the changes it underwent, as reflected in the literature of the last nine centuries'.[50] His intent exemplified a topos in nineteenth-century national literary histories.

Those countries that lacked a firm national identity or suddenly lost their belief in their identity were the first to produce national literary histories. The first important German literary history, Georg Gottfried Gervinus's five-volume *Geschichte der poetischen National-Literatur der Deutschen*, had appeared in 1835–42, before German unification in 1870, and the first French one, by Gustave Lanson, was published in 1895, when France was still recovering from defeat in 1870–71. De Sanctis's Italian literary history came out when Italy was already unified, but its conception dates from the 1840s, when unification was still only a dream.

Such great national syntheses were preceded in almost every country by factual chronological compilations of authors and works, sometimes complemented by ample annotations. Witness Pál Wallaszky's *Conspectus Reipublicae Litterariae in Hungaria* (1785), Sámuel Pápay's *A magyar literatúra esmérete* (1808), Ulrich Ernst Zimmermann's *Versuch einer Geschichte der Lettischen Literatur* (1812), Felix Bentkowski's *Historya literatury polskiey* (1814) or Jungmann's *Historie literatury české* (1825). Such publications were not yet fully-fledged histories in Friedrich Schlegel's terms, but in two important respects they were more inclusive than their more sophisticated successors. First, they listed as 'literature' a variety of philosophical, historical and scientific writings. More importantly, they often recognised only political, but not linguistic, borders. Wallaszky's history included, for instance, everything that was written in Hungary in any language, including Latin. In the course of the nineteenth century this inclusiveness and liberality narrowed as histories gradually eliminated what was not fiction and not written in the national vernacular. Wallaszky's successor Pápay, for example, included in his history only texts written in Hungarian, although he still recognised a 'universal' Hungarian literature. The same holds for Bentkowski's *Historya*. Ferenc Toldy's *A magyar nemzeti irodalom története* (1851) was already a critical and rational history in the modern sense but it included only fiction written in Hungarian, recognising but explicitly excluding the non-Hungarian literature written in Hungary.[51] By the end of the century, such exclusions became self-evident. Only very recently have attempts been made to include foreign language writings in national literary histories.

This narrowing of scope could not resolve, however, some of the key issues in drawing historical and geographical borders around national literary histories. The position of oral literature in the historical chronology and with respect to 'high' literature, for instance, remained uncertain. Was it the first phase of national literary history, as Alexander Balan and several of his Bulgarian colleagues thought?[52] If so, oral poetry should have disappeared once writing emerged, which was untrue, and unacceptable precisely to those who believed that truly modern national poetry had to be based on folk poetry. For these and other reasons, many literary historians did not include oral literature in the canon of national literary history. The Hungarian János Horváth, for instance, believed that oral literature became part of history only once it was philologically recorded.[53] Antal Szerb and other modernist historians left it out, in order to link 'high' literature to its European context rather than to its presumed native roots.[54]

The nationalist momentum of the nineteenth century drove literary histories with irresistible force towards monolingualism and monoculturalism. Yet these histories remained problematic, not the least because language itself came to be conceptualised in shifting configurations, as the cases of Czechoslovakia and Yugoslavia amply demonstrate. While literature and literary scholarship today no longer have the social force they possessed when Europe's nations awakened, they continue to shape conceptions of national identity through the narratives about the national past they have institutionalised. It remains for the twenty-first century to retell these institutionalised narratives of the nineteenth century and to reconstruct the literary institutions of the national awakenings.

Notes

1. The following article brings together a number of ideas that are worked out in greater detail in my contributions to the 'History of the Literary Cultures of East-Central Europe', vol. 3, of which I am the editor, together with Marcel Cornis-Pope. The volume has been published by Benjamins (Amsterdam) in 2007.
2. 'Szaktudományunk [&] a nemzeti eszme áramlási korában fejlődött ki, s annak nem tudományos megfigyelőjeként, hanem részeseként mutatkozik.' J. Horváth, *A magyar irodalom fejlődéstörténete*, 1922–23, in *A magyar irodalom fejlődéstörténete*, Budapest, 1980: 58. Unless stated otherwise, all translations are my own.
3. Schlegel programmatically announced: 'Art is based on knowledge and the science of art is its history.' Quoted in *Kritische Friedrich-Schlegel-Ausgabe*, vol. 2, ed. E. Behler, Paderborn, 1958: 290 ff.
4. Ibid., 182–83.
5. See J. Neubauer, 'Epigenetische Literaturgeschichten bei August und Wilhelm Schlegel,' in *Kunst – die andere Natur*, ed. R.Wegner, Göttingen, 2004: 211–27
6. *Kritische Friedrich-Schlegel-Ausgabe*, 291.
7. *Vorlesungen über schöne Literatur und Kunst*, 3 vols, ed. J. Minor, 1884; also, *Vorlesungen über dramatische Kunst und Litteratur*, 3 vols, Heidelberg, 1809–11.
8. See Ernst Behler in *Kritische Friedrich-Schlegel-Ausgabe*, vol. 6: xviii.
9. Ibid., xxi.
10. For his report, see *Kritische Friedrich-Schlegel-Ausgabe*, vol. 6: xxiv, and J. Baxa, 'Fr. Schlegels Vorlesungen über die Geschichte der alten und neuen Literatur im Urteile der Wiener Polizeihofstelle', *Der Wächter* 8, 1925–26: 354–59.
11. *Kritische Friedrich-Schlegel-Ausgabe* 6: 4.
12. Ibid., 7.
13. Ibid., 9.
14. Ibid., 11.
15. Ibid., 10.
16. Ibid., 15–16.
17. Ibid., 169.
18. Friedrich Schlegel's Sanskrit studies in Paris led to his epochal essay 'Über die Sprache und Weisheit der Inder' (1808).

19. Quoted in H. Jelínek, *Histoire de la Littérature Tchèque: Des origines à 1850*, vol. 1, 5th ed. Paris, 1951: 305.

20. 'Minden nemzetnek van egy szent városa, melyre kegyelettel, büszkeséggel gondol.' M. Jókai, *Kárpáthy Zoltán* 1854, Budapest, 1971: 142.

21. Letter of 15 August 1905 to Irmy Jurkovics: *Letters*, ed. J. Demény, Budapest, 1971.

22. Preface to Karadžić, *Pismenica serbskoga jezika po govoru prostoga naroda* (Vienna, 1814); quoted in D. Wilson, *The Life and Times of Vuk Štefanović Karadžić 1787–1864*, Oxford, 1970: 105.

23. J. Kollár, 'O literárnej vzájemnosti mezi kmeny a nářečími slavskými', *Hronka*, 1836. German trans. *Über die litterarische Wechselseitigkeit zwischen den verschiedenen Stämmen und Mundarten der slawischen Nation*, Pest, 1837.

24. *Hlasové o potřebě jednoty spisovného jazyka pro Čechy, Morawany a Slowáky*, Prague, 1846.

25. *Elementa linguae daco-romanae sive Valachicae*, Vienna, 1780. The other foundational Romanian linguistic publication was Samuil Micu-Klein's, and Petru Maior's *Lexicon românescu-latinescu-ungurescu-nemțescu* (Pest, 1825), a Romanian–Latin–Hungarian–German Dictionary, but also the first etymological and explanatory dictionary in Romanian.

26. 'azt, akinek szép nyelve nincsen elkeverve mással, […] Úgy ír ahogy beszél - egyszóval; aki Köztünk lett, köztünk nőtt, köztünk maradt meg.' Ferenc Kazinczy, *Vitkovicshoz* (1811), ll. 19–28. See http://mek.oszk.hu/00700/00727/html/vers02.htm#13 (page viewed 26/01/2006).

27. F. Palacký and J. Šafařík, *Počátkové českého básnictví, obzvláště prozodie*, Prague, 1818. Dobrovský stated his theory in 'Böhmische Prosodie', a postscript to Pelcl's *Grundsätze der böhmischen Grammatik*, 1795.

28. See esp. Part IV, Book 16, Chapter 4.

29. First version published in 1821 under the title *Básně* (Poems).

30. A more extended treatment of the topic with respect to East-Central Europe may be found in the section 'The Historical Novel' in *History of the Literary Cultures of East-Central Europe. Junctures and Disjunctures in the 19th and 20th Centuries*, vol. 1, eds M. Cornis-Pope and J. Neubauer, Amsterdam, 2004: 463–511. The 'classic' study on the subject, Georg Lukács's *The Historical Novel* (1937) is in great need of revision, both because of its outdated Marxist approach and its total neglect of Eastern Europe, where the genre had, arguably, its greatest impact. Nevertheless, Lukács's work still offers a number of indispensable insights.

31. *Mala prostonarodnja slaveno-serbska pjesnarica* was published in 1814 and *Narodna srbska pjesnarica* in 1815.

32. Quoted in D. Wilson, *The Life and Times of Vuk Štefanović Karadžić 1787–1864*, Oxford, 1970: 113.

33. My following discussion relies on Milan Otáhal's excellent article, 'The Manuscript Controversy in the Czech National Revival', *Cross Currents*, 5, 1986: 247–77.

34. Quoted in Otáhal, 'Manuscript Controversy', 254.

35. Ibid., 252.

36. Ibid., 254.

37. See Otáhal (pp. 249–50) for a short survey of artistic works inspired by the manuscripts.

38. *Athenaeum* 3 (1886).

39. Otáhal, 269.

40. Otáhal, 272.

41. S. Verković, *Veda Slovena. Le Veda Slave. Chants populaire des Bulgares de Thrace & de Macédonie de l'époque préhistorique & préchretienne*, vol. 1, Belgrade, 1874; vol. 2, St. Petersburg, 1881.

42. 'Erőteljes néppoézis maradványai a messze hajdanból. Csak nekünk nincs semmink!! Mythológiát csinálni kell, régies eposzt csinálni kell, különben űr és pusztaság.' J. Arany, *Összes művei*, vol. 10, Budapest, 1962: 609 (author translation).

43. J. Arany, 'Naiv eposzunk', *Összes művei*, vol. 10, Budapest, 1962: 264–74: *Buda halála*, Pest, 1864.

44. J. Kriza, ed., *Vadrózsák*, 1863; rpt. Bucharest, 1975.

45. 'A nyelvjárási s hanglejtési legkisebb árnyalatokat is kiszínelni akarva, tán főbb sajátságok, a kifejezés, a beszéd igaz székelyessége ellen fogtam véteni.' Ibid., 36 (author translation).

46. 'az újra föleszmélt nemzet lelke mélyebben szállott önmagába, hogy saját nemzeti lényét a romboló vészek ellenében minden gyökszálaiban erősítse és megszilárdítsa', ibid., 34 (author translation).

47. P. Slaveikov, *Săbrani săchineniya*, vol. 5, Sofia, 1958–59: 104.

48. F. de Sanctis, *Storia della letteratura italiana*, vol. 2, Bari, 1925: 433.

49. See ibid., 2: 421.

50. P. Chmielowski, *Historya Literatury Polskiej*, 6 vols, Warsaw, 1899–1900: 23.

51. T. Ferenc, *A magyar nemzeti irodalom története*, 2 vols, Pest, 1851; rpt. Budapest, 1987.

52. A.T. Balan, *Bălgarska literatura*, Plovdiv, 1896.

53. Horváth, 63.

54. A. Szerb, *Magyar irodalomtörténet*, 2 vols, Cluj/Kolozsvár, 1934.

Chapter 6

Towards the Genre of Popular National History: Walter Scott after Waterloo

LINAS ERIKSONAS

This chapter opens with an invitation to consider two phenomena: history and genre. Most of the contributions to this volume take genre as a static element in the universe of historical enquiry. They see genre mostly as a prescriptive form that through its narrativity lends meaning and engenders common traits to a corpus of texts – textual or visual – claimed to be of the same *genre*.

In 1986 Ralph Cohen, the founding editor-in-chief of *New Literary History*, the flagship journal of postmodern literary criticism, opened a discussion on the issue with the article 'History and Genre'.[1] In his essay Cohen rebuked Fredric Jameson's neo-Marxist dialectical critique of genre as presented in the latter's *The Political Unconscious*, where Jameson argued that genre criticism and with it genre itself as a methodological tool had been thoroughly discarded by modern literary theory and practice and were, generally speaking, a thing of the past.[2] Jameson's criticism was based on three assumptions: firstly, that texts do not compose classes, secondly, that members of a genre do not necessarily share common traits and, thirdly, that genre cannot function as an interpretive tool. In his attempt to bring about the regeneration of genre theory Cohen argued that it was possible to talk about genre and history provided genre was interpreted as a process rather than a structure; he used the process theory to show the feasibility of this historical approach to genre.

Dominic LaCapra lent his support to this line of thinking by endorsing the view that the processual dimension of the concept of genre deserved more attention. Both he and Cohen agreed that in terms of relations of genres to one another 'genres generally come in hierarchies, and the objection to a mixture of genres often occults or conceals an attempt to retain or reinforce a dominant position or an authoritative position'.[3] Hence, the mutation of genres throughout history also reflects changes in the degree of authority attributed to a certain genre.

In 2003, *New Literary History* restarted the debate about genre, reflecting the new interest in the applicability of the genre concept for the humanities.[4] Cohen has summarised his old-new ideas about genre in the following dictum:

> A genre can become transformed, leading to new genres; or it can cease to be practiced. Membership in a genre is inevitable, but whether such membership is identified as essential is not. Texts that may at one time be considered essential members of one genre may at another be considered members of several genres.[5]

Fredric Jameson, who also contributed to this renewed discussion, was now somehow less sceptical about genre but maintained his reservations regarding this branch of enquiry. He still holds that the generic question is not the most productive one to consider and that 'problems of representation along with ideological analysis offer surer paths towards an understanding of a group of texts'.[6]

It has long been established that texts, once they become attributed to a genre, are dependent on the changes that occur in the way a specific genre is perceived in society. Biblical literature, for example, is a genre that depends on the religiousness of society and the ways that society sees apt to relate to the Church. A pamphlet written in a popular style and featuring Biblical characters would belong to this genre. However, popular tastes are malleable and society might, in the future, prefer a more learned or, on the contrary, a more profane and perhaps more poetic way of reading about God. Thus, the same text might extend, for instance, the original genre of popular Biblical tracts to one of religious national poetry. Therefore, if we want to see the original genre in the processual dimension, as Cohen and LaCapra propose, we have to discuss the way a given genre has changed in relation to a particular group of texts over time – not the other way around.

If we turn our attention to historical texts and apply these insights to the case of popular historical narratives, we can begin to see a new historical method of approaching genre and history. Hence, by defining genre as a process rather than a discursive structure it becomes possible to interpret genre historically and distinct from literary criticism. For the purpose of a small analytical experiment, which seeks either to prove or refute the process theory of genre, this chapter will examine the national historical predilections of Walter Scott, the most famous nineteenth-century historical novelist. Scott has traditionally been considered as the founding father of the genre of historical novels (in which capacity Ann Rigney pays fleeting tribute to him in Chapter four). This chapter will examine different stages of Scott's historical endeavours, which until now have been pigeonholed by fitting them into various unconnected genres. Instead, the historical approach will be adopted in order to explain the historical process of genre change that started with Scott's wartime epic poetry and ended with his national popular history.

The chapter begins by tracing the origins of Scott's historical sentiments in his poetic period that terminated after a visit to the battlefield of Waterloo in 1815. Furthermore, the 'Waterloo effect' will be discussed in parallel with Scott's post-Waterloo penchant for military history, acknowledging his attempt to narrate national history through battles and heroes. Second, it will discuss the change of the original genre of poetry to a popular form as documented through a literary competition organised with the knowledge of Scott in 1819. Third, it will explain the aborted attempt to use the genre of historical literary sources and Scott's inroads into factual history through his commissioned History of Scotland. Finally, it will show how the original genre, war poetry, had permutated through a number of generic changes into the genre of popular national history, which itself oscillated between the genres of juvenile literature and popular history.

Originating Genre: War Poetry

Until the Napoleonic Wars, Scott was not interested in the genre of history writing. Instead, he collected ballads and wrote fictional accounts about the celebrated deeds of semi-fictional Scottish characters, mostly in verse. At this time, epic poetry was considered the most authoritative type of literature.[7] The situation started to change with the war on the Continent.

By the time of the Peninsula Wars, Scott was already considering visiting a real battlefield and experiencing the reality that he could use for narrating fictional plots. In 1810 and again in 1811 he mentioned his intention of planning to go to Spain to observe the battle at hand, noting 'I should have picked up some very curious materials for battle scenery'.[8] He regretted being unable to go, and instead had to content himself with first-hand battle accounts written by others. However, he found such texts uninspiring and vague, commenting:

> I don't know why it is I never found a soldier could give me an idea of a battle. I believe their mind is too much upon the tactique to regard the picturesque; just as we lawyers care very little for an eloquent speech at the bar if it does not show good doctrine.[9]

Once the news of Napoleon's defeat at Waterloo reached Scott, he could wait no longer, and he arrived at the site ahead of many other visitors.[10] Originally, his plan was to render what had happened on 18 June 1815 on a field near the Walloon village Waterloo in verse, through the genre in which he had already excelled. However, the gruesome reality was too difficult to grasp. Less than a month before, some 30,000 corpses, the dead from both sides, had been put under the turf. How could one imagine, let alone rhyme, the scene of carnage? The contrast between the tranquil surroundings of Waterloo and the realisation of one of the greatest losses of human lives in history to date was significant.[11] This sense of unease is evident in the drawings of the battlefield made soon after the battle; they show barren hills and plains with few shrubs and no signs of life (see Figure 6.1).[12]

Similarly, when animal painter James Howe came to Waterloo to capture the battlefield on canvas, the result was his elegiac painting 'Scots Greys in bivouac before Waterloo' (exhibited in London in 1816) conveying a sense of suspended tranquillity before the battle (see Figure 6.2).

It is not surprising many observers found it difficult to connect the scale of the battle and human tragedy with the actual battlefield that looked so ordinary. The gap, as Scott saw it, stimulated 'a moral interest, deeper and more potent even than that which is produced by gazing upon the sublimest efforts of Nature in her most romantic recesses'.[13]

In order to create an epic narrative of the battle Scott had to gather supplemental evidence and interview eyewitnesses, from Napoleon's Walloon servant, who briefed Scott on the battlefield, to the victorious Duke of Wellington in Paris. The poet was keen on recording every detail, all that could breathe more life into his verses on the battle.[14] The poem 'The Field of Waterloo', written in August 1815, was Scott's poetic dispatch from the scene of the legendary battlefield.[15] Although the poem, published two months later with a run of 6,000 copies, went into three editions the same year, it was not well received by critics. Their reaction to 'The Field of Waterloo' was indeed disappointing. Scott was not a novice to poetry, his previous narrative poems such as *The Lady of the Lake* (1810) had been very well received and reviewed across Britain. Nevertheless, unlike his earlier poetic creations, 'The Field of Waterloo' was dull, repetitive, packed with violent scenes and the minutiae of

Figure 6.1: 'The Field of Waterloo', signed 'J.W.', a pen and wash topographical drawing of the field of Waterloo (Source: National Museums of Scotland).

Figure 6.2: James Howe (1816) 'Scots Greys in bivouac before Waterloo' (Source: National Museums of Scotland).

the battle. In short, the poem was a difficult read and failed to render the subject matter within a popular format. One can only guess whether the Waterloo experience had anything to do with the fact that Scott abandoned poetry after the failure of his second, equally badly received, post-Waterloo poem 'Harold the Dauntless' (1817). Literary scholars attribute this change of genre to Scott's pecuniary considerations, as he had chosen to write what would yield more profit – historical novels. However, the change of genre could also be explained by the fact that post-war society already demanded a more prosaic genre.

Transitional Genre: Historical Literary Sources

Source editing is one possible explanation for Scott's move away from poetic renditions to a more 'hands-on' approach to historical reality. In post-1815 Europe, historical source editing became an occupation for many successful writers (as John Neubauer mentions in Chapter five). Since his visit to Waterloo, Scott had become obsessed with matters military and the battlefield had become the running theme of his narratives. So when looking for historical literary sources to be tapped he did not have to go far.

Historical battlefields abound in Scotland, but in Scott's time the two most important ones for Scottish identity were Stirling and Bannockburn.[16] During the former battle, in 1297, the Scottish army led by heroic William Wallace had crushed the English adversary while in the latter, in 1314, Robert the Bruce, another national hero of Wallace-like stature, had terminated the English threat to conquer Scotland. Their stories were committed to parchment at the end of the fifteenth century, during a period of renewed conflict between Scotland and England, and published a century later by Protestant leaders after Mary I, Queen of Scots, had been deposed.[17] These published versions took the form of a verse story about the exploits of William Wallace, known as *Wallace Book*, and its follow-up, *Bruce Book* or the *Bruce*, an epic poem written by John Barbour. The two narratives became founding texts; no history of Scotland was possible without at least a passing reference to them.[18]

Therefore, it was no surprise that Walter Scott too started his quest for national history with Wallace and Bruce. His interest pre-dated Waterloo but it was only after the writer's visit to the battlefield that Scott had started to revive the idea of national popular history. Scott's turn to national historical endeavours was not surprising, particularly when one considers his previous interest in these two historical battlefields and the heroic stories linked to them. In 1796, Scott visited the field of Bannockburn. It was not an unusual journey at the time; after the French revolution a flow of visitors to the ancient sites on the Continent had stopped and the energy of Grand Tours was now being revitalised by opening 'new' ancient sites around Britain.[19]

In 1801, Scott revisited Bannockburn, and in 1808 he even took his wife on an excursion to Stirling 'chiefly to show that interesting part of Scotland and on viewing the field of Bannockburn I certainly said that one day or another before I died I hoped to make the earth yawn and devour the English archery and knighthood as it did on that celebrated day of Scottish glory'.[20] Scott's interest in Wallace had culminated during the Peninsula War. In his wartime letters, he mentioned Wallace and El Cid, a Spanish medieval hero, and how the two were needed to aid the precarious situation of the British army in Spain.[21] In 1809, when Scott's beloved dog Camp died, Lady Francis Dunlop Wallace, whose family claimed descent from Wallace, procured for the writer a terrier of high pedigree. Scott reciprocated the gift by naming the dog after heroic Wallace, noting 'so I have christened him Wallace, as the donor is a descendant of the Guardian of Scotland'.[22] The very presence of the terrier thus reminded Scott of the Scottish national hero. When the dog died in 1812, it was a significant loss for Scott, as was recorded in his letter.[23]

Although sentimental about pets, Scott was rather less so about the verses others wrote about the celebrated hero. When Margaret Hodson, a promising young poet, took the liberty of adapting the structure of Scott's poem *Marmion* (1808) for her metrical romance *Wallace; or, the Fight of Falkirk*, describing Wallace at the battle of Falkirk (1298), Scott was not amused.[24] In

1810 he wrote to another poet, Joanna Bailley, who was soliciting his support on behalf of Hodson:

> Her Wallace is really very fine – it will not please Scotch folks because Wallace is one of those characters that get beyond the reach of poetry, which when applied to them is apt to fail in a certain degree for the reasons which Johnson applies to sacred poems.[25]

In Scott's view, heroic narratives, being by their nature almost sacred, defied the creative intrusion of the poet. It was indeed a common understanding of the Romantic Age that people were guardians of popular memory, reflected in folklore (to which such heroic narratives belonged), and that popular memory was to be preserved intact. This contrasts with today's understanding of the institutionalised memory, which is brought down and installed from above.

Yet, in 1811 Scott had decided to move ahead with writing a narrative poem on the subject of Robert Bruce. His aim was not to paraphrase the existing narrative but to expand the background of the hero's biography by adding some impressions gained from his recent journey through the Highlands. But when, after four years of writing, Scott's poem about Bruce, entitled 'The Lord of the Isles', was finally published (1815), it failed to reach the same heights of popularity as his most successful poem 'The Lady of the Lake'. Although the former sold well (13,750 copies as compared to 10,000 of *Rokeby* from 1813), it, nevertheless, failed to capture the popular imagination to the extent of the historical literary sources, the heroic narratives *Wallace Book* and *Bruce*, upon which it was based.

During his work on the poem, Scott realised that the existing editions of these two heroic narratives were outdated and were in need of revision. Thus, in 1814 he approached John Jamieson, an antiquarian and author of the *Etymological Dictionary of the Scottish Language* (1808), with the suggestion to prepare a new edition of the two narratives (Scott was successful in raising funds and made it possible for the two volumes to appear in print in 1820).[26] He introduced the texts to be edited to Jacob Grimm in a letter of November 1814 as such:

> There are two poems in ancient Scottish, both classical, and almost epic. One relates to the exploits of Robert the Bruce, who recovered Scotland, from the English yoke, and is well-nigh historical in its details. The other relates to the great champion of our freedom William Wallace. It is legendary, but makes up in a high spirit of poetry what it wants in historical authenticity. Both [of] them being still of late great favourites with the common people have been repeatedly reprinted, but in a very degraded and corrupt state.[27]

However, when published, the new edition of these historical literary sources failed to capture the public's imagination. By the time the books were published, the genre of critical source editing had been integrated into the emerging historical discipline and hence lost its literary appeal. Scott's quest for popular history then took an unprecedented turn.

Searching for a Popular Genre: People's Poetry

Instead of editing historical literary sources, Scott chose to adopt contemporary, more authentic voices – people's poetry – the genre of a kind. In 1818, he anonymously published an advertisement inviting fellow Scots to submit verses reflecting on the national historical theme 'Sir William Wallace's inviting Bruce to the Scottish throne' after the battle of Falkirk. According to the traditional accounts, Wallace invited Bruce to take up the Scottish throne during their talk across the Carron River after the battle. The advertisement placed in the Tory *Blackwood's Edinburgh Magazine* ran as follows:

> Dear Sir,- Enclosed you will find a bill of £50, to be divided into three sums of £25, £15, and £10 as prizes for the best lines, in verse or prose, on the subject of Sir William Wallace's inviting Bruce to the Scottish throne; which I could wish to be so expressed, as not to give offence to our brethren south of the Tweed.
> Perhaps there could be introduced into the composition, the propriety of erecting a tower or monument to the memory of Wallace, on Arthur Seat or Salisbury Craigs. If such an object could be accomplished, I would leave £1000 by my will to assist it.
> My name need not be mentioned – only say a native of Edinburgh, and a Member of the Highland Society of London, who left his native place at twelve years of age. The rest I leave to your better judgement.[28]

Although the author of the advertisement discreetly chose to remain anonymous, all circumstantial evidence points in Walter Scott's direction. He was born in Edinburgh and stayed there for twelve years before being sent to school in Kelso, he was a member of the Highland Society of London, and the River Tweed separates Scotland from England within his own region.[29] Moreover, one of Scott's letters dated in 1819 mentions his meeting with the delegation of local weavers from Galashields, their communication conducted standing on different banks of the river. This reminded Scott of the scene from *Wallace Book* where the heroes Wallace and Bruce addressed each other across the Carron, and indeed this episode was chosen as a theme for the literary competition.

The competition generated an enormous interest. The poems submitted were collected by the antiquarian David Laing and, upon his death, bequeathed to Edinburgh University Library. According to Laing's notes, about seventy entries were received, of which thirty-eight compositions have been preserved. Some authors made themselves known, whilst others remained anonymous, but most entries would suggest a greater level of patriotism than creative talent.

Among the dozens of first-time poets who were trying their hand in lyrical engagement, lured either by the potentially significant prize money or by a patriotic sentiment, there were at least two established poets of the time who competed for the first prize; a Scotsman, James Hogg (1770–1835), and an English poet, Felicia Hemans (1793–1835), to whom the prize was eventually awarded. The September issue of *Blackwood's Edinburgh Magazine* informed readers that 'this prize was lately adjudged to Mrs Hemans, adding that 'Scotland has her Baillie – Ireland her Tighe – England her Hemans'.[30] The prize-winning poem was surprisingly more battle-orientated than Hogg's musings. Hemans' lines lacked a sense of historicity and were steeped in the Ossianic mood:

> The morn rose bright on scenes renown'd,
> Wild Caledonia's classic ground,
> Where the bold sons of other days
> Won their high fame in Ossian's lays,
> And fell – but not till Carron's tide
> With Romans blood was darkly died.[31]

Despite the initial design to award three best poems on the subject, as the anonymous benefactor had clearly stated in his advertisement, of seventy entries the jury had selected one clear winner, Hemans. No other awards were made and plans for a de facto commissioned monument to Wallace appear to have been forgotten. That Hogg's submission did not win, despite his being a literary contributor to the magazine, was perhaps due to his poem's rather battle-free narrative.[32] Here is an extract:

> The land of Caledonia hight
> My hero's name is Wallace wight
> Wallace! Unstained illustrious name!
> My country's honour and her shame!
> Can there a Scottish heart be found,
> That glows not at the very sound
> Of such a name: is breast so base
> That burns not at our hero's praise?[33]

The literary competition was an attempt to raise public awareness of historical literary narratives. It showed to all involved how differently people responded to the theme of national heroes. Evidently, there was a need to produce an inclusive and popular national history, and Scott seized the initiative.

Aborted Genre: Factual History

It is difficult to estimate how much the Waterloo experience had contributed to the writer's subsequent choice of genres but it is possible to establish is his growing interest in military dimensions of national history. After his return from the Waterloo battlefield, in late October 1815, Scott's 'The Field of Waterloo' was published and *Peter's Letters to His Kinfolk*, which contained further literary dispatches from post-Waterloo Belgium and France, followed. However, by December of that year the writer had already become occupied with the idea of writing history for his native country, Scotland. Scott's essay 'Culloden Papers', published in January 1816 in Edinburgh's *Quaterly Review*, provided a sneak preview of future publications.[34] His point of departure for Scottish history was to be the 'Scottish Waterloo', the Battle of Culloden (1746) which had ended the Jacobian threat supported by France.

However, as Scott began considering future approaches towards the narration of national history, he realised that 'the task of digesting, elucidating, and arranging these materials would engross more time than he could spare'.[35] The task was postponed but the novelist continued collecting materials for a history to be written one day, a task in which antiquarians and other enthusiastic correspondents around the country helped him. As Scott processed the collated historical materials, his heroes Wallace and Bruce started to feature more frequently in his historical novels. More importantly, the associated battle scenes became a more permanent feature in his fictional landscapes, and his penchant for the military detail became more pronounced. This could be seen from his letters in which he enthusiastically discussed various military matters, as the following letter suggests: 'The whole superiority of the English in their wars both with the French and Scotch turned on the long-bow. Bruce dispersed their archers at Bannockburn with a body of light horse stationed for the purposes, an example which no subsequent Scottish general had sense to imitate.'[36]

Scott was not the first to promote this genre of popular history, and his effort was influenced by the publication of John Croker's *Stories Selected from the History of England from the Conquest to the Revolution* (1817).[37] Croker was a political bedfellow of Scott: both were staunch Tories, staunch supporters of the government and had also been to the field of Waterloo soon after the battle and conducted field research there. Indeed, Croker was already experienced in military matters and, during the Peninsula War, had been appointed the secretary to the Admiralty in October 1809, a position he served through four premierships. Modelled on Scott's *Marmion*, his poem on the Battle of Talavera (1809) was applauded by Wellington, who was pleasantly amused to find out that a battle could be turned into something so entertaining. Like Scott, after Waterloo Croker abandoned poetry and turned to history writing in the national vein. During his visit in Belgium and France in 1815, he began collecting materials for his planned book on the French revolution. However, Croker also sought to produce a popular history of England that would inculcate within children a sense of patriotism. Scott would follow his example a decade later but with more significant consequences for national history.

In 1823, the young and ambitious Patrick Fraser Tytler, a lawyer-turned-historian, came to stay with Scott at Abbotsford. Scott proposed that Tytler write a history of Scotland. The need was great, the writer explained, because the existing histories were dull (Hailes' *Annales*), inaccurate, full of unnecessary minutiae (John Pinkerton's *An Enquiry into the History of Scotland*, 1814) and outdated (William Roberton's *History of Scotland*, 1759 was still in print at the time).[38] Furthermore, the historical literary sources alone, as proven by the existing texts on Wallace and Bruce, did not suffice.

Tytler took Scott's advice and started meticulously preparing a new history of Scotland. Its first volume was published five years later, in 1828, and chronologically covered the period, defined by its subtitle, 'from Alexander III until the union of crowns 1603'. Scott expected that, with Tytler's engagement, Scottish national history would be successfully articulated. Therefore, he turned his attention towards researching for a biography of Napoleon – the fallen hero of Waterloo. Napoleon featured significantly in the works of those who had visited the Waterloo battlefield, but it was hardly surprising given the aura he carried during this period. Yet, even during his most creative years as a historical novelist in the 1820s, Scott never completely rejected Scottish history. Disappointingly for Scott, Tytler failed to deliver, as his history of Scotland was written in the traditional way, following the chronology of the ruling sovereigns and lacking the elevated promotion of battles. It was not the popular genre of national history Scott sought.

Crystallised Genre: Popular National History

Therefore, without disparaging Tytler's work publicly, Scott decided to take matters into his own hands, and, out of the material he had gathered, produce a popular book along the lines of Croker's historical episodes for children. *Tales of a Grandfather: Being Stories Taken from Scottish History* was conceived as a fictionalised account of important events in Scottish history narrated in prose with the help of historical source material. Although the book was dedicated to Scott's grandson ('humbly inscribed to Hugh Littlejohn', ran a paternal subtitle) and was primarily aimed at the juvenile audience, its impact on Scottish history writing, whether intentional or not, was unprecedented. A book intended for children turned into a Scottish history for the masses.

Tales of a Grandfather: Being Stories Taken from Scottish History introduced a new scheme into Scottish historical writing, national history narrated as a series of key battles. The posthumous edition of 1836, which gathered all parts together, was divided into five volumes. Each volume covered a distinct historical period established on the basis of the battles which Scott viewed as watersheds in Scottish history. Therefore, volume 1 covered the period roughly from 'a great battle fought between Danes and the Scots' ('and Macbeth and Banquo, the Scottish generals, defeated the Danes, and drove them back to their ships, leaving a great number of their soldiers both killed and wounded') to the battle of Flodden in 1523 (as was believed in Scott's time; today the established date of the battle is 1513). The volume also incorporated a very lengthy passage dealing with Wallace and Bruce, taken from the 1820 edition of the Wallace and Bruce historical literary narratives.

Volume 2 continued this historical approach founded on the battles of Scotland, continuing its overview from the battle of Flodden and drawing to a close with the last battle fought by Montrose against the Covenanters in 1644. The period covered in the third volume commenced with the battle of Auldern (Montrose) and ended with the battle of Killiecrankie and the battle of La Hogue (1692). Volume 4 focused on the period ending with the battle of Glenshiel that sealed the fate of the Jacobite uprising in 1716. The volume culminated with the description of the 1707 union and, again, the main argument drew on the imagery of the battlefield:

> The promoters of the Union founded their arguments not merely on the advantage, but the absolute necessity, of associating the independence of the two nations for their mutual honour and defence; arguing, that otherwise they must renew the scenes of past ages, rendered dreadful by the recollection of three hundred and fourteen battles fought between two kindred nations, and more than a million of men slain on both sides.[39]

The final volume encompassed the dramatic period marked by the battles of 1719 and 1746 (Culloden), and Scott concluded his history with the 1815 peace treaty.

The historical foundations of Scott's *Stories Taken from Scottish History* and the origins of the materials he drew on are of significant importance and interest. The chronology of individual volumes shows that, in writing this fictionalised history, Scott drew on his historical novels to provide the narrative framework that he then supplemented with more detail on battles and main heroic characters. Thus, volume 1, which culminates with the Battle of Flodden, echoes his poem *Marmion* (1808) and *A Tale of Flodden Field* (1809), volume 2 reads as if it sprang out of *A Legend of Montrose* (1819), while volume 3 is strongly influenced by *Old Mortality* (1816). Volume 4 starts chronologically around 1689, the period that is described in *The Pirate* (1822), and ends with the episode that brings to one's mind the narrative of *Rob Roy* (1817). In addition, the final volume, which deals with the Jacobite uprisings, has its narrative basis partly in *Waverly* (1814) and *Redgauntlet* (1824). This would suggest that Scott, having been dissatisfied with the efforts of Tytler but unable to produce a factual history himself, fused his literary creations together with the material he gathered on various battles into one comprehensive text. Though he gave the book a modest title, *Tales of a*

Grandfather, aiming at the juvenile readership, the immediate success of the book proved that he had written a Scottish history for readers of all ages.

The book was soon translated and published in Germany, France and the US. Its impact on popular national history writing in those countries is beyond the scope of this article but there is evidence to suggest that the genre of national popular history presented in the form of a juvenile book influenced approaches in other countries.[40]

Oscillating between Genres

In Scotland, the publishing history of the book shows that the national sentiment embedded in *Stories Taken from Scottish History* generated and sustained its popularity for almost a century. Indeed, it was the most popular Scottish history book between 1828 and 1915. Already by 1836, the title for the Edinburgh edition had been amended to give it more credibility and confirm its status as a work of national history: *The History of Scotland from the Earliest Period to the Close of the Rebellion 1745–46, Contained in Tales of a Grandfather.*[41] The new title moved the book from the genre of juvenile literature and placed it under the rubric of the emerging genre of popular history. The publisher probably deemed that the book would sell better and be better appreciated if it bore the title *The History of Scotland* rather than *Tales of a Grandfather*. The book was republished in 1855 and 1864 under this more solemn title, though not in Berlin, where the German edition (in English) bore the slightly amended title *Tales of a Grandfather Taken from the History of Scotland*.

The original title, *The Tales from a Grandfather*, was restored in 1869, although popular editions of the book, such as *History of Scotland Adapted from Sir W Scott's Tales of a Grandfather* (1873), continued to be issued. This indicates that the book oscillated between the two genres of juvenile literature and popular history. The 1874 Glasgow edition represented a further step towards increasing the credibility of Scott's history by publishing the book as a school textbook entitled *History of Scotland for Junior Classes: Adapted from Sir Walter Scott's Tales of a Grandfather*, also including a historical map of Scotland. The popular historical credentials of the book were strengthened further in 1907, when the 200th anniversary of the 1707 Union was celebrated in Scotland. A special edition of the book was issued under the augmented title *From the Tales of a Grandfather: A History of Scotland from Early Times to the Union of the Parliaments: Condensed from Sir Walter Scott's Tales of a Grandfather by T.D. Robb with the Complete Act of Union Appended*.

It is evident that throughout the nineteenth century Scott's tales were accepted by people as the concise national history of Scotland. In 1911, as the home rule movement gained strength and the Wallace and Bruce narratives resurfaced as the symbols of new Scotland, Scott's history once again influenced popular discourses. Passages about the battle of Macbeth and the valiant feats of Wallace and Bruce were extracted and put together under the title *Wallace and Bruce: With the Story of Macbeth; from Tales of a Grandfather*. In 1920 another extract was selected and presented to the public, *Mary Queen of Scots: Adapted from Sir W. Scott [An extract from Tales of a Grandfather]*. In 1923, the history came full circle when a new full edition of the book was published under the original title. However, the interwar and Second World War periods saw Scott's *Tales* lose their significance and appeal to the public, and they have not been re-issued in the post-war period in a separate edition. Instead, academic histories such as Peter Herbert Brown's *A History of Scotland for Schools* (1910), published in various editions and Robert Rait's *History of Scotland* (1914) came to occupy their place.

Conclusions

In conclusion, one can say that the genre of popular national history witnessed its heyday in the period between the 1830s and the 1860s at the time when 'scientific history' made its claim on the past. Once national histories had developed into a particular genre, Scott's popular histories fell under the new extended genre of historical novels that became increasingly distinct from more orthodox approaches to nation-building. This also explains why Scott, though an earnest advocate of a distinct Scottish history, lacks resonance within the pantheon of modern Scottish nationalism.[42] The chapter has shown that the historical approach to genre is a useful way of gaining new insights into the way narratives are received and positioned vis-à-vis other texts that are perceived to represent the same genre. It further indicates that the genre changes of narratives occur due to dynamics that lie outside textual boundaries.

Notes

1. R. Cohen, 'History and Genre', *New Literary History* 17, 2, 1986: 203–18.
2. F. Jameson, *The Political Unconscious: Narrative as a Socially Symbolic Act*, Ithaca, NY, 1981.
3. D. LaCapra, 'History and Genre: Comment', *New Literary History* 17, 2, 1986: 219–21.
4. The revival of interest in genre has been reflected in R. Cohen, 'Genre Theory, Literary History, and Historical Change', in David Perkins, ed., *Theoretical Issues in Literary History*, Cambridge, MA, 1991: 85–113.
5. The most recent debate about genre took place on the pages of two issues of *New Literary History* in 2003; see R. Cohen, 'Introduction: Notes Toward a Generic Reconstitution of Literary Study', *New Literary History* 34, 3, 2003: v.
6. F. Jameson, 'Morus: The Generic Window', *New Literary History* 34, 3, 2003: 431–51.

7. K. Trumpener, *Bardic Nationalism: The Romantic Novel and the British Empire*, Princeton, 1997.

8. The Letters of Sir Walter Scott, 2–405.

9. Ibid.

10. He was accompanied by his son John, who kept a journal that was published posthumously: *Journal of a Tour to Waterloo and Paris, In Company of Sir Walter Scott in 1815*, London, 1842. For more on Scott's Waterloo visit, see D.E. Sultana, *From Abbotsford to Paris and Back: Sir Walter Scott's Journey*, Stroud, UK, 1993.

11. 'The Battle of Waterloo was one of the bloodiest in modern history. During the fighting of June 18, French casualties totalled about 40,000, British and Dutch about 15,000, and Prussian about 7,000; at one point about 45,000 men lay dead or wounded within an area of 8 sq km. Additional thousands of casualties were suffered by both sides during the three-day campaign that preceded the final battle'; 'Waterloo, Battle of,' Microsoft® Encarta® Online Encyclopaedia 2005; http://encarta.msn.com

12. 'The Field of Waterloo', signed 'J.W.', a pen and wash topographical drawing of the field of Waterloo, SCRAN ID 000-000-607-257-C, www.scran.ac.uk

13. Quoted from Semmel, 'Memory after Waterloo', 20.

14. Even French battle songs from the song-book he picked up from the field would come to use. Scott included their selection in a series of letters from Belgium published under the title *Paul's Letters to His Kinfolk* (1816), W. Scott, *Paul's Letters to His Kinfolk*, Edinburgh: Printed by James Ballantyne and Co. for Archibald Constable and Company, Edinburgh; and Longman, Hurst, Rees, Orme, and Brown, and John Murray, London, 1816.

15. *The Field of Waterloo: A Poem*, Edinburgh; Printed by James Ballantyne and Co. for Archibald Constable and Co. Edinburgh; and Longman, Hurst, Rees, Orme, and Brown, and John Murray, London, 1815. Also, *An authentic and interesting narrative of events in and near Waterloo: containing the most interesting particulars of that dreadful battle and the present situation of the village of Waterloo yet published: to which added from the poem, called 'The Field of Waterloo'*, by Walter Scott, London, n.d. [1816].

16. The third battlefield – Culloden – would soon join the two through the efforts of Scott (see below).

17. W. Geddie, *A Bibliography of Middle Scots Poets; with an Introduction on the History of Their Reputation*, Scottish Texts Society, Edinburgh, 1912, 61–62, 133–34.

18. G. Brunsden, 'Aspects of Scotland's Social, Political and Cultural Scene in the Late 17th and Early 18th Centuries, as Mirrored in the Wallace and Bruce Tradition', in *The Polar Twins*, ed. Edward Cowan and Douglas Gifford, Edinburgh, 2001, 75–113.

19. Robert Burns, the celebrated Scottish poet, had visited the battlefields of Falkirk, Stirling and Bannockburn already in 1787. Bannockburn had inspired his memorable line 'Scots Wha Hae Wi' Wallace Bled' supposed to be addressed by Bruce to his soldiers before the Battle of Bannockburn against Edward II. The last and most memorable stanza in his poem was directly taken from *Wallace Book*: 'A false usurper sinks in every foe/And liberty returns with every blow'.

20. The Letters of Sir Walter Scott, 2–116.

21. Ibid., 2–93.

22. Ibid., 2–205.

23. Ibid., 3–186.

24. Margaret Holford Hodson, *Wallace; or, The Fight of Falkirk*, London, 1809.

25. The Letters of Sir Walter Scott, 2–302.

26. *The Bruce and Wallace: Published from Two Ancient Manuscripts Preserved in the Llibrary of the Faculty of Advocates*, ed. J. Jamieson, vols 1–2, Edinburgh, 1820.

27. The Letters of Sir Walter Scott, 3–437.

28. 'Literary Premium', *Blackwood's Edinburgh Magazine*, 21 (Dec. 1818): 336. The competition had also been advertised on the pages of the main Scottish periodicals such as

the Scotsman and the Glasgow Herald, undoubtedly extending and broadening the social range of Scott's patriotic appeal.

29. In 1814 his neighbour the Earl of Buchan erected a colossal statue of William Wallace on the grounds of his estate at Dryburgh facing England across the historic border at the River Tweed. It was the first nationalist monument to be raised in Scotland. Scott's reaction to the monument is not known.

30. 'Meeting of Wallace and Bruce', *Blackwood's Edinburgh Magazine*, 30 (Sept. 1819): 686–87.

31. Ibid.

32. This poem was first published in James Hogg, *Collected Poems*, ed. John Wilson, vol. 4, Edinburgh, 1888: 280–91.

33. James Hogg, Wallace (a poem), Edinburgh University Library, Special Collections, La.II.216.

34. Walter Scott, 'Culloden Papers', *The Quarterly Review*, 28 (Jan. 1816), Art. I.

35. 'Patrick Fraser Tytler', in *Biographical Dictionary of Eminent Scots*, ed. R. Chambers; the text available online at http://www.electricscotland.com/history/men/tytler_patrick.htm

36. The Letters of Sir Walter Scott, 5–129.

37. J.W. Croker, *Stories Selected from the History of England from the Conquest to the Revolution: For Children*, London, 1817. The book was reprinted four times within the two years of publication.

38. The episode is related by Robert Chambers in his edited *Biographical Dictionary of Eminent Scotsmen*, Edinburgh and London, 1856. The entry on Francis Tytler which contains this information has been transcribed and is available at http://www.electricscotland.com/history/significant_scots.htm

39. *Tales of a Grandfather*, vol. 4 in *The Prose Works of Sir Walter Scott*, 25, Edinburgh, 1836, 80.

40. For example, N.A. Polevoi, who wrote historical novels under the influence of Scott, also published *History of the Russian Nation* (1833); Cf. D. Ungurianu, 'Fact and Fiction in the Romantic Historical Novel', *Russian Review* 57, 3 (Jul. 1998): 380–93.

41. W. Scott, *The History of Scotland from the Earliest Period to the Close of the Rebellion 1745–46, Contained in Tales of a Grandfather*, Edinburgh, 1836.

42. On the fortunes of the popularity of Walter Scott's writings during the nineteenth and twentieth centuries, see C. Parsons, 'Sir Walter Scott: Yesterday and Today', *Proceedings of the American Philosophical Society* 116, 6, 1972: 450–57.

Chapter 7

Families, Phantoms and the Discourse of 'Generations' as a Politics of the Past: Problems of Provenance – Rejecting and Longing for Origins

SIGRID WEIGEL

The Rediscovery of Family Ties

The discourse of 'generations' has for some time dominated the German *Zeitgeist*. Recently, however, the inception of a new era within this discourse has entered the culture pages of the newspapers, this most sensitive of seismographic instruments when it comes to registering even the tiniest shifts in collective states of mind. In the political sphere, the contract between the generations is becoming the object of negotiations that could possibly end up blowing apart the structures of the social welfare state altogether. At the same time, however, a whole series of films and literary publications are revealing the awakening amongst the younger generation of a new interest in the older one.

The success of Wolfgang Becker's film *Good Bye, Lenin!* (2002), for example, is being heralded as the document of a new peace between the generations, under the sign of which the parents' traditional caring role vis-à-vis their children is reversed. This is despite the fact that it was only the year before that the satirical film *Tanguy* (2001) by French film-maker Etienne Chatiliez gave expression to the notorious and in the meantime all too familiar complaint of today's fifty-year-olds that their offspring are reaching their late twenties without contemplating giving up the comforts of 'Hotel Mama'. It may of course be the case that the contrast between the two films can be put down in part to other causes – that the nostalgic story in which a son stages a resurrection of everyday life in the GDR in a 79 square metre apartment for his mother's sake is simply confirming the sociological hypothesis which suggests that generational conflict is less of an issue in eastern Germany because it is overshadowed by the contrast between the old and new federal states.[1] This reading would suggest that the allegorical marriage between East and West, an image both popularised *and* ironised in the mass media in 1989 through countless cartoons, would have to be regarded as having failed, since it had been overtaken by obviously more powerful recollective images of previous genealogies. In other words, the family ties and sense of origin would have proved more dominant than the contractually formed new national community would.

However, in the West, too, there is a marked reawakening of interest in the older generation. Here too the link is via research into the German past, albeit in this case the past of fifty years ago. Recently there has been a run of novels by authors born in the post-war era that explore the history of the war and post-war periods via the medium of generational narratives. This goes for writers now in their fifties, such as East Berliner Reinhard Jirgl and Stephan Wackwitz from Stuttgart, as well as for younger writers like Tanja Dückers, who was born in 1968. Dückers' *Himmelskörper* (*Heavenly Bodies*, 2003) is expressly concerned with the rediscovery of the extent to which one's own situation is determined by one's place in the sequence of generations in the family genealogy. Wackwitz's novel *Ein unsichtbares Land* (*An Invisible Country*, 2003), meanwhile, which revolves around the memories of a grandfather, in staking its claim to being a 'family saga' presents itself so to speak as the spectre of a literary genre long since given up for dead. The form of Jirgl's novel *Die Unvollendeten* (*The Incompleted*, 2003), which presents scenes of the expulsion of the German population from the Sudetenland, in its representation of a community of three generations of women cites a narrative model characteristic of the nineteenth century. It is a model that reached its zenith and simultaneous end-point in Thomas Mann's *Buddenbrooks: The Decline of a Family*, which was published in 1902. In the twentieth century, the form was only used in the context of a programmatic literature of remembrance by marginalised groups, as in the feminist project of reconstructing a female genealogy[2] or, for example, in Dieter Forte's trilogy about a family from the Ruhrgebiet, whose line Forte traces back to the twelfth century.[3]

There are, of course, literary alternatives to the novel of multiple generations that encapsulates history in the narrative model of a seemingly natural genealogy – 'from generation to generation', as the saying goes. In the nineteenth century, this saying became the discourse-forming pathos formula of an epoch of temporalisation, historiography and the theorisation of heredity, strongly under the influence of evolutionary theory. Thus, narrating national history also followed a sort of evolutionary structure since the image of the society was presented by a sequence of generations. Historical developments were in literature mediated by changes in families and the experiences of their members. This mode of writing formed a typical bourgeois narrative in which the family romance functions as a model for the nation, particularly for a specific historical epoch of the nation. Whereas the nineteenth century was dominated by this narrative model structured by generations following each other, there emerged a new kind of generation literature in the twentieth century especially after the First World War. Since then, there have been stories of specific generations who consider themselves to have undergone a unique experience with national relevance and who identify and entitle themselves by a specific event, e.g. Generation First World War, Hitlerjugend-Generation, Generation of 68, etc. It is only through this representative type of generation novels that the autobiographical experience has become a reason and legitimacy for nationally relevant narrations. Here a specific generation appears as the protagonist of a national history although individual experience can never include the whole story. As a result, stories of generations have also become the family romance of the nation in the Freudian sense, i.e. narratives including fantasies and images produced to cover blind spots within the genealogy or to substitute gaps in memory. When generation stories function as national narratives historical experiences tend to be presented as analogy in a familiar framework, and thereby history tends to be brought into line with natural rhythms.

Nowadays, however, one has to look beyond German literature to find the literary alternatives to such generational narratives. To Rafael Chirbes' *La Larga Marcha* (*The Long March*, 1998), for example, a novel which presents a panorama of two generations – that which lived through the Spanish Civil War and the post-1968 generation – without recourse to the model of the family novel or the representation of generational succession. In its two parts, Chirbes' novel sets up a contrast between synchronically organised sequences of scenes from the lives of different families and classes. This device enables Chirbes to show the lack of communication and awareness between the two 'political' generations, as well as unspoken correspondences that connect the stories in unsettling ways. In this way, he succeeds in demonstrating, through striking scenarios, the synchronicity between historically asynchronous episodes and events.

To return to recent German literature, however, the interest, already outlined, in the grandparents' generation is indeed a novelty. It is of course the case that a number of publications from the decade before had already given the lie to the claim that the literature of younger writers took no interest in the German past. It is true that in the 1990s, as the passing of the years gradually diminished the source of the survivors' memories, a new literature emerged, authored by younger writers who had not participated in the historical events they described. These were texts in which scenes, events and figures from the history of National Socialism, the Shoah, exile and the aftermath were brought back into the limelight through the conscious and skilful use of fictional methods. These are works that no longer fall into the category of autobiography and authenticity, but which are based on precise archival research. In novels such as Marcel Beyer's *Flughunde* (*The Karnau Tapes*, 1995) and Norbert Gstrein's *Die englischen Jahre* (*The English Years*, 1999), fiction does not appear opposed to facts – as the formula, as popular as it is erroneous, 'fact and fiction', would suggest. On the contrary, it is precisely the fictional scene of literature which makes it possible to articulate things retrieved from the archives, to address the hidden and repressed traces of history, and to give voice to the silenced and the uncanny lodged within the familiar.

Family Secrets and Phantom Images

The most recent literature follows in the wake of this liberation from the norms and the myths of a postulate of authenticity, to which such precarious products as the simulated eyewitness account of Wilkomirski are to be ascribed.[4] This, at any rate, is how Tanja Dückers has described it in an interview: 'My generation is the first to be able to dare to take a sober look at this topic. I would find it very dubious if the older generation got up on its high horse over the issue of authenticity on account of my generation not having lived through the war.'[5] It is all the more remarkable that this new attention to history, while freed from the obsession with authenticity, has been accompanied by the return of genealogical investigations. Yet a number of works from this body of recent literature differ very considerably from the traditional family novel in which the family sets the rhythm for the historical process in a quasi natural-historical generational progression. In contemporary literature, the family is not infrequently the scene of a secret or unresolved past, in which the gaps in memory or in recounted family history become the basis from which uncanny effects unfold, in particular with regard to the central figures' own familial background.

The new generational novel is often a novel that revolves around a family secret in which the forefathers are entangled. Thus, the protagonists of Tanja Dückers' *Himmelskörper*, for example, while clearing out the apartment of their grandparents, stumble upon some documents that set them on the trail of a family secret from the Nazi period. In Marcel Beyer's *Spione* (*Spies*, 2000), meanwhile, the image of the grandmother itself takes on phantom-like features, as a prohibition on memories surrounding the grandfather's deceased first wife transforms the children of the family into spies who fill the blind spots within the family memory with fantasies, speculations and suspicions.

'The phantom (le fantome, the ghost, the spirit) – in all its forms – is an invention of the living', according to the psychoanalyst Nicolas Abraham; an invention which 'must turn into an object the gap which the obscurity of a segment in the life of the love-object has produced in us [...] This means, it is not the dead who haunt us but the gaps which have remained behind in us as a result of other people's secrets'.[6] Phantoms, then, are not simply what are silenced, secret or obscure in our tradition; they are not the buried memories of our forefathers, or what is concealed in the crypts. Rather, they are what the imagination sets in the place of the mysterious gaps in the stories handed down to us. They are the product of our fantasy – and thus fictions. The fiction of the phantom is related to the life and the secrets of others to whom we are bound by interest or by love, or, more precisely, to the obscurities in what they have told of themselves or transmitted in some other way. In short, it is related to the family narrative they have handed on. In this sense, the phantom refers not to one's own unconscious, but to what is repressed in one's ancestors' stories.

Abraham posits this difference in images of varying strangeness. He says that the phantom affects us like a foreign body and not like a repression which 'Freud calls the *familiar* and *old-established* in the mind [...] which has become *alienated* from it or the uncanny'.[7] The character of the phantom as a secondary fiction is given a genealogical foundation in Abraham's conceptualisation, when he states that the phantom cannot be traced back to a lost object and refers not to the person who conceals a grave within him or herself, but rather to this person's descendants. It is the latter whose fate it becomes to 'objectify such hidden graves in the figure of the phantom'. It is the graves of the others which, in the form of phantoms, haunt the survivors. In the case studies cited by Abraham, it is always familial constellations that are at issue, phantoms formed in relation to the family narratives of parents, and mostly ones that circle around narcissistic injuries and reinterpretations of one's own origin. For example, in one case he mentions, 'The family narrative of the father was a repressed fantasy', or in another, 'The appearance of the phantom thus indicates the effects upon the descendant of what was injurious or even a narcissistic catastrophe for the respective parent.'[8] Hans-Ulrich Treichel's novel *Der Verlorene* (*Lost*, 1998) deals with a complex case of this kind. In this novel, it is a brother lost by the refugee parents during their flight at the end of the war whose infant photograph and, even more, whose phantom image comes to dominate the narrator's childhood. The mother's all-consuming desire to find her lost son sets in motion a dynamic of genealogical research whose methods, ranging from family likeness to anatomical measurement and genetic certification, get closer and closer to the racial-political practices characteristic of the Nazis.

The rediscovery of family ties as a link that produces an immediate relation to the past of the war and of Nazism for those born subsequently serves not infrequently in recent writing as a means of accessing a historical knowledge that has been hushed up. Very often it is literally pictures missing from photograph albums that initiate or accompany the search for the traces of the past, together with hidden documents, manically preserved souvenirs or written records that do not tell the whole story. In this sense, Stephan Wackwitz's story of the reappearance of a grandfather's camera reads like an allegory of the relations between the generations in the long epoch of Germany's post-war history. The camera, which for many years lay in a depot of property confiscated by the Allies from former German soldiers, still contains a film from 1939. However, the old film will not deliver up its images of the past, because it had 'decomposed in the darkness of that half-century and would only show the black of the kind which reigns upon the bottom of the sea'.[9] If the younger generation's investigations of history through the medium of family origins confront the grandsons with the images that can no longer be developed from the recollective apparatuses of their ancestors, then this corresponds with the experience of having grown up in a ghostly reality. Wackwitz again comments, 'But it is not only because the earlier life of my parents lay in a time beneath the sea or the rubble of destroyed towns that the country in which I grew up often seemed ghostly to me as a child.'[10]

The rediscovery of family origins in recent German literature does not so much serve the appropriation of the past via the relation between the generations. Put differently, it does not support the usual form of the transmission of history within the family structure. Rather, it seems to take place as part of an attempt to secure a subjective position and to accept an uncanny inheritance in a history that otherwise remains abstract and obstructed by the moralising discourse of victims and perpetrators.

The Discourse of Generation as Politics of Identity and Lifestyle

The revaluation of the family line in recent German generational discourse as described so far really does signal a new departure, given that the period prior to this saw the flowering of a quite different way of conceptualising generation. This was 'generation' as a title, even a label, of a group sharing common birth years, whose name then came to characterise the political and cultural disposition of a set of people whose mentality or lifestyle had been shaped by a particular historical experience or situation. A new controversy emerged recently about the historical role of the 1968 generation, which looked, in part, like a re-run of the way in which the political camps divided during that period – in accordance with the rule that the talk of generations usually follows from the perspective of a particular generational attitude. However, even before this controversy, it had become habitual in the debates about the *Zeitgeist* to invent new generations on an almost daily basis. If the media are dominated at the moment by metaphors such as 'Generation Unemployed' or 'Generation Scrapheap',[11] only a short while ago names such as 'Generation X', 'Generation Golf', 'Generation East', 'Generation Berlin' or 'Generation@com' were prevalent.

Florian Illies' book *Generation Golf* (2000) first emerged as a bestseller from this discourse. Seen from the perspective of those born between 1965 and 1975, Illies' book depicts the 1980s as the most boring decade of the twentieth century, the decade *after* the upheaval of 1968 and the German Autumn of 1977 and *before* the *Wende* of 1989. West Germany appeared to this particular age group as a comfortably feathered nest, though they had no mission and no prospects in this period. Moreover, it was a time in which leisure activities were largely unaffected by the oncoming new media age, 'Well-fed, admittedly, but otherwise completely without orientation, a whole generation born between 1965 and 1975 stumbled its way into the 1980s.'[12] The defining characteristics of this generation were, according to Illies (himself born in 1971), a certain dress sense, a particular set of consumer habits and a general attitude of indifference: 'Generation Golf's complete apathy towards every kind of theoretical construction, and its preference for practical philosophy are surely shaped decisively by the demise of the Lego age.'[13]

Illies' book predicates upon the distinction drawn between the 'Generation Golf' and the generation of 1968. It had been preceded by a debate in the newspaper review sections, staged as a controversy between the '68ers' and the '89ers' or as a fight between the thirty-year-olds and the fifty-year-olds. When Ulrich Greiner described this debate in a 1994 article in *Die Zeit* as a 'conflict between generations',[14] he was coining a new usage of the phrase 'generational conflict'. Therefore, the conflict was no longer that between fathers and sons (or mothers and daughters), but one arising out of the need of groups relatively close to each other in age to be seen as distinct from one another. It is this sense of generational conflict that opens up the possibility of replacing the rhythm of natural, familial reproduction with a succession of generations that change with ever-increasing rapidity. *Generation Berlin* was published soon after, based on a title coined by Heinz Bude first in 1998 in an article in the *Frankfurter Allgemeine Zeitung* and then as a book in 2001. It provided a name to the sense of themselves and their place in the world shared by those born around 1960, whom he set apart, in essence, from the 'protagonists of protest', i.e. the '68ers'. According to Bude, they were a generation hitherto assigned to the backstage of history but now waiting in the wings to 'make the Berlin Republic their own'.[15] Since then, the term 'generation' has become free territory in the media for all kinds of quite arbitrary metaphorical usages. In the process, the battle of the generations in the media sphere seems to have taken over from the older pattern of generational conflict as the form by which the relation to the past and issues of lifestyle and life preferences are negotiated.

Jochen Hörisch introduced a rather differently articulated liaison between generation and the media when, under the title *Mediengenerationen* (*Media*

Generations), he reformulated the aforementioned 'quarrel between 68ers and 89ers' by means of an analogy between the history of technology and that of mentalities. Hörisch proposed that the technical development of hardware and software provides the conditions that shape the consciousness and attitudes of users. He saw the change in the computer generations as instrumental in shaping the respective youth culture, and thus substituted the media for a historical index in demarcating the generations.[16] The rhythm for the change from one generation to the next in this interpretation is set by the speed of media development. Indeed, the generation of the 'video kids' has been supplanted by that of the net surfers and of the avatars before their parents have even had the chance to learn their ABC in the new vocabulary of digitalisation.

The examples given here have in common that the term generation is used to refer to an identity politics that differentiates between lifestyles and attitudes. Illies' *Generation Golf* made this use of the term popular and simultaneously set its self-ironic standard. The understanding of generation is dominated here by the observation of a similarity amongst those of the same age and the difference vis-à-vis those who are only a little older. However, retrospective appraisal serves not to position oneself within the genealogy, but at the most to generate a nostalgic review of one's own short history. As Illies self-ironically remarks, 'we have, although we are barely adults, already developed a strange tendency to indulge retrospective review, and some of us write at 28 already books about our own childhoods, in the vain belief that these will be able to tell the story of an entire generation'.[17]

With this formulation, Florian Illies takes the aspect of identity politics within the conceptualisation of generation to its absurd extreme. It is not by chance that this happens in a book that was published in 2000, at the end of the millennium. For, insofar as the 'Generation Golf' is determined by a lack of events or formative experiences, one could see in it also the embodiment of a kind of negative conceptualisation of generation. In the 'Generation Golf' we see taken to its negative extreme the form of conceptualising generation which can be said to be the master trope of the twentieth century: generation understood as a cohort whose biography was shaped in a particular phase by decisive historical events, usually of a catastrophic nature. This way of conceptualising generation goes back to Karl Mannheim's 1928 essay *Das Problem der Generationen* (*The Problem of Generations*), in which the experiences of the First World War took on the form of sociological theory.

The Doubled Semantics of the Term 'Generation' and the Forgetting of Genealogy in Modernity

The concept of generation is ambiguous, since the term stands at the intersection of multiple dimensions of meaning. It refers to a stage of life and so to the fact of belonging to a particular age group. Also, when the relation between generations or the succession of the generations is at issue, it contains a temporal or genealogical dimension: the human race owes its existence to the succession of the generations. In an older, nowadays largely neglected usage, generation also means production, (pro)creation or begetting (lat. *generatio* or gr. *genesis*), a meaning which has passed into the bioscientific concept of generation or development of an organism. Etymologically, 'generation' is derived from the family of words surrounding the Greek *genos* (species, race, family), which can also be translated as the genus of the human being or age of man. Founded in the fact of ageing, mortality and sexual reproduction, generation is an order that guarantees the continuation of history in the figure of the production of ever-new lineages, and organises genealogy in terms of provenance and succession.

In this sense, the concept of generation already conceals within itself a complex interplay of nature and culture, since 'generation' stands at the threshold between emergence and continuation, between provenance and legacy, between procreation and tradition, between origin and memory. For cultural studies and for the question of narrating a nation the concept of generation is thus of eminent interest. It can be regarded as the medium of genealogy, so to speak, which regulates the boundary between the procedure of reproduction as described by biology and a process of tradition understood as culture. However, the term always carries with it the danger that cultural phenomena will be regarded as being produced by natural laws and historical-theoretical questions will be treated as if they were derivations of biologically defined rhythms – that diachrony is reduced to demography, in other words.

In the current usage of the term, one meaning has, however, become dominant. It has arisen because of a paradigm shift from a genealogical to a synchronic perspective that aims to capture what it is that unifies a specified age group. Here 'generation' is used to mean a generational community or cohort. A similarity in attitudes, lifestyles and patterns of behaviour is traced back to experiences held in common by people born around the same time or shaped by particular life histories, while at the same time, distinctions are drawn between this and other generations. This understanding generally takes as its reference point Wilhelm Dilthey's definition of generation as a 'narrow circle of individuals who, despite the differences arising out of other factors, are bound together into a homogeneous whole through their dependence on the same great facts and changes which occurred in their formative years'.[18] Through participating, as a result of being born at a particular time, in specific historical events, which in turn come to constitute a given generation, the individual thus becomes both a part of a group and also, as it were, its natural representative. In this way, the individual's biographical narrative becomes the micro-narrative of history, and, conversely, the individual life history becomes narratable within a structure of generationally specific life-stages. This generational model can be seen, as such, in terms of the interplay between subjective and epochal history that has a tendency to harmonise individual biography and historiography. It is on the basis of this narrative structure that 'generation', as the term which designates a group or identity, becomes an instrument so well-suited to that variant of historiography which calls itself social or oral history. Oriented around biographical or collective memory, it makes of the representative of a generation an eyewitness or witness of history.[19]

The concept was elaborated theoretically in Karl Mannheim's 'cohort model'. His notion of generation is the product of a form of German romantic-historical thinking directed towards a sociology rooted in the cultural sciences, which is elaborated with reference to Dilthey. It combines the idea of 'an interior time that cannot be measured but only experienced in purely qualitative terms', a 'sphere of interior time which can [only] be grasped by intuitive understanding', with the phenomenon of synchronicity (contemporaneousness) and a 'state of being subjected to similar influences'.[20] On the evidence of its diction, Mannheim's model can be translated without any difficulty into the ontic language of Heidegger's *Sein und Zeit* (*Being and Time*). Thus, Mannheim does not specify contemporaneousness as a social given for a certain age group, but assesses it as 'subjectively experienceable time'. Here, the idea of generational synchronicity becomes compatible with Heidegger's concepts of destiny (*Geschick*), togetherness and appearance within the same time: 'The inescapable fate of living in and with one's generation completes the full drama of individual human existence.'[21]

From a theoretical point of view, it is perhaps more significant that in Mannheim's approach the sociological sphere is introduced as the medium between nature and mind/intellect (*Geist*). He ascribes to social and cultural forces, quite literally, the medial position between the 'natural' and the 'mental' spheres, as the level of those 'socializing forces' which mediate between the 'vital' (or biological) and the 'intellectual'. This triple layered model is reproduced directly in the three levels of his conceptualisation: generational 'location' (*Lagerung*), generational 'actuality', and the generational unit. As he attempts in the final section of his essay to introduce dynamism into this static model, however, Mannheim's rhetorical devices and metaphors reveal a significant return of the kind of rhythms associated with natural occurrences that the author had repudiated at an earlier point in his essay. The social dynamic is expressed above all in images of currents, tides, the rhythm of waves and of emergence – in other words, with the aid of metaphors from the sphere of nature.[22]

It has frequently been stressed that the establishment within the social sciences of 'generation' as meaning the social uniformity of the experiences of an age group can be explained by the aftermath of the First World War. However, the strongly nationalist overtones have hitherto been largely overlooked. The nationalist elements in the way in which war experiences were dealt with and within the post-war consciousness were not least responsible for the fact that the concept of the generational community that emerged in the process lent itself to appropriation by the total state, as Werner Krauss has shown.[23] In Mannheim's work, the nationalist arguments are located on the level of his methodology. In the course of Mannheim's development of a sociological approach, with reference to 'understanding' as a method derived from the social and cultural sciences, the nationalist connotations that were latent in Dilthey are made manifest. In France, according to Mannheim, positivism had been able to dominate not only in the natural sciences, but also in the humanities. The situation in Germany was different. Here, only the natural sciences had been constituted under the sign of positivism.[24] This distinction between the arts and the sciences is only briefly addressed, but the schema of 'measurable versus understandable' which underpins Mannheim's entire essay can be read as a cipher of Dilthey's opposition between the two. A proper debate about the natural sciences is never actually taken into consideration, despite the theoretical apparatus of evolutionary thinking, which had so influenced the development of knowledge in the nineteenth century, being derived from the biological definition of generation.

Rather, Mannheim's opposition to positivism ends up blocking out the natural sciences' notion of generation altogether. The result is that the category of the social is introduced as a means of avoiding the immediacy of the 'biological', although at the same time the description of the social sphere remains contaminated by natural metaphors. What this means, though, is that a significant prehistory of the concept of generation is left out of the picture. For the fact is that neither Mannheim nor, for that matter, Dilthey established a new concept. What they did was radically reformulate a concept introduced (in Germany) around 1800. At that point, the revalorisation of the 'young generation' under the influence of the development of biological theories of inheritance and of the French Revolution led to the emergence of a genealogical meaning of the term. This enjoyed a notable career in the formula 'from generation to generation'.[25] In Mannheim's sociological reinterpretation, however, the genealogical meaning is replaced by a dimension of synchronicity (contemporaneity) which takes over the functions of social classification and of identity-formation. Although the origin of the term is forgotten in the process, it is the condition of possibility for a usage that underpins the rejection or denial of one's own parentage. It is this concept of generation that has also quite literally written the history books in post-1945 Germany.

The Young Generation: The Refusal of Provenance after 1945 and the Belated Generation Conflict of 1968

The discourse of generations was of central importance for the politics of the past in Germany after 1945. It is one of those scenes in which the negotiation of political and moral power is carried out. Self-definition as a representative or member of a generation has stood in for and superimposed itself upon the paradigm of victims and perpetrators (or accessories). In this sense, the discourse of generations can often be understood as an oblique form of national discourse in which the refusal to accept guilt and the desire for blamelessness find expression. The changing rhetoric and reference to different contours of the concept of generation, meanwhile, is symptomatic of the shifts in the self-understanding of subjects and their relation to the past. 'Generation' functions as a medium of the politics of memory.

In the period immediately following the Second World War, cultural-political discourse was shaped definitively by the programme of a 'young generation' that was linked to its radical refusal of its provenance. A programmatic statement in these terms is to be found in the journal *Der Ruf* (1946–47), which bore the subtitle *Unabhängige Blätter für die junge Generation* (*Independent Journal for the Young Generation*) and functioned, so to speak, as the articles of an association for German post-war literature and the *Gruppe 47*. This programmatic article was authored by Alfred Andersch and entitled 'Young Europe Forms Its Features'. It begins by linking the familiar rhetoric of the 'zero hour' with the phantasm of a young generation without parentage, the offspring of an immaculate conception: 'From out of the most extreme reaches of destruction there sprang, as once Athena from the head of Jupiter, a new, youthful-fresh and virginally Athenian spirit.'[26] The construction of the young generation in these terms is the precondition for the authors' definition of their own self-understanding via the synchronicity and common cause with other, non-German groups, as opposed to their position vis-à-vis the recent past:

> From here [i.e. from the resistance] there stretches a thin, very precarious tightrope across the abyss to another group of young Europeans which has in the past few years likewise given its all with total dedication and personal sacrifice. We are speaking of young Germany [...] It seems to us – despite the crimes of a minority – that it is quite conceivable that a bridge might be built between the Allied soldiers, the men of the European resistance and the German soldiers from the front, between the political inmates of the concentration camps and the former Hitler Youth (they have long since ceased to be it!).[27]

It is notable, and indeed symptomatic, with regard to the unity conjured up by Andersch, which is supposed to bring together recent enemies, that among the groups he lists one above all is missing, namely the Jews and emigrants.

This gap in the originary scene of the discourse of the generation marks the symptom of the hushed-up extermination within the projection of this young generation without origins and its role as the foundational generation of the Federal Republic. Nor is it coincidental that this construction appears in the context of a clear attempt to distance themselves from America:

> We see in general only two methods with the aid of which this bridge-building might be possible. One is on everybody's tongue at the moment. It is called 're-education' [...] There remains, then, only the other course, the independent one which the young generation of Germany must tread alone. Transformation as our own achievement [...] Generally, America and Europe seem to have exchanged roles: with its two-hundred-year-old republican tradition and its capacity for fostering and guarding the spirit of freedom, America is about to become the maternal breeding-place of a European renewal. For Germany this means that the emigration must bear fruit for us. The emigration can in any case only live from the expectation of the return home. We demand and expect the union of the emigration with Germany's young generation. Because this young generation of Germans, the men and women aged between 18 and 35, separated from their elders by the fact that they bear no responsibility for Hitler and from those younger than they by the experiences of the frontline and imprisonment, in short, through having given their all – they are accomplishing the turn towards the new Europe with passionate rapidity.[28]

The metaphorical and rhetorical use of 'young generation' stands here for a complete sealing off from the recent past. The image of the generation without provenance serves to legitimise the refusal of responsibility for the past, supported by the phantasm of being a part of 'young Europe' and thus of participating in the aura of the resistance. At the same time, there is articulated the self-definition as a 'child' of America that needs to cut loose from the latter's tutelage (re-education).

The editors of *Der Ruf* speak in the name of a generation that from a historical perspective must be defined as the generation of the Hitler Youth or the anti-aircraft support, a generation which the history books have described as the 'white generation'. In fact, however, there is a very marked discrepancy between the platform they adopted as representatives of a young and 'guiltless' generation and the editors' actual age. Hans Werner Richter, born in 1908 (and so 31 years old when the war began and 38 already in 1946), and Alfred Andersch, born in 1914 (and so 25 at the start of the war and 32 years old by 1946), belonged to a generation which was not after all as young as all that. The leitmotifs of their founding programme – such as rebirth, renewal and radical rebuilding, dedication and self-possession, the experiencing of the war in religious terms and the experience of freedom – linked up very clearly to the rhetorical pathos formulae of the Youth Movement and Existentialism. They are very clearly contaminated by the mentality of the inter-war years. With their assistance, all the differences in historical provenance and all the incompatibility of the positions occupied during the historical catastrophe that had just passed were determinedly pushed aside. Moreover, in order to create a unity capable of eradicating all differences, another opposition was posited as absolute, namely that between the older and the younger generations. In this sense, the *Young Generation* is the cover name for a historical memory divided along the demarcation line of guilt. Under this name, a heroic collective of soldiers attempts to wriggle its way out of the historical responsibility for Nazism: 'The astonishing feats of arms of *young* Germans in this war and the 'deeds' of rather *older* Germans, currently the object of the trials in Nuremberg, are in no way connected. The warriors of Stalingrad, El Alamein and Cassino, whose efforts were acknowledged even by their opponents, are *innocent* of the crimes of Dachau and Buchenwald.'[29]

Therefore, it is not wholly accurate to suggest that the knowledge of Dachau and Buchenwald played no role in the cultural discourse of the immediate post-war years, as Martin Walser recently claimed in his defence of his works of post-war literature. Rather, the nursery years of his literary career were spent under the influence of a grouping which in the same breath laid the responsibility for history at the door of the 'rather older Germans' and defined itself as a guiltless, innocent 'young Germany': 'We mean the young Germany. It stood for the wrong cause [...] But it stood.'[30] In the rhetoric that reciprocally substitutes this generation for Germany, the age-group comes to stand as it were for the entirety, as the latter's first representative. The image of the virgin head-birth as applied to this generation severs the umbilical cord of its origins in the war. In this way, it defines itself as the starting-point of a new and unbegotten genealogy. Under such circumstances, every survivor's testimonial must appear to this generation as suspect or disturbing, to the extent that it is a reminder of a tradition in which, however disrupted or discontinuous, genealogy is seen as a form of memory that crosses, but also connects the generations.

Seen against the horizon of this post-1945 discourse, the 1968 movement becomes readable as a late echo of it, as a delayed forced confrontation between the generations. The uprising and protests of 1968 took place amongst other things under the sign of a generation conflict, in which the older generation of those who took part in the war was explicitly confronted with its position as the perpetrator generation. The so-called 'father literature' (*Väterliteratur*) embodies this trend. With the formulation *Täter-Väter* (perpetrator-fathers), which represents in condensed form the identification of Nazi history with the generation of the fathers, the so-called 'coming to terms with the past' or *Vergangenheitsbewältigung* is transferred into the genealogy of one's own family. In this body of literary work, the sons (and daughters) direct their rhetoric of accusation and attack against their parents, a constellation which produces, from the historical point of view, a precarious effect. By presenting in this literature their own understanding of themselves as the victims of the *Täter-Väter*, the children take over the position of the real victims of Nazi history and so contribute once more to the repression of the historical victims.

The overlaying of history with the familial perspective marks as it were the return of impurity into the dimension of genealogy and provenance. Moreover, symptomatic here is the symbolism of guilt (*Schuld*) and debts (*Schulden*) and more generally the role of money in the discourse of the 1968ers. The demonising of money in the anti-capitalist pathos formulae of the movement may be interpreted as a contra-phobic reaction on the part of the children to the idea of an inherited guilt with which, even though provenance always involves impurity, they wished at least to protect themselves from the grubbiness of money.[31]

Counting the Generations: *Télescopage*

Since the 1980s, that is, at a considerable distance now to the events concerned, the history of the National Socialist period has come increasingly to be represented in the narrative of the second and third generation – that is, it is counted and recounted in terms of generations. As so often happens, the counting of the generations starts at two. It is only in relation to the second and third generations, i.e. only retrospectively, that a first generation is posited, mostly implicitly and without being expressly described as such. It happens remarkably seldom that anything is said in the name of the first generation. Yet we have any number of accounts that claim to be speaking from some kind of originary place, in that they ascribe their own origins to those historical events that the history of the aftermath takes as its reference point, so that they come in retrospect to figure as *the* history.

If talk of the second and now the third generation has invalidated modern concepts of historiography, post-1945 history has at the same time drawn closer and closer to biblical notions. On the side of the descendants of the perpetrator collective, the figure of the return of guilt inherited from the parents displays a close proximity to the notion of original sin. The responsibility of those born after the events is not derived directly from the events themselves, but relates in a *mediated* way to the history of the war and the Final Solution. However, it is directly connected to the parents' mistakes and failures in the aftermath of 1945, to the consequences of their refusal to acknowledge their guilt and their inability to mourn. Only the history of the aftermath, perceived by those most affected as a kind of 'propagation' of denied or refused guilt, has brought forth those symptoms which in psychoanalytical case studies since the 1980s have been described as 'transgenerational traumatisation' and analysed as the 'Continuing Effects of National Socialism in the Unconscious'.[32]

Since transgenerational traumatisation affects a generation who did not participate in the events from which the trauma arises, it means that the retrospective symptom-formation, which according to Freud characterises every trauma, has now broken through into historical time. Here, the temporal dimension of the individual life history is exceeded, while the symptom-formation continues across the generations. At the same time, the impossibility of relating the discourse of the second and third generation unambiguously to particular age groups points to phenomena of displacement and encapsulation in the memory of the generations. This is a kind of *télescopage* in the language of the unconscious, a figure of a distorted genealogy, where a bond is created between the generations, which continues to work actively within the memory.[33] In this way, the category of generation has become, in the aftermath of 1945, a category of memory, and genealogy now takes up a position within the unconscious.

The traditional historical-philosophical concept of generation marks the intersection of continuum and periodisation. The figure of the 'transgenerational', on the other hand, unites the break in the continuum and genealogy, though not in terms of a break *in* the genealogy but rather as a way of conceptualising the legacy of a 'break in the history of civilisation' and its consequences. Against the backdrop of the semantics of generation after 1945, the generational narratives whose return has been observed recently can be interpreted not just as narratives of origin that connect aspects of identity politics and the politics of the past. The fact that the concept of generation plays the dominant role must also be interpreted as a response to the displacements in the elementary 'structures of relationality' that up until now have been seen as the foundation of our culture as well as the agents of its reproduction and development. These structures are now coming into question in view of the achievements of reproductive medicine and genetic technologies (such as in vitro-fertilisation, surrogate motherhood, cloning, and so on). This alone can explain the success of Michel Houellebecq's novel *Particules élémentaires* (1999). In this book, memories of the 'sexual revolution' of the 68ers contrast with fantasy perspectives on the development of genetic technology and a programme for asexual replication. On the metaphorical level, the novel expresses on the one hand the desire to regress and at the same time the wish for an undifferentiated maternal sexuality. The bioscientific interventions in a generational succession hitherto regarded as natural are evidently activating old myths as well as new longings for origin.

Notes

1. Cf. K.O. Hendrich, 'Katalysator Katastrophe: Betrachtungen über den Generationskonflikt' [Catalyst Catastrophe: Observations on the Generation Conflict], *Frankfurter Allgemeine*

Zeitung, 19 Dec. 2002: 8. The article is a discussion of the findings of the recent Shell study into today's youth.

2. For example, in Ingeborg Drewitz's *Gestern war heute*. *Hundert Jahre Gegenwart*, Düsseldorf, Claassen, 1978.

3. D. Forte, *Das Muster*, Frankfurt am Main, 1992; also her *Der Junge mit den blutigen Schuhen*, Frankfurt am Main, 1995; and *In der Erinnerung*, Frankfurt am Main, 1998.

4. Cf. S. Weigel, 'Zeugnis und Zeugenschaft, Klage und Anklage. Zur Differenz verschiedener Gedächtnisorte und -diskurse' [Witness and Witnessing, Lament and Accusation: Differences in the Standpoints and Discourses of Memory]', J. Tanner and S. Weigel, eds, *Gedächtnis, Geld und Gesetz. Vom Umgang mit der Vergangenheit des Zweiten Weltkriegs*, Zürich, 2002: 39–62.

5. 'Der nüchterne Blick der Enkel. Wie begegnen junge Autoren der Kriegsgeneration? Ein Gespräch mit Tanja Dückers' [The grandchildren's sober gaze: How do young authors encounter the war generation? A conversation with Tanja Dückers], *Die Zeit*, 30 Apr. 2003: 42.

6. N. Abraham, 'Aufzeichnungen über das Phantom. Ergänzungen zu Freuds Metapsychologie [Notes on the phantom: a supplement to Freud's Metapsychology]', *Psyche* 8, Aug. 1991: 691–98.

7. Ibid., 697, my italics.

8. Ibid., 694, 696.

9. S. Wackwitz, *Ein unsichtbares Land. Ein Familienroman*, Frankfurt am Main, 2003: 17.

10. Ibid., 28.

11. The latter as the title under which the 'dip in careers for academics' is being discussed, *TU intern* (Journal of the Technische Universität Berlin), Feb/March 2002: 3.

12. F. Illies, *Generation Golf*, Berlin, 2000: 18.

13. Ibid., 20.

14. *Die Zeit*, 16 Sept. 1994.

15. H. Bude, *Generation Berlin*, Berlin, 2001: 25.

16. 'Today generations switch identities as quickly as the software programmes and the chip generations'; J. Hörisch, ed., *Mediengenerationen*, Frankfurt am Main, 1997: 14.

17. Illies, *Generation* Golf, 197.

18. W. Dilthey, 'Über das Studium der Wissenschaft vom Menschen, der Gesellschaft und dem Staat' [On the study of the human, social and political sciences], in his *Gesammelte Schriften*, vol. 5, Stuttgart and Göttingen, 1964: 37.

19. Cf., for example, *Die Hitlerjugend-Generation. Biographische Thematisierung als Vergangenheitsbewältigung*, ed. G. Rosenthal, Essen, 1986; *Generation und Gedächtnis. Erinnerungen und kollektive Identitäten*, eds K. Platt et al., Opladen, 1995; H. Bude, *Das Altern einer Generation. Die Jahrgänge 1938–1948*, Frankfurt am Main, 1995.

20. K. Mannheim, 'The Problem of Generations', in his *Essays on the Sociology of Knowledge*, ed. P. Kecskemeti, London, 1952: 281–82.

21. M. Heidegger, *Sein und Zeit*, Halle/Saale, 1927: 384, as quoted in Mannheim, 'Generations', 282.

22. Ibid., 312–20.

23. W. Krauss, 'Das Ende der Generationsgemeinschaft' [1946/47], in his *Literaturtheorie, Philosophie und Politik*, ed. M. Naumann, Berlin and Weimar, 1984, 399–409.

24. Mannheim, 'Generations', 280–81.

25. Cf. S. Weigel, *Genea-Logik. Generation, Tradition und Evolution zwischen Kultur- und Naturwissenschaften*, München, 2006.

26. A. Andersch, 'Das junge Europa formt sein Gesicht', in *Der Ruf. Unabhängige Blätter für die junge Generation* 1 (15 Aug. 1946), München 1976: 19.

27. Ibid., 21–22.

28. Ibid., 24.

29. A. Andersch, 'Notwendige Aussage zum Nürnberger Prozeß' [Necessary statement on the Nürnberg trials], *Der Ruf*, 26.

30. Andersch, 'Das junge Europa', 21.

31. Cf. S. Weigel, 'Shylocks Wiederkehr. Die Verwandlung von Schuld in Schulden oder: Zum symbolischen Tausch der Wiedergutmachung [Shylock's return: the transformation of guilt into debt or: the symbolic exchange of reparation]', in S. Weigel and B.R. Erdle, eds, *50 Jahre danach. Zur Nachgeschichte des Nationalsozialismus*, Zürich, 1995: 165–92.

32. This is the title of an essay by Werner Bohleber, 'Das Fortwirken des Nationalsozialismus in der zweiten und dritten Generation nach Auschwitz', *Babylon. Beiträge zur jüdischen Gegenwart*, 7, 1990: 70–83.

33. Cf. S. Weigel, 'Télescopage im Unbewußten. Zum Verhältnis von Trauma, Geschichtsbegriff und Literatur' [Télescopage in the unconscious: the relation between trauma, the concept of history and literature], in E. Bronfen, B.R. Erdle and S. Weigel, eds, *Trauma – Zwischen Psychoanalyse und kulturellem Deutungsmuster*, Köln, 1999: 51–76.

Part III

Narrating the Nation as Film

Sold Globally – Remembered Locally: Holocaust Cinema and the Construction of Collective Identities in Europe and the US

WULF KANSTEINER

Nations might exist in many forms but they certainly, perhaps even primarily, exist as narrative constructs. Nations share that characteristic with other identities with which they coexist, for instance, gender, regional or transnational identities.[1] All these forms of social identity can be further understood, according to the classic definition of Henri Tajfel, 'as that part of the individual's self-concept which derives from his knowledge of his membership of a social group (or groups) together with the value and emotional significance attached to that membership'.[2]

Obviously, social identities are subject to considerable contestation about the composition of a group, its particular attributes and values, and its relationship to other groups. Among other axes of communication, these discussions involve elite designers of collective identity and their audiences, who encounter identity designs in a wide range of media settings and have considerable freedom regarding their response to them. In fact, like many elite products intended for popular consumption, most identity concepts fail in the court of public opinion, because they never reach their designated audience or do not reflect popular tastes and interests.

Three important developments, which have reshaped communication about collective identity in the course of the twentieth century, will concern us in this essay. First, public negotiations about national and other identities have been increasingly conducted through narrative visual media, especially film and television. Second, in particular towards the end of the last century, elite master narratives in the West have called for the construction of transnational identities that can ameliorate or even replace more traditional forms of collective identity and foster solidarity across national boundaries.[3] Finally, the Holocaust has played an important role in both of these developments. Over the course of several decades, Holocaust iconography and narratives have become one of the most successful cultural inventions of the post-Second World War era. As a result, Holocaust subject matter has become an important part of mass communication. At the same time, references to the events of the 'Final Solution' play a key role in the aforementioned elite advocacy for transnational identities. Since the end of the Cold War, the Holocaust has emerged as an important symbolic reference point that is invoked to justify a wide range of political initiatives, including the use of military power for the enforcement of new standards of political conduct.[4]

The following inquiry analyses these developments by taking a closer look at the way that historians of film have conceptualised the relationship between national identity and visual representations of the 'Final Solution' in Europe, Israel and the US. According to most accounts that relationship evolved in two overlapping stages. In the post-war decades, more or less oblique references to Nazi genocide supported the reconstruction of national identities after the catastrophe of the Second World War, before Holocaust history became an independent genre of popular media in the late 1970s. As a result of that success and rapidly changing production and distribution networks, visual reinventions of the Holocaust took on a life of their own that cut across national identity barriers. Some social theorists, including Jürgen Habermas and Ulrich Beck, are convinced that these developments have helped establish a universal memory of the Holocaust that interacts with conventional national collective memories and identities, and fosters national self-reflexivity and the legitimacy of international human rights.[5] However, many questions remain about the allegedly salutary effects of Holocaust memory. Since identities are inscribed in films and TV productions on at least three levels – i.e., artistic intent, narrative form and content, and through audience reception processes – it remains difficult to determine to what extent transnational interpretations have displaced or productively coexist with conventional national perceptions of European history.[6] It is equally challenging to find out what precise role Holocaust narratives have played in the recalibration of collective identities after the Cold War.

I hope to be able to provide some answers to these questions by relating innovative philosophical and sociological insights into the accomplishments of Holocaust culture to more conventional film historical analyses of post-war images and narratives of the 'Final Solution'. Since film historians have carefully analysed different national cinematic traditions and taken a close look at the representation of the Holocaust, their publications show how national master narratives have intersected with Holocaust subject matter. In the course of our comparative analysis, we might be able to understand with more precision in what respects Holocaust interpretation has assumed a transnational dimension since the 1980s. In addition, we can historicise our own collective memories of the 'Final Solution' and address the important ethical question of whether the history of film yields guidelines for the responsible manipulation and appropriation of the memory of events like the 'Final Solution'. Even a superficial glance at existing film scholarship indicates that the important choices in this matter do not pitch national against transnational paradigms of interpretations. More important is the degree of self-reflexivity that different national and transnational strategies of representations attain in the process of cultural production and consumption.

Post-war Cinema in Eastern Europe

After the Second World War, many non-Jewish Europeans continued to imagine Jews outside the social mainstream, but such prejudices did not prevent European nations from incorporating elements of Jewish suffering into their collective memories. As a result, the death camps, conceived as part of the general category of Nazi war crimes, became symbols of national suffering despite the ambivalent relations that post-war European and Israeli societies developed towards the survivors and the victims of the 'Final Solution'. Good examples for the creative use of Holocaust story elements during the invention/revision of post-war national identities are the negotiations about Polish and Czech identities during the late 1940s and 1950s, the attack of the Gaullist myth of resistance in France in the 1970s, and the Zionist master narrative in Israel. In the US, Britain and the Soviet Union, representations of Nazi atrocities helped to justify the war efforts and legitimate the victor's post-war political agendas. However, the images quickly disappeared from the news and did not return to movie screens for many years, if at all.

Given the Allied control of the German media, it is not surprising that public representations of Nazi crimes followed a similar pattern in East and West Germany. After a short, intense media campaign about the camps and German responsibility, the topic was no longer addressed explicitly, although it probably remained an important reference point for all post-war attempts to provide the former citizens of the Third Reich with a sense of collective belonging. With the exception of Israel, cinema was an important venue for the reconstitution of collective identity in all these postwar settings. Even in Israel, ideological uses of the Holocaust echoed development in Europe, since the history of Jewish resistance against National Socialism was embraced on a conceptual political level, while the non-heroic experiences of the average survivor and their concrete suffering were deliberately omitted from public memory.[7]

Polish and Czech films were the first cinematic traditions to visualise the events of the 'Final Solution' in an effort to come to terms with the terror of the Nazi years and create new national identities that reflected the post-war geopolitical status quo. The task required Czech and Polish film-makers to acknowledge the political expectations of their new Soviet overlords, although film executives still had considerable flexibility until the Soviet bureaucracy penetrated Eastern Europe in the late 1940s. In Poland particularly, film-makers also sought to connect to traditional national themes of historical interpretation, for instance, a pronounced sense of Polish victimhood that had been powerfully confirmed by war, occupation and Poland's forced westward 'migration' after 1945. Post-war Polish cinema reflected both strategies of historical interpretation and thus indirectly acknowledged the widening gap between the official memory of the Polish state and the communicative memory of the Polish population that evolved in parallel and often in opposition to that official ideology.

Already the first representations of the camps related positively to official Communist discourse because Polish film-makers, like other Polish intellectuals, either identified with Marxist interpretations of the Nazi phenomenon or quickly adapted to the new political climate. The two approaches to Soviet rule reflect the respective strategies of the film directors Wanda Jakubowska and Aleksander Ford, who created *The Last Stage* and *Borderstreet*, the two best-known post-war feature films about Nazi crimes. Jakubowska did not need much encouragement to provide *The Last Stage* with a pro-Soviet twist, while Ford assumed the party line after his first cut of *Borderstreet* was rejected by state authorities. These voluntary or enforced ideological affinities – and, in the case of Jakubowska, her personal experience as a non-Jewish camp survivor – explain why the films downplayed the specific anti-Semitic aspect of Nazi persecution.[8] However, the same effect, i.e. stripping many victims of their Jewish identity, also resulted from applying long-standing themes of Polish culture to the task of memory management.

While acknowledging or even emphasising the difficult ethnic relations in pre-war Poland, Polish film-makers unequivocally represented Jews as part of the national collective. In the case of Ford, that strategy was a conscious critique of the virulent anti-Semitism of the war and post-war years. Yet despite his best intentions, he thus reduced the suffering of Jews to yet another example of the long-term suffering of the Polish people that was already one of the overriding themes of Polish culture prior to the war. Depending on the self-critical edge of the films, the catastrophe of occupation and genocide was played out either as a drama of failed solidarity among Poles or as a tragedy of an overwhelming attack of the national collective from the outside. Either way, the retroactive obfuscation of the very different experiences of Poles and Jews stripped the latter of their Jewish identity.[9]

The ambivalent, yet honest filmic exploration of the Nazi legacy ended once Moscow tightened its control of Polish affairs and brought the blessings of Soviet realism to its satellite states. However, an intense concern with contemporary history returned to the Polish screen after Stalin's death. From 1956 to 1963, during the most remarkable years of post-war Polish cinema, a new generation of directors deconstructed the simplistic official discourse of Communist heroism as well as the more traditional theme of Polish victimhood. The feature films of those years, directed by Andrzej Wajda and others, focused primarily on the war experience, but there were also some renewed attempts to come to terms with Auschwitz, most notably in Andrzej Munk's movie fragment *The Passenger*.[10] As the young directors of the Polish School worked their way through the historical-literary theme of Polish martyrdom, they inadvertently exposed the great advantages and disadvantages that a powerful national tradition of historical interpretation represents for the task of historical reinvention. On the one hand, the presence of a long-term cultural tradition for the representation of national suffering differentiated the Polish from many other national European cultures. This explains why Polish directors were capable of visualising the camps before artists in other countries. On the other hand, that very tradition made it impossible to grasp the anti-Jewish essence of the Nazi genocide because such an acknowledgment would have detracted from Polish suffering and raised the spectre of Polish anti-Semitism.

After the collapse of Communism in 1989, Polish intellectuals finally had a chance to address openly the difficult topic of Polish–Jewish relations and initiate a process of public mourning for Jewish victims and their culture. The recovery of a lost and repressed history – what Harold Segel has called 'the ongoing postcommunist archaeology of the Jewish past in Poland'[11] – has resulted in important reinterpretations of Polish national identity, for instance, through nostalgic reminiscences of multinational pre-war Poland and an unprecedented number of Polish Holocaust feature films and documentaries.[12] The Holocaust films have helped adapt Polish identity to new political and commercial realities without representing a radical departure from traditional themes of Polish culture. Some contemporary Polish directors exploited the Holocaust to spice up conventional movie genres; others, including Andrzej Wajda, presented affirmative readings of Polish–Jewish martyrdom that downplayed the prominence of Polish anti-Semitism.[13] Nevertheless, freedom of expression has also permitted the production of a few exceptionally self-critical movies, for example, Jan Lomnicki's *And Only This Forest* (1991).[14]

The developments in post-war Czechoslovakia represent the closest parallel to the Polish case. Czech film-makers also approached the catastrophe of occupation and genocide from the perspective of the victims of history.

Like their Polish counterparts, they were offered two windows of opportunity to confront the legacy of Nazism outside the confines of the official Communist paradigm of historical interpretation. The first window remained open for about three years after the collapse of the Nazi regime until the Communist takeover in February 1948 and the second existed from 1959 until the Soviet invasion of Czechoslovakia in August 1968. During both phases Czech film directors succeeded in developing a compelling visual language for the representation of the Nazi camps. Already in 1948 Alfred Radok, whose Jewish father had been murdered by the Nazis, made an expressionist film about Terezin (Theresienstadt) called *Distant Journey*, which developed many of the visual themes of today's Holocaust iconography. Radok integrated a love story between a Gentile and a Jewish doctor with long non-narrative passages describing everyday life and brutality in the camps. Combining new film with documentary footage, he assembled the images of roll calls, barbed wire, watchtowers, piles of clothing and gas chambers that reflected the future Holocaust paradigm with surprising accuracy.[15] Unfortunately, Radok's prescient vision only reached a small audience because the authorities withdrew the *Distant Journey* shortly after its release and cut short Radok's career as a film-maker.[16]

A number of other modernist Czechoslovak films about the Final Solution followed in the 1960s, including Zbynek Brynych's *The Fifth Horseman is Fear*, which showed what terror the Nazi assault caused among Jewish victims and Czech bystanders while also making abundantly clear that the everyday experiences of the perpetrators and bystanders remained normal and tolerable compared to those of the victims.[17] The most successful Czechoslovak Holocaust film of the 1960s was the realistic *The Shop on Main Street*. Its directors Jan Kadar and Elmar Klos provided a naturalistic and suspenseful study of the range of reactions with which the Slovak population responded to the Nazi inspired Slovak destruction of local Jewish communities.[18] Like many of the Eastern European films about the war years *The Shop on Main Street* reflected its director's familiarity with the Nazi terror system, as Kadar had been imprisoned in several concentration camps.[19]

The Eastern European Holocaust films of the 1940s and 1960s emerged from a complex political and film historical constellation. The film-makers tried to negotiate their way through a maze of different influences relating to national artistic traditions, ethnic identities and prejudices that had been violently reshaped by a harrowing wartime record of victimisation and collaboration, the ideological demands of Soviet Communism and, during the 1960s, the promises of an emerging international network of film festivals and distribution systems whose managers appreciated the new Eastern European voices. Yet the films that were produced under comparable circumstances differed in one important respect. In contrast to contemporary Polish productions, the Czechoslovak movies clearly acknowledged Jewish suffering and remained for many years the most honest filmic representations of the history of Nazi genocide.[20] One might want to attribute these differences to personal factors; while all Eastern European film-makers had directly witnessed or experienced Nazi brutality, the Czechoslovak directors appeared to have had first-hand experience of Nazi anti-Semitism, which explains why they had less inclination to equate war crimes with crimes of genocide. Nevertheless there is also a complementary, more intriguing explanation. Since all Eastern European film-makers had to come to terms with Soviet anti-Semitism, the differences in the representation of the 'Final Solution' might primarily reflect specific national sensibilities and traditions. While a strong sense of Polish identity unified the country against German invaders, the same sense of self rendered the survivors impervious to Jewish suffering. According to the same logic, Czechs and Slovaks could perceive the specificity of the Jewish catastrophe because they had never developed a similarly robust sense of collective identity and had reacted much more ambivalently to German occupation. Considered from this perspective, Polish misremembering and Czechoslovak historical honesty attest to the troublesome dynamics of ethnic exclusion that particularly successful politics of national identity set into motion.

The Eastern European accomplishments in Holocaust representation are particularly noteworthy because they attest to a measure of independence from Soviet influence. Polish and Czechoslovak elites might have adopted many Communist customs, but they did not copy Soviet historical culture, which focused exclusively on the war and the Western front. In the late 1940s and early 1950s, Soviet film celebrated Stalin's military prowess in a series of simplistic and repetitive Second World War epics.[21] After Stalin's death, Soviet cinema regained visual and narrative complexity and called into question the previous paradigm of heroism. The terrible experiences of the war years were for the first time documented from the perspective of the average Soviet citizen. The new everyday histories of the war acknowledged the suffering of civilians and soldiers, for example in Nazi POW camps, but the Holocaust never appeared on the Soviet movie screens.[22] Most likely, the depictions of the Nazi concentration camp universe would have struck too close to home in a post-Stalinist dictatorship that discontinued the worst Stalinist abuses but never openly acknowledged the full extent of the Soviet crimes.

With the end of state censorship in the late 1980s, Soviet and later Russian film-makers could for the first time openly and critically address the historical legacy of the Soviet Union. In a phase of intense reckoning with the past, a new generation of film directors helped create a public memory of the Gulag.[23] Even at this stage, however, Russian media never participated in the reinvention of the Holocaust that began on a modest level in Eastern and Western Europe in the 1950s and became such an important reference point of the Western imagination after the end of the Cold War. It might be tempting to identify the lack of an indigenous Russian Holocaust culture as one of the reasons why Russia has not assimilated the global human rights discourse that derives so much legitimacy from the memory of the Holocaust. However, there are other, more important factors that explain the continuing ideological divide between the West and a diminished East, including the lack of democratic traditions and the many skeletons that are still harboured in Moscow's closets. These skeletons invite additional national self-reflection but have been most recently covered by a patina of nostalgia.[24]

Post-war Cinema in France, Germany and the US

Eastern European films about the 'Final Solution' differed substantially in their representation of the victims, but in terms of artistic intention, they remained tied to a specific locale. The films initially attained credibility because they addressed the identity dilemmas caused by social and geographical proximity to Nazi genocide and the rapid succession of Nazi and Soviet occupation. That credibility helped some of the films transcend the context from which they had emerged and circulate in the West without having necessarily been designed for that purpose. The Eastern European Holocaust films shared the concern for regional and national identity problems with many post-war productions, although Western European film-makers paid even less attention to Nazi genocide. The British mourned the loss of empire in a series of spy movies, French and Norwegians recalled and reinvented their heroic resistance against German occupiers, and West Germans returned to the front to wrest at least some moral surplus value from the unmitigated national disaster of the Second World War.[25] The specific national focus of these war stories and Eastern European Holocaust films like *Borderstreet* or *The Shop on Main Street*, becomes particularly obvious if they are compared to the 1955 French documentary *Night and Fog*, which represents the first film about Nazi genocide that transcended the arena of national identity politics.

In only thirty minutes, *Night and Fog* accomplishes two seemingly contradictory objectives. On the one hand, the film provides a succinct introduction into the concentration camp universe and the process of industrial genocide. To underscore the relevance of these events for contemporary audiences Resnais lifts the Holocaust from its immediate historical context, for instance, by never referring explicitly to Jews or Germans. The film's ahistoricity and compact format, both in terms of viewing time and thematic accessibility, explains why *Night and Fog* has become such an exceptionally successful educational tool. On the other hand, the documentary also represents an accomplished meditation about the limits of human imagination. The juxtaposition of static black and white photos of the crimes with innocuous looking colour film footage of the camps' post-war appearance and the at times cryptic voice-over commentary explore the limits of representation that have emerged as a result of the Nazi genocide.[26]

The didactic and philosophical accomplishments of *Night and Fog* made the film interesting to viewers from different national and intellectual backgrounds. In this way, the documentary laid the foundation for the internationalisation of the intellectual memory of the Holocaust that Claude Lanzman accomplished two decades later. Ironically, the documentary's international appeal was an effect of its faithful reproduction of the representational taboos of French post-war historical culture that featured no references to collaboration or Jewish victims.[27] Even the first cut of *Night and Fog* was not well suited to call into question the strategies of self-exculpation that dominated the European media in the 1950s – with one notable exception. Resnais had included a very short segment showing a French guard assisting in the deportation of Nazi victims. French authorities quickly forced the producers to remove the visual evidence of collaboration so that the version that was presented to the public lacked even this small, specific element of French self-reflexivity.[28] Resnais' dehistoricisation strategies and, to a lesser extent, the vigilance of French censors, turned *Night and Fog* into a prototype for an aesthetically accomplished, but politically ineffective liberal Holocaust memory that displayed similar shortcomings as many anti-fascist memories on the other side of the Cold War divide. The interaction between nationalist defensiveness and international political ideologies rendered Jewish victims invisible and shielded European audiences from historical self-doubt.

The collective memories offered to victors and victims of Nazism did not differ substantially from those offered to Hitler's former supporters. West and East German film-makers had serious problems inventing new visions of national belonging because many traditional themes of German identity had not survived the collapse of the Third Reich. In addition, they showed little interest in revisiting their past crimes that had been the subject of a short-lived, yet intense, Allied media campaign in the years after liberation. Under these circumstances, directors and audiences embraced escapist entertainment, for instance, the *Heimatfilm* that was particularly popular in the West.[29] However, film-makers also enthusiastically adopted the ideologies championed by their occupiers and replicated the historical blind spots that these ideologies entailed. Consequently, the films released in post-war Germany showed very clearly that the new transnational ideological frameworks of anti-fascism and anti-totalitarianism systematically detracted attention from the history of Nazi genocide, although this shortcoming was more pronounced in West than East Germany.

West German media turned the war into an important visual paradigm for national reconstruction. The films of the 1950s focused on the suffering of German civilians and the suffering and alleged heroism of the Wehrmacht, sometimes revamped as a Cold War warrior *avant la letter*, to develop a temporary West German identity.[30] The Holocaust did not fit into that anti-totalitarian vision of the past, although Jews sometimes appeared in the margins of a media paradigm that was primarily concerned with German misery. On those occasions, either Jews were featured as passive objects of German rescue and resistance efforts or they became the targets of German attempts to make amends and heal the wounds of the past. Incidentally, the reconciliation stories tended to focus on the same question that already concerned and confused the Nazis, i.e., the question of so-called mixed marriages. One of the first post-war films, *In jenen Tagen*, illustrates this point. Käutner's famous movie presents a fragmented collective of survivors, including 'half- or privileged Jews', that has retained its sense of humanity despite the national catastrophe.[31]

Starting in the 1950s, photographs of the Holocaust resurfaced in West Germany popular culture, but they were not integrated into the narrative universe that unfolded on the movie screens.[32] Moreover, allusions to the 'Final Solution' were often contained or displaced by an official philo-Semitism that rapidly took hold of West Germany's mainstream media and corresponded very nicely to the dominant anti-totalitarian agenda.[33] The strategies of narrative and visual containment did not change decisively when the introduction of television revolutionised the social rituals of collective entertainment in the late 1950s and early 1960s.[34]

The Sozialistische Einheitspartei Deutschlands (SED) leadership in East Berlin tightly controlled the politics of memory to make sure that public representations of the past reflected the new anti-fascist orthodoxy.[35] However, since representations of the camps could serve as excellent props for Communist interpretations of Nazism, East German cinema paid more attention to Nazi crimes than its West German counterpart did.[36] Many of these productions were of dubious aesthetic and political value; they featured triumphant socialist heroes and simplistic story lines linking the profit interest of German industrialists to the gas chambers at Auschwitz.[37] At least during some stages of the history of the German Democratic Republic (GDR), Deutsche Film-Aktiengesellschaft (DEFA) personnel with an interest in exploring Nazi anti-Semitism were supported generously by state agencies, including Jewish directors and scriptwriters who had decided to stay in the GDR during Stalin's anti-Semitic purges. It worked to their advantage that they were not burdened by strong commitments to traditional forms of national identity. In this respect, like their colleagues in Czechoslovakia, DEFA directors could take some liberties in developing a consistent socialist interpretation of Nazi history and pursue their interests in Holocaust representation within the margins of the powerful paradigm of anti-fascism.[38]

Many intellectuals in East Berlin adopted Soviet paradigms of historical exegesis for the same reason that West German elites embraced the anti-totalitarian worldview of their new partners in the West. Both sides quickly reinvented themselves as opponents and victors over Nazism to avoid having to come to terms with past crimes and mistakes. However, in the hands of skilful film-makers with a certain degree of political independence, the socialist paradigm assumed a compelling self-critical twist. Since neither commercial nor national political interests forced East German intellectuals to exculpate the citizens of the Third Reich, some GDR films achieved both, presenting an internationalist, socialist vision of the Nazi crimes and providing impressively honest inquiries into the history of the 'Final Solution'. As in the cases of Polish and Czechoslovak cinema, DEFA productions already engaged with the topic of Jewish suffering in the immediate post-war years, but the best East German Holocaust films stem from a later period.[39] One of them is Konrad Wolf's 1958 feature film *Sterne*, which chronicles the political awakening of a Wehrmacht soldier who falls in love with a Jewish camp inmate, fails to rescue her, and realises belatedly that only decisive, concerted political actions can succeed against fascism. Thus summarised, *Sterne* sounds like a typical socialist propaganda film, but the movie also clearly showed the misery of Jewish victims on their way to Auschwitz and explored the mindset of the German bystanders of the Holocaust, a topic that was, in general, carefully avoided in East and West Germany.[40] A second particularly noteworthy East German production is the 1974 film *Jacob the Liar*, based on a novel by the East German author and Jewish child survivor Jurek Becker. The film is an accomplished visual document but it tells the story of the Lodz ghetto in the form of a tragic fairy tale devoid of concrete historical context. *Jacob the Liar* thus already attested to the risks of Holocaust aestheticisation, although in this case the aestheticisation came from an unlikely source, the haven of historical materialism in East Berlin.[41]

Western Europe received substantial help in the task of collective 'guilt management' from a US film industry determined to penetrate European markets under particularly favourable circumstances. Hollywood commanded unprecedented resources in terms of star power, financial capital and government backing, and faced European competitors that had been devastated by the war and European consumers curious about the blessings of American modernity. In this situation, it was only a question of time before US films would play a decisive role in European mass culture.[42] Yet European audiences only gradually shifted their preferences from national codes and rituals of film culture to Hollywood products. In some contexts, for instance in Germany, that transition was only concluded by the early 1970s.[43]

In the first post-war decade US films about the Nazi years focused primarily on the war,[44] but in 1959 *The Diary of Anne Frank* reflected and reinforced the common denominator in questions of historical taste which Western audiences could use to work through their own wartime experiences. As the first international Holocaust-related media event, the story of Anne Frank represented the post-war consensus of many national historical cultures:

no camps, no brutality and no Jewishness, but a distinctly generic representation of innocence and tragedy in times of crisis.[45] The melodrama offered a perfect projection screen for a wide range of interests and sensibilities. In the US, these interests included the mainstreaming of the Jewish minority.[46] In Europe, the re-imported diary of Anne Frank allowed audiences to embrace its reconciliatory, redemptive message without having to take responsibility for the cultural product itself. Thus, already in the 1950s Hollywood displayed an uncanny ability to codify and visualise a sense of history shared by different collectives and different media in the capitalist West. The universalisation, democratisation and popularisation of the Holocaust through US films that began with *The Diary of Anne Frank* continued in the 1960s and 1970s until it reached its apex with the media event *Holocaust* in 1978.[47]

The above brief summary of the (mis)representation of the 'Final Solution' in post-war cinema reveals an interesting, contradictory situation. Images and narratives that later became part of the Holocaust genre only appeared in the margins of the two important transnational paradigms of political interpretation. State-sponsored socialism and free-market anti-totalitarianism spent considerable time attributing the catastrophe of the Second World War to each other without exploring the genocide of European Jewry in any detail or with any historical precision. It seems that more accurate and, to this day, compelling visualisations of Nazi crimes emerged from countries that had been subject to particularly brutal Nazi repression and, even more crucially, whose cultural elites approached the legacy of Nazi crimes with a diminished sense of national belonging. Even in these settings, the Holocaust never took centre stage and was integrated instead into larger campaigns of national renewal and political reform. In essence, it was precisely the intersection and competition between conventionally conceived national identities and ambitious transnational political agendas that rendered the 'Final Solution' invisible. It should be noted, however, that the Communist paradigm was more compatible and permissive of Holocaust representations than its anti-totalitarian counterpart, especially when Communist leaders and intellectuals sought to distance themselves from the radical anti-Semitic and anti-Israeli inclinations of their Soviet allies.

Inventing the Holocaust

The development of French cinema since the 1970s adds an interesting new dimension to the interplay between national and international factors in the construction and reception of Holocaust representations. In 1971, the film-maker Marcel Ophuls challenged the dominant Gaullist myth of French resistance and spearheaded the most important turning point in the collective memory of Vichy. The strategies of representation that Ophuls developed in *The Sorrow and the Pity*, including controversial indictments of French collaboration in the implementation of the 'Final Solution', allowed a new political generation to destabilise a defensive paradigm of historical identity and replace it by a more variegated memory of France's wartime record.[48]

Ophuls' deconstruction of the Gaullist fiction of national unity followed in the footsteps of important literary works of the immediate post-war years, for instance, Marcel Ayme's 1948 novel *Uranus*. However, Ophuls and fellow film-maker Louis Malle managed to displace the myth on a national scale and thus laid the foundation for the self-critical and self-reflexive French historical culture of the 1980s and 1990s that focused specifically on the victims of Vichy's anti-Semitic policies. The new genre of historically self-reflexive feature films include Claude Chabrol's *Une affair de femmes*, Louis Malle's *Au revoir les enfants*, and Christian DeChalonge's *Docteur Petiot*.[49]

The Sorrow and the Pity was clearly a national media event, but that label does not fit the next extraordinary French historical documentary, Claude Lanzmann's *Shoah*, which was released in 1985. *Shoah* reflected French intellectual traditions, but at the same time radically transcended national frameworks of collective remembrance.[50] In design and especially reception *Shoah* became a non-national, even anti-national media event, despite the Zionist inclinations of its director. The potential for international success was inscribed clearly in the film itself. Lanzmann did not directly engage with French, German, Polish or Israeli national identity. Instead, *Shoah* offered an inquiry into the memory of the Holocaust that glorified the idiosyncratic perspective of the critical intellectual who, among other accomplishments, resisted the manipulation of history for ideological purposes and sidestepped national strategies of historical appropriation.[51]

However, the success of *Shoah* among intellectuals was also the result of a radically changed reception environment. After the surprising success of the TV mini-series *Holocaust*, many academics, for the first time, paid serious attention to the role of popular visual media in the shaping of collective historical consciousness. Now they were looking for a visual document that reflected their own reservations about popular historiography in general and popular Holocaust historiography in particular, and *Shoah* fitted that bill in every respect. Lanzmann showed in concrete terms how the uniqueness and non-representability of the 'Final Solution', which had become a key theme of academic Holocaust scholarship in the 1980s, could be visualised in film.[52] Moreover, *Shoah* and Lanzmann helped expose intellectual and aesthetic shortcomings of popular Holocaust films like *Holocaust* and *Schindler's List*.[53]

Lanzmann's nine-hour-production never reached large audiences but it represents an extremely important moment in the development of Holocaust memory because *Shoah* for the first time demonstrated in concrete terms how an independent, transnational intellectual memory of the Holocaust might look like. *Shoah* has attained almost canonical status in discussions about Holocaust culture, despite the fact that critics, often only with considerable delay, have raised serious questions about Lanzmann's moral integrity as a film-maker and the allegedly salutary psychological effects of his film.[54]

The generational constellation that prompted the anti-Gaullist appropriation of Holocaust history in France brought about a very different visual language of memory in West Germany. The directors of the New German Cinema attacked the apologetic Second World War image created by their predecessors after 1949, but they left the Holocaust largely unrepresented. Alexander Kluge's work best illustrates this ambivalent silence in the films of the post-war generations. On the one hand, Kluge obsessively revisits the Nazi past to foster self-reflexive memories of the war years. His fixation with the battle of Stalingrad provides the best example for this focused, yet extremely selective attack on the identity of the war generation.[55] On the other hand, Kluge rarely invokes the Holocaust and on the few occasions that he includes references to Nazi anti-Jewish policies, he refuses to develop them in any sustained or meaningful fashion.[56] Like Lanzman, the representatives of the New German cinema never reached a mass audience. Nevertheless, their reluctance to visualise Auschwitz – a reluctance they shared with the mainstream media they despised so much – highlights a cross-generational taboo and helps explain the exceptional impact of *Holocaust*.

Holocaust is one of the best-researched media events in film and television history. This might be the reason why the TV series plays such an ambivalent role in narrative accounts about the rise of global Holocaust memory. On the one hand, *Holocaust* marks an unprecedented universalisation of the Holocaust on the level of TV aesthetics, story line and distribution; it represents a key turning point towards, perhaps even the first example of, the development of a popular transnational memory of the Holocaust in the second half of the twentieth century. On the other hand, plenty of evidence about the reception of *Holocaust* calls into question this narrative emplotment of a media event that appears to have had different effects in different national settings.[57] Historians of film who write from conventional, national points of view have documented these particularistic readings of the *Holocaust* series. Histories of French film and French memory, for example, focus primarily on indigenous media events. The broadcast of *Holocaust* on French television in February and March 1979 represents just one among many other historical debates and scandals that have erupted in France's public sphere since the early 1970s.[58]

It is tempting to attribute this special emphasis on indigenous culture to the historians' idiosyncratic, perhaps even nationalistic predilections. However, an alternative explanation seems more compelling to me; when *Holocaust* traversed Europe's national historical cultures in the context of a carefully calibrated PR campaign, it caused significant debates that often sounded very similar from one country to another but that became part of different memory trajectories in different national settings. In France, *Holocaust* intersected with an already well-established intellectual culture of self-criticism that assumed more sociological depth through the broadcast of the mini-series, but the string of French memory scandals would probably have continued with similar intensity with or without *Holocaust*.

In the Federal Republic, the US import functioned as a fabulous memory catalyst. The broadcast of *Holocaust* and the intense emotional reaction of millions of viewers catapulted self-critical strategies of remembrance into the national limelight that had previously only flourished in sub-cultural contexts and had received little media attention. In this sense, *Holocaust* represented a decisive turning point in the evolution of West German memory of the Nazi past because all sectors of West Germany's historical culture hastened to respond to popular demand and thus produced an unprecedented phase of intense and surprisingly popular historical self-reckoning.[59] The memory wave of the 1980s still represents a key achievement of the Federal Republic and it seems unlikely that it would have developed as quickly and with the same intensity without *Holocaust*.

Austrian viewers reacted in similar ways as German audiences and at least temporarily *Holocaust* called into question some of the most cherished and time-tested strategies of Austrian self-exculpation. These doubts lingered in some segments of Austria's historical culture and helped bring about the memory reversal of the mid-1980s. However, after the broadcast of *Holocaust* the majority of the population and the elite once more embraced the conviction that Nazism was a German not an Austrian problem and that Austria should be counted among the victims not the perpetrators of the Nazi era. These strategies of representation finally lost their legitimacy as a result of the Waldheim affair in 1986 when Austria's president was exposed as an enthusiastic member of Hitler's army and subsequently shunned by the international diplomatic community.[60]

Holocaust provided a common frame of reference for audiences around the world and helped establish the history of the 'Final Solution' as a new subgenre of mass entertainment. This outcome was probably not anticipated by the creators of the mini-series. They had planned and committed an act of genre normalisation by integrating the extraordinary topic of Nazi genocide into the visual language of the well-established, popular genre of the soap opera. However, the overwhelming success of *Holocaust* inadvertently created a new genre with its own icons and narrative formats. The most important of these formats, already developed in *Holocaust*, was the survivor story that confronted viewers with accounts about extreme human suffering paired with extraordinary, fortuitous tales of resistance and liberation. The success and integrity of the new genre depended on a specific generational constellation. The majority of viewers who embraced Holocaust subject matter as a form of entertainment had not experienced the Nazi era, but knew many people who had. The wave of Holocaust material that swept across movie and television screens in Europe, the US and other parts of the world during the 1980s and 1990s reflected considerable curiosity (as well as a sense of superiority) about these contemporaries of Nazism and their feelings and actions during and after the catastrophe.

Above examples illustrate that *Holocaust* advanced self-reflexive memory paradigms in Europe, but in its country of origin *Holocaust* stood at the beginning of a trajectory of collective remembrance that had very different political effects. The US media products that helped European societies address the burden of the past in a more honest fashion forged a close link between American exceptionalism and Holocaust exceptionalism in the US itself.[61] The stories that have been developed in this tradition, from *Holocaust* to *Schindler's List* and *The Pianist*, reflect the good intentions of their creators and provided belated recognition for the survivors of the 'Final Solution'. However, by casting the US in the role of the premiere anti-Holocaust nation, the new genre undercut the measure of self-reflexivity that had developed in the US public sphere in the aftermath of the Vietnam War.[62]

The Limits of the Holocaust Paradigm

For the last two and a half decades, Holocaust narratives have circulated in an increasingly integrated global market place, with different effects on local and national communities. In some contexts, for instance in Great Britain, Holocaust themes surfaced with some delay and never became a popular staple of mass entertainment. In other countries, for example Germany, Holocaust films had a great run as a movie and TV subgenre but are now reintegrated into more powerful and well-established genres of movie entertainment, with the effect that new generations of film-makers call into question some of the aesthetic principles that have dominated Holocaust interpretation since the late 1970s. This process of genre normalisation is also noticeable in Israel, whose film-makers made few contributions to the first wave of Holocaust movies, but where the 'Final Solution' has always been an integral part of the nations' historical culture and has recently attracted the attention of a new cohort of directors. In all these contexts, the evolution of popular Holocaust interpretation has been influenced by important political developments, for instance the political integration of Europe or the US invasion of Iraq, which have changed the production and reception parameters of all mass media products and added a new twist to the ongoing globalisation and Americanisation of Holocaust memory.

British directors and television makers have developed considerable ambition in exploring historical topics, but made few original contributions to the Holocaust genre and only imported the transnational Holocaust paradigm with some delay.[63] It is tempting to attribute this lack of an indigenous Holocaust culture to the fact that the British, in contrast to many other European nations, never had to endure occupation and deportation at the hand of the Nazis. However, the relative disinterest in Holocaust remembrance is also caused by a peculiar combination of national and postnational themes of collective memory that are either incompatible with the Holocaust genre or fulfil similar functions as the Holocaust genre on the continent. Since the war years, British elites and British mass media audiences have taken great pride in the fact that the UK repelled the Nazi onslaught and helped defeat Hitler's dictatorship. A simplistic heroic memory of that accomplishment has been celebrated in a series of war, spy and adventure films. These have helped the British public come to terms with the UK's diminished role in international affairs and made international audiences swoon over gentle, well-spoken British officers who outwit and outdress their opponents under the most adverse conditions, for instance, in a Nazi POW camp.[64] After a successful run of several decades, war films are no longer a prominent part of British production schedules. Contemporary audiences, in the UK as well as abroad, tend to reflect about British national virtues in more peaceful settings, for instance through heritage films like *Howard's End* or *Pride and Prejudice*, which have also done wonders for the British tourism industry.[65] However, the heroic memory of the Second World War is still a dominant theme in British official and popular culture, as the fiftieth and sixtieth anniversary celebrations of the end of the war have amply demonstrated. Holocaust subject matter only appeared in the margins of the celebrations without undercutting the patriotic stories of national valour and resilience. The type of self-critical stories about lost rescue opportunities, which are part of continental Holocaust memory and could be legitimately raised about British wartime policies as well, are not part the British Holocaust imagination.[66]

One should be careful, however, about dismissing the British refusal to join the Holocaust bandwagon as merely another example of English arrogance. Unlike US popular culture, British mass media have reserved more self-reflexive forms of mass entertainment for the task of coming to terms with English human rights abuses that visibly and sometimes violently inserted themselves into British society. The legacy of colonialism has been addressed in British black cinema, in many movies about Northern Ireland, and a number of particularly accomplished films about the lives of former colonial subjects in the UK.[67] The fact that British film-makers engaged with the colonial legacy before their colleagues in other European countries might explain the relative dearth of Holocaust products;[68] postcolonial cinema provided the type of introspection that other Europeans derived from Holocaust and Second World War stories.[69]

The development of a postcolonial cinematic tradition also explains why British film historians have been particularly willing to embrace the concept of postnational cinema in their study of British film culture. They have emphasised the heterogeneity at work in films of the 1980s – for instance, in *My Beautiful Laundrette* or *Bhaji on the Beach* – and projected hybridity back into history.[70] From the perspective of the postmodern-inclined film historian, the film-making profession has always been a diasporic community and even the Ealing films of the 1940s, which have long been regarded as a backbone of national British cinema and identity, are more accurately understood as original 'signifiers of difference and insecurity' as Andrew Higson put it in 2001.[71] Yet the critics' focus on diversity and contestation, which questions the very notion of a stable, consensual national community, also inadvertently stresses the power of any audience to inscribe itself and its interests into complex cultural products. Some audiences might prefer to see stable and consensual national values where critics perceive postmodern fluidity and fragmentation.

In the late 1980s, partly inspired by the survivor paradigm, German movies explored the interaction between different post-Holocaust generations. These family dramas focused on problems of the second and third generations whose members are caught in complex, over-determined emotional relationships that turn them into belated victims of Nazism. That applies, for instance, to Harlan's *Wundkanal*, which deals with the challenges of the second generation; Graser's *Abrahams Gold*, focusing on the third generation; and Hofmann's more optimistic *Land der Väter, Land der Söhne*.[72] Germany's post-unification cinema has experienced an impressive revival that reflects two interesting trends. There exist an increasing separation of labour between US blockbusters and inexpensive German productions, often relationship comedies, which reflect 'local' tastes and sensibilities. Moreover, German film-makers and audiences seem to have developed a new appreciation of genre cinema and that appreciation has also taken hold of NS and Holocaust subject matter. Consider, for example, Vilsmaier's historical spectacle *Stalingrad* and the biopic *Marlene* by the same director, or the Holocaust love stories *Meschugge* and *Aimee and Jaguar*, the thriller *Nichts als die Wahrheit* and the melodrama *Gloomy Sunday*.[73]

Recent developments in Germany parallel those in Israel, whose cinema has traditionally paid little attention to the Holocaust.[74] Yet since the late 1980s, a number a second generation Holocaust documentaries have been produced which call into question the Zionist interpretation of the 'Final Solution' and try to liberate its legacy from the control of Israel's right-wing political establishment. For example, in the documentary *Choice and Destiny* director Tzipi Reibenbach follows the daily routines of two Holocaust survivors and, by displacing the official memory of heroic Holocaust resistance, transposes the events from the European past into the Israeli present. While the film pays tribute to the extraordinary experiences of the survivors in concrete and respectful terms, it also integrates them into Israeli everyday life and thus undercuts the notion that the 'Final Solution' represents an event *sui generis* that resists conventional strategies of representation.[75]

The integration of the 'Final Solution' into conventional parameters of film-making and political advocacy provides a measure of the normalisation of the memory of the Holocaust in Western cinema. This filmic equivalent of the historicisation of National Socialism is best illustrated by the development of Holocaust comedy, most prominently in *Life Is Beautiful*.[76] It is difficult to imagine that there are still representational taboos in Holocaust film that have not been broken and that would interfere with the further demise of the special Holocaust aesthetic that existed for over two decades.

Globalisation, Americanisation and Self-reflexive Memory

Because of the process of European political and economic integration, film production in Europe has been integrated to such an extent that it seems to make little sense to focus any longer on distinct national traditions of film-making. The integration is particularly advanced on the level of financing and distribution but has also increasingly influenced production and the choice of subject matter.[77] Film historians who are particularly interested in questions of aesthetics are indeed well advised to abandon national frameworks of reference and develop transnational story lines instead.[78] However, transnational paradigms are not necessarily similarly useful for the analysis of film reception. Even audiences who consume the same media products may react very differently, especially if the products in question raise questions about the viewers' collective identity. In the European context, audience interaction with fiction film is played out in a complex triangular space delineated by a large number of imports, especially from the US; a smaller but still significant number of indigenous products, often produced and distributed via public television; and the viewers' diverse interests and identities that they bring to their media experience. Any accurate description of the interactions and identity effects that take place within that space has to combine transnational, national and even regional/local perspectives without, as a matter of principle, privileging one above the others.

Yet that shortcoming, i.e. the privileging of one of these perspectives above others, is noticeable in many intellectual attempts to re-conceptualise processes of international political and cultural exchange after the end of the Cold War. Francis Fukuyama and Samuel Huntington, as well as Volker Beck and Jürgen Habermas, have speculated about human interaction in times of accelerated globalisation and have *a priori* emphasised the role of transnational factors in the constitution of personal and collective identities.[79] Among other problems, the models raise serious empirical questions. Even in the European context, where elites have aggressively fostered the development of transnational identities, there is no indication that these efforts have produced anything approaching a European identity among significant parts of the population, with the exception of the elites who supported these initiatives in the first place.[80]

Volker Beck's concept of the age of second modernity has been specifically applied in an analysis of the dynamics of international Holocaust culture and offers a good reference point to raise some questions about Beck's and similarly structured models. In their application of Beck's thesis Daniel Levy and Natan Sznaider trace the evolution of Holocaust memory in Europe, Israel and the US and come to very optimistic conclusions about the future of Holocaust remembrance and the construction of transnational collective identities. In their assessment, the development of Holocaust memory illustrates in exemplary fashion how the dialectic, conflicted relationship between global and local identities has displaced the previously dominant paradigm of national identity. As a result, collective memory processes have become more diverse and fluid and follow a promising transnational trajectory. A global memory of the 'Final Solution' that breaks the straightjacket of national memory pays more attention to the victims than the heroes of history, assumes an inherently self-critical quality that national memories never encouraged to the same degree. Furthermore, it makes it more difficult for political elites to avoid the moral imperatives of Holocaust memory and refuse to acknowledge and compensate the victims of past human rights abuses.[81]

With hindsight, it is easy to recognise that Levy and Sznaider told only one side of the story of the Americanisation and globalisation of Holocaust memory. Critics in the US and Europe have deplored the trivialisation and Disneyfication that the history of Nazism has experienced at the hands of the US film industry. However, US-made Holocaust movies have indeed played a positive role in the evolution of Europe's national historical cultures. Films like *Holocaust*, *Sophie's Choice* and *Schindler's List* forced European elites to address the legacy of genocide and collaboration in terms and formats that rendered the process of historical self-reflection intelligible and interesting to the general European public. European film and TV makers learned from the US formats, sometimes by consciously avoiding their mistakes, how to engage their audiences in the ambivalent task of historical reckoning. In this way, US films became part of diverse historical cultures although they never commanded a hegemonic influence even if some European intellectuals perceived it that way. US Holocaust products had such a positive effect in Europe because the Americanisation of the Holocaust never happened there.

The other side of the Americanisation of the Holocaust is much more problematic. The wave of popular Holocaust representations that signalled the integration of American Jewry into the US mainstream also led to the nationalisation of the memory of the 'Final Solution'. Through TV, film and museums, especially the Holocaust Memorial Museum in Washington DC, large segments of the American public have embraced the legacy of Nazi genocide as a defining component of their group identity. There is nothing unusual about this development. In an age of mediated, 'prosthetic memories' people often identify with historical events and narratives to which they have no 'natural' connections, through family lineage or other forms of personal interaction. Mediated memories might even help create empathetic relations across ethnic, racial and national divides that are impossible to develop on a large scale through non-mediated communication.[82] It is also not decisive, although more troubling, that US Holocaust memory has a strong national bend; we have seen above that national group identities can coexist with self-critical memories of the 'Final Solution'. However, there are serious reasons for concern about the specific way that US Holocaust memory defines the role of the American nation in the history of the twentieth century. Within the parameters of US Holocaust remembrance, the nation is cast either in the role of victor over Nazism and helper of Jews or, in the most self-critical format, as distracted bystander and reluctant helper who failed to intervene and bomb Auschwitz as quickly as possible. This description is certainly historically accurate, but by becoming an important element of US national identity, US Holocaust memory systematically discourages the perception of the US as a historical perpetrator. Thus, US Holocaust memory distracts from historical events that, for purposes of self-reflection, probably deserve more attention than the Holocaust, i.e. the genocide against American Indians, slavery and the long record of US imperialism.

In the late 1990s James Young warned about the danger 'of turning Holocaust memory into a kind of self-congratulatory spectacle' and making it 'a substitute for real action against contemporary genocide'.[83] Events in subsequent years have not necessarily alleviated these fears. While the US and its Western partners intervened relatively quickly to stop human rights abuses in former Yugoslavia, they have largely ignored the genocide in Sudan. Moreover, the 'self-congratulatory spectacle' of US Holocaust memory has had other unanticipated and similarly problematic side-effects: the way the US continues to be featured in Holocaust narratives on film and in museums makes it less rather than more likely that US consumers of such narratives begin to wonder about the legitimacy of the US war in Iraq and the concentration camp in Guantanamo, Cuba. It is quite possible that the disconcerting disregard for human rights and civilian casualties which the US has displayed in this conflict is linked to a moral short-circuit that has many discursive sources but is also based on a trivialised Holocaust memory. By encouraging the perception of conflicts in terms of extremes (Nazis versus Jews) some forms of Holocaust remembrance seem to undermine rather than advance self-reflexivity. In fact, diligent champions of Holocaust memory like Israel and the US might feel particularly justified in abandoning diplomatic and legal constraints when they consider themselves victims of history and rally under the banner 'Never again'. Unfortunately, this troublesome self-righteousness, which derives legitimacy from the manipulation of Holocaust memory, could also afflict the post-Cold War international human rights discourse and trigger the collective use of military force in situations that can be solved by peaceful means.[84]

The simple fact that collective memories of atrocities like the Holocaust circulate in inter- and transnational contexts says little about the political and ethical effects of these memories. But we might be able to identify and replicate productive forms of collective memory by studying the interaction between transnational, national and local discourses that have produced particularly compelling, self-reflexive ways of thinking about and visualising the past. The brief history of film considered above contains at least four concrete and promising examples: Czech feature films of the 1960s, the French documentary film tradition of the 1970s and 1980s, the West German media landscape before and after unification, and the second generation Holocaust cinema in Israel. All these examples developed as a result of complicated political and generational constellations that caused intense conflicts about collective identities. All four case studies thus indicate that memory diversity is a value in itself. Since identity and memory paradigms, including transnational paradigms, may have destructive and discriminatory effects, we are most likely to reproduce self-critical cultural practices if dominant paradigms are continuously challenged (and occasionally overturned) by identity concepts that substantial differ from them in content and form.

In addition, all these encouraging models of Holocaust remembrance originated within societies that had transformed historical proximity to the events of 'Final Solution' into strong emotional investments in its collective remembrance. It seems, therefore, that the absence of historical proximity makes it much more difficult to develop self-reflexive collective memories of events that took place outside one's own preconceived geography of identity. Is it possible that our historical survey of Holocaust film history has exposed the political and ethical limits of prosthetic memories? Do the existential divides between historical perpetrators, victims and bystanders thwart our efforts to invent media-based memories of historical catastrophes that help prevent their recurrence? In my assessment, it is too early to make that call. We have certainly reached the limits of the dominant paradigm of Holocaust remembrance that, for very good reasons, has focused attention on the victims. The Holocaust memory of the future would have to develop similarly sophisticated and sympathetic, but at the same time very critical perspectives on the perpetrators and bystanders of the 'Final Solution' to counteract the moral short-circuiting that currently seems to take place in American historical culture. Only a series of popular mass media events about perpetrators and bystanders would tell if Holocaust films can instil self-critical perpetrator perspectives as easily as they inspired survivor empathy in the past.

It is certainly possible, however, that the prospect of compelling, popular and self-reflexive Holocaust perpetrators films is no longer a realistic option. Maybe self-reflexive memories – individual, collective as well as prosthetic – have a limited shelf life. The positive examples cited above developed under very specific social circumstances that made it possible for adults of the Nazi era to be challenged by their peers or members of subsequent generations. The levels of commitment, empathy and critical energy that informed these struggles were the result of intimate knowledge about the contemporaries of Nazism who had inadvertently communicated their hopes and fears to subsequent generations in ways that might never be matched by even the most sophisticated media experience. Perhaps this means that we should soon let go of the Holocaust and deal with our many new catastrophes about which we can attain intimate knowledge. That might give us a chance to turn historical proximity into the type of self-reflexive media product that some film-makers and their audiences created in the aftermath of the 'Final Solution'.

Notes

1. See the helpful surveys in H. Friese, ed., *Identities: Time, Difference and Boundaries*, Oxford and New York, 2002; see also the excellent critique of identity discourses in L. Niethammer, *Kollektive Identität: Heimliche Quellen einer unheimlichen Konjunktur*, Reinbek, 2000.
2. H. Tajfel, *Human Groups and Social Categories*, Cambridge, 1981: 255.
3. The German philosopher Jürgen Habermas, for example, has projected his long-standing advocacy for German constitutional patriotism onto the European Community, hoping that a transnational European identity might help accomplish a level of solidarity and justice across Europe that could never be realised in the era of the nation-states. In theory, Habermas' proposal sounds like a good idea, although he remains quite vague about the concrete political steps that might create a new large-scale democratic sense of belonging. Moreover, Habermas displays at times a troubling partiality for old Europe, i.e., France, Germany, and the Benelux countries, which he trusts to be able to craft a cosmopolitan democratic order which can challenge US unilateralism. See Habermas' response to the US invasion of Iraq that he published together with Jacques Derrida in many European papers, 'Unsere Erneuerung: Nach dem Krieg – Die Wiedergeburt Europas', *Frankfurter Allgemeine Zeitung* (31 May 2003). See also Habermas' similar responses to German unification and the NATO invasion in Yugoslavia, *Die Normalität einer Berliner Republik*, Frankfurt am Main, 1995: 187–88; also 'Bestialität und Humanität: Ein Krieg an der Grenze zwischen Recht und Moral', *Die Zeit* (29 April 1999). Habermas shares his optimism and his terminology with his colleague Ulrich Beck, who is also quite confident that the 'second age of modernity' will usher in a new type of self-reflexive cosmopolitanism; see Beck's article 'The Cosmopolitan Perspective: Sociology of the Second Age of Modernity', *British Journal of Sociology* 51, 2000: 79–105.
4. On the development of the new paradigm see, for example, E. Barkan, *The Guilt of Nations: Restitution and Negotiating Historical Injustices*, New York, 2000. The post-Cold War Holocaust memory was collectively embraced by the political elite of the West in the 2000 Stockholm Holocaust conference; see, for example, M. Jeismann, *Auf Wiedersehen Gestern: Die deutsche Vergangenheit und die Politik von morgen*, Stuttgart,

2001: 139–51. It played a key role in the decision for military intervention in former Yugoslavia especially during the discussions in Germany; see M. Schwab-Trapp, *Kriegsdiskurse: Die politische Kultur des Krieges im Wandel 1991–1999*, Opladen, 2002; and Habermas, 'Bestialität und Humanität'.

5. Habermas and Derrida, 'Unsere Erneuerung'; Beck, 'The Cosmopolitan Perspective'. See also D. Levy and N. Sznaider, *Erinnerung im globalen Zeitalter: Der Holocaust*, Frankfurt am Main, 2001.

6. Empirical research about identity effects of feature films has only begun relatively recently. See, for example, the two volumes edited by M. Stokes and R. Maltby, *American Movie Audiences: From the Turn of the Century to the Early Sound Era*, London, 1999, and especially *Identifying Hollywood's Audiences: Cultural Identity and the Movies*, London, 1999.

7. Y. Zerubavel, *Recovered Roots: Collective Memory and the Making of Israeli National Tradition*, Chicago, 1995: 76; O. Bartov, *Mirrors of Destruction: War, Genocide, and Modern Identity*, Oxford, 2000: 192.

8. F. van Vree, 'Auschwitz liegt in Polen: Krieg, Verfolgung und Vernichtung im Polnischen Film, 1945–1963', in W. Wende, ed., *Geschichte im Film: Mediale Inszenierungen des Holocaust und kulturelles Gedächtnis*, Stuttgart, 2002: 44–64, esp. 49–54.

9. M. Haltof, 'National Memory, the Holocaust and Images of the Jew in Polish Cinema', in J. Falkowska and M. Haltof, eds, *The New Polish Cinema*, Trowbridge, 2003: 81–97.

10. On the Polish School see, for example, B. Michalek and F. Turay, *The Modern Cinema of Poland*, Bloomington, 1988: 19–34; and, on Munk's *The Passenger*, esp. 125–28.

11. H. Segel, *Stranger in Our Midst: Images of the Jews in Polish Literature*, Ithaca, 1996: 1.

12. Haltof, *Polish National Cinema*, 222–40.

13. Wajda's most prominent critic was Claude Lanzman, who called Wajda's *Korczak* outright anti-Semitic; see A.P. Colombat, *The Holocaust in French Film*, Metuchen, 1993: 113–16.

14. Haltof, *Polish National Cinema*, 234–36.

15. I. Avisar, *Screening the Holocaust: Cinema's Image of the Unimaginable*, Bloomington, 1988: 54–64.

16. Radok was only allowed to make two more comedies, P. Hames, *The Czechoslovak New Wave*, Berkeley, 1985: 41–42.

17. Avisar, *Screening the Holocaust*, 70–75.

18. Ibid., 79–86; Insdorf, *Indelible Shadows*, 172–75.

19. R. Taylor, N. Wood, J. Graffy and D. Iordanova, eds, *The BFI Companion to Eastern European and Russian Cinema*, London, 2000: 117.

20. That is also the assessment of the Polish film historian Marek Haltof; see Haltof, *Polish National Cinema*, 226.

21. D. Gillespie, *Russian Cinema*, Harlow and London, 2003: 133–35; E. Margolit, 'Der Film unter Parteikontrolle', in C. Engel, ed., *Geschichte des sowjetischen und russischen Films*, Stuttgart, 1999: 68–108, esp. 99.

22. O. Bulgakova, 'Der Film der Tauwetterperiode', in Engel, *Geschichte des sowjetischen und russischen Films*, 109–181, 118–128; D. Shlapentokh and V. Shlapentokh, *Soviet Cinematography 1918–1991: Ideological Conflict and Social Reality*, New York, 1993: 135–43; Gillespie, *Russian Cinema*, 136–38.

23. A. Lawton, *Before the Fall: Soviet Cinema in the Gorbachev Years*, 2nd ed., Xlibris, 2002: 187–222; E. Binder, 'Der Film der Perestroika', in Engel, *Geschichte des sowjetischen und russischen Films*, 256–307, esp. 268–81.

24. Ibid., 308–327, esp. 316–20.

25. S. Dürr, *Strategien nationaler Vergangenheitsbewältigung: Die Zeit der Occupation im französichen Film*, Tübingen, 2001, esp. 174–75; T. Soila, A. Söderbergh-Widding and G. Iversen, *Nordic National Cinema*, London, 1998: 122–24.

26. A. Insdorf, *Indelible Shadows: Film and the Holocaust*, 2nd ed., Cambridge, 1989: 39–41, 212–13; and Avisar, *Screening the Holocaust*, 6–18.

27. L. Rice, 'The Voice of Silence: Alain Resnais' *Night and Fog* and Collective Memory in Post-Holocaust France, 1944–1974', *Film and History* 32, 2002: 22–29.

28. Avisar, *Screening the Holocaust*, 16.

29. J. Trimborn, *Der deutsche Heimatfilm der fünfziger Jahre: Motive, Symbole und Handlungsmuster*, Köln, 1998.

30. W. Becker and N. Schöll, *In jenen Tagen...: Wie der deutsche Nachkriegsfilm die Vergangenheit bewältigte*, Opladen, 1995; and P. Reichel, *Erfundene Erinnerung: Weltkrieg und Judenmord in Film und Theater*, München, 2004.

31. Reichel, *Erfundene Erinnerung*, 174–81.

32. H. Knoch, *Die Tat als Bild: Die Fotografien des Holocaust in der deutschen Erinnerungskultur*, Hamburg, 2001.

33. F. Stern, *The Whitewashing of the Yellow Badge: Antisemitism and Philosemitism in Postwar Germany*, Oxford, 1992.

34. W. Kansteiner, 'Entertaining Catastrophe: The Reinvention of the Holocaust in the Television of the Federal Republic of Germany', *New German Critique* 90, 2003: 135–62.

35. A. Leo and P. Reif-Spirek, eds, *Helden, Täter und Verräter: Studien zum DDR-Antifaschismus*, Berlin, 1999.

36. P. Reichel, *Erfundene Erinnerung*, 192.

37. This applies for instance to the films *Der Rat der Götter* and *Ernst Thälmann* from 1950 and 1954/55 respectively; see D. Kannapin, *Antifaschismus im Film der DDR: Defa Spielfilme 1945–1955/56*, Köln, 1997: 131, 167.

38. T. Jung, 'Jenseits der Erinnerungspolitik oder Der schwierige Umgang mit dem Holocaust in der DDR', in K. Berghahn, J. Fohrmann and Helmut Schneider, eds, *Kulturelle Repräsentationen des Holocaust in Deutschland und den Vereinigten Staaten*, New York, 2002: 167–91, esp. 171.

39. Kannapin, *Antifaschismus im Film der DDR*, 90–110.

40. Reichel, *Erfundene Erinnerung*, 207–14; Jung, 'Umgang mit dem Holocaust in der DDR', 181–82.

41. Reichel, *Erfundene Erinnerung*, 206.

42. R. Wagnleitner, 'American Cultural Diplomacy, the Cinema, and the Cold War in Central Europe', in D. Ellwood and R. Kroes, eds, *Hollywood in Europe: Experiences of a Cultural Hegemony*, Amsterdam, 1994: 196–210.

43. J. Garncarz, 'Hollywood in Germany: The Role of American Films in Germany, 1925–1990', in Ellwood and Kroes, *Hollywood in Europe*, 94–117.

44. P. Beidler, *The Good War's Greatest Hits: World War II and American Remembering*, Athens, 1998.

45. J. Doneson, *The Holocaust in American Film*, Philadelphia: Jewish Publication Society, 1987, 57–83; see also H. Loewy, 'Märtyrerromanze: Die "befreite" Anne Frank', in Wende, *Geschichte im Film*, 94–122.

46. P. Novick, *The Holocaust in American Life*, Boston, 1999: 117–20.

47. Doneson, *Holocaust in American Film*, 119.

48. H. Rousso, *The Vichy Syndrome: History and Memory in France since 1944*, Cambridge, MA, 1991: 98–114; and G. Austin, *Contemporary French Cinema*, Manchester, 1996: 22–24.

49. R. Fournier Lanzoni, *French Cinema: From Its Beginnings to the Present*, New York, 2002; see also R. Golsan, 'The Legacy of World War II in France: Mapping the Discourses of Memory', in C. Fogu, W. Kansteiner and N. Lebow, eds, *Identity and Memory in Postwar Europe*, Durham, NC, forthcoming; and H. Frey, *Louis Malle*, Manchester, 2004: 119–27.

50. For an exploration of the relation between *Shoah* and *The Sorrow and the Pity* and Lanzmann and Ophüls, see Colombat, *The Holocaust in French Film*, 323, 328–41. Colombat's and Ophüls' emphasis on the ahistoricity of *Shoah* also indicates basic parallels between Lanzmann's and Resnais' strategies of Holocaust interpretation.

51. Dominick LaCapra has compellingly analysed Lanzmann's subject position as a secular Jewish, anti-historiographical (at times even anti-intellectual) intellectual intent on vicariously participating in the trauma of Holocaust survivors. That perspective explains Lanzmann's arrogance and ruthlessness vis-à-vis some of his interview partners and his sacralisation of the Holocaust; see D. LaCapra, *History and Memory after Auschwitz*, Ithaca, 1998: 100, 111, 118–19, 132–35.

52. The uniqueness theme was most vigorously debated during the German historians' debate; see P. Baldwin, ed., *Reworking the Past: Hitler, the Holocaust, and the Historians' Debate*, Boston, 1990. For canonical readings of *Shoah* as a testimony to the uniqueness and non-representability of the Holocaust, see S. Felman and D. Laub, *Testimony: Crises of Witnessing in Literature, Psychoanalysis, and History*, New York, 1992: 224 and passim; and G. Koch, *Die Einstellung ist die Einstellung: Visuelle Konstruktionen des Judentums*, Frankfurt am Main, 1992: 159–60. At least initially, intellectual praise was almost unanimous in Europe and the US, with the exception of Poland, where critics rejected Lanzmann's emphasis on Polish anti-Semitism and omissions of Polish rescue efforts during the Holocaust; see Colombat, *The Holocaust in French Film*, 299.

53. M. Hansen, 'Schindler's List is not Shoah: The Second Commandment, Popular Modernism, and Public Memory', *Critical Inquiry* 22, 1996: 292–312, esp. 301.

54. LaCapra, *History and Memory after Auschwitz*, 137–38; and especially the excellent, detailed critical reading of *Shoah* from a psycho-traumatological perspective, provided by H. Weilnböck, 'Claude Lanzmanns *Shoah* und James Molls *Die letzten Tage*: Psychotraumatologische Analysen von Bearbeitungen der Shoah im Film', in W. Schmitz, ed., *Erinnerte Shoah: Die Literatur der Überlebenden*, Dresden: Thelem, 2003: 444–94.

55. E. Wenzel, *Gedächnisraum Film: Die Arbeit an der deutschen Geschichte in Filmen seit den sechziger Jahren*, Stuttgart, 2000; see also A. Kaes, *From Hitler to Heimat: The Return of History as Film*, Cambridge, MA, 1989: 105–35; and the critical remarks about Kluge in O. Bartov, *Murder in Our Midst: The Holocaust, Industrial Killing, and Representation*, Oxford, 1995: 139–52.

56. The best example for such underdeveloped Holocaust references is Kluge's first feature film *Yesterday Girl* released in 1966. Kluge tells the story of a young Jewish woman fleeing from East to West Germany, where she is rejected and remains in a state of social alienation. Kluge informs the viewer that the protagonist was born to Jewish parents in Leipzig in 1937 but the film contains no information on her family's life and/or death in the Third Reich. In fact, the woman's Jewish ancestry seems to be of no consequence for the story-line of *Yesterday Girl*; see M. Wolfgram, 'West German and Unified German Cinema's Difficult Encounter with the Holocaust', *Film and History* 32, 2, 2002: 24–37.

57. This ambivalence is very noticeable in Levy and Snaider, *Erinnerung im globalen Zeitalter*. The authors emphasise that *Holocaust* marked the transformation of particularistic into universalistic modes of Holocaust memory (p. 132). But they also have to acknowledge that audiences reacted very differently, for instance in Germany and Israel, and therefore they choose to have the new paradigm of transnational Holocaust memory take shape in the 1990s when *Schindler's List* was released on a global scale (p. 174).

58. Rousso, *Vichy-Syndrome*, 144–47.

59. M. Thiele, *Publizistische Kontroversen über den Holocaust im Film*, Münster, 2001: 298–338.

60. O. Marchart, V. Öhner and H. Uhl, 'Holocaust revisited: Lesarten eines Medienereignisses zwischen globaler Erinnerungskultur und nationaler Vergangenheitsbewältigung', *Tel Aviver Jahrbuch für Deutsche Geschichte*, 2003: 307–34.

61. J. Shandler, *While America Watches: Televising the Holocaust*, Oxford, 1999; and P. Novick, *The Holocaust in American Life*.

62. US cinema only engaged with the Vietnam War once it was over. Starting the late 1970s, Hollywood has produced self-critical as well as affirmative accounts of the Vietnam War, but rehabilitation of the US military has taken centre stage since the mid-1980s (*Rambo*),

the same time that the Holocaust paradigm took shape in the US; see S. Ross, ed., *Movies and American Society*, Oxford, 2002: 280–302.

63. British Holocaust culture developed only in the 1990s; see T. Kushner, *The Holocaust and the Liberal Imagination: A Social and Cultural History*, Oxford, 1994: 264–65.

64. C. Monk and A. Sargeant, *British Historical Cinema*, London, 2002; and J. Chapman, 'Action, Spectacle and the *Boys Own* Tradition in British Cinema', in R. Murphy, ed., *The British Cinema Book*, 2nd ed., London, 2001: 217–25. In the 1980s the Second World War and the Blitz returned to British screens in a number of coming-of-age stories like *Hope and Glory*; see P. Powrie, 'On the Threshold between Past and Present: "Alternative Heritage"', in J. Ashby and A. Higson, eds, *British Cinema, Past and Present*, London, 2000: 316–26.

65. A. Sargeant, 'Making and Selling Heritage Culture: Style and Authenticity in Historical Fictions on Film and Television', in Asby and Higson, *British Cinema*, 301–315.

66. J. Petersen, 'How British Television Inserted the Holocaust into Britain's War Memory in 1995', *Historical Journal of Film, Radio, and Television* 21, 2001: 255–72.

67. Self-critical voices about British imperialism are still underrepresented and often depend on imports. In the 1980s, for instance, films about the Ulster conflict were for first time produced in Ireland and no longer just in the US and the UK. The new Irish cinema emphasised the incomprehensibility of the war in Northern Ireland and thus deliberately employed rhetorical devices of Holocaust memory. M. Walsh, 'Thinking the Unthinkable: Coming to Terms with Northern Ireland in the 1980s and 1990s', Asby and Higson, *British Cinema*, 288–300.

68. In France, self-critical films about colonialism and its aftermath develop in the shadow of the Vichy syndrome and focus primarily on the experiences of the colonisers; see S. Hayward, *French National Cinema*, London, 1993: 252–53.

69. It is interesting to think about a causal link between the self-critical, postcolonial coverage in the mass media in the UK and the British population's opposition to the invasion of Iraq. Apparently, a reasonably self-critical public sphere can be sustained despite (or perhaps precisely because of) the absence of a strong popular Holocaust memory.

70. A. Higson, 'The Instability of the National', Ashby and Higson, *British Cinema*, 35–47.

71. Ibid., 44.

72. S. Reinicke, 'Nachholende Bewältigungen oder: It runs through the family: Holocaust und Nazivergangenheit im deutschen Film der Neunziger', in Deutsches Film Institut, ed., *Die Vergangenheit in der Gegenwart: Konfrontationen mit den Folgen des Holocaust im deutschen Nachkriegsfilm*, Frankfurt am Main, 2001: 76–83.

73. S. Hake, *German National Cinema*, London, 2002: 180–92.

74. There are some notable exceptions which were produced in the aftermath of the Eichmann trial; see A. Kronish, *World Cinema: Israel*, Trowbridge, 1996: 24–25.

75. Y. Loshitzky, *Identity Politics on the Israeli Screen*, Austin, 2001: 32–71.

76. J. Bleicher, 'Zwischen Horror und Komödie: *Das Leben ist schön* von Roberto Benigni und *Zug des Lebens* von Radu Mihaileanu', in Wende, *Geschichte im Film*, 181–99; see also the critical remarks in K. Niv, *Life Is Beautiful but Not for Jews: Another View of the Film by Benigni*, Lanham, 2003. The normalising effects of comedy might also explain the surprising success of 2004 German release *Go for Sugar* (Alles auf Zucker). *Go for Sugar* by the German-Jewish director Dani Levy does not deal with the Holocaust; it is a family comedy about two estranged Jewish brothers with very different religious convictions who are forced to reconcile after their mother's death. But German audiences clearly appreciated the revival of Jewish humour in Germany and the opportunity to shed some of their post-Holocaust anxieties; see K. Grieshaber, 'New Film Lets Germans Laugh with (Not at) Jews', *New York Times* (9 March 2005).

77. A good example for this trend is Volker Schlöndorff's film *The Ogre*, based on the novel by Michel Tournier, which can no longer be attributed to a specific national intellectual tradition and is consciously geared towards an international art cinema audience.

78. See, for example, P. Sorlin, *European Cinema, European Societies 1939–1999*, London, 1991.

79. See note 3 above and F. Fukuyama, *The End of History and the Last Man*, New York, 1992; and S. Huntington, *The Clash of Civilisations and the Remaking of the World*, New York, 1996.

80. See the empirical chapters in parts II and III of R. Herrmann, T. Risse and M. Brewer, eds, *Transnational Identities: Becoming European in the EU*, Lanham, 2004.

81. Levy and Sznaider, *Erinnerungim globalen Zeitalter*, 219–24, 228, 232.

82. Alison Landsberg emphasises the empathetic potential of mediated memories although she remains surprisingly uncritical of the political effect of US Holocaust memory; see A. Landsberg, *Prosthetic Memory: The Transformation of American Remembrance in the Age of Mass Culture*, New York, 2004: 19–21, 142–50.

83. J. Young, 'America's Holocaust: Memory and the Politics of Identity', in H. Flanzbaum, ed., *The Americanization of the Holocaust*, Baltimore, 1999: 68–82, esp. 82.

84. For some observers this negative scenario was already played out in the late 1990s when NATO members bombed Serbia without UN mandate and justified the intervention by comparing Serbian atrocities to Nazi genocide.

Chapter 9

Cannes 1956/1979:
Riviera Reflections on
Nationalism and Cinema

HUGO FREY

The French creators of the Cannes International Film Festival had always
envisioned the event functioning as a subtle assertion of patriotism. From the
outset Cannes was conceived as a national-Republican response to Fascist Italy's
Venice festival (originating in 1932). However, as is often recounted, the German
invasion of Poland on 1 September 1939 brought a sudden halt to the first Cannes
festival fortnight.[1] War in Europe meant that a competitive celebration of cinema
was no longer a priority. Re-launched in 1946, a series of successful mountings
of the festival eventually did bolster the myth of French cultural superiority. In
Paris Jean-Paul Sartre, Albert Camus, Juliette Greco and Saint-Germain-des-
Prés's 'existentialism' demonstrated a continued ability to produce a
philosophical and artistic tradition with universal pretensions. Hosting Cannes
fulfilled a comparable public rhetorical effect. Year in year out, the festival
projected a vision of a glossy, modern and upwardly mobile country that was
leading the world in film, fashion and celebrity. Alongside other quasi-industrial,
quasi-spectacular, often sporting phenomena (the Paris Air-show, the Tour de
France, the Paris-Dakar motor race), Cannes signified a healthy and vibrant
society that was, superficially at least, at ease with itself. By 1954, French
nationalists had been humiliated by the loss of Indochina and new tensions were
evident in Algeria. Delivering a good festival reminded everyone and anyone that
the Republic excelled in the cultural field. There at least it was business as usual.

The purpose of this chapter is to examine and to compare two historically significant festivals (1956 and 1979) to better understand how cinema and nationalism interact; and, secondly, to reflect on how scholars evaluate that relationship. More precisely, in the light of evidence from the festivals I will reconsider the pertinent concepts at the heart of this growing sub-field of film studies. The role of nationalist discourse in film, national industrial marketing and organisation, and questions of 'negotiations of nationhood through cinema' will be analysed. New issues like the influence of post-1960s critical history film-making on national identity formation will be teased out. Generally speaking, I will be examining how the film festival, including those works entered in the competitions, functions to promote and disseminate nationalism. For the record, and in line with the persuasive work of Ernest Gellner, I understand nationalism as a political ideology which is historically specific and is neither timeless nor inevitable.[2] As these very brief remarks implicitly indicate, the essay does not revisit the long running political science debate on the meaning of national identity. Instead, the more modest contribution I will offer is that of the cultural historian. Like a yacht moored offshore, my reflections will bob along on the tide, sweeping from contextual discussion of individual films to more general or theoretical intervention s and, on again, to further historical analysis.

1956: A High Watermark of the Nationalist-cinema Nexus

Several of the films presented 'in competition' were marked by nationalist discourses and so elicited patriotic home audience responses. Briefly sampling the general content of the entries indicates how much of mid-1950s cinema was shaped by nationalism or national cultural traditions. For example, the Austrian film delegation entered works that reflected that country's affiliation with the production of classical music. Similarly, the Netherlands relied on offering material that explored distinctively Dutch geographical and anthropological features, presenting Bert Haanstra's documentary piece, *En de Zee was niet Meer*.[3] In a rather predictable intervention, Franco's Spain evoked a tradition of sporting prowess, giving audiences a film about bull fighting, *Tarde de Toros* (directed by Ladislao Vajda). Just as conventionally, the British delegation included the patriotic espionage film, *The Man Who Never Was*. Directed by Ronald Neame, it retold the 'true story' of how ingenious British intelligence officers, led by Ewen Montagu (played by Clifton Webb), invented a brilliant intelligence smokescreen for the Allied invasion of Sicily in 1943.

The two now highly regarded entries to the festival, Ingmar Bergman's *Smiles of a Summer Night* (Swedish delegation) and Satyajit Ray's *Pather Panchali* (Indian delegation), are relevant. Today, many critics view these films as being key works in 'world cinema' but the initial celebration of the films functioned along nationalist lines. These films were quickly interpreted by American, British, French and other journalists as being indicative of Sweden's and India's newfound ability to produce quality works of art. On a secondary level, aspects of the content of these films were suggestive of national cultural traditions. Bergman's light dramatic comedy features typically Scandinavian scenes of mid-summer festivities. Regarding Ray's *Pather Panchali*, the first film of his *Apu Trilogy*, comparable national markers are evident. Thus, Darius Cooper contends in his analysis of the film that it is founded on Indian 'Rasa' philosophy and aesthetics.[4]

In the light of this historical context, Anthony Smith's work on the rhetoric of nationalism in cinema represents a plausible thesis.[5] As the political scientist explains in his brief but compelling essay on the subject, key modes of visual communication such as dramatic historical reconstructions, visualisations of symbolic landscapes or celebrations of national heroes, were commonplace in early nationalist fine art and literature. By the twentieth century, and the birth of the cinema, the same West-European national communities used the cinema to comparable effect. Now, major works of cinema evoked patriotic heroes, and directors used the camera to imply the superiority of their respective ethnic and cultural communities. Likewise, the cinema allowed the people to view themselves and to learn the accepted norms of social conduct. Almost all of these processes, originally outlined in general terms by Smith, were evident in the film entries to the Cannes competition (1956). Some of the films on show that year relied on images of ethnoscapes and landscapes (the aforementioned Dutch anthropological work), while others provided a nostalgic vision of a community's way of life. Some of the entries were overtly patriotic, not bothering to conceal their political colours. Works like the British war film *The Man Who Never Was* combined more than one of the devices identified by Smith in a single movie. For example, it was set in the important cityscape of blitz-torn London, while it also featured the heroic military figure, Montagu. Furthermore, director Neame included scenes in which Churchill himself was implied to be the key decision-maker behind the espionage strategy.[6] These episodes were contrasted with negative representations of enemies: Hitler being portrayed as falling for the British ruse. The work therefore typified how classic nationalist discourse was relayed through dramatic cinematography.

The general nature of the entries to the festival also supports Alan William's perspective that film is most powerful when it reflects and redistributes pre-existing stereotypes.[7] Certainly, there was nothing inventive about either the Austrian delegation's use of Mozart/Salzburg or the Spanish selection of a film dedicated to bull fighting. As noted above, the British selection of an episode from the Second World War reworked already popular myths. Therefore, Williams wisely comments that cinema communicates by 'preaching to the converted'. However, as Susan Suleiman suggests in her work on the political novel, redundancy is a vital component in any persuasive communication.[8] Processes of visual and narrative repetition are critical in maintaining the circulation of social ideas and prejudices, giving new images to longstanding social and political attitudes and in so doing keeping them up to date.

Another good example here is Alfred Hitchcock's *The Man Who Knew Too Much*, entered in Cannes 1956 as part of the American delegation. The film does not include any particularly original political implications: it is a patriotic spy thriller, and a remake of an earlier work from the 1930s. However, this does not mean that it is insignificant. Hitchcock's reaffirmation of traditional American values in the context of a Cold War storyline maintained the relevance of these concepts for the new generation. To repeat, Hitchcock did not originate the fundamental stereotypes. However, his *mise-en-scène*, the construction of individual scenes, produced some of the most powerful individual signifiers of American identity from throughout the 1950s. For example, the details of James Stewart's and Doris Day's *haute couture* costumes perfectly captured the aspirations of a post-war generation starved of such luxuries. These heroic characters, their smiles, body shape, make-up and costumes embodied the new 1950s-style American dream. Hitchcock's rendering of the pure physical movement of the two stars, their grace and elegance, even when escaping from foreign terrorists, implied national-genetic and moral superiority. The kitschy concluding scenes from the picture, complete with Day's charming rendition of the song 'Que sera sera', are brilliantly entertaining. Even when a film is communicating a relatively conservative and well-established political subtext, in the hands of a Hitchcock it is such a flexible form that it can produce unforgettable new sounds and images.[9] Works such as these gave audiences new visual codes through which to continue to believe their old prejudices. They made interwar values still appear central to modern times.

Commercial activity represents a second arena of significant patriotic intervention. Each delegation arrived on the Riviera as a named national party and provided documentation that quite literally waved the flag with pride. Films were presented 'in festival' as representatives of a wider artistic and industrial team. Those teams metaphorically stood in place of the nation-states. Relatively crude paraphernalia was deployed by the delegations to explain their nation's artistic prowess. For example, the British Film Institute archives reveal how the film industry spared no expense in the production of marketing material. Rank and Ellstree studios framed their products though the rosy filter of national pride that used icons such as Britannia. Like the British, the Soviet marketing material was advanced, patriotic and in its case pitched to evoke noble notions of Soviet 'humanism'.[10] Thereby, the festival served as a crossroads for 'national cinemas' to meet and to boast of their wealth to each other.[11] Various other forms of patriotic intervention were common. Lavish parties were thrown to impress rivals with generosity. Details of cuisine were selected to symbolise popular national traditions. The Swedish and Austrian delegations provided guests with high quality schnapps, and the United States had cases of bourbon on offer. The Russians provided the vodka and the British the Scotch whiskey.[12] Invitation lists to parties were subject to passages of international diplomacy. In 1956, the Russian group apparently snubbed the prominent British delegation because they felt that a recent British-made film had insulted Soviet pride.[13]

As Andrew Higson and Susan Hayward have argued, the broad concept of national cinema as industrial label/marketing device is a central point of intersection between cinema and nationalism.[14] The format of the festival, a kind of international race for first prize, meant that delegations competed with each other and in so doing turned Cannes into a mythological space for the expression of patriotic loyalty. Journalists played the most significant part in this framing of the event. Most Western-European societies accessed Cannes, and other cinematic events, via the popular and extensive writings of this key group. The core concept of national competition over a festival fortnight gave the press the easiest of narrative structures through which to file their reports. It was a plot line that they applied indiscriminately to the analysis of film content, the social events and other episodes besides. I find that film journalists are as significant a social group in the alignment of cinema with nationhood as any governmental or industrial participants. For it is precisely this group that most commonly presents individual films or genres as being national forms.[15]

In addition, one can confirm the theoretical importance of the concept of 'banal nationalism'. Michael Billig's analysis of the subtle, almost unnoticeable reassertion of patriotic values through everyday socio-cultural forms, is probably as significant a theorisation as the now widely cited work of Benedict Anderson.[16] Cannes 1956 illustrates how forms of banal nationalism are demonstrated in one significant historical example. Consistency, repetition and normalisation are the key terms to understanding the phenomenon. Furthermore, I suggest that Cannes sheds light on how closely bound up nationalism is with social entertainment. In times of peace, and particularly in social contexts like festivals or sports events, it is evident that 'being patriotic' is experienced by citizens and described by reporters as a pleasurable sensation. Contemporary historians who focus on the 1930s and 1940s have quite understandably neglected this aspect of the ideology in favour of nationalism's relationship to militarism and conflict. However, Cannes 1956 underlines how important the national–entertainment–pleasure nexus was within just over a decade of the conclusion of the war. The association of nationalism with social or pleasurable cultural activity is an insidious phenomenon because it brilliantly conceals the ideology's propensity for violence and destruction.

Here too questions of gender stereotyping and nationalism intersect and blur together. The very bodies of the 'stars' were the subject of international rivalry during competition. For example, the festival was frequently framed in the press as a 'Miss World'-style national beauty pageant. Thus, most of the female stars were presented as champions of their country's relative 'sex appeal'. Rather surprisingly, the British delegation had launched the competition before they had arrived in Nice. Days before reaching France Diana Dors declared to journalists; 'I AM GOING TO CANNES TO BOOST BRITISH SEX APPEAL' (capitals in original quotation). Competition was fierce: Kim Novak waved the Star-Spangled Banner and the French media discovered a sixteen-year-old named Brigitte Bardot. Attempting not to be outdone, the Russian participants touted the actor Irina Skobetseva. British journalist, Anthony Carthew was impressed by Irina's naivety and exotic novelty value. Writing for the readers of *The Daily Herald* he explained: 'She looks sad because she is worried about her clothes. I told her that since she was prettier than most of the French stars and all of the British ones, she need not be troubling her blonde head.'[17] In addition to the dated sexism of the reportage, the material captures how entwined film culture and nationalism had become. Women stars were dressed, made-up, posed and photographed to signify implied national superiority. Some journalists, like Carthew, were prepared to flirt with the 'foreign' women, and to pay them compliments, but these gestures were simply that. One does not have to accept all of the recent psychoanalytic theorisation on the subject to acknowledge that popular nationalist statements were articulated in close relation to similarly crude constructions of gender roles.[18]

The record of Cannes 1956 fully supports the scholarship of those writers who highlight the significance of the national-cinema link.[19] However, it indicates that there are tensions as well. Films entered in the festival included internationally financed co-productions. Directors, actors and technicians were part of a semi-global industry. Alfred Hitchcock is again the obvious example to take-up. Born in England, by 1956 Hitchcock had started his 'American' phase of film-making. Moreover, his work was having a growing influence on film journalism and production in France. As is well known, his influence on François Truffaut, Louis Malle and Claude Chabrol was great, if not overwhelming. Similarly, festival entries that year included work that was shaped by cross-national cultural traditions. The Soviet entry, an interpretation of *Othello*, indicates how literary adaptation can go beyond strict national literary canons to penetrate frontiers. The second British entry to the festival is another telling case. That piece was a quasi-documentary/quasi-historical reconstruction of the Austrian mountaineer Heinrich Harrer's memoirs, *Seven Years in Tibet*. Harrer's recollections of his experiences of life with the young Dalai Lama had been a publishing phenomena of 1953. Now, a British producer and director brought them to the cinema to win filmgoers across Europe and North America.

Production histories, hybrid or cross-national source materials and international reception questions indicate how the association between cinema and nationalism is sometimes more tenuous than might be popularly imagined (or asserted by patriots). However, scholars who reveal these ambiguities in their work must not in turn forget the dominant force of nationalists. Surely, Hitchcock's *The Man Who Knew Too Much* was meant to be a product that found global audiences. Agreed, it was perhaps interpreted in subtly different ways by French, Italian, British or American audiences. It was based loosely on 'a universal' story-pattern of 'good triumphing over evil', and so tenuously supports Pierre Sorlin's claim regarding the universality of film-culture.[20] Nevertheless, none of these 'international/hybridity factors' change the central visual and narratological valorisations articulated in the content of the work. *The Man Who Knew Too Much* remains a proudly pro-American thriller and it always will. If the discourse of a film is nationalist then no matter how many production/reception ambiguities one lists it is wise to prioritise its core ideological content. Much can be learned by the genuine transnational ambiguities that are evident in film production but these factors should be handled with sensitivity. Deconstructing the idea that a film comes with a straightforward national identity label is a noble scholarly task. However, it is unfortunate if emphasis on 'transnationalism' and 'universality' is made at the expense of better understanding the patriotic content, context or function of a film.

To add a more theoretical afterthought, the social world contains many living nationalists who are ready to position any film inside their ideological vision. To my knowledge, far fewer people might be called 'transnationalists' who are ready to enjoy cinema for the diversity of its production funding or global artistic talent. That is to say, nationalism is a working ideological body of knowledge, held by individuals and groups, which interprets cinema (and everything else) to its own advantage. Conversely, transnationalism is an analytical category developed by scholars in universities. Unlike nationalism it is not in any meaningful sense a popular belief system that acts on, and in, the social-political world.

Cannes 1956 Continued: Internal and External Negotiations of the National

Repeatedly, it is claimed that cinema and nationalism come together in 'dynamic' and 'ever-shifting' ways. Both Williams and Higson agree that cinema does not offer a single hegemonic, unchanging vision of national identity.[21] Instead, they argue that film is a space where national identities are displayed and argued over. The theoretical watchword is 'negotiation'. Film is therefore one site where competing internal ideas on the national community are raised, contested or rejected. As I will explain, Cannes demonstrates the importance of this thesis and adds to it. Individual films, including international co-productions, function as locations for debating nationhood. The divided British press response to the Cannes entry *The Man Who Never Was* represents a rich body of evidence regarding the phenomenon. Furthermore, it will also be wise to point to new dynamic factors. Besides 'complex internal national negotiations', one discovers 'international, external negotiations' taking place at Cannes. Typically, nation-states respond to each other's film production. This level of 'external' negotiation of meaning is a currently neglected aspect in the secondary literature, which I will argue merits renewed attention.

Every significant British press review of the historical war film *The Man Who Never Was* confronted what was perceived as a significant problem. Film historians Sue Harper and Vincent Porter have succinctly explained the issue: 'Zanuck (of Fox) [father of producer André Hakim, also of Fox] insisted on casting two Americans, Gloria Grahame and Clifton Webb as the leads – the former was under long-term contract to Fox. Director Ronald Neame had no say in the matter'.[22] In the spring of 1956, the casting decision to use Americans to portray British war heroes generated a backlash of British xenophobia and anxiety concerning Anglo-American relations. Right-wing and left-wing reviewers were united in their dislike of this aspect. Thus, *The Daily Worker* columnist claimed that his viewing of *The Man Who Never Was* underlined all his worse fears that Britain was now nothing better than a subjugated state in a wider American Empire. Writing for the *Spectator* magazine, J. Graham, might well have agreed with these sentiments, if not the exact words of his leftist colleague. Graham informed his conservative readers: 'He (Clifton Webb) disguises his accent a bit, but he never gets away from the fact that he isn't an Englishman, that he doesn't talk like one, or look like one'.

Less overt comments were made to similar effect elsewhere and it was commonly noted that one or both of the American stars were inadequate. However, a less anti-American, more internationalist, form of Britishness was aired in response to the picture. Neo-liberal celebration of Anglo-American co-operation was implied in some of the reviews. For these critics it was accepted and understood that a British film had to make casting compromises to win over the lucrative American market. Dilys Powell, doyen of critics, was at pains to stress that the film was 'not over-Americanised' because of the casting. Elsewhere, the *Daily Telegraph's* reviewer described Clifton Webb's performance as being 'with intelligence and assurance'. Others accepted that younger domestic audiences wanted 'stars' and that British acting talent was unable to fulfil that reasonable desire.[23]

The discussion of Britishness, and by implication Anglo-American relations, which was presented in response to *The Man Who Never Was*, exemplifies how potentially quickly cinema triggers social thinking and debate on the qualities of nationhood. Single films, as well as series of works, or genres, are common vectors for the negotiation of internal divisions over the qualities of national identity. The above examples are especially telling because they exemplify how a single film is able to provoke a clash between differing nationalist readings. Indeed all kinds of other patriotic concerns ran riot in response to the picture, its heroic wartime story and the perceived casting issue. For example, fake military identification cards issued by cinemas to promote the work caused a minor security scare in the naval city of Portsmouth. The offending fake ID cards were withdrawn.[24]

Significantly, for a minority inside the Conservative Party the seemingly bland patriotic celebration of a wartime espionage intrigue was deemed a threat. Conservative MP for Nottingham Central, Lieutenant-Colonel Cordeaux claimed that the film had too quickly revealed Secret Service strategies to the public. For this politician the defence of the realm was placed in some peril because the film revealed far too much, even while flying the flag for English military ingenuity. Lieutenant-Colonel Cordeaux explained: 'people soon forget that there might be another [war] in which Britain would want to use devices that were successful last time'.[25] Questions were tabled in the House of Commons in a last ditch attempt to prohibit screening, although release went ahead. To appease these contradictory responses the same film was subsequently entered at Cannes under the auspices of the British delegation and given a 'Royal première' screening back in London.

These remarkable episodes are instructive for they offer a working model of the central processes involved in the broader notion of film acting as a space for 'negotiations of the national'. One can hypothesise from the case study that films that seek to respond to, or directly portray, episodes of symbolic importance to nationalists, form *the critical sites* for producing internal intellectual and press discussions. These same types of film afford the potential for the release of pent-up frustrations regarding the status of the nation, and invite public responses that exceed the patriotic content of the work itself (e.g.: Lieutenant-Colonel Cordeaux's national security campaign). Films like these function as loadstones for nationalist intellectuals to react to. Cinema, especially 'national problem' films, that in this case are due to the casting decisions, give nationalists a new and popular subject on which to speak with authority and confidence. They provide nationalist intellectuals with a popular point of access to the public in ways that complex social-economic questions simply do not. Products like *The Man Who Never Was*, combining patriotic historical reconstruction, contemporary international relations via the American actors, and issues of national intelligence, would seem to be almost the perfect vector to generate furious internal debate. In particular, films that strike a problematic note (in this, casting the Americans) are potentially highly provocative. They not only fulfil traditional nationalist agendas but introduce controversy as well.

Let us next raise the question of 'international' negotiations of the meaning of nationhood. The festival that year, and every other, was supposed to establish a space for intra-national artistic harmony. Cannes was meant to be a celebration of film-making and international understanding. Thus, a working stipulation for all delegates was that films that were entered in the competition should not provoke hostility or offend any other delegation. In 1956 this well-meaning criteria was impossible to uphold and did little to ease tensions. The most widely recorded example of controversy relates to Alain Resnais's *Nuit et brouillard* (*Night and Fog*) (see also Wulf Kansteiner's analysis of the film herein). As Richard Raskin has recorded, Franco–West German diplomatic pressures were placed on the festival organisers not to include the Holocaust documentary in the event.[26] Both the French Foreign Ministry and the German embassy in Paris pressed that the film be ignored because it was feared too offensive to German national sensitivities. Although never given as a formal reason for its exclusion, individual reputations within the French film industry were compromised equally. So, one might note that the prize jury at Cannes included the 'collaboratrice' – Arletty and one of the official French films in competition was directed by Henri-Georges Clouzot, an artist famous for his work under the Vichy regime.

Several other films were marked by comparable 'international' disputes and subject to petitions for withdrawal. The controversies surrounding *Nuit et brouillard* were not unique, nor part of an exclusively French or German 'syndrome' regarding war and Holocaust memory. The allegedly offensive content of several films came to endanger the integrity of the festival. For example, the Japanese delegation to Cannes lobbied against the inclusion of the British *A Town Like Alice*.[27] A now long forgotten film on the 'war in Malaya', it had depicted a Japanese soldier crucifying an Australian serviceman. Following the organiser's etiquette of not showing material that might offend other participants, and presumably Japanese diplomatic lobbying, the work was grudgingly withdrawn. Paradoxically or perhaps deliberately based on a combination of self-righteous diplomacy and ironic sleight of hand, the British replaced *A Town Like Alice* with *Seven Years in Tibet*. The travel writing the film adapted recounts how a former enemy military personnel (Harrer) escapes from a British prisoner-of-war camp in India. The British delegation's inclusion of this work implied that, unlike the inflexible Japanese, or West Germans, they were prepared to handle any cinematic material relating to the 'last war'. In selecting the film the British ensured that the former Nazi army soldier, Harrer, was 'in competition' at Cannes the very year when *A Town Like Alice* and *Nuit et brouillard* were deemed unacceptable.

Two new disputes developed during the festival itself. The Finnish entry, *Unknown Soldier*, offered an account of the 1941 Winter War against the Soviet Union.[28] The Soviet delegation objected to its projection and the festival organisers upheld the complaint. In retaliation to that decision, the Finnish delegation quit the Riviera. Having spent much diplomatic energy removing

Nuit et brouillard so as to encourage full German participation, a new set of controversies ensured the Germans subsequent departure. Contemporary press coverage implies that the Russians had complained about the inclusion of the German film, *Himmel ohne Sterne* (*Sky without Stars*; dir. Helmut Käutner), because it narrated a negative account of Soviet controlled East Berlin. When the Cannes authorities chose to 'ban' that film to protect the Soviets Dr Bernhard von Tieschowitz, head of the German delegation, abandoned all involvement in the event.[29] One might note that the aforementioned film also again raised issues of wartime violence, including reference to the bombing of Dresden.

The micro-history of international lobbying, walkouts and prohibited films underlines how cinema produces 'international negotiations' on the meaning of nationhood. A more systematic pattern can now be developed to map out these episodes. Evidently, one national film industry's production of a negative vision of the history/society of another country is potentially likely to cause offence. In turn, the offended national community might well use the perceived, very public, external critique as a means of evoking a defensive sense of unity at home. It is possible that this kind of obstinacy will produce renewed antipathy from the producer-nation (as was the case in some British press comment on the 'Japs'' disgraceful attitude to *A Town Like Alice*). As we have seen, direct diplomatic pressures ensue. The use of censorship barriers provides a final defence for the offended nation to prohibit internal display of the foreigner's cinematic criticism. The model sketched out here underlines the genuine potential for international controversy.

However, when critical films successfully cross borders they might serve a powerful educational function. Empirical evidence of the latter scenario is limited. I sense that more often than not governmental censorship boards have restricted 'critical' outsider products or limited their distribution. For instance, I know of no 'foreign critical film' devoted to Britain or Britishness, or France or Frenchness, that has not either been censored or provoked critical journalistic response. Although still controversial, internal critiques of nationalist themes remain more successful and generally speaking more accepted among nationalists precisely because they are perceived of as being somehow a part of a pre-existing community debate. In a world composed of nation-states, the acceptance of critical discourses from 'foreign' sources represents the hardest lesson of all. Nationalists, extreme or more moderate, prefer to listen to internal, 'home', critiques to the warnings of outsiders, even when they might play a more valuable pedagogic role.

There are exceptions and deviations from the model that I have been outlining. West-German reception of non-West-German films dedicated to the Holocaust is a potential case in point. By the 1970s, the initial rejection pattern illustrated in the Cannes 1956 delegation's reaction to *Nuit et brouillard* evolved into a more complex public mood. For example, major North-American productions like the television serial *Holocaust* and the movie *Schindler's List* generated some favourable West-German responses, although far from exclusively so. Similarly, more recently, the *avant-garde* Israeli participation at the Berlin film festival, *Don't Touch My Holocaust* (directed by Asher Tlalim, 1994) was awarded with a 'Forum Entry' showing in 1995. Episodes such as these would indicate that in this area of historical film-making some West Germans have accepted and approved of 'critical' outsider cinema dedicated to the Nazi genocide. However, any final judgement on this matter would have to be compared to the history of reactions to popular 'insider' German films, and then analysed on that basis.

One can add that generational factors must play a part in the international reception processes on which I am speculating. On the face of it, the German and Austrian generation that was engaged as adults in the war and Holocaust would be the least likely to accept 'foreign', 'former-enemy', cinematic criticism, out of longstanding loyalty to the idea of the national community (and of course due to the ideological context of their formative years).[30] Equally, later post-war generations appear likely to be more receptive to listening to pertinent critical information from beyond the frontiers of the nation-state. This addition to the general model sketched above therefore poses the question of how cross-generational unity, or conflict, is itself established. Thus, the role of a range of social institutions, such as the Church, the education system or other youth organisations, like the Scouts movement or the popular sports-club scene, are potentially crucial formations that shape generational relations. When these kinds of institutions function to produce cross-generational harmony it is likely that nationalism will continue and that critical foreign cinema will be perceived as anti-national, and in turn attacked or at best ignored. If, however, these social institutions encourage internationalism, or alternatively fail to maintain unity because they preach too strict a message, then, generational discord will push the young to question the old. Challenging outsider films that undermine the 'glory' of the nation-state will be welcomed by the younger generation and then used as a stick to beat fathers and mothers.

Patterns relating to the 'international relations of cinema' seem oddly distinctive from the development of traditional historiography. In the latter field, it has been far more common to see 'foreign critical publications' becoming key works in the very states that the historians analyse.[31] The classic example here is American historian Robert Paxton's groundbreaking work on Vichy France. His highly critical account of Pétain's regime has become an essential textbook on most French university history courses. As readers will recall, Paxton was even invited to act as a specialist witness in French crimes against humanity trials in the 1990s.[32] There are also certainly other examples that show that Paxton's transnational role is relatively common: for example, the numerous works of British-based historians devoted to Nazism that are translated, published and read in Germany and Austria. Why then can elite 'critical' historiography move across national borders more easily than their cinematic equivalents? Here is a speculative and short answer to a complex question. The epistemological truth claims of professional historiography mean that work in this field is more difficult for nationalist elites to dismiss, as compared to entertaining cinematic works that rarely make overt scientific truth claims (documentary film being the obvious exception). University-level historiography is part of an internationalised scientific community in which nationalist ideology is less significant an ideological factor than in the popular entertainment-media industry and the affiliated print media. Rightly or wrongly, it is also probably the case that governments and nationalists are more sensitive to the persuasive power of a mass medium like cinema than to the introduction of the printed word. The patronising assumption at work is surely that cinema may have a greater emotional and psychological impact on the masses than a mere scholarly publication.

Cannes 1979: New Times/New Conceptions of Identity

Some things never change, or so it seems. The Cannes festival fortnight always witnesses an influx of international celebrities and assorted media people to the South of France. Hotel prices and restaurant bills rise accordingly. Delegates arrive and depart as named representatives of their national film industries. However, work entered in competition at Cannes 1979 was very different to that from the 1950s. In the 1950s, films had celebrated national ideologies or, as we have just noted, managed to offend other national groups. By the 1970s a radical shift occurred. Films like *Apocalypse Now* and *Die Blechtrommel* (henceforth for ease, *The Tin Drum*), which dominated proceedings in 1979, recounted episodes from the past that were ambiguous, problematic or psychologically disturbing. National delegations produced distinctly more critical works about the sovereign powers they represented at the festival. The idea of the history film as an epic of positive national adventure was temporarily suspended. Alternative modes that shaped national identities in new ways emerged in their place.

Apocalypse Now provided one of the first of the United States' more reflexive and critical considerations of the Vietnam War. To summarise, it charts the secret mission of a CIA operative, Captain Willard, to assassinate a rogue officer, Kurtz, who has disappeared on the edge of the Vietnamese/ Cambodian border. The film follows Willard's mission by moving through a number of set pieces which are evocative of the American experience in Southeast Asia and that loosely also reflect the source text, the Joseph Conrad novella *Heart of Darkness*. The officer and the small boat of soldiers he travels with witness the barbarity of the American war effort, they encounter and murder Vietnamese civilians and finally reach the compound of Colonel

Kurtz. Although much of the material is spectacular, especially the famous US helicopter attack sequence, the general message of the film questions the morality of the war. Coppola depicts American military incompetence and illustrates the graphic terror and pain of combat. The film relies on the powerful metaphor 'war is insanity'. There are also strong implications that American society had itself slipped into a kind of madness. Explaining the meaning of the work to a press conference in Cannes, Coppola said that his audiences should leave the cinema knowing what the Vietnam War meant on a psychological and emotional level. He added that he had wanted Americans to see a 'face of horror' and to accept that they were looking in the mirror.[33]

In retrospect, aspects of the film are somewhat conservative. As Gilbert Adair notes, there is a racist subtext that denies any systematic interest in the Vietnamese characters and that reduces the black GIs to simplified clichés.[34] In a comparable vein, Tomasulo is right to argue that some of the film's battle sequences glorify violence in a troubling fashion.[35] However, the basic intention, and much of the content of *Apocalypse Now*, problematises purely patriotic attitudes towards American identity. As everyone would accept, even those who now read *Apocalypse Now* as a crypto-conservative evocation, it is a very different perspective on Vietnam from that offered in reactionary work from John Wayne or Sylvester Stallone.

By 1979, the tone of *Apocalypse Now* typified a common form of historical cinema being produced in the United States and Western Europe. The fellow winner at Cannes that year, *The Tin Drum*, sheds further light on the general trend. Adapting Günter Grass's novel from the 1950s, Volker Schlöndorff's film presents German history as a nightmarish experience. Oskar, dwarf-like, and obsessed with playing his toy drum, witnesses the rise of Nazism, the persecution of Jews, as well as the chaos of war and later Soviet invasion. The depiction of Danzig's German-and-Polish-speaking communities in the film is far from sympathetic. Schlöndorff's work strongly invites audiences to read Oskar's madness as a symbol of the folly of the course of German history in the twentieth century. As in Coppola's film, there is a loose conservative subtext as well. The treatment of the only Jewish character in the film is rather stereotypical, and so is the portrayal of the Soviet forces, who are shown to be mainly 'Asiatic' types. Too much audience sympathy is elicited for Oskar and so there is a less critical side to this version of history as well. Shlomo Sand asserts that Schlöndorff's decision to conclude the film's narrative in 1945, unlike in the original novel, implies that the Nazi phase was a parenthesis in German history.[36] Nonetheless, Schlöndorff's feature still demonstrates how much history film-making had developed since the 1950s or early 1960s. Pure realist depiction was now completely out of fashion; any kind of simplistic, nationalist storytelling was abandoned, and works were supposed to look like rich psychologically informed problem plays. Epic commemorations of positive episodes from the past were mainly consigned to history.

Exceptionally high-quality scholarly work has been produced on the so-called 'Nazi-retro' films, including Saul Friedländer's brilliant work on the subject.[37] However, the wider trend of critical history film-making, encompassing radical westerns (*Soldier Blue*; *Pat Garret and Billy the Kidd*; *Bring Me the Head of Alfredo Garcia*), gangster films (*Bonnie and Clyde*; *Chinatown*; *The Godfather I and II*; *Once Upon a Time in America*), literary adaptations or social dramas (*They Shoot Horses Don't They*; *The Great Gatsby*; *Pretty Baby*; *Thieves Like Us*) is overlooked. Moreover, neither subform of 1970s 'retro cinema' has registered in the film/national identity debate. Anthony Smith's model of nationalist cinema rhetoric (film producing nationalist ideology by glorifying history, celebrating national heroes, showing ethnoscapes, and so on) is inadequate in the light of the problematic 1970s material. Similarly, Jeffrey Richards's interpretation that the increase of violence in British film in this period simply reflects growing social unease is equally limited. Such remarks tell us more about this scholar's nostalgia for a pre-Thatcherite Britain than they explain how the new history cinema reshaped perceptions of national identity.[38]

How can one characterise the impact of the critical turn in history film-making? The films presented softer-edged, problematic anti-heroes with different attitudes to patriotism from those more conventional hero figures of the 1950s. If heroes existed at all, they were youthful rebels, cynical detectives or sexually liberal playboys with seemingly few patriotic concerns (the rock-stars Mick Jagger and Bob Dylan starring in several pictures from the era). These men signified a libertarian radicalism that questioned everything about society, including whether the nation should be followed, 'right or wrong'. These films functioned with non-linear, more fantastical, or surrealist, approaches to the representation of time. Notions of chronological national history were undermined and by implication the idea of national progression or 'mission' were made to look obsolete. Greater emphasis was placed on the experiences of individuals interpreted through pseudo-psychoanalytic perspectives.

Such highly personalised forms of narrative replaced concepts of ethnic unity or national collective social bonds. In sum, these discourses tempered or 'softened' national loyalties. They evoked more nuanced patternings of nationhood that acknowledged nation-states' historical records of shame. On the critical wing of the new genre, these films de-legitimised nationalist ideology altogether. More commonly, as with our two brief examples from Cannes 1979, they functioned to open a public space for national guilt and self-reflection – feelings that severely undermined sympathy for hard nationalism. The 1970s historical fantasies prepared Western Europe and North America for models of national-identity affiliation that remain common to the present day. Currently, most liberals retain some sense of national identity but see this as a fairly attenuated allegiance. Works like *Apocalypse Now* implied just this kind of sentiment. The critical history films made it far more problematic to believe in, or to enjoy, heroic patriotic cultural material, except with a dose of irony. Nonetheless, it is necessary to recognise that nationalists, to bolster notions of successful national cinema production in turn, recuperated even this new material. Thus, one found the ironic scenario of works that were hostile to traditional versions of sovereignty still being used to demonstrate the vitality of national cultural production. Here, the meaning of the content of the film was an unimportant side issue. Nationalists simply celebrated how *their* film industries were creating impressive pieces of cinema.

Finally, when considering 1979, it is important to highlight the domination of American film. Besides Coppola's triumph, Woody Allen provided his celebratory hymn to New York, *Manhattan*, and Terence Mallick entered *Days of Heaven*. On the fringes of the festival, the veteran Elia Kazan offered a master-class where he memorably suggested that the director should 'take a little distance ... like God'. Later, the Prize Jury President, Françoise Sagan, complained that the event had gone too far in accommodating American interests. By the end of 1979, she was to claim that undue pressure had been placed on her committee to award Coppola the *Palme d'Or*. Organiser, Robert Favre Le Bret issued strong denials. Next, he retaliated by releasing Sagan's large expenses claim sheet that contained an unpaid 600 dollar hotel telephone bill.[39]

Hollywood's domination of much of the world's cinema screens, of which Cannes 1979 is but one minor illustration, brings with it serious implications for our theme. In short, and one cannot really do justice to the subject in the few paragraphs available here, that phenomenon has had a paradoxical and complex effect on questions of national identity. As already was the case in 1956, a common response to Hollywood has been for national film industries and national film critics to respond by becoming increasingly inward looking to use home advantage to find a niche market. In echoes of the walkouts in Cannes 1956, and reactions to US actors in *The Man Who Never Was*, the rise of American production has raised nationalist intellectual hackles, especially when Hollywood films have made 'mistakes' with other nations' historical records. Thus, one reaction to Hollywood's power has been a defence of national cinema production. This process has itself varied from nation-state to nation-state. Much has probably depended on the relative strength of the film industry and film culture (specialist critical press, and relative popularity of film going) in question.

Mid-sized Western-European nation-states and their film industries have risen to the challenge through a variety of strategies. To generalise, France has attempted to use its credibility as an intellectual and artistic homeland to generate an elite international audience for its film-makers and their products. On the other hand, Britain has sought to use its close linguistic, cultural and historical links to the United States to offer quality literary adaptations that are welcomed in the US and are distinctive from Hollywood cinema. Film-making, supported by the export of quality television series produced by the BBC make for an intriguing and uniquely British film marketing formula. However, much of the European cinematic response to Hollywood is based on unpredictable market factors and variable fashion effects. For example, the Danish film industry witnessed unprecedented success in the 1990s because of a new generation of radical directors who have been able to produce quirky and disturbing cinema that has gained a wide artistic following – the so-called *Dogme* school. Few would have predicted in the early 1980s how fashionable this form of cinema would become. Today, it is easier to foresee that when a movement such as this enters a phase of decline it will prove difficult for Danish cinema to repeat the act.

Irrespective of the rearguard action against Hollywood, national audiences across Western Europe rush to new films from Coppola, Scorcese, Spielberg, Lucas and others. Based on ticket admissions data alone it seems that audiences have relished the American material and neglected domestic fare. The sheer fantasy of American production, including everything from *Star Wars* to the films of Joel and Ethan Coen, has overwhelmed European cinemas without remission. Any contemporary consideration of national identity formation through cinema therefore has to engage with the influence of Hollywood and issues of Americanisation. While the European Union might like to think that it has done much to integrate Europe, at least as much erosion of national cultural distinctions is attributable to Hollywood's ability to produce global pro-US myths.

The main question that this poses is whether audience acceptance of US cinema profoundly changes nation-state citizens' fundamental links to their sense of national identity. Those who love or fear Hollywood probably exaggerate the breaking of the traditional bonds. Taking a different position, Ian Jarvie has argued that this is all just another historical process that should not be too worrisome.[40] However, his comments are surely too modest. One does not have to be a reactionary nationalist intellectual to note the importance of Americanisation. Community realignments to neo-liberal American values on the back of Hollywood's success represent a significant trend in some parts of Europe. As noted above, it is a trend that itself can cause a rise in defensive nationalism, and of course anti-Americanism. To be more optimistic, the very same Hollywood fare might prove useful in quashing extreme forms of popular nationalism by providing quirky, postmodern formations in its place. The sheer dominance of American cinematic material might well eventually erode traditional loyalties and produce new citizen-consumers who are more at home with American cultural-reference points than with domestic literary traditions or once famous episodes from their own national histories. Nationalist intellectuals and journalists frequently label such processes as episodes of cultural decline, or in the British popular rhetoric, 'dumbing down'. From an anti-nationalist perspective the new familiarity with

American popular culture in Europe can be interpreted as a liberationary process for the working class and the lower middle classes, who for decades have in part felt marginalised by overpowering internal elite cultural activity, of which, ironically, the Cannes festival was itself a small exotic part.

Conclusion

Frequently, critics assert that understanding historical context is essential to grasping nationalist–film relations. However, instead of rich historical analysis, theorists in this area focus on just two types of work. The more traditional scholars analyse film classics that are obviously important: D.W. Griffith's *Birth of a Nation* or Abel Gance's *Napoléon*. These scholars' range of analysis is restricted by this selection. The alternative trend is to analyse well-known populist fare and here a prime example is the recent spate of books devoted to *James Bond*. Again, there are clear limitations associated with the tendency. Historically important but not so immediately fashionable works are forgotten and that is a pity because this denies genuine breadth of coverage. This chapter has aimed to revise the above propensity by analysing a body of film festival material, reportage and a range of individual films.

Although not overtly articulated above, and now without naming individual scholars, I consider that too much existing theoretical discussion is oriented around questions of whether 'national cinema' is good or bad, right or wrong, pervasive or more or less non-existent. These are not very refined analytical questions. I have demonstrated that it is potentially more useful to map out how the national–cinema relation works, and the quality of its performance in selected contexts.

The content of a high proportion of individual films can be quickly linked to nationalist discourses. Festivals like Cannes 1956 were major opportunities for this material to be displayed. Scholars, Smith in particular, are correct to analyse cinematic nationalism through comparisons with nationalist tropes once common in fine art. One must also remember that important cinematic works fall outside of Smith's categorisations; the films themselves are more important than the categories used to understand them. Similarly, cinema should not be underestimated because it repeats existing prejudices. Stereotypes are updated through new images. Films can turn old-fashioned attitudes into original and seemingly up-to-date perspectives. Alfred Hitchcock's *The Man Who Knew Too Much* was one brief example of this reworking process.

Common concepts such as 'national cinema' or 'negotiations of the national' are plausible in the light of the case studies. It is important to underline how the nationalism associated with cinematic operations is utterly banal. Clichéd national stereotypes were offered and used in the 1950s; sexist discourses are mingled with patriotic sentiments and applied to 'stars'. More specifically, I have highlighted how journalists' reportage plays a vital role in relaying nationalist readings of cinema to mass readerships. Concepts such as transnationalism, hybridity and universal story-types are of importance. They provide new ways of looking at film and culture. However, I have argued that work on these aspects should not be conducted at the expense of continued reflection on the role of nationalism.

The case of the British war picture *The Man Who Never Was* shows that films that confront symbolically resonant issues are most likely to trigger public negotiations of 'nationhood'. Works that offer nationalists a question to argue over (the appropriateness of foreign actors, the plausibility of historical detail, the orthodoxy or revisionism of an interpretation of an event) are fundamental. These 'national issue films' have attracted nationalist interventions. Any genre can light the flame, so to target historical-works as being especially significant (as claimed by Pierre Sorlin) is an unnecessary refinement. One should recognise that 'international negotiations of nationhood' are common. The history of *Nuit et brouillard* and *A Town Like Alice* at Cannes 1956 represents one sample of the international relations of cinema. Cross-cultural communication between nation-states does not mean a reduction of nationalist thinking. Intra-nationalist antagonism is generated when a foreign director offers challenging depictions of other states or communities. Issues of censorship, distribution policy and review/reception are used to welcome films and their messages, or to expel them back from whence they came. Although my examples are drawn from the 1950s, I see no reason why the model cannot be tested against works from throughout the twentieth century.

Post 1960, a major shift in historical film-making took place. In this era, most history films were based on quasi-critical narratives about the national pasts, typified herein by the examples of *Apocalypse Now* and *The Tin Drum*. These works created popular anti-heroes with few political allegiances. I have argued that works like these contributed to the development of softer identifications with nationhood. These films did not destroy nationalism (American/German) but they established new kinds of nationalist ideology that were more nuanced, less belligerent, more considered and accepting of collective guilt. These films and the identities they inspire do not map onto conventional secondary discussions of nationalist communication in film. Where once there were 'epic historical re-constructions', 'national heroes' and 'poetic landscapes', one finds more personalised narratives, damaged anti-heroes and alternative visions of time and place.

Some major works of cinema have of course not followed the aesthetic and narrative patterns established in the 1970s. For instance, fairly traditional heritage films were a common feature of the British mediascape in the Thatcherite 1980s. Comparable conservative developments can be found in mainstream Hollywood production. In the work of some film-makers, it is almost as if the 1970s cinematic aesthetic had never even happened, as if these directors had failed to spend an hour or two to watch *Apocalypse Now*, let alone *The Tin Drum*. Indeed, this strange kind of aesthetic forgetting is as true of some films from the political left wing, for instance Ken Loach's *Land and Freedom*, as it is of more neo-conservative heritage material. Nevertheless, the legacy of the 1970s continues to influence many other contemporary directors, young and old. Audiences too have come to have certain aesthetic expectations because they have enjoyed the more daring positions, moral complexities and artistic choices, of directors such as a Coppola or a Scorcese, a Schlöndorff, Fassbinder or Wenders, a Louis Malle or a Jean-Luc Godard, a Bertolucci or a Fellini. In other words, I think that the impact of the radical retro-films from the 1970s has yet to run its course.

Paradoxical scenarios have developed. Nationalists, to signify more general collective cultural strengths, have recuperated anti-patriotic films and works that are sceptical about nationhood. Critical films become the pride and joy of national film industries. This phenomenon reminds us that it is nationalists, groups and individuals, who project their views of the world onto art and other cultural forms. In brief, notwithstanding my comments above on how certain works have a greater propensity to attract nationalists, the content of a film need not matter for it to be raised up for patriotic consideration.

The impact of Hollywood and Americanisation is significant. Cinema has acted as a key means for the United States to tell stories about itself to mass audiences around the world. Anti-American nationalist reactions have developed, as too have generations of cinema audiences who thrill to the latest Hollywood import. It is silly to panic about this process. Conversely, it is negligent to deny its existence, or to ignore its multiple and complex effects. To take this position is to abandon the issue to the conservative right-wing which is more than willing to think about identity, culture and nationhood. More work is needed in this critical field and as the new century unfolds it is clear that the question of America and Hollywood will demand our attention for years to come.

Notes

1. For general histories of the festival, see Pierre Billard, *D'or et de palmes*, Paris, 1997; the official guide, anon., *Cannes Memories: Festival International du film de Cannes: Album Officiel du 50ᵉ Anniversaire*, Montreuil, 1997; Serge Toubiana, *Cannes-Cinéma: Cinquante ans de festival vus par Traverso*, Paris, 1997; Kenneth Turan, *Sundance to Sarajevo: Film Festivals and the World They Made*, London, 2002. See also the recently published, Kieron Corless and Chris Darke, *Cannes*, London, 2007.
2. Ernest Gellner, *Nationalism*, New York, 1998.
3. For further discussion of this film-maker, see Kees Bakker, 'Haanstra' in Ian Aitken, ed., *Encylopedia of Documentary Film*, New York, 2006: 535–36.

4. Darius Cooper, *Satyajit Ray: Between Tradition and Modernity*, Cambridge, 2003; for Bergman, see Jesse Kalin, *The Films of Ingmar Bergman*, Cambridge, 2003; Marc Gervais, *Ingmar Bergman: Magician and Prophet*, McGill, 1999: 42–44.

5. Anthony Smith, 'Images of the Nation: Cinema, Art and National Identity', Mette Hjort and Scott Mackenzie, eds, *Cinema and Nation*, London, 2000: 45–60.

6. Remarkably, Neame caste a young, then unknown, Peter Sellers to 'voiceover' for Churchill. See Ronald Neame with Barbara Roisman Cooper, *Straight from the Horses Mouth – Ronald Neame an Autobiography*, London, 2003: 149.

7. Alan Williams 'Introduction' in Williams, ed., *Film and Nationalism*, London, 2002: 6–8.

8. Susan Suleiman, *Authoritarian Fictions: The Ideological Novel as a Literary Genre*, New York, 1983.

9. See Elsie B. Michie, 'Hitchcock and American Domesticity', in Jonathan Freeman and Richard Millington, eds, *Hitchcock's America*, Oxford, 1999: 29–53.

10. Various national delegation catalogues are held at the British Film Institute Library for the Cannes 1956 festival, specifically the complete British delegation catalogue, Dutch materials and the Soviet catalogue.

11. The economic motivations to make film a nationalist cultural product are fully displayed at Cannes in the mid-1950s. My micro-history case study begins to confirm the 'economic thesis on the origins of national cinema'. See, for example, Valentina Valenti and Paul Willemen, 'Introduction' in their own edited collection, *Theorising National Cinema*, London, 2006.

12. Toni Howard, 'Whingding of the Movie Queens', *Saturday Evening Post* (18 August 1956): 51.

13. Leonard Mosely, 'Russians Snub Diana Dors', *Daily Express* (3 May 1956) – the offending film was the comedy about a sanitary engineer who is mistaken for an atomic scientist, *Top Secret*. For the record it is worth recalling that Cannes 1956 took place just a few months prior to the Suez crisis and the Hungarian uprising.

14. Andrew Higson, 'The Concept of National Cinema', *Screen* 30, 4, 1989: 39–47; Susan Hayward, *French National Cinema*, London, 1993: 1–17. See also Valentina Valenti and Paul Willemen, eds, *Theorising National Cinema*.

15. Valentina Vitali and Paul Willemen, *Theorising National Cinema*, assert in the 'Introduction' to their collection that film historians have much to answer for because of framing film production through national historical narratives. This might well be so. However, to be fair, one has to note that journalists set the popular tone rather more emphatically and on a daily basis as compared to the influence of early film scholars or historians. The boundaries between film history writing and journalism were of course permeable and that is a subject that merits further research.

16. Michael Billig, *Banal Nationalism*, London, 1995.

17. Anthony Carthew, 'Enter Irina, Looking Like a Scarecrow', *Daily Herald* (2 May 1956).

18. See, among others, Susan Hayward 'Framing National Cinemas' in Hjort and Mackenzie, eds, *Cinema and Nation*, 88–102.

19. In addition to the works cited above, see also Michael Walsh, 'National Cinema, National Imaginary', *Film History* 8, 1996: 5–17.

20. Pierre Sorlin, *Italian National Cinema*, London, 1996. Sorlin argues for the 'universal' nature of film in his framing discussion: 1–15. Various samples of the 'film is global or transnational' thesis are found in Alan Williams's and Mette Hjort and Scott Mackenzie's collections. See also Geoffrey Nowell Smith and Steven Ricci, eds, *Hollywood and Europe: Economics, Culture, National Identity 1945–1995*, London, 1998.

21. Higson, ibid.; Williams, ibid.; see also John Hill, 'British Cinema as National Cinema' in Vitali and Willemans, eds, *Theorising National Identity*.

22. Sue Harper and Vincent Porter, *British Cinema of the 1950s*, Oxford, 2003: 131.

23. For brevity of referencing, see the extensive dossier of reviews held as 'Press Cuttings' Microfiche, *The Man Who Never Was*, BFI Library, London, England.

24. It should be noted that security tensions were disproportionately high in the naval town that year. Just a few weeks after the film identity cards scare (13 March 1956) the city was the setting for the Lionel 'Buster' Crabb affair in which a British diver disappeared while investigating the Soviet vessel 'Ordzhonikidze' which was moored in harbour and which had brought the Soviet leader Khrushchev for meetings with Prime Minister Eden.

25. 'M.P. and Film', *The Times* (9 March 1956); 'M.P. to Urge Ban on Film', *Daily Telegraph* (9 March 1956); and for the Portsmouth scare, 'Identity Card for Film', *The Times* (13 March 1956). The same M.P., Cordeaux, was to protest against the portrayal of Nottingham working class life in the film *Saturday Night and Sunday Morning*. The discussion of film by politicians in national parliamentary chambers remains a completely under-researched subject among scholars in 'film studies'. Thanks go to Virginia Manvell for the useful reference to Cordeaux's attack on *Saturday Night and Sunday Morning*.

26. See, 'French Asked Not to Show Film at Cannes', *The Times* (19 April 1956). The most detailed historical account of the diplomatic wrangling leading up to the festival is found in the excellent: Richard Raskin, *Nuit et Brouillard: On the Making, Reception and Function of a Major Documentary Film*, Aarhus, 1987: 33–36; perceptive contextual work is also found in Christian Delage and Vincent Guigueno, *L'historien et le film*, Paris, 2004: 60; recent further important contributions include, Ewout Van der Knaap, *De Verbeelding van Nacht und Nevel*, Groningen, 2001; Ewout Van der Knaap, ed., *Uncovering the Holocaust*, London, 2006. As is well known, the film was not shown 'in Festival' but was screened 'out of competition'.

27. See among others, 'No Town Like Alice', *Daily Mail* (28 March 1956); 'Don't Be Beastly', *The Star* (29 March 1956); 'A Matter of Honour', *Evening News* (29 March 1956); in particular, the thoughtful article 'Only Amiable Films Need Apply', *The Times* (20 April 1956). The British–Japanese episode is noted briefly in Raskin, *Nuit et brouillard*: 35.

28. 'Finns Quit Festival', *Daily Telegraph* (8 May 1956); 'Finnish Film Out of Festival', *Star* (7 May 1956).

29. See 'Film Festival Walk-out', *The Sunday Times* (29 April 1956); 'Cannes: Objection to Showing of West German Film', *Times* (30 April 1956); and 'Vexed Germans Scram Cannes…', *Variety* (2 May 1956). See also Raskin, *Nuit et brouillard*, 42–43

30. For generational questions in West German memory and historiography of the Nazi period, see Wulf Kansteiner, 'Between Politics and Memory: The *Historikerstreit* and West German Historical Culture of the 1980s', in Richard Golsan, ed., *Fascism's Return: Scandal, Revision, and Ideology since 1980*, Lincoln, 1998: 108–11. Work therein builds on the earlier studies of Karl Mannheim and Helmut Schlesky; for full refereneces, see Kansteiner's extensive footnote no. 72: 127–28.

31. For a wide-ranging international comparison of historiographic interchange since 1945, see Stefan Berger, 'A Return to the National Paradigm? National History Writing in Germany, France and Britain, 1945 to the Present', *Journal of Modern History* 77, 3, 2005.

32. Robert Paxton, *Vichy France: Old Guard and New Order 1940–1944*, New York, 1972; see also Henry Rousso, 'L'historien, lieu de mémoire', in Rousso, ed., *Vichy, L'événement, la mémoire, l'histoire*, Paris, 2001: 453–85; and Ruth Zylberman, 'Robert Paxton. Un Américain tranquille à Vichy', *L'Histoire* 203, 1996: 20.

33. 'Deux conférences de presse sur *Apocalypse Now*', *Positif* 220/2, July/August, 1979: 6–9.

34. Gilbert Adair, *Hollywood's Vietnam*, London, 1989: 101–20.

35. Frank Tomasulo, 'The Politics of Ambivalence: *Apocalypse Now* as Prowar and Antiwar Film', in Linda Dittmar and S. Michand, eds *From Hanoi to Hollywood*, London, 1990: 145–58. For a more general analysis in this area, see H. Bruce Franklin, *Vietnam and Other American Fantasies*, London, 2000; and the equally persuasive Philip D. Beidler, *Late Thoughts on an Old War: The Legacy of Vietnam*, London, 2004. I have a great deal of sympathy with many of the critical views expressed on Vietnam war culture in the US presented in these works but consider *Apocalypse Now* to be too ambiguous to be read as simply a piece of reactionary cinema.

36. Shlomo Sand, *Le XXe Siècle à l'écran*, Paris, 2004: 267. For analysis of Schlöndorff's career, see Thomas Elsaesser, *New German Cinema*, London, 1989: 123; Thilo Wydra, *Volker Schlöndorff und seine Filme*, Munich, 1998.

37. Saul Friedländer, *Reflets sur le Nazisme*, Paris, 1982.

38. Jeffrey Richards, *Films and British National Identity: From Dickens to 'Dad's Army'*, Manchester, 1997: 170–72, wherein Richards reduces Hollywood production to 'musclemen' and 'violence chic' and in so doing overlooks the popular and more complex work noted herein. The 'abyss of Thatcherism' leads Richards to similarly pessimistic comments on the legacy of British cinema of the 1950s and 1960s; see his essay in Bart Moore-Gilbert and John Seed, eds, *Cultural Revolution?*, London, 1992: 218–35. Thoughtful discussion on identity questions and 1970s Hollywood film is found in several contributions to Thomas Elsaesser, Alexander Horwath and Noel King, eds, *The Last Great American Picture Show*, Amsterdam, 2004.

39. '7 Months Later, Sagan Says *"Apocalypse" Win Was "Pressured"'*, *Variety* (19 December 1979).

40. Ian Jarvie, 'Free Trade as Cultural Threat: American Film and TV Exports in the Post-War Period' in Geoffrey Nowell-Smith and Steven Ricci, eds, *Hollywood and Europe*: 42–44.

PART IV

NARRATING THE NATION AS ART AND MUSIC

Chapter 10

From Discourse to Representation: 'Austrian Memory' in Public Space

HEIDEMARIE UHL

In the field of memory studies one can distinguish, within ideal-typical contexts, two dominant concepts that Aleida Assmann has vividly characterised as a relationship of tension between 'solid' and 'liquid':

> We constantly encounter the 'liquid' forms of memory in the discursive and visual surroundings of communication society: narrations about the past of the collective – the nation – in various formats: from the fictional plot of TV crime thrillers (for instance, the episode of the 'Tatort' (Scene of a Crime) series produced by ÖRF (Austrian Radio and Television) about the restitution of the 'Aryanized' paintings of Egon Schiele to historical writings; from political statements, for example, on the assessment of May 1945 as the liberation or the occupation – the latter being a comment made by a politician from the Austrian Freedom Party (FPÖ) – to the documented stories told by witnesses about the crimes of the Nazi regime.[1]

In contrast, the 'solid' forms of social memory are visibly manifested in the public representations of memory in monuments and on commemorative plaques, in museums and exhibitions, during anniversaries and on days of remembrance. Furthermore, through the associated rituals, we observe the 'crystallisation' that Jan Assmann described as 'cultural formations', where public memory is visibly expressed by way of 'fateful events of the past', i.e. defined both for contemporaries and for future generations as the binding historical points of reference for the collective. According to Assmann, these signs are directed above all at the present and future of communities: 'A society becomes visible for itself and for others through its cultural tradition. Which past it decides to make visible and cause to appear in the value perspective of its identificatory appropriation tells us something about what it is and what it wants.'[2]

While Assmann speaks of 'society' and 'collectives', in his concept of 'lieux de mémoire' Pierre Nora defines sites of memory as 'sites, in every sense, in which the memory of the [...] nation is particularly condensed, embodied or crystallised'.[3] As such, he views memory as an 'inventory of national identity', a construction of identity that refers, by definition, to positive points of reference, to the historical 'heritage' of the nation.[4] National memory is generally drawn from events with positive associations or from historical points of reference that have as their theme a 'common' experience of suffering.

The argument I would like to put forward here is that historical narratives of the nation, especially, in the successor states of the Third Reich , in the European states affected by the Nazi regime and also elsewhere, have undergone transformations since the 1980s, at the time when the question of the 'guilt of nations'[5] entered the agenda of memory culture. The question of guilt refers both to the content, i.e. the historical points of reference, and to the intentions or imaginations connected with national memory.

According to historian Tony Judt, we may refer to this process as the deconstruction of political myths constructed in the European post-war period. Since 1945 the view of history in practically all countries that had been in the National Socialist sphere of influence was characterised by a partial amnesia that presented each nation's population as either victims of cruel oppression by the Nazi dictators or as a heroic resistance movement. Since the beginning of the 1980s, public discussions in many of these countries have revolved around the question of the involvement of each country's own society in the Nazi regime apparatus and their participation in the National Socialist politics of annihilation. Indicative of these discussions were the German historians' and the Waldheim disputes, which both took place in 1986, debates concerning the 'Wehrmacht exhibition' in the latter half of the 1990s and the persisting controversies regarding the involvement of the local population in the murder of Jews in Jedwabne in Poland.[6] The emotional charge and conflict potential of these debates can be explained, as Jan Assman has already noted, by their relevance to the present day. The matter under discussion, then and now, is not the past itself but rather the ethical, moral foundations of current political culture.

Since the beginning of the 1980s, the renegotiations of national historical identity with regard to the place of National Socialism in national memory have become a signature of European political culture. The heroic, pathos-laden memory of national resistance, the 'struggle for freedom', was criticised by many as 'false memory', as forgetting and suppressing joint responsibility for the Nazi crimes. Therefore, it was now necessary to find new forms of commemoration for a 'negative memory' and the 'guilt' of the nation.[7]

The realignment of the treatment of the past became manifest in the signs made by a new culture of memory in public spaces. This has seen the installation of the Holocaust monuments in Vienna, Berlin, Paris and other European capitals, and also in smaller towns; the institution of national Holocaust remembrance days in Germany, France, Italy, Great Britain, Sweden and the USA; and new museums and exhibitions such as the Holocaust Museum which opened in Budapest in 2004. These all indicate that the Holocaust, the 'breach of civilisation' (as Dan Diner put it), has become a focus of memory culture in many countries as a historical point of reference for a European self-image that sees itself as an antithesis to National Socialism. Against this backdrop, 27 January, the day of liberation of the Auschwitz concentration camp, and since 1996 official remembrance day in Germany for the victims of the National Socialist tyranny, has increasingly become a remembrance day of European dimensions.

In the following chapter I will describe this transformation process by looking at the example of changes in 'Austrian memory' in relation to the Nazi period (1938–1945).[8] This will highlight and analyse the change of the historical point of reference in memory culture from the 'Austrian struggle for freedom' to the new commemorative culture for the victims of the Holocaust. The eclipsing and paling of heroic, pathos-laden memory rituals in the name of the nation, and the cultural formations of a 'memory of guilt' are presented below through the examples of four monuments in Vienna. These are: the monument for the victims of the city of Vienna, planned and erected between 1945 and 1948; the memorial for the Austrian struggle for freedom (1965); the disputed memorial against the war and Fascism in Albertinaplatz (1988); and the Holocaust monument in Judenplatz designed by the British artist Rachel Whiteread (2000).[9]

What these monuments all have in common is the fact that they are designed as representations of the memory of the entire collective, i.e. the City of Vienna or the Republic of Austria, and that they were designed as representatives of the memory of the entire nation, and thus express a hegemonic narrative. However, the fact that these monuments must be seen as material statements in a contested space becomes visible in the conflicts concerning the representation of the National Socialist period in cultural memory, which constitute the context of these monumental projects.

Commemorating the Austrian Struggle for Freedom in the Period Immediately after the War

The first monumental memorial acknowledging the National Socialist regime in Vienna was erected just a few weeks after the end of the war by the Soviet occupation authorities in order to commemorate the fallen soldiers of the Red

Army. This extensive memorial, featuring an almost twelve-metre bronze figure of the Soviet soldier was the only major monument commemorating the Nazi period in the city until the 'Monument against War and Fascism' was erected in 1988.

Although the Soviet liberation monument, unveiled on 19 August 1945, was dedicated to the fallen Red Army soldiers, the Russian inscription on the colonnades reads 'Eternal salvation to the heroes of the Red Army who fell in battle against the German-Fascist land-looters for the freedom and independence of the peoples of Europe'.[10] The unveiling ceremony was also an opportunity for the leading Austrian politicians, such as Chancellor Karl Renner (Social Democratic Party), People's Party State Secretary, and later Federal Chancellor Leopold Figl and the Communist State Secretary Ernst Fischer, to emphasise the interpretation of the Nazi era that conformed to the victim theory as the ideology underlying the foundation of the Second Republic. This was expressed, for instance, in Leopold Figl's speech: 'For seven years the Austrian people languished under Hitler's barbarism. For seven years these Austrian people were subjugated and oppressed, no opinions were allowed, no declaration of belief, brutal terror and violence coerced people into a situation of blind servitude.' Yet 'faith in Austria', he maintained, had become the driving force of patriotic resistance supported by all sections of the population: 'In factories and offices, at the front and at home, silently and successfully Hitler's state was being sabotaged [...] We, true Austrians, (stood) on the side of the soldiers of the Allied forces.'[11] Figl's remarks corresponded to the experiences of the political elites of the founding generation of the Second Republic. As a leading figure of the corporative state, he had been imprisoned in the concentration camps Dachau and Mauthausen and jailed in Vienna, and only the fast advance of the Soviet army saved him from a certain death sentence.[12] These experiences were communicated to the entire 'Austrian people'.

The inauguration of the Viennese liberation monument gives an exemplary insight into the way the war and National Socialism were dealt with in public discourse immediately after the war. The view of the Nazi era followed the victim theory, as expressed in the declaration of independence on 27 April 1945. Employing a literal reference to the Moscow declaration of the Allied foreign ministers of 30 October 1943, Austria was described as 'the first free country to fall a victim to the Hitlerite aggression'. The '*Anschluss*' (annexation) of March 1938 was referred to as an occupation which 'was forced upon the Austrian people, who were rendered helpless' by a 'large-scale military intervention'.[13]

During the first years of the Second Republic, monuments were set up to commemorate the victims of the resistance. Commemorative ceremonies were held and political declarations made by the three founding parties of the Second Republic, the Austrian People's Party (ÖVP), the Social Democratic

Party (SPÖ), and the Communist Party (KPÖ), all honouring the struggle for freedom as the foundation stone of an independent and democratic Austria.

However, the 'anti-fascist' political consensus regarding the assessment of the past soon started to crumble. This began as early as November 1945 with the National Assembly elections, which produced the landslide victory for two of the major parties. Contrary to the general expectations, the Communist party, who associated most strongly with the resistance fight, and who singularly continued to identify unreservedly with the Austrian struggle for freedom, gained only five per cent of the vote. The process of consolidating relations with the Western occupying powers also diminished the cogency of a sense of justification based on resistance. At the outbreak of the Cold War, the policy of isolating the Communist Party intensified.[14] The amnesty laws of 1948 created new underlying conditions, while at the same time the ÖVP and the SPÖ intensified their efforts to win over former National Socialists, mainly in an attempt to tap into the considerable pool of voters of 'less incriminated persons' who were eligible to vote for the first time in the national elections of 1949.[15] Although the *Verband der Unabhängigen*, or Federation of Independents, the precursor of today's Freedom Party (FPÖ), proclaimed itself champion of the ex-National Socialists, both major parties also endeavoured to gain votes from the nationalist camp. The abatement of the anti-fascist 'spirit of 1945', and the revaluation of former National Socialists following their social rehabilitation, made a 'truly political taboo' of the subject of resistance by the end of the 1940s.[16]

This new political orientation was also reflected in new monuments. The last notable regional monuments were dedicated to victims of the Nazi regime at the end of the 1940s, and they were increasingly beset by political conflicts between the main parties, who were trying to distance themselves from the Communist Party and the *KZ-Verband* (Concentration Camp Inmate Association), whose key demands still included honouring the resistance. One particularly cogent example of different ideological interpretations of the National Socialist period that characterised the culture of commemoration in Vienna from the end of the 1940s until the 1980s is the monument for the victims of fascism which was unveiled at the main cemetery of Vienna on 1 November 1948.

The unveiling was an official commemorative ceremony led by Vice-Chancellor Schärf (SPÖ) as a representative of the Federal government, the Minister of Education Felix Hurdes (ÖVP), and the mayor of Vienna, Theodor Körner (SPÖ). The monument, designed by Fritz Cremer, was intended to express the struggle for freedom, the condemnation of fascism, and mourning for the victims.[17] Although the inscription on the monument was dedicated to 'The Victims for a Free Austria 1934 to 1945', and was beyond doubt intended to be a 'Socialist' monument commemorating the Social Democratic uprising that was quashed by the corporative state dictatorship in February

1934, the ceremony was greatly influenced by an attempt to reconcile both camps. Mayor Körner did not explicitly make reference to the 'sore point' of the period 1934–1938. Instead he spoke of a 'monument that commemorates the tragedy of an entire people and that is dedicated to all the dead' who 'fell victim to political oppression and finally cruel tyranny of superior strength in the fateful years from 1938 to 1945 in the battle for a free Austria'.

Although the unveiling of the monument took place against the background of the rapprochement between the former civil war opponents of 1934 who now shared the government in the Grand Coalition, the divergent views about the recent conflict were being expressed at the parties' separate commemorative ceremonies. Immediately after the ceremony, the Socialist participants, 'a mighty column', behind the forest of flags, headed by Vice-Chancellor Dr Schärf and mayor Mr Körner', moved on to the grave of the executed fighter of the February 1934 uprising, Georg Weissel, to attend the inauguration of a memorial stone donated by the trade union. The commemoration was concluded with the 'Internationale'.[18]

The same day, a commemorative cross was unveiled at the Vienna central cemetery, erected by the Communist Party's *KZ-Verband*. The speakers commemorated victims of a felonious regime, vowing to 'avenge their blood guilt'. However, the condemnation was, above all, addressed to those who were reluctant to take into account the interwar period and the integration of the National Socialists: 'Are we to forget the days [of the February uprising of 1934] when cannons were aimed at people's homes? Are we to forget the days in March 1938 when they started to trample on human dignity? Are we to forget that we were treated like animals and humiliated?' The Communist Party's commemorative ceremony was the only one at which a representative of the Jewish community commemorated the Jewish victims. In general though the Holocaust did not become part of the narrative of the Austrian victim theory until the 1980s.[19]

The commemorative ceremonies of November 1948 illustrate the culture of memory pursued by official representatives of Vienna as a field of symbolic politics whose logic was based upon party political interests. Reference to the Nazi past opened up possibilities of consensus and reconciliation for the Social Democrats and the People's Party. In their search for a historical identity transcending party borders, they sought to establish common ground on the basis of the facts related to the oppression of both parties, the imprisonment of their leaders in concentration camps and the resultant 'Geist der Lagerstraße' (the spirit of solidarity that unified concentration camp inmates of all political persuasions who had overcome their political differences).[20]

Yet, since the late 1940s, the monuments for the victims of the Austrian freedom struggle had played only a limited role in the Austrian culture of commemoration. The monument landscape in the Federal provinces had been dominated by memorials of the fallen soldiers since the end of the 1940s.

However, in Vienna commemorations of the victims of National Socialism, apart from specific party rituals, were much disputed. An example of these tensions is provided by the installation of a commemorative plaque for the cabaret artist Fritz Grünbaum by the Dachau and Buchenwald camp associations in 1955. Members of the concentration camp inmate associations who had been imprisoned together with Grünbaum wanted to set up a monument, but soon realised that 'none of the authorities or individuals contacted were prepared to take any action in this matter'. Particularly, the director of *Kabarett Simpl*, although he himself had been 'persecuted because of his ancestry', was opposed to installing a commemorative plaque, fearing demonstrations and a drop in the number of visitors. The plaque was only put up after lengthy negotiations with the local landlord. However, the inscription avoided any suggestion that Grünbaum had been persecuted, either for political or 'racial' reasons. Instead, it read, 'He was a good Austrian and lost his life in a concentration camp for this declaration of belief.'[21]

Analysis of the monument landscape in Vienna shows that the civil war in February 1934 and the political resistance to National Socialism were the main points of reference in the anti-fascist culture of commemoration in the post-war period. In contrast, Commemoration of the murdered Jews of Vienna generated only marginal public interest. Mostly, such commemorations were monuments set up by the Jewish communities, often in semi-public or indoor areas, as, for example, the commemorative plaque for the 'Jewish men, women and children who lost their lives in the fateful years of 1938–1945', unveiled in 1946 in the synagogue in Seitenstettengasse in the centre of Vienna.[22] The lack of high-profile Jewish memorials reveals the fact that the 'Jewish issue' constituted a 'void' in Vienna's culture of commemoration.[23]

Commemorating the Fallen Soldier as a Culture of Commemoration: Creating Identity in the Federal Provinces

While it was politically complicated to set up monuments for the Austrian fight for freedom outside Vienna, a strong movement for building war memorials appeared at the beginning of the 1950s. Not only were such memorials created later than the memorials for the resistance, they were also intended to provide an antithesis to this view of history. The 'Hero Memorials' for the soldiers who fell in action were initially seen as a change of paradigm with regard to how to deal with the National Socialist era. 'From now on', one newspaper commentary on the memorial of 1949 stated, 'the soldiers who fell in the Second World War will also take a place of honour in the memories of our people'. Not, however, as victims of the war as 'it is not true that all the hundreds of thousands of people were driven to death by a cunning system' but rather as 'brave heroes fulfilling their duty'.[24]

The war memorials from this period should not be seen only as commemorations of the fallen soldiers but equally as signs of the rehabilitation of the former Wehrmacht soldiers. Between 1949 and 1950, this category of monuments came to be the standard practice of collective memory. While only a small number of resistance memorials were built in Austria (with the exception of Vienna), in the 1950s practically every village or town in the country had a war memorial erected, or extended its monument commemorating the fallen soldiers from the First World War. This monument movement was supported by the *Kameradschaftsbund* (War Veteran Association) and its precursor organisations, a veteran association in which the former servicemen from the two World Wars promoted the 'positive image of the soldiers of World War Two'.[25] The support that this undertaking met with in the public was reflected in the monuments, as they expressed the fact that 'the homeland was again standing by its fallen sons who fell in fierce battle by renewing and redesigning war memorials.'[26]

It must be noted that, since the early 1950s, the activities of the war veteran associations had encouraged growth into mass organisations numbering tens of thousands of members. They were supported by all political parties, a situation in which tactical electoral considerations played a significant role. However, this defence of the 'honour' of the soldiers of the *Wehrmacht* also severely challenged the legitimacy of the resistance. If fulfilling one's duty is a standard of honourable behaviour, then resistance against the Nazi regime is pushed into the realm of 'betrayal, revolt and resistance against the legal power', as *Der Kamerad* wrote in April 1963. The *Kameradschaftsbund* made no secret of this stance: 'As front-line soldiers we have nothing, absolutely nothing, in common with our compatriots who took up arms and killed, struck dead or betrayed our own comrades.'[27]

By 1963, however, the first reactions emerged that opposed the view of history that married the rehabilitation of the soldiers of the *Wehrmacht* with the defamation of the resistance. This was instigated by the refusal of the *Kameradschaftsbund* of Lower Austria to take part in the dedication of a memorial in Maria Langegg commemorating both fallen soldiers and priests murdered in concentration camps. This was because they did not want the 'honest soldiers who wore the cloth, kept their oath and died for it' to be put on the same level as 'all kinds of manifestations of a contrary nature'.[28] The minister of the interior Franz Olah (SPÖ) thereupon issued a decree banning the *Kameradschaftsbund* from organising a march. Although this ban was lifted after the resignation of the provincial chairman of the *Kameradschaftsbund* of Lower Austria, this incident indicated the emergence of socio-political change in connection with the incipient student movement that expressed its political views in the form of its 'anti-fascist commitment' (for instance, in demonstrations against acquittals in war crimes trials).

In the mid-1950s, social upheaval began to emerge in Austria, and new post-war generations encouraged both main parties to develop new political models. Differences between the political camps were exacerbated by debates surrounding issues of 'modernisation' and 'democratisation', which became the buzzwords of a new phase of reform marked domestically by the end of the Grand Coalition, followed by a single-party Conservative government (1966) and, after 1970, Socialist governments ('the Kreisky era'). The growing consolidation of an Austrian consciousness was confirmed in 1965 by the National Assembly, unanimously voting to adopt October 26 as a national holiday,[29] the politicisation of the student youth, the so-called generation of 1968; and the emergence of a new type of critical journalism also contributed to long-term changes in the underlying conditions of historical awareness.[30]

Against the background of the Taras Borodajkewycz affair, the discussions on commemoration also began to show signs of change. The German-National and anti-Semitic statements made by the professor at the Vienna Academy of World Trade sparked off demonstrations of supporters and opponents alike during which one demonstrator, the former Communist resistance fighter Ernst Kirchweger, was killed at the beginning of April 1965.[31] This coincided with the 20th anniversary of the Austrian declaration of independence, when a room dedicated to the memory of the Austrian fight for freedom was inaugurated at the Äußeres Burgtor of Vienna's Hofburg, the first state monument commemorating the resistance to be erected by the Republic of Austria.[32] The political declarations made on this anniversary contained unmistakeable and clear denunciations of National Socialism. Representatives of the second republic were clearly shocked by the political violence surrounding the Borodajkewycz affair. In his noteworthy speech at the joint commemorative meeting of the National Assembly and Federal Council in parliament, the president of the National Council, Alfred Maleta (People's Party), affirmed that 'we will not let this house that we have built be set on fire'. Maleta acknowledged that 'the former National Socialists must be integrated in democratic society', but also unambiguously stated that: 'We pardoned people, but we will not accept views of history close to National Socialism.'[33] The memorial room for the 'victims in the fight for Austria's freedom' (as the inscription reads) is located in the immediate vicinity of the war memorial of the corporative state for the military victims of the First World War; the monument was consecrated in 1934 and after 1945 it was also re-dedicated to the soldiers who fell during the Second World War.

At the unveiling ceremony, representatives of the Social Democrats and the People's Party unanimously declared their belief that the Resistance to National Socialism was crucial in legitimating Austria's Second Republic. Thus, the government, for the first time, gave to the political victims of National Socialism the same status as the fallen soldiers of the *Wehrmacht*. As a signal from the official representatives of Austria, the memorial room marked the end of the period in which the official view of history was characterised by the rapprochement with the former National Socialists and by the renewal of the consensus of the political elites of both major parties with regard to how history should be seen in order to fit the victim theory. Since then the two parallel monuments have become a symbol of the separate cultures of commemoration and contradictory narratives of the Nazi past, something that has also been underscored by separate commemorative ceremonies at state festivities. On the one hand, the commemoration of the struggle for freedom, and, on the other hand, the commemoration of the fallen soldiers of the Wehrmacht constitute two separate and distinct sides of the public commemoration culture in Austria.

Landmarks of a New Culture of Commemoration since the 1980s

The deconstruction of the Austrian political post-war myth of the victim theory was provoked by the Waldheim debate. In the debate surrounding the war record of the ÖVP-candidate for the federal presidency and former general secretary of the UN, Kurt Waldheim,[34] Austria was finally, in 1986, confronted with 'its own' Nazi past. Waldheim's remark that 'I did nothing more during the war than did hundreds of thousands of other Austrians, which was to fulfill my duties as a soldier'[35] abruptly brought the contradictions of the post-war conceptions of history to light, especially regarding the judgement about Austrians in the German Wehrmacht.

With regard to the culture of commemoration, for the first time Austrians began to consider that there had been other victims of National Socialist crimes such as Austrian Jews, Roma, Sinti, homosexuals and disabled and other victim groups affected by enforced euthanasia programmes. The Hrdlicka monument at Albertinaplatz square and the Holocaust monument at Judenplatz square became part of a broader movement of symbolic reparation. The origins of what are probably the most notable monuments in Vienna constructed since 1945 clearly illustrate both the potential for conflict of public commemoration of the 'dark sides' of history and the problems involved in looking for a new consensus about the past beyond that of victim theory.

The first design for an 'anti-fascist monument' was submitted by Alfred Hrdlicka in 1978 in a competition for the redesign of Stock-im-Eisen-Platz square in the immediate vicinity of St Stephens's cathedral. The idea was taken up by Vienna's then councillor of cultural affairs, Helmut Zilk. During the search for a suitable location – 'a busy square frequented by pedestrians' – the choice finally fell on the centrally located Albertinaplatz square near the opera. In August 1983 a contract was concluded between the municipal authorities of Vienna and Alfred Hrdlicka concerning the erection of a monument at Albertinaplatz square, and in September the same year the monument was unanimously approved by the Vienna council. The initiative was backed those opposed to the project began to voice their opinions in the influential newspapers *Die Presse* and *Kronenzeitung*. The latter was vociferous in its criticism in the months prior to the unveiling on 24 November 1988, conducting an all-out campaign against the monument, which had also become a bone of contention between the main political parties. The opposition parties, the People's Party and, above all, the Freedom Party, now declared themselves against the project leaving only the Social Democrats to back it.[36] The 'kulturkampf' between the right and the left focused on the location of the monument in the city centre. However, in addition to the superficial question of the location, the opposition was primarily concerned about the design of the monumental ensemble, which rendered the theme in a drastic, realistic manner and focused on the indictment of the perpetrators, not the commemoration of the victims.[37]

Hrdlicka's 'monument against war and fascism', which along with the performance of Thomas Bernhard's 'Heldenplatz' at the Burgtheater were among the much-disputed cultural manifestations of a 'different Austria' during the year of commemoration in 1988, lacks contemporary significance when considered within the context of the intense debates that accompanied its creation. However, the ambivalence of its perspective on the Nazi past, which revealed the blind spots of an 'anti-fascist' understanding of history, raises some significant questions. Does a combined commemoration of the victims of war and tyranny blur the difference between perpetrators and victims? Does the reproduction of the government's declaration of April 1945 as a keystone in the historical reconstruction, represented by the monument, give new birth to the victim theory?

It was, however, the figure of the 'street-washing Jew', a reference to the pogrom-like violence in March 1938 when Viennese Jews were forced to clean corporative state slogans from the streets, that proved to be the real bone of contention. Not only Jewish critics saw this portrayal as a 'perpetual repetition of that humiliation'.[38] For Ruth Beckermann it transports what is the actual message of the monument, the marginalisation of the Jewish view, which is also handed down in the debate on history in terms of social criticism: 'Whatever this monument wants to tell the people of Vienna, it tells me: you lay in the dirt. You crawled on your bellies. And that is the way we see you today [...] This monument is suited for the city without Jews.'[39]

The Holocaust monument in Judenplatz square in the first district of Vienna places this commemoration at the heart of the symbolic area of the city, also as a sign that 'Vienna is conscious of its historical guilt and its living obligations to the Jewish citizens of this city and this country'.[40] The Viennese monument commemorating the expulsion and murder of the Jewish population – like the monument for the murdered Jews of Europe installed in Berlin – draws our attention to the fact that the Holocaust has become a focus of official commemoration, while at the same time it can be seen as a response to experience with the Hrdlicka monument. The discussion was initiated by Simon Wiesenthal, who advanced the argument that the street-washing Jew was a 'monument of humiliation'.[41] With regard to its purpose, the memorial for the Jewish victims of National Socialism was not an indictment of the 'society of perpetrators'; rather it was intended to be a worthy place of commemoration for the victims of the Holocaust. The concept of the design refrained from any figured representation as this could not 'do justice to the monstrosity of this crime'.[42] In view of the doubts as to whether art is capable of expressing what we cannot comprehend, for Amnon Barzel, one of the judges of the art competition, 'emptiness itself becomes a possible element in designing a Holocaust monument'. Rachel Whiteread's award-winning design is based on this idea of emptiness – encased in an inaccessible library whose books are turned to the outside.[43]

The Vienna Holocaust monument indicates quite clearly that a memory that had hitherto been absent has now become a central aspect of Austrian memory. The caesura in Austrian memory is not only visible in the flagship projects, such as the Holocaust Monument on Judenplatz square in Vienna and the rebuilding of the synagogue in Graz (2000) that had been destroyed in 1938. It is also visible in a number of smaller tokens of commemoration, such as the 'stumbling stones' bearing the names of expelled and murdered Jewish citizens that have been put into place in Leopoldstadt, a traditionally Jewish residential district in Vienna.

At the same time, memorials that fail to express a clear dissociation from the Nazi regime meet with increasing concern among the general public, as can, for example be seen in the conflict concerning the 'Siegfriedskopf'. The Siegfriedskopf was unveiled in 1923 as a monument commemorating students and teachers of Vienna University who had died in the First World War; in the 1990s, it had increasingly become a symbol of the fight for the representation of commemoration at the university. Against the opposition of fraternities, the monument was relocated and, redesigned by artists, put into a new context as a historic document – thus making it virtually impossible to use it in the honouring of heroes rituals of 'Burschenschaft' fraternities.

'We have arrived in the twenty-first century', said the President of Vienna University in July 2006 when the newly designed Siegfriedskopf was unveiled.[44] This may hold true for the culture of remembrance as a whole. After the post-war myths had collapsed, and after the phase of new negotiations triggered by the Waldheim debate, the Austrian memory has obviously arrived at a new consensus which characterises a European-wide culture of commemoration that revolves around Auschwitz as a 'breach of civilisation'[45] and historic point of reference for a 'negative memory'. This does not mean that there are no counter-tendencies. However, it is exactly the public response to cases of reactivation of the victim thesis, or to ceremonious commemorations of former officers of the Wehrmacht, that has led to the Holocaust being considered of 'central importance for the identity and memory'[46] of Austria and Europe and to this view prevailing in public discourse.

Notes

1. A. Assmann, 'Fest und Flüssig. Anmerkungen zu einer Denkfigur', in A. Assmann and D. Harth, eds, *Kultur als Lebenswelt und Monument*, Frankfurt am Main, 1991: 181–99.

2. J. Assmann, 'Kollektives Gedächtnis und kulturelle Identität', in J. Assmann and T. Hölscher, eds, *Kultur und Gedächtnis*, Frankfurt am Main, 1988: 16. This is the final sentence of Assmann's essay on the correlation of cultural memory and collective identity from 1988 that marked the start of scientific interest in memory in the German-speaking humanities.

3. P. Nora, 'Vorwort', in his edited *Zwischen Geschichte und Gedächtnis*, Berlin, 1990: 7.

4. Ibid., 7–9; P. Nora, *Realms of Memory: Rethinking the French Past*, vols 1–3, ed. L.D. Kritzman, trans. A. Goldhammer, New York, 1996–1998.

5. E. Barkan, *The Guilt of Nations: Restitution and Negotiating Historical Injustices*, New York, 2000.

6. See M. Flacke, ed., *Mythen der Nationen. 1945 – Arena der Erinnerungen*, Mainz 2004, a catalogue of the exhibition 'Myths of the Nations. 1945 – Arena of Memories', German Historical Museum Berlin; C. Cornelißen, L. Klinkhammer and W. Schwentker, eds, *Erinnerungskulturen. Deutschland, Italien und Japan seit 1945*, Frankfurt am Main, 2003.

7. R. Koselleck, 'Formen und Traditionen des negativen Gedächtnisses', in V. Knigge and N. Frei, eds, *Verbrechen erinnern. Die Auseinandersetzung mit Holocaust und Völkermord*, Munich, 2002: 21–32.

8. W. Kannonier-Finster and M. Ziegler, 'Einleitung und Ausgangspunkte', in W. Kannonier-Finster and M. Ziegler, *Österreichisches Gedächtnis. Über Erinnern und Vergessen der NS-Vergangenheit*, 2nd ed., Vienna, Cologne and Weimar, 1997: 21. In the meanwhile, a great number of books have been published on this issue, among them H.P. Wassermann, *'Zuviel Vergangenheit tut nicht gut!' Nationalsozialismus im Spiegel der Tagespresse der Zweiten Republik*, Innsbruck, Vienna and Munich, 2000; H. Pick, *Guilty Victim: Austria from the Holocaust to Haider*, London, 2000; A. Pelinka, *Austria: Out of the Shadow of the Past*, Boulder, CO., 1998; G. Bischof and A. Pelinka, eds, *Austrian Historical Memory and National Identity*, Contemporary Austrian Studies 5, New Brunswick, NJ, 1997; P. Utgaard, *Remembering and Forgetting Nazism: Education, National Identity, and the Victim Myth in Postwar Austria*, New York and Oxford, 2003.

9. See 'Dokumentationsarchiv des österreichischen Widerstandes', *Gedenken und Mahnen in Wien 1934–1945. Gedenkstätten zu Widerstand und Verfolgung, Exil, Befreiung. Eine Dokumentation*, revised by Herbert Exenberger, Heinz Arnberger with the assistance of Claudia Kuretsidis-Haider, Vienna, 1998; H. Uhl, ed., *Steinernes Bewusstsein. Die öffentliche Repräsentation staatlicher und nationaler Identität Österreichs in seinen Denkmälern*, vol. 2, Vienna, Cologne and Weimar, 2006.

10. See J. Seiter, '"In Erz und Granit aber werden ihre Taten dauern…": Denkmäler, Monumente und Grabmäler für Soldaten und Angehörige der alliierten Armeen nach 1945', in Uhl, *Steinernes Bewusstsein*.

11. 'Mahnmal unerbittlicher Gerechtigkeit', *Das Kleine Volksblatt* (21 August 1945), 1f.

12. See R. Kriechbaumer: 'Leopold Figl', in H. Dachs, P. Gerlich and W.C. Müller, eds, *Die Politiker. Karrieren und Wirken bedeutender Repräsentanten der Zweiten Republik*, Vienna, 1995: 125–33.

13. Proclamation of 27 April 1945, in *Staatsgesetzblatt für die Republik Österreich*, 1 May, 1945. See G. Bischof, 'Die Instrumentalisierung der Moskauer Erklärung nach dem 2. Weltkrieg', *Zeitgeschichte* 29, 11–12, 1993, 345–66; R.H. Keyserlingk, *Austria in World War II: An Anglo-American Dilemma*, Kingston, OT, and Montreal, 1988.

14. See G. Bischof, *Austria and the First Cold War, 1945–55: The Leverage of the Weak*, Basingstoke, 1999.

15. The SPÖ has for some years been going through intense soul searching in an effort to exorcise the 'brown stains' in its party history, particularly with regard to the Federation of Socialist Academicians' (BSA) courting of erstwhile Nazis. See W. Neugebauer and P. Schwarz, *Der Wille zum aufrechten Gang. Offenlegung der Rolle des BSA bei der gesellschaftlichen Reintegration ehemaliger Nationalsozialisten*, Vienna, 2005.

16. See B. Bailer-Galanda and W. Neugebauer, 'Das Dokumentationsarchiv des österreichischen Widerstandes (1963–1983)', in *40 Jahre Dokumentationsarchiv des österreichischen Widerstandes 1963–2003*, Vienna, 2003: 26–70.

17. See K. Klambauer, 'Das Mahnmal der Stadt Wien', in Uhl, *Steinernes Bewußtsein*.

18. 'Wien ehrt die Opfer des Faschismus', *Arbeiterzeitung* (3 November 1948), 3.

19. Quoted in 'Der Mund der Toten ist verschlossen, der unsere aber spricht!', *Volksstimme* (3 November 1948), 7.

20. On the 'political truce' between the Social Democrats and the People's Party and the instrumentalisation of commemoration of February 1934, see E. Klamper, '"Ein einig Volk von Brüdern. Vergessen und Erinnern im Zeichen des Burgfriedens"', *Zeitgeschichte* 24, 5–6, 1997: 170–85.

21. See 'Geschichte einer Gedenktafel', *Der Neue Mahnruf* 9, 1971: 4.

22. *Gedenken und Mahnen in Wien*, 65.

23. See R. Mitten, 'Die "Judenfrage" im Nachkriegsösterreich. Probleme der Forschung', *Zeitgeschichte* 19, 11–12, 1992, 356–67.

24. 'Helden und Opfer. Totengedenken im vierten Jahr nach Kriegsende', *Murtaler Zeitung* (29 October 1949), 3.

25. 'Zeitgemäße Aufgabenstellungen', *Kleine Zeitung* (27 September 1977), 16.

26. 'Dem Andenken der Gefallenen', *Kleine Zeitung* (5 June 1951), 4.

27. 'Widerständler stören Bürgerfrieden', *Der Kamerad* 6, 11, 1964: 1.

28. *Niederösterreichische Landzeitung*, F. 37, 12 Sept. 1963, quoted in W. Hacker, ed., *Warnung an Österreich. Neonazismus: Die Vergangenheit bedroht die Zukunft*, Vienna, Frankfurt am Main and Zürich, 1966: 171.

29. The introduction of a national holiday met with opposition above all from German-National groups and the Freedom Party. See G. Spann, 'Zur Geschichte des österreichischen Nationalfeiertages', *26. Oktober. Zur Geschichte des österreichischen Nationalfeiertages*, Vienna, Bundesministerium für Unterricht, Kunst und Sport, Abteilung für Politische Bildung, n.p.: 27–34.

30. On the turning-point at the end of the sixties, see E. Hanisch, *Der lange Schatten des Staates. Österreichische Gesellschaftsgeschichte im 20. Jahrhundert*, Vienna, 1994: 456f.

31. See G. Kasemir, 'Spätes Ende für wissenschaftlich vorgetragenen Rassismus. Die Affäre Borodajkewycz', M. Gehler and H. Sickinger, eds, *Politische Affären und Skandale in Österreich. Von Mayerling bis Waldheim*, Vienna and Munich, 1995: 486–501.

32. As early as 1958, a plaque had been set up by resolution of the Council of Ministers with the inscription 'In memory of the victims in the fight for Austria's freedom. The Austrian Federal government at the Äußeres Burgtor'. See 'Österreich ehrt seine treuesten Söhne', *Arbeiterzeitung* (17 July 1959), 1. On the debates concerning this plaque, see H. Uhl, 'Konkurrierende Gedächtnislandschaften. Widerstand gegen das NS-Regime, Zweiter Weltkrieg und Holocaust in der Denkmalkultur der Zweiten Republik', in Uhl, *Steinernes Bewusstsein*.

33. 'Maleta: Wir lieben dich, Vaterland!', *Wiener Zeitung* (28 April 1965), 1f.

34. See R. Mitten, *The Politics of Prejudice: The Waldheim Phenomenon in Austria*, San Francisco and Oxford, 1992; R. Wodak et al., *'Wir sind alle unschuldige Täter'. Diskurshistorische Studien zum Nachkriegsantisemitismus*, Frankfurt am Main, 1990; M. Gehler, 'Die Affäre Waldheim: Eine Fallstudie zum Umgang mit der NS-Vergangenheit in den späten achtziger Jahren', in R. Steininger and M. Gehler, eds, *Österreich im 20. Jahrhundert*, vol. 2. *Vom Zweiten Weltkrieg bis zur Gegenwart*, Vienna, Cologne and

Weimar, 1997: 355–414. Kurt Waldheim was cleared by a commission of historians of any suspicion of having committed any war crimes in February of 1988.

35. Kurt Waldheim in an election booklet of April 1986, quoted in *Neues Österreich, Pflichterfüllung. Ein Bericht über Kurt Waldheim*, Vienna, 1986, dust jacket.

36. On the history of the Hrdlicka monument, see U. Jenni, 'Vorgeschichte und Entwürfe der antifaschistischen Denkmäler in Wien', in her edited, *Alfred Hrdlicka. Mahnmal gegen Krieg und Faschismus in Wien*, vol. 1, Graz, 1993: 83ff.

37. M. Wagner, 'Kommunikation mit dem Betrachter', in ibid.: 29.

38. B. Coudenhove-Kalergi, 'Auf dem Judenplatz', *Profil*, 37 (11 September 1995), 88. See also M. Bunzl, 'On the Politics and Semantics of Austrian Memory: Vienna's Monument against War and Fascism', *History and Memory* 7, 2, 1996: 30.

39. R. Beckermann, *Unzugehörig Juden und Österreicher nach 1945*, Vienna, 1989: 14.

40. Michael Häupl, Hannes Swoboda, Ursula Pasterk, *Zum mahnenden Gedenken, in: Judenplatz Wien 1996. Wettbewerb Mahnmal und Gedenkstätte für die jüdischen Opfer des Naziregimes in Österreich 1938–1945*. Vienna 1996, 8. (Statement made by the mayor of Vienna and other representatives of the City council.)

41. Simon Wiesenthal, 'Zur Geschichte der Juden in Österreich', in ibid., 14.

42. Häupl, Swoboda, Pasterk, in ibid., 8.

43. Amnon Barzel, 'Die Gestaltung der Erinnerung', in ibid., 21.

44. http://www.dieuniversitaet-online.at/beitraege/news/kunstlerisch-gestaltet-wissenschaftlich-aufgearbeitet-siegfriedskopf-im-arkadenhof/10.html

45. Dan Diner, ed., *Zivilisationsbruch: Denken nach Auschwitz*, Frankfurt am Main 1988; Dan Diner, *Beyond the Conceivable: Studies on Germany, Nazism and the Holocaust*, Berkeley, LosAngeles and London, 2000.

46. Tony Judt, *Geschichte Europas von 1945 bis zur Gegenwart*, Munich and Vienna, 2006: 953.

Chapter 11

Personifying the Past:
National and European History
in the Fine and Applied Arts
in the Age of Nationalism

Michael Wintle

National narratives have been expressed in a variety of different ways, most commonly and perhaps most importantly in print. However, identities and narratives can also be expressed visually, with an often immediate effect that rivals other media in the representation of complex human messages and emotions. This chapter will pay particular attention to 'the visual' in the process of narrating the nation. Chronologically the highpoint of national self-assertion among European nations was reached around the time of New Imperialism in the decades before the First World War, a period of intense nationalism. This was also a peak period in the assertion of Europe as an idea based on power and civilisation: of Eurocentric Euro-assertion, helped by the mechanism of the European empires. That Euro-assertion went back to the time of the Renaissance, and had always had a strong visual component;[1] it became particularly strong in the nineteenth century, not least because of technological developments that allowed images to be circulated as never before. An examination of some of the visual evidence of the experience of nationalism in Europe, and of the assertion of Europe in images, will permit a juxtaposition of the nationalist with the European at the height of both European self-confidence and nationalistic feelings in Europe.

The chapter will begin with a discussion of the pros and cons of using visual evidence in history, followed by a survey of the tradition of representing the continent of Europe in graphic images. Then we shall examine the rise of nationalist narratives in Europe within that medium of visual images, focusing particularly on personification. In conclusion, we shall evaluate the impact of the rise of nationalism in Europe on the self-image of Europeans and of Europe as a whole.

Visual Images

The empirical evidence employed in this chapter in order to examine assertions of nation and Europe does not fall within the conventional range of learned publications, printed media, political statements or even literary productions. Instead, shifts are sought out in ideas about Europe and the nations in the *visual* representation of the continent and its constituent countries, ranging from paintings and sculpture to flags, cartoons and maps. Traditionally, professional historians used to eschew the use of visual material as hard evidence. There used to be a distinct lack of theorising amongst historians about the way in which visual material could contribute to historical studies. However, since the 1980s at least, there has been a small but slowly increasing tendency to employ visual sources, starting for example with British political prints from the eighteenth century, such as those by James Gillray and others.[2] Such material can be difficult and complex to use, for it is often simply 'exploring gut prejudices' in public opinion, and therefore, rightly or wrongly, 'reflecting' contemporary thought. On the other hand, we also know that prints were also used to *affect* and influence public opinion, rather than simply *reflect* it, for governments had long used prints as a vehicle for official propaganda.[3] This means that the cartoons were not just reflecting, but also directing public opinion. Whilst this form of evidence can prove problematic, that should not necessarily restrict analysis. In recent years certain museum exhibitions have collected some of the kinds of images which are useful for examining nationalism, for example a very extensive one at the Deutsches Historisches Museum in Berlin in 1998.[4]

In disciplines adjacent to history, scholars have gone some way towards codifying 'visual methods' in research. The principal conclusion concerns the need to apply rigorous source criticism to visual sources. We must not only ask about the content of an image, but who made it, when, why, who read it, and how. For 'seeing is not natural'; the ways in which we interpret what our eyes see is governed by our culture, and is temporally and spatially particular. That is to say, we learn in our specific variant of society to select certain aspects of images for attention, and to screen out others. Therefore, unpacking that filtering process can tell us as much about a person or people as can the image itself. The significance of the same image can change radically: as a photograph, painting or cartoon 'travels' over space and time, it can mean quite different things to different people.[5] The same point – the need for rigorous source criticism – has also been made by the cultural historian Peter Burke, in his 2001 book, *Eyewitnessing*, which dealt with the use of the visual in history.[6] The quality of a work of art has nothing to do with its value as historical evidence. Most images used for official purposes are a form of theatre rather than reality, and 'documentary' pictures invariably have an agenda or moral aspiration. Images show us contemporary views of things rather than reality, but that is after all the currency in which most historians trade.

There is a long and distinguished tradition of *iconographical* interpretation in the history of art. Erwin Panofsky's essay, 'Iconography and Iconology', published in 1939, is a classic example.[7] Many of those concerned with the study of fine art have moved in more recent decades further towards integrating their work on visual evidence much more closely with the history of society as a whole. Much of the theoretical discussion has come to centre on the question of agency, a key question for historians who wish to use visual evidence. Do artists, engravers, cartoonists and the like simply offer up a mirror of contemporary politics and social relationships, or are they ideological crusaders with their own (or their patrons') agenda making aspirational statements about how they think things *should* be seen?

The answer is of course a mixture of the two. Few artists, at whatever level, have nothing whatsoever to say. Therefore, any piece of visual evidence, from Old Master to penny print, is going to present a point of view, with all the loaded bias and selection that that entails. However, the issues on which comment is evinced in visual material are usually thrown up by political and cultural debate already in existence elsewhere, and in that sense, art is adding to an ongoing debate, and so largely reflecting it. There is an interaction at work here, as there is with most questions of agency in history. The artist engages with a contemporary problem, reflects the issues of his or her time, but also contributes to the agenda and even shifts the scrimmage by his or her own comment.

Over the last thirty years, there has been an increasing interest in the academy in 'visual culture'. There is now a recognition that many of the images that surround us in our daily lives are charged with meaning, and as a whole can be highly active in the social and political process.[8] This 'visual culture' covers an immense range of subject matter and methods, from iconography and semiology to reflexivity and discourse analysis.[9] The crucial insight that seems to link all the various strands of the study of visual culture is that vision, or seeing, is socio-culturally conditioned, and spatially and temporally specific. Once again, the eye is not an objective organ: it selects. Similarly, all artefacts made for visual consumption, from high art to advertisements, and from wallpaper to the built environment, have a cultural content, whether it is overtly intended (as in advertisements) or not (as in some decorative art).

A scholarly and systematic use of visual images as historical evidence alongside written and printed sources is not only illuminating and interesting, but also even essential. This kind of 'visual history' not only employs photographs and paintings, but almost every kind of visual image available, certainly including the adornment of public space of all sorts: cartoons, prints, currency, flags, ceramics, greetings cards, maps and films. It cannot, it goes without saying, operate in isolation: the pictures, emblems and icons must be taken alongside the written evidence, in order to come to a well balanced conclusion.[10]

Traditions of Representing Europe

Returning to the subject of Europe and its nations, two of the most powerful ways of representing the continent are in personification and in maps. This chapter will concentrate on the former. Personification is an ancient rhetorical, literary and artistic convention, and the representation of countries and continents in the form of a human figure is almost universal in Western culture. By the time of the rise of modern nationalism, Europeans had a very assured view of themselves. There was a tradition of personifying the continent of Europe as a being superior to her sister continents, which had been widespread since the Renaissance.[11] That self-assurance took several forms, which can be summarised as a general superiority in everything from science to force of arms, and a moral superiority as the dutiful bearer of the 'White Man's Burden', complete with *mission civilatrice*.

The expansion and colonising activities of Europeans since the time of the 'discoveries' of the fifteenth and sixteenth centuries had resulted in, and been supported by, this portrayal of European superiority. One of the early classics of such visual propaganda was the *Iconologia* of Cesare Ripa, published in illustrated form in 1603,[12] as a handbook for artists seeking authority for their decorative work using personifications of the muses, the elements, the virtues or – in this case – the continents. Europe was shown as the Queen of the World, with a crown and sceptre, the true church, military hardware and a white charger to show prowess in battle, books and owls, scientific instruments, cornucopiae and rich clothes. Her sister continents, meanwhile, were characterised in these illustrations with accoutrements such as exotic animals, beads, incense, riches ready to offer up to Europe, and in the case of America, a severed head to indicate cannibalism and barbarism. Asia was usually richly dressed like Europe (though without the crown and other regalia), but Africa and America were generally naked. Moreover, this tradition continued for several centuries. In the 1750s, Giambattista Tiepolo was still drawing on Ripa in portraying America in terms of cannibal feasts in his crowning masterpiece, the staircase ceiling frescoes representing Apollo and the Four Continents in the Prince-Bishop's Residence at Würzburg.[13]

A panel dominated by beautiful young women and alligators represents America. To the left there is a reindeer, various muscular men with turbans and moustaches, three Indians featured with feather headdresses, and a parrot. There is a huge cornucopia, and the central figure is a larger-than-life young female (Figure 11.1), with no clothes and an anatomy which manages to be simultaneously athletic and voluptuous. She has a highly coloured South American feather headdress, earrings of gold, a heavy gold necklace, and a massive gold ingot with a sun pattern on her chest. She has a bow at her back, sandals, a modesty drape, and a satisfied, sensuous, languid smile. Behind her to the left (her right) is a young white European, perhaps the artist. America sits on an enormous alligator, which is decorated with scallop shells and an exotic carpet. Behind her are figures of all races, including Orientals, Negroes, Arabs and Caucasians. To the right of this, there is a standard with a dragon, and then a moustached, feather-bonneted man carrying a bundle of sticks, and to his left

Figure 11.1: Giambattista Tiepolo, America, from the fresco of Apollo and the Four Continents, 1753, in the Residence of the Prince-Bishop, Würzburg. (Source: D. Kutschbach, *Tiepolo: eine Reise um die Welt*, Munich, 1996.)

a muscular figure with a dead alligator over his shoulder. Slightly further to the right, we see, in the foreground on the balustrade, a young Western man in eighteenth-century dress (unlike the rest of the illustration), holding up a board that could be the painting or could be a mirror. We seem to be following him on his journey through the world. Immediately above him is a young white female figure, carrying a wine jar of sorts on her head; she has feathers in her hair, and a naked torso. Finally, to the right of her, we have a scene of four men roasting meat on an open fire, which is reminiscent of the usual cannibalistic forms used earlier in portraying America. There is little doubt about the implicit meaning of this image: America is well endowed, available and ripe for possession; her culture is primitive, exotic, naturalistic and voluptuous. All this is in contrast to European sophistication, learning and civilisation. In this riot of detail, the 'otherness' of the image of America dominates, especially in terms of sexuality.

By the time of the nineteenth century, the cannibalism had disappeared, though the hierarchy of the continents continued unabated. For the Universal Exhibition at the Trocadero Palace and Gardens in Paris in 1878, Alexandre Schoenewerk was commissioned to create a huge metal sculpture of Europe in

Figure 11.2: A. Schoenewerk, Metal sculpture of Europe, made for the Paris Universal Exhibition of 1878; now at the Musée d'Orsay, Paris (author's photograph).

this tradition (Figure 11.2). Many will have seen the sculpture there, and many see her now for, since 1986 she has stood, some two metres tall, outside the entrance to the Musée d'Orsay on the Seine embankment in Paris, where the tourists queue to gain entry to that temple to nineteenth-century art and design. She has strong classical associations, and could well be modelled on Minerva; the inherited greatness of the Ancients is the point offered. Her accoutrements pronounce her to be proficient in war and its technology (helmet and weapons), but also in peace (she bears an olive branch). At her feet are books and a palette, to show her superiority in science and the arts. She is clearly the dominant member of the group of continents, in terms of power and sophistication of all sorts.

To compare Europe with, for example, the statue made by Mathurin Moreau to symbolise Oceania (Australia, New Zealand and Polynesia), is very instructive (Figure 11.3). The personification of the Pacific Ocean continent is a naked, brute, female aborigine. She has a sheepskin to symbolise her wool exports, a wallaby for her indigenous species, and nothing less than a spiked club to indicate her (and this new world's) dumb violence and primitiveness.

Figure 11.3: M. Moreau, Metal sculpture of Oceanie, made for the Paris Universal Exhibition of 1878; now at the Musée d'Orsay, Paris (author's photograph).

The club seems to put paid to Enlightenment ideas about the noble savage: this is simply a portrait of base life. There was therefore a very clear pecking order in the visual portrayal of the continents, which had been established in the Renaissance, and which had remained more or less in place ever since.

The other version of the European self-assertion, *vis-à-vis* the other continents, was in the form of a belief in an obligation to civilise the rest of the world in the ways of Europe, be it in law, religion, public life, politics or civil society; in other words, the 'White Man's Burden'. One of the most direct ways of communicating this kind of superiority was the representation of the colonised continents as children, and of Europe as their mother. Figure 11.4 displays an image that is one of the most eloquent of all the images of Europe and the other continents, and it touches on empire in the sense of protection in the most saccharine way. The porcelain figurine from Berlin dates from the 1760s. Europe is portrayed as a mother figure, with crown, orb, sceptre and rich clothes. The other continents, meanwhile, are cast as little children at her feet. America has a

Figure 11.4: German soft-paste porcelain model of the four continents, Berlin Porcelain Manufactory, 1769. The Metropolitan Museum of Art, New York, Gift of the Estate of James Hazen Hyde, 1959 (59.208.8)

feather bonnet, arrows and beads; Africa is Negroid, with a toy sword and shield; Asia has a censer and the crescent of Islam on his turban. As a piece of ceramic art, its claims may be modest, but it is a very telling emblem indeed of European identity. The mother-child relationship was of course an ideal way in which Europeans could project their imperial fantasies. The condescension defined them as superior in every way, as an adult is to a child, but it provided the excuse of charity or love or succour for weaker fellow humans that made it all justifiable. The device was to continue into the nineteenth and twentieth centuries as well, for the need for Europe to rear and educate the other continents was too valuable a piece of propaganda to be neglected.

Many a graphic representation of imperial European condescension, in national form, to less favoured peoples of the world decorated the public parks and buildings of Western Europe. A telling example, which is a statement of both European superiority and national assertiveness, comes from the bombastic central hall of the Congo Museum near Brussels. This is a monument to King Leopold's infamous 'Red Rubber Regime' in Central Africa, which was built in the first decade of the twentieth century at the

Figure 11.5: A. Matton, 'Belgie schenkt bescherming aan Congo', c. 1910, in the main hall of the Congo Museum, Tervuren.

height of New Imperialism, and is still today an astonishingly unreconstructed bastion of colonial bravado and condescension. In its vast central hall, gilded statues by Arsène Matton promulgate the message loud and clear: the title of the sculpture is 'Belgium bestows protection on the Congo' (Figure 11.5). Belgium is the comely maiden; the Africans are naked children. Belgians – and imperial Europeans in general – clearly had found an important part of their own identity by discovering or rather inventing their relationship with their colonies, and defining that relationship as one between parent and infant.

This process of the 'othering of Europe' is nicely displayed in a portrait by the renowned New Zealand painter Charles Goldie (1870–1947) (Figure 11.6). It dates from 1910, and is of a Maori Tohunga, or priest of the Tuhoe tribe. On the face of it, this is a deeply sensitive and complimentary portrait; indeed its title reads, 'A noble relic of a noble race'. It certainly does not appear to be negative about its subject. However, under the surface, things are not quite what they seem. The sitter for this portrait evidently had a splendid set of tattoos, which is what attracted Goldie in the first place. However, Goldie virtually took him off the streets, paid him some money, and dressed him up in various more-or-less authentic clothes of which he had a trunkful in

Figure 11.6: Charles F. Goldie, 'A noble relic of a noble race', 1910. Location: Auckland Art Gallery.

his studio. He then proceeded to paint this tragic, noble figure, almost tear-jerking in its pathos. He was a specialist in the genre and did many dozens of such pictures, which sold exceedingly well: he became a wealthy man. It is essentially a white man's picture, a European's picture, even if it was painted in Auckland on the other side of the world. In a colonial society, like New Zealand just before the First World War, this painting was as much a statement of white, colonialist, Orientalising, condescending values in reverse, as it was a litany for an order that was well and truly past.

The Rise of Nationalism and the Visual Representation of the Nation

At the same time as the zenith of this irrepressible European self-confidence, during the nineteenth century, there was also an increase in the visual portrayal of nation-states, linked directly to the rise of nationalism. There was a longstanding tradition of personifying towns, regions, provinces and countries, as well as continents, and this use of geographical imagery to laud and glorify a particular location became particularly popular with major trading ports such as Amsterdam. In the triangular tympanum at the back of the great City Hall of that town (now a royal palace), built in 1648, there is a frieze by the sculptor and designer Artus Quellinus showing the four quarters of the world bringing their tribute to the city personified (Figure 11.7). On the left, we see Africa and Europe. Africa is a naked Negro woman, accompanied by a lion and an elephant, and offering ivory and bales of trade goods, while Europe is clothed and crowned, with her war horse and bull, bunches of grapes (showing advanced agriculture and diet) and books of learning. The difference in status is clear: one is primitive, exotic and productive of luxury raw materials, while the other is sophisticated, learned and mighty in war. On the right, we are shown Asia and America. Asia stands opposite Europe, holding a camel's bridle. She is richly dressed, and has an exotic turban headdress and censer. Next to her, a child offers the first tulip to Amsterdam, reminding the good burghers of the disastrous tulip mania speculation in 1636–37, only a decade previously. America has a feather headdress and an alligator, into the jaws of which a child is placing a lump of sugar. Silver mines and tobacco surround her, and indeed a lit pipe is featured: it all points to the productive, subservient nature of the other continents. All are paying tribute to the Maid of Amsterdam, who stands above two river gods, and so Europe is only the second star of this collection. However, the point to be taken is that Amsterdam is also a European; this is an important document in the portrayal of European superiority.[14]

　　In the eighteenth century, Britain played a leading role in developing and displaying the characteristics of a modern nation, as Linda Colley has shown us.[15] On the coin of the realm, for example, the display of the monarch and

Figure 11.7: Artus Quellinus, Amsterdam and the continents, 1648, frieze in the west (rear) tympanum of the Royal Palace, Amsterdam. (author's photograph)

various national icons and symbols was an important part of nation-building. John Bull was also a popular image throughout the eighteenth century.[16] However, it was the female personification of the nation in the form of Britannia that was really to symbolise the nation. From the enormous range of possible examples, Figure 11.8 shows a Derby soft-paste porcelain figure of her, in enamel and gilt, dating from about 1765. Her accoutrements trumpet her claims to international supremacy and national pride. She also has the attributes of war, with a lion, a globe, trumpets, cannon, a helmet, cannon balls, breastplate and shield. The nation, in this case eighteenth-century Britain, is visibly emerging, bursting with pride and self-assertion. This kind of imagery is very similar to much found in the written texts, but adds an extra dimension, all the more immediate because of the directness of visual communication.

With the arrival of the nineteenth century, virtually all the nations of Europe produced such national personifications with which to promote their national sentiments and values. It was the century of nation-building, and the concept of the nation, in most cases inhabiting the state, increasingly had to be sold to the people, who were gradually becoming enfranchised and whose

Figure 11.8: Figurine of Britannia, Derby soft-paste porcelain, enamelled and gilt, c. 1765. Location: Fitzwilliam Museum, Cambridge, C.89.1932.

loyalties were therefore crucial to the elites. A leading role in personifying the nation was also taken by France. Since the seventeenth century the kingdom had been regularly portrayed by a Minerva-like figure, and indeed her kings themselves had been displayed as the embodiment of France (if not of the nation or people), especially in the case of Louis XIV. From the time of the Revolution a more popular figure arose, particularly associated with the French populace, in the form of the maid of freedom, Marianne, always with a tricolour for the Revolution and usually with a Phrygian bonnet standing for freedom. Figure 11.9 shows her in the iconic painting by Eugène Delacroix, celebrating the Revolution of July 1830, as Liberty leading the people on the barricades. This is the French nation personified as a bare-breasted (the 'slipped chiton', for liberty), revolution-capped, tricolour-brandishing, militant, republican, female freedom fighter. There was considerable controversy attached to the figure of Marianne in the course of the nineteenth century, because of her association with the common people as opposed to the more virtuous and sophisticated Minerva, but she eventually became established as the ubiquitous symbol of republican France and the French people, dominating much of the country's public space.[17]

However, although Britain and France were trailblazers in nation-building and in the visual representation of the nation, they were by no means alone in

Figure 11.9: E. Delacroix, 'Liberty leading the people', 1831. Location: Musée du Louvre, Paris.

236 Michael Wintle

the use of a heroic female personification to represent the nation visually. At the end of the nineteenth century and in the run-up to the First World War, there were several representations of the newly formed Germany as a medieval mother-warrior, enhancing a German self-image of martial prowess and gothic, almost feudal traditions.[18] 'Mother Denmark' also made frequent appearances, at least from 1813, as we see in Figure 11.10. It shows her with the Danish flag, in a painting on a large circular wooden panel (63cm diameter), inscribed with the date 5 May 1813.[19] The nation's representative is shown in front of a pile of weapons, with a plumed helmet and shield, plus an enormous Danish flag.[20]

There are several examples from Greece, perhaps the most romantic of the nationalist movements of the nineteenth century. Delacroix was a leader in the genre, as we have seen, and his 1826 picture entitled, 'Greece on the ruins of Missolonghi'[21] is an iconic portrait of the ancient but reborn nation in its

Figure 11.10: Mother Denmark with the flag, 1813. Location: Klampenborg, Royal Copenhagen Society for Danish Brotherhood (351).

struggle for independence from the Ottoman overlord. Delacroix shows Greece personified as a young woman in traditional dress, kneeling in devastation on a rock surrounded by dead bodies and soldiers. The Greek nationalists had taken the town of Missolonghi, and the Ottomans sent an Egyptian army in to crush the uprising in 1825. The siege lasted a year before the town fell to the Ottoman troops, whereupon all the defenders were put to the sword. Theodorus Vrysakis produced another emotive painting of Greece personified in 1858, in which the long-haired young maiden gathers her children around her, in the form of a collection of national heroes on their knees; she wears an olive garland, while dawn breaks over the Olympian mountains in the background.[22]

In another nation in another empire, Hungarians staged a nationalist uprising in 1848 against the Habsburg Empire. It was put down with the help of Croat and Russian forces; more than a hundred Hungarian officers were

Figure 11.11: 'Der rote Drache', *Der Stürmer*, no. 4 (1937). Source: E.H. Gombrich, 'The Cartoonist's Armoury', in idem, *Meditations on a Hobby Horse and Other Essays on the Theory of Art*, London, 1963, 127–42, ill. 114.

executed. In 1861 Mihály Kovács painted 'The Subjugation of the Hungarians' to commemorate the event: Hungary was depicted as a young maiden with two children at her skirts, being overpowered by naked, brutish soldiers, stealing her crown and smashing her coat of arms.[23] To return to Southeastern Europe, Bulgarians received partial autonomy within the Ottoman Empire in 1878, with a German prince. It was the occasion for a painted personification of Bulgaria, now in the National Library in Sofia, in which a young woman stands on a hilltop overlooking a beautiful, densely populated valley: with sword in hand, she is guarding the motherland against any possible foe. She has a lion with her, and sports the national flag, with various symbolic documents, heraldic arms and artefacts strewn around, including a broken shackle to show her newly won freedom.[24] These paintings helped communicate to contemporaries, and indeed to us, the intense, Romantic, nostalgic, nature and landscape-based feelings of nationalism which were often current in the nineteenth century.

A final example from this huge genre is taken from the twentieth century, in Spain at the time of the Civil War in the 1930s (Figure 11.11). The nation is personified here in a fascist cartoon of 1937, which shows her as a maiden under threat of a fate worse than death. She is tied to a Communist stake, and is being threatened by a dragon that bears the crudely (but presumably effectively) caricatured physiognomy of the Nazi version of a stage-Jew. Oddly, the dragon carries a pentagonal star (not a star of David); the drawing is entitled 'The Red Dragon'.

As a variant on the tradition of representing the regions and nations by personification and other forms of geographical imagery, there was also a pedigree of representing Europe as a 'family' of nations, from the time of the Renaissance onwards. Figure 11.12 shows a decorated French fan of 1733, depicting a procession at a grand ball of the European nations, all dressed up in their party clothes or national costumes, amicably accompanying each other, two by two, to a great court party. These early versions of the Europe of the nations originated as commentaries on differences in costume and appearance; costume geographies were an important printed genre from the sixteenth century onwards.[25] In the nineteenth century, the general concept of people with interesting differences living peacefully side-by-side began to be displaced, especially at the hands of the cartoonists, by representations of the nations of Europe more often than not at each other's throats. This was perhaps understandable in wartime, for instance during the Napoleonic confrontation (again one thinks of the work of James Gillray). However, the rise of nationalism in the nineteenth century made it endemic and more sharply focussed.

Towards the end of the nineteenth century, the cheap periodicals and newsprint, now emancipated from stamp tax in much of Europe, began to produce images that, with hindsight, seemed to map or even steer the imperial nations of Europe in their long slide down into imperialist rivalry and

Figure 11.12: Fan showing the nations of Europe, 1733. Location: Bibliothèque Nationale, Cabinet des Estampes, Paris.

DISINTERESTED ADVISERS.

Bear, "YOU *MUST* FEEL, DEAR TURKEY, OUR *ONLY* OBJECT IS YOUR GOOD!"

Figure 11.13: 'Disinterested advisers', cartoon in *Punch* (20 November 1875).

eventually open conflict in the First World War. Figure 11.13 shows a cartoon of 1875, with the European nations as predatory animals, from *Punch*. The victim of their attentions is the Ottoman Empire, portrayed as a tethered turkey in a fez, about whose security the crowned heads of Europe are offering expertise as 'disinterested advisers', while they circle their prey: the Russian bear, the British lion, and the Austrian and German eagles. The nations of Europe are here portrayed as predatory, vainglorious and mutually inimical. Many illustrated periodicals in most European countries issued such cartoons in the last third of the nineteenth century[26] and indeed right throughout the twentieth. They have reflected, but also influenced, the way in which the public views national differences.

Meanwhile, Europe as a whole continued to be personified, occasionally positively, as an arbiter or figurehead, but more often with a negative connotation. She seemed impotent to control affairs, and was even shown as a victim of aggression from new powers around the world, like the United States or Japan. The Spanish–American War of 1898 was the definitive occasion on which a mature United States established its claims on the world stage as a fully fledged imperial power, at the direct expense of one of the old European imperial nations, Spain. American victories resulting in the loss of the remnants of the Spanish empire – Puerto Rico, Cuba and the Philippines – occasioned a wave of patriotic cartoons. These placed Uncle Sam and Teddy Roosevelt as personifications of rampant America on a par with the personifications of the European powers (John Bull, the Kaiser, the Tsar, the Austrian Emperor), and were often anything but complimentary about the latter. Spain in particular was singled out for detrimental portrayal, as a tired, lecherous old bandit: one cartoon in particular, entitled 'Spaniards search women on American steamers', showed a naked young (American) woman being manhandled by Latin types on a boat deck.[27] In the East, the cartoonists also played upon the rising power of Japan and even China. In one called 'Die ostasiatische Frage', which appeared in the German magazine *Kladderadatsch* on 5 May 1895, Europe was cleverly shown as a map in the shape of a woman,[28] a tradition which goes all the way back to the work of a fourteenth-century heretical monk, Opicinus Canistris. His hand-drawn maps were perhaps the first to fit a human body into the space of the continent of Europe.[29] In the German case from 1895, the woman embodying or personifying Europe was an old hag whose feet protruded beyond Asia, in the form of Formosa and Korea, countries that were deemed European spheres of influence. Here, however, they were being sawn off by a vigorous-looking Japan, which had imperialist designs of its own. Such images implied, reflected and amplified challenges to European supremacy.

Sometimes, indeed, the symbols of majesty and authority that had earlier accompanied the personification of Europe were taken over in the era of rising and rampant nationalism by the anthropomorphic representations of the nations, rather than of the continent as a whole. Figure 11.14 shows the cartouche of a late eighteenth-century map of Britain by John Rocque, in which we see a Britannia figure with many of the attributes of the personification of Europe of previous generations. A trident has been added as symbolic of Britannia's special domination of the oceans, and it is carried by a lion, the king of beasts, which was Britain's animal signifier. Otherwise, there are the traditional figures of Hermes on the right, for trade, a personification of the arts on the left with her myriad accoutrements referring to all the sciences and fine arts, and a figure of war in the background. It is an image very close to the tradition of portraying the European continent, from the time of Cesare Ripa onwards. In this way, the national personification of individual European countries began to take over and take on aspects of the traditional European imagery. Another example makes the point, again from Britain, but this time in the form of a poster in celebration of the life and death of the Yorkshire-born explorer Captain James Cook.[30] The heroic navigator of the Pacific Ocean is shown being raised to immortality and fame by Neptune. Below him, personifications of the four quarters of the world present to Britannia their various stores. Britannia has almost identical imagery to that which usually characterised Europe. Black Africa offers gold, jewels and ivory; exotic Asia brings rare woods and incense, while feather-bonneted America is on her knees in obeisance. Europe is the only crowned continent,

Figure 11.14: Cartouche of a map of England and Wales, by John Rocque, later eighteenth century (author's collection).

and therefore the senior one, but she stands back on this occasion, for helmeted Britannia and her lion have prominence and pride of place here. However, the Eurocentrism of such images had lost none of its self-assurance. The unthinking certainty of European superiority was undiminished.

Conclusion

The visual sources used in this chapter – paintings, ceramics, maps, cartoons – have not only assisted our analysis of the narration of national and European identity, but also directly assisted in the narration itself. This chapter has joined the growing trend to expand the range of sources which most historians use, to include more of the visual. All sources are problematic in one way or another;

what is essential is that we have rigorous source criticism, and awareness of the possible pitfalls. The visual sources can tell us things that we did not know before, especially about mentality, social history and cultural history. These claims are not by any means made here for the first time. Many art historians have long been moving towards a practice of history based on art as one source material amongst others, while historians of technology and of material culture, for example, have done pioneering work on using non-standard sources to open up a range of new perspectives on the past. In the end, the message remains the same: historians must cross-reference all their sources alongside others, and the actual type of source employed is almost without limit.

One of the most important issues is the question of agency. It is not hard to maintain that the visual sources used here 'reflect' events in the real world of economics and politics. That model is basically a Marxist one, in which culture follows economics and politics, and where the agenda is set in the real world, to be simply 'reflected' or reacted to in the world of art. However, is that really the whole story? Is it not the case that culture can also set the agenda? Does culture matter, to put it in terms of a political science debate? Where does agency lie? Who sets the agenda? These images are best analysed as a form of media, and as with all media they reflect the current state of affairs – sometimes in a somewhat distorted manner – but they also exert their own independent influence. The artists, designers, architects and cartoonists who devised, developed and perpetuated these images were reflecting current trends, but they were also generating them, in the way that the mass media does today, in particular television.[31]

Finally, we have seen the arrogant, Eurocentric self-projection of Europe in the colonial and imperial age. We have also seen that there has been a long-lived tendency to personify the nations as well as Europe. Generally, the two levels of representation – nations and Europe – were not mutually inimical. Both could be and were happily promoted alongside each other. It is true that in the period before the First World War there was a tendency noticeable in the cartoons, especially, to denigrate Europe's ability to control events. However, this was at a time when there was, simultaneously, a massively positive portrayal of Europeanness in all visual forms, and when almost all visual imagery, including the nationalistic forms, was more assuredly Eurocentric than it ever was before, or since. It was only the disasters of the twentieth century, in the form of World Wars, Holocaust, decolonisation and Cold War, that would finally introduce a measure of restraint into the European narration of its self-image.

Notes

1. See M. J. Wintle, 'Renaissance Maps and the Construction of the Idea of Europe', *The Journal of Historical Geography* 25, 2, 1999: 137–65.

2. See, for example, J. Brewer, *The Common People and Politics 1750–1790s*, Cambridge, 1986; and R.S. Porter, 'Seeing the Past', *Past and Present* 118, 1988: 186–205.

3. M. Duffy, *The Englishman and the Foreigner: The English Satirical Print 1600–1832*, Cambridge, 1986: 43–44.

4. See the catalogue: M. Flacke, ed., *Mythen der Nationen: ein europäisches Panorama*, Berlin, 1998.

5. M. Banks, *Visual Methods in Social Research*, London, 2001: esp. 7–11.

6. P. Burke, *Eyewitnessing: The Use of Images as Historical Evidence*, London, 2001.

7. In E. Panofsky, *Meaning in the Visual Arts: Papers in and on Art History*, Garden City, NY, 1957: 26–54. For commentary, see Burke, *Eyewitnessing*, 35f.

8. M. Barnard, *Art, Design and Visual Culture: An Introduction*, London, 1998: 166–67, 190, and throughout.

9. There are many handbooks of visual culture and analysis available, which amply demonstrate the amazing diversity of these concepts: one example among the many is T. van Leeuwen and C. Jewitt, eds, *Handbook of Visual Analysis*, London, 2001.

10. Banks, *Visual Methods*, 177.

11. See Wintle, 'Renaissance Maps'.

12. C. Ripa, *Iconologia overo descrittione di diverse imagini cavate dall'antichità, & di propria inventione, trovate, & dichiarate*, Rome 1603; I have used the 1644 Dutch edition: C. Ripa, *Iconologia, of uytbeeldingen des verstands*, Amsterdam, 1644.

13. S. Alpers and M. Baxendall, *Tiepolo and the Pictorial Intelligence*, New Haven, 1994: 123, 130.

14. E. Vanvugt, *De maagd en de soldaat: koloniale monumenten in Amsterdam en elders*, Amsterdam, 1998: 25–27.

15. L. Colley, *Britons: Forging the Nation 1707–1837*, New Haven, CT, 1992.

16. Porter, 'Seeing the Past', 198. See also P. Langford, *Englishness Identified: Manners and Character 1650–1850*, Oxford, 2000: 11.

17. See M. Agulhon, *Marianne into Battle: Republican Imagery and Symbolism in France, 1789–1880*, Cambridge, 1981: 42; M. Agulhon and P. Bonte, *Marianne: les visages de la République*, Paris, 1992: 26–27; and M. Warner, *Monuments and Maidens: The Allegory of the Female Form*, London, 1985: 277.

18. E.g. Lorenz Clasen, 'Germania auf der Wacht am Rhein', c. 1900, now in the Kaiser Wilhelm Museum, Krefeld; and Friedrich August von Kaulbach, 'Germania', 1914, now in the Deutsches Historisches Museum, Berlin.

19. 5 May 1813 is the date of an important battle at Gersdorf (Saxony), the date of Kierkegaard's birth, and the date in 1945 of the liberation. See Flacke, ed., *Mythen der Nationen*, 83.

20. See also, for example, Elisabeth Jerichau-Baumann's painting of Denmark, 1851, in the Carlsberg Glyptotek, Copenhagen.

21. In the Musée des Beaux-Arts, Bordeaux (Bx E 439-Bx 1852-2-1). Illustrated in Flacke, ed., *Mythen der Nationen*, 340.

22. Athens, National Art Gallery and Alexandros Soutzos Museum (3202). Illustrated in Flacke, ed., *Mythen der Nationen*, 162.

23. In the István Dobó Museum, Eger (55119). Illustrated in Flacke, ed., *Mythen der Nationen*, 398.

24. Illustrated at T.C.W. Blanning, ed., *The Oxford Illustrated History of Modern Europe*, Oxford, 1996: 34.

25. See, for example, A. de Bruyn, *Omnium pene Europae, Asiae, Aphricae atque Americae gentium habitus*, Antwerp, 1581.

26. Many examples are to be found in R. Douglas, *'Great Nations Still Enchained': The Cartoonists' Vision of Empire 1848–1914*, London, 1993.

27. See various collections of cartoons available on the Internet, and in particular http://www.humboldt.edu/~jcb10/spanwar.shtml, consulted 12 April 2003. I am grateful to Yu-Chun Kao, an MA student at the Universiteit van Amsterdam in 2002/3, for bringing these cartoons to my attention.

28. Illustrated at Wintle, 'Renaissance Maps': 160.

29. See M.J. Wintle, *The Image of Europe: The Portrayal of Europe in Cartography and Iconography throughout the Ages*, Cambridge, 2008, forthcoming: chapters 4, 5.

30. Designed by M. Hamberg (Kew, c. 1780); copy held in the Museum of Archaeology and Anthropology, Cambridge.

31. The point has been made with regard to maps and the media by the great cartographic historian Brian Harley, in J.B. Harley and D. Woodward, eds, *The History of Cartography*, vol. 1: *Cartography in Prehistoric, Ancient and Medieval Europe and the Mediterranean*, Chicago, 1987: 4–5.

Chapter 12

The Nation in Song

PHILIP V. BOHLMAN

Prelude: The Bards of Ukraine

Two bards sing this chapter into being, resonant with the narratives they intoned to sing in the Ukrainian nation in the seventeenth and nineteenth century (Figures 12.1 and 12.2).[1] The two bards, a Cossack nobleman, domesticated through the elevation of folk art in the seventeenth century, and Wernyhora, memorialised through the monumental style of the Romantic Polish painter, Jan Matejko (1838–1893), sing of the Ukrainian nation in styles and with national imaginaries that are as strikingly similar as they are different.[2]

The Cossack bard turns to music during a moment of rest, the emblems of his power – horse and sceptre, ornate sword and lavish garb – momentarily laid aside in exchange for the national instrument of Ukraine, the *bandura*. He plays with abandon and sings, mediating between the song that has entered his consciousness and the inscribed text written across the base of the painting itself. In the Cossack's song, Ukraine is self-assured, bounded by evidence musically mustered for a quintessential Ukrainianness, that leaves little question about its cultural and national authenticity. This song of Ukraine does not simply rise from the soil of the nation: the song, through its transcribed text at the Cossack bard's feet, provides the very land of the nation, and by singing the song of Ukraine, the Cossack bard lays claim to the nation itself. The *bandura* is no less a product of the country, for it appears here and in imagery to the present in countless variants, each one crafted by the

Figure 12.1: Cossack Playing Bandura (seventeenth century). Source: National Museum of Ukrainian Art, Kyiv.

peasant-musician who proclaims an allegiance to a collective unified through song.[3]

In contrast, the epic bard, Wernyhora, displays a restless and troubled presence on the canvas. The haunting hagiography with which Matejko treats his bard and the music he imagines into being bears witness to the Wernyhora's association with a different sort of mediation, the political and ideological mediation that has the potential to accommodate cultural differences along national borders. Flanked by symbols of Poland on the left and Ukraine on the right, Wernyhora has dropped his modern *bandura*, the hurdy-gurdy sometimes called a *lira*, to the rocky, infertile ground below him.[4] The centrality of song notwithstanding, Matejko renders its contents unclear. Will the Polish nobleman with notebook and pen inscribe it in Polish? Alternatively, will it retain its Ukrainian character and thus its familiarity to the peasant woman and the Orthodox priest? The nation itself, embodied by Wernyhora rising from the earth, transcends the border, overtly aspiring towards the very sacrality that envelops the bard's head in the halo of the moon.

Figure 12.2: Wernyhora (1883) – Jan Matejko (1838–1893). Source: National Museum of Art, Kraków. Used with permission.

The national music of Ukraine contrasts as much as the nation itself in the two images of Ukraine sounding the prelude to this chapter. The reason these images of the nation differ might seem at first glance obvious. Historically, one painting dates from the seventeenth century, and it expresses a premodern (or early modern, in more general European historical terms) set of national metaphors. The other painting reflects late-nineteenth-century nationalist metaphors. Aesthetically, one painting is imbued with folk-like qualities, the other with the painterly skill of a renowned nationalist painter. The political difference – one painting is Ukrainian, the other Polish – is so obvious that it might be too easy to overlook why the nationalist attributes of 'Ukrainian' and 'Polish' themselves are so different as almost to defy simple comparison.

What kind of Ukraine is being sung here? The music that we can draw from the paintings provides conflicting and complex answers to that question. There is little about the Cossack bard that suggests a sacred image of his Ukraine, whereas Wernyhora rises, Christ-like, from the music at his feet. The Cossack's national instrument is consciously a folk-music instrument, and its maker might well have been a peasant, though there is also no reason to believe that he himself could not have constructed the instrument. Wernyhora's *lira* variant of the *bandura* functions like a machine, and thus it is highly unlikely that he could have built it himself.[5] Even if we today do not hear the music off the surface of the respective canvasses, it is evident that the

Cossack is singing an epic, with line-by-line structure, which is highly personal and reflective of the mythical world of the Cossack in Ukrainian history. Wernyhora sings of the present, a song of border conflicts resolved, a song text rendered in Polish by the modern nationalist collector of song but understandable to Poles and Ukrainians alike. The solo voice and the collective voice will inevitably sing of Ukraine from different genres.

At the end of the nineteenth century, Wernyhora had entered the national narratives of border conflict between Poland and Ukraine, not just in Matejko's historical masterpiece, but also in dramatic works, such as Stanisław Wyspiański's 1901 play, *Wesele* ('The Wedding Feast').[6] At the beginning of the twenty-first century, in 2004, Matejko's Wernyhora made another appearance as the symbol of reconciliation between Poland and Ukraine, this time as the cover art for the book, *Viyny i myr* ('Wars and Peace'). This was distributed by the publishers to Ukrainian schools and universities in the most contested regions of western Poland with the explicitly activist agenda to narrate a new nationalism of European unity.[7]

It is the premise of this chapter that music narrates every nation in diverse ways, and that the power of music to narrate nationalism in varied forms arises from the vast array of genres that constitute national and nationalist musical repertoires and styles. The relation between multiple forms of the nation-state and the multitude of musical narratives in music, moreover, is no accident. The rise of musical modernity, I argue here, follows a path that often parallels the rise of the modern nation and nationalism. The expansion of nationalism as a global response to postcolonialism has no less found its parallel in the cosmopolitanism of musical nationalism in the newly emerging Third World nations.[8] My point is not that all modern music is national or nationalist, rather that it has the potential to narrate the nation. How and where music narrates the nation, therefore, depends on the variety of meanings and subject positions in music that are open to debate at any and all moments. Even in the most seemingly incontestable genres of musical nationalism, such as the national anthem, the nation constantly assumes different forms and meanings for different groups of citizens. The national chorus historically has a constantly shifting membership.

From the outset, it is crucial to recognise that the narrative power of musical nationalism results from, even depends on, a paradox. Music is fundamentally non-representational, which means, by extension, that it can narrate only what given subjectivities will it to narrate. Music lends itself to genres that not only invent and construct meanings for the nation, but also multiply and deconstruct those meanings. The narrative genres of national music are malleable, voraciously absorbing new texts and spawning new forms of collective performance. The borders between genres are flexible and permeable, but that means that repertoires often mix and that hybrid styles are the rule rather than the exception. Music's representational paradox, thus, generates the narrative energy fuelling the history upon which modern nationalism is borne.

Narrative Genre between the National and the Nationalist

The present chapter unfolds as a series of sections devoted to specific genre pairs, which frame a space in which music narrates the nation in ways that are related yet distinctive. The choice of genre pairs is not meant to imply underlying dialectic, though dialectic too is one of the narrative processes that music history juxtaposes with national history. Instead, the pairs expand the space in which multiple images of the nation and its narratives are allowed to emerge through changing historical moments. The essay resists isolating genres and practices of music that display narrativity, as opposed to those that do not. Quite the contrary, the essay takes the non-representational paradox of music and turns it on its head, theorising just why musical genres become narrative the moment they are enlisted in the service of the nation. The pairs also result from classes of comparison that function in distinctive ways. Epics and ballads contrast with each other in ways quite unlike national anthems and military music; the sacred and the secular complement each other in ways that do not bear direct comparison with folk music and popular music. As different classes of genre, however, all these pairs yield crucial spaces in which music comes to represent the nation.

In the pages that follow, as I did in the opening comparison of the two Ukrainian bards, I make a distinction between forms of musical representation and narrativity that I refer to as the 'national' and the 'nationalist'. The Cossack bard is intensively national, Wernyhora extensively nationalist. That distinction, not surprisingly, also reinforces the ways in which genre accrues to music in the forms of overlapping but contrastive pairs. Some of the most general distinctions between the national and the nationalist in music appear in the next section of this chapter. Such distinctions are admittedly coarse at first glance, but they allow themselves to be extracted from scholarship on music and nationalism.[9] The coexistence of national and nationalist forms of musical narrativity empowers music to be particularly malleable as a means for shaping a nation in many images. The distinctions between and among the national and nationalist genres of music are great and small, sometimes stereotypical but more often subtle. The genres that constitute national and nationalist music overlap at times, but at other times differ sharply from one another. In both cases, nonetheless, the turn to music to shape an image of the nation is conscious.

The differences between national and nationalist music reveal themselves in a number of ways, including the ways in which the nation uses music to draw attention to its borders. In national music, reinforcing borders is not a primary theme, whereas nationalist music often mobilises the cultural, even political, defence of borders. In both instances, the producers and consumers, the creators and performers, of national and nationalist music are distinctive, as are those who collect, disseminate, or even study and write about them.

Each nation in the modern world can claim repertoires of national and nationalist music, but the ways in which those repertoires interact with each other – the performative processes filling in the space between the national and the nationalist – are specific to an individual national and the historical moment that generates and transforms given genres.

Despite the differences and distinctions, the interrelation between national and nationalist music bears witness to modern history in many ways. Modernity, for example, invests folk music with national traits and national anthems with nationalist character. Most nations, individually and in collectives, also express a belief in the capacity of music to be international, hence to cross borders while defining them. In historical moments such as the early twenty-first century, when great emphasis is placed on strengthening unity (e.g., through the expansion of the European Union into Eastern Europe), time and money are expended on the creation of music for international venues (e.g., the yet-to-be-resolved debate about the Schiller/Beethoven 'Ode to Joy' as the EU anthem).[10] The difficulties with which the national can be extricated from the nationalist again make it abundantly clear that music rarely represents the nation without narrating its history and ideals in one way or another.

National and nationalist music assume their functions, and even acquire their aesthetic and sonic individuality, from the ways in which they connect history to the nation. History is more oblique and malleable in national music, which possesses the potential to shape it and make it more tangible through narrative genres. In nationalist music, history is rarely oblique, primarily because the nation is insistently mapped on the narrative functions of music. In both national and nationalist genres, music articulates a sort of imbalance that results when history or the nation put each other at risk. When it becomes national or nationalist, music also assumes a new sort of power, potentially redressing the imbalance, but to various ends, which in turn yield the range of genre traits that provide the general framework below.

The National and the Nationalist in Music

Traits of the National

- Musical genres emphasise internal characteristics
- National culture is generated from within
  - Metaphors stress the origin of the nation, particularly in nature
  - The national language is treated as distinctive
  - The generation of national culture itself is realised through symbols of reproduction in musical genres (e.g., weddings, life cycles, courting dances)
- Music represented by the local and the individual on the stage

- Individual musicians presented as creative, particularly within oral tradition
- Festivals emphasise local choruses
- Pageants arise from local performances

Traits of the Nationalist

- Musical genres emphasise external characteristics
  - Nationalist culture threatened and made insecure from without
  - Survival, rather than origins, are of primary importance
  - Blurred borders cut through places where languages are insecure
- Symbols of cosmopolitanism proliferate in music, but generate a sense of loss
  - Music represented by collectives and competition on the stages
  - Emphasis placed on the size of ensembles
  - Festival choruses claim mixed local and regional membership
- Minorities, especially from outside national borders, display commonality

The national and the nationalist, however, do not fall into distinctively different categories, but rather they shift, blur and come to influence each other. The relation between them, moreover, is unstable, with the national changing over time to become nationalist. The same song, moreover, may be national or nationalist, depending on where and when it is performed, at which historical moment or towards which ideological end. Songs narrate the nation so powerfully, moreover, precisely because they change, with old melodies acquiring new texts ('contrafacts') and new performers borrowing and altering previous repertoires for their own purposes ('covers'). The permeable and shifting boundaries, nonetheless, do not eliminate the distinctions between the national and nationalist. Instead, the distinctions become more complex and more emblematic of the changing landscapes of the modern nation.[11]

Inventing Musical Genre to Narrate the Nation

The musical myths about the birth of nations notwithstanding, musical genres that narrate the nation do not simply appear *sui generis* in national histories. The Cossack's *bandura* no more grew as an organic product of the Ukrainian soil than the Finnish *kantele* emerged from the northern seas in the Finnish national epic, the *Kalevala*, or than the most classical instrument of South Indian music, the *vina*, truly embodied the goddess Sarasvati. As images of the nation, these myths about music draw our attention to the nation. The metaphors they provide may seem at first glance to reside in the shrouds of myth, but they acquire their meaning because they respond to a historical awareness of a shared history. They are invented to serve the nation by participating in the narration of its history.

No genre is more widely associated with the nation and nationalism than folk song. Its association with tradition and the past – with the imagination of myth and the premodern traces of the nation – nonetheless belies its modernity and its narrative potency to proliferate as new and fertile genres and subgenres. The very concept of folk song – *Volkslied* – owes itself to a specific historical moment and narration of Enlightenment, Johann Gottfried Herder's two volumes, *Voices of the People in Songs* and *Folk Songs*.[12] That Herder wrote extensively about folk song, both as a philologist and an active collector, and that other musical genres preoccupied him throughout his life, is surely less well known than his other contributions to modern concepts of the nation and nationalism.[13] Herder's common engagement with folk song and the nation is significant for many reasons, of course, but suffice it to say here that he succeeded in juxtaposing genre and nation, and did so by specifying performative processes of narration. The folk song of a nation afforded certain types of narrative connections: between dialect in oral tradition and national languages in literate traditions; between the internal expression of individual feeling and emotion, and the external perception and performance of collective experience; between musical forms relying on personal creativity and those rallying a nation's unity; between the local and the global.[14] Through performance, folk song could do all of these things, which, when unified, unleashed many of the modern narratives that ascribe meaning to the nation.

Song expressed national aspirations even before the rise of the modern nation-state. The performers of 'proto-nationalist' genres of music sang tales of great leaders and the people they rallied into collective action. Such genres chronicled the conflicts of power and battles with mighty enemies, and they charted the landscape of struggles and great events that would inscribe the fate of the nation on its history. It is in these genres, moreover, that national bards invent and then play upon musical instruments, unfettering myth from nature and affixing it to the tales of the nation. In musicological parlance, as in the theoretical terminology that provides the context for the contributors to the present volume, we refer to the genres of national music that preceded the nation as 'narrative', for they told stories about the past. Those stories, often passed orally from singer to singer and from community to community, were also part of a much larger historical complex, within which the threads of nascent national identity were woven together to form the whole that unified people in the early stages of nationhood.

Among the proto-national genres of music, the epic and the ballad most commonly possessed the power to transform local stories into national histories. Narrative genres of folk song shape the narrative and national spaces that form between myth and history, thus creating textual structures for representing the nation-state, in both premodern and modern forms. It is crucial that epic and ballad, as narrative genres, reflect different social contexts and cultural meanings throughout the world, thereby designating national distinctiveness at the same time as national similarity. The narratives in the epic and ballad make it possible to understand the foundations from which nations formed and to see why some of a nation's oldest stories remain embedded in the narration of its most recent histories.

The epic is the story of the nation writ large through the deeds of a single individual, whose remarkable deeds mobilise the nation and whose leadership in a mythological age provides a metaphor for a modern nation's coming of age. The names of proto-national heroes resonate through great epic cycles: Moses in the *Torah*, Rama in the *Ramayana*, Odysseus in the *Odyssey*, the Cid in *El Cid*, Siegfried in the *Niebelungen*, and Väinämöinen in the *Kalevala*. The epic hero acquires extraordinary power through song, and that power only increases through the intervention of modern poets and musicians with national and nationalist motivations, be they those of the Enlightenment translations of *El Cid* by Johann Gottfried Herder, the creation of a national myth through Elias Lönnrot's collection of runes for the Finnish *Kalevala*, or Richard Wagner's operatic cycle, *Der Ring des Nibelungen*.[15]

In epics, the nation usually appears as unstable and in fragments, which in turn are evident in the formal poetic and musical structures of the genre. The basic unit of the epic is the line of text and melody, which, however, grows from internal formulaic structures, usually the division of the line into several phrases and metric patterns that connect text to melody. Epic singers are often specialists and professional singers, and their names, as with Homer, may become known when their versions begin to circulate in canonical variants. Epic singers frequently perform long stories from memory and possess poetic license to dissect and recombine narrative units that personalise their performative styles. The singer's specialty often means that singers acquire special status in their communities, even as local and national historians. The special skills required for epic performance are underscored by the music, for example, when epic singers, as is often the case, accompany themselves on an instrument (e.g., the Ukrainian *bandura* in the opening figures). Melody, rhythm and metre, moreover, complement the nuance of language, often meaning that the music itself complements the narrative structures of the language. Language and melody together acquire the attributes of a poetic language that can give specific meaning to the nation at the formative stages represented in the epic.[16]

If epics chronicle the *longue durée* of a nation's formative stages, ballads more often narrate the lives of individuals and the events that constitute a national mosaic. In cultures where ballads predominate as narrative genres (e.g., Central and Northern Europe, North and South America) ballads persist into the nationalism of the present because of the ways in which oral tradition has interacted with written tradition. In southwestern Europe, for example, ballad repertoires such as the *romancero* bear witness to the ways in which narrative genres ply the borders that separate modern nationalism from its precursors. Jewish *romancero* repertoires accompanied the Sephardic Jews in their largely Mediterranean diaspora after their expulsion from the Iberian Peninsula at the end of the fifteenth century. Sephardic ballads, sung in the Jewish variant of Spanish, Ladino, recount historical events from throughout the Mediterranean diaspora, especially conflicts between European Christians and Muslim empires in North Africa, the Balkans and Ottoman Turkey.[17]

In the ballad, it is not a few great heroes whose deeds are celebrated, but rather the lives of the 'every person' and the tragic realities of daily life. The characters in a ballad narrative, therefore, are frequently stereotypes, and the narrative itself often contains a moral. The musical structure and form of a ballad also make it possible for a broad cross-section of society to be familiar with them, if not to participate, say, during the folk-music revivals of the 1950s and 1960s, in their transmission as singers. Each verse of the strophic form – ballads are musically identifiable through their use of verses, often with one or two lines of refrain, or multiple lines of chorus – sets the stage for a scene in the larger drama that unfolds as the ballad's narrative. Characters interact with each other, entering and exiting from the verses, with the main characters eventually reaching a denouement, often marked by the tragic confrontation with reality. In the twenty-first century, United States folk- and country-music ballads still voice responses from both the right and the left political wings, for and against the War in Iraq, no less than they did in previous moments of war and political conflict, from the Second World War through to the Vietnam War.[18]

Military Music and National Anthems

Military music mobilises the nation to undertake action in the name of the nation. Its conscious goal is to perform moments in which the nation recognises itself in the collective actions of a military force, and in the more abstract performance of that collective through ensembles dedicated to the ritual performance of military music (e.g., parades and political ceremonies). Although it is explicitly nationalistic, military music has many functions, and it assumes complex forms. In the broadest terms, military music expresses nationalism on two levels, which literally and figuratively represent the nation through military action. On the first level, musical practices accompany soldiers as they go to war. In this literal sense, music does not so much represent the nation as mobilise the nation. The modern nation-state thus uses military music to ritualise the ways in which the nation interacts with its armies. The nation establishes ensembles, particularly choruses and wind ensembles whose members are also members of the military, to perform at specific moments that focus the nation on the conditions of its defence or its entry into combat itself.[19]

The metaphor of the military musical ensemble is remarkably widespread in premodern and modern nation-states throughout the world. Such ensembles are particularly recognisable because of a characteristic sound – even genres of national music that crosses national musical borders, as in the Ottoman 'Janissary music' that influenced Central European symphonic music in the eighteenth century – or because of the military uniforms in which musicians perform.[20] The music of military ensembles demonstrates universal and national characteristics, but it is surely the more specific traits that are most critical in their evocation of nationalism. The historical use of pipe bands by the United Kingdom serves as an example of a military music with specifically nationalist symbolism. From the mid-nineteenth century to the present, British military bands have made extensive use of Highland bagpipes. Though the pipe band itself performs the characteristic of one of Britain's more contested regions, Scotland, it came to the service of the nation at the time of greatest colonial expansion.

Military music need not be unequivocally militaristic to represent the nation. It may generate more metaphorical uses in the creation and inscription of national repertoires. Certain genres and repertoires that came into being with specific military references may spin off new genres, which might variously be called 'quasi-national anthems' or 'unofficial national anthems'. Unofficial national anthems serve all the functions of a national anthem, but they do not have the top-down sanction to represent the nation beyond its borders. The unofficial anthem enjoys a wide range of ritual functions, stretching from performance at the beginning of athletic events (e.g., in England, where 'Three Lions' rather than 'God Save the Queen' is often sung at football matches) to the marking of national crises (e.g., in the United States after the 9/11 attacks, when 'God Bless America' and 'Amazing Grace' were more widely sung than 'The Star Spangled Banner'). Unofficial anthems may produce even more collective performance than their official cousins, perhaps because they have more immediate historical or modern relevance, or even because they are easier to perform or to sing as a collective. Sanctioned to represent the nation or not, unofficial national anthems usually contain particularly powerful historical narratives, which invest them with a common narrative of nationalism.

With few exceptions, official national anthems are less well known and historically much less stable than are unofficial anthems. Origin myths swirl about national anthems, generating abundant questionable and often false attributions of authenticity.[21] National anthems are notoriously unstable, with version upon version competing for official sanction and trying to keep up with changing governments.[22] Anthems move around from nation to nation, with notable cases of exchange from one nation to another; the melody that was first Austria's national anthem, Franz Joseph Haydn's 'Kaiserhymne' (originally the theme of the second movement of the String Quartet, Op. 77, no. 3, Hob. III: 77) was dropped by Austria after the First World War, only to be picked up by Germany in 1922. Nor is it uncommon for anthems to be exported as contrafacts, in some cases on the coat-tails of colonial administrations (e.g., 'God Save the Queen', which served as the melody for numerous postcolonial nations in the British Commonwealth), but more often because certain tunes have a global popularity, if for military and nationalist ends. Just what, one might query, is and is not national about national anthems?

There are many reasons why national anthems are musically ambiguous, even if we imagine that their nationalist cultural work is potentially of great significance. First, national anthems do move around, and they often possess the generic characteristics that make melodies suitable for contrafacts and cover versions, assigning new texts to pre-existing versions.[23] Second, external forms that together yield the subgenres that fit together as the genre of the national anthem itself are remarkably similar on their musical surfaces. They are either strophic or repetitive in form, using the contrast between an opening theme or chorus and a middle section, usually a bridge of some kind or, in a march, a trio section (the B section in an ABA form). Third, melodic themes, leitmotifs and gestures do seem to migrate from anthem to anthem. The opening of the Irish anthem, for example, uses the same arch-like gesture that begins the German anthem. Fourth, through ceremonial and ritual uses the tempo becomes generalised. In performance, marches do not lend themselves to marching and hymns do not quite possess the sacred aura produced by congregational singing in a sanctuary. Fifth, anthem composers have historically avoided melodies and formal techniques that would exoticise their nations. Nineteenth-century attempts to find an appropriate *raga*, or Indian melodic mode, for 'God Save the Queen' as an anthem in colonial India, for example, were abandoned.

Are the national anthems of the world more similar than different?[24] Does the fact that their histories intersect – as melodies and discrete musical compositions or as the symbols of political change – exaggerate or eviscerate their contemporary roles as genres narrating the nation? To answer such questions, it may be helpful to think about myths that surround, buttress and shroud national anthems, and reflect upon these myths comparatively, much as the origins of European nations have been increasingly narrated through both myth and history.[25] At times national anthems chronicle history, but just as often they rely on the narrative ambiguities of myth. If the myths woven into national anthems are similar, it may well be a result of the fact that they compete with each other in an international arena, where the borders between genres acquire the functions of the borders between nations.

Mixing and Sampling: Music of the People and Popular Music

At the beginning of the twenty-first century, the shear abundance of musical genres narrating the nation has increased appreciably. More styles and repertoires contain nationalist music, and more musicians – music makers, performers, national subjects actively engaged in narrating the nation through music – give voice to nationalism. Surely, one reason for the explosion of nationalism in music must be the proliferation of nationalism itself in a postcolonial age of globalisation. By extension, there is greater cause for singing for or against the nation as it provides the contexts for the lives and activities of its citizens. Globalisation, with its impact on transnational circulation of music and its technological capacity to transform musical genres, must also account for the further transformation of postmodern musical narratives, in other words the sampling and mixing that allows music to have different meanings for different subjects. In the twenty-first century, music narrates the nation in hybrid forms, and musical genre moves across historical, geographical and linguistic borders, generating new processes of narration by mixing the old with the new. New music – modern and postmodern – narrates the nation, not simply keeping pace with modernity, but realising modernity through modern technologies and postmodern contests, from popular-song contests to the shuffle of iPod repertoires created from hip-hop songs narrating the Orange Revolution.

It is crucial to recognise that the mixing and sampling of new genres that narrate the nation does not simply happen. Actors upon the stages of postcolonial nationalisms perform the new genres, and they do so because music's capacity to narrate the nation is fundamental to their postmodern subject positions. There is perhaps no clearer example of such subject positions than the growth of choralism, in other words, the participation in a large choral collective that shares a common cause. No other case of choralism as nation-building is surely as familiar as that in the Baltic States of Estonia, Latvia and Lithuania, where choruses amassed during the 1980s to bring about the so-called 'Singing Revolution', with its open agenda of national independence from the Soviet Union. The importance of the chorus for the consolidation of the nation in music has a long history, with many local and national variants, from the growth of the German singing society in the nineteenth century to the emergence of *kibbutz* choruses in Israel and Celtic choruses along Europe's Celtic fringe.[26]

In the 1990s, however, the phenomenon spread across Europe with an especially renewed vigour and, in many cases, ideologically motivated agendas. Choruses restored Jewish culture to the destroyed communities of Central and Eastern Europe, and 'guest workers' from Turkey transformed traditionally solo and male-dominated repertoires into choral repertoires for the performance in the working-class neighbourhoods of the European metropolis. The symbolism of the new choralism at the end of the twentieth century was overt, intentionally rendered as nationalist as possible. Because the chorus can embody a religious or cultural community, as well as people with a common historical and national background, it possesses the power to express their unity through song. The new choralism, moreover, has responded to a historical irony of expanding nationalism, that is, to the political fissures that might otherwise prevent unity. The postmodern chorus, not only in a reunified Europe, but also in postcolonial Africa and Asia, is mobile, connecting the local to the global processes of choral tours and CD distribution. The singing nation embodied by the new choralism at once gives a virtual presence to a collective and community that once were and might again become real.[27]

The sampling and mixing of genres has also meant that popular music has become increasingly national and nationalist in the twenty-first century, sweepingly reversing the modernist teleology of popular music as a global phenomenon that effectively ameliorated national differences. The reversal is evident even on the surface of many rock repertoires, which on the national level have begun to replace performance in English with local, urban dialects and lyrics in the national language. Prior to the turn of the present century, national entries in the Eurovision Song Contest, the largest of all international popular music competitions, were overwhelmingly in English or French. Since 2000, however, during a period when all the victorious national entries were from Eastern or Southeastern Europe, national languages have enjoyed a resurgence, even when singing in a national language for Slovenian, Macedonian or Turkish performers effectively eliminates any chance of winning. Hybrid styles do not abandon the national for the international, retaining instead the former by choosing traits from the latter that enhance local meaning and ideology.[28] African American and Afro-Caribbean popular styles, for example, may be integrated into Eastern European or East Asian rock repertoires as a means of sharpening a message of resistance. At the beginning of the twenty-first century, hip-hop currently enjoys a universal presence in popular repertoires, but in each repertoire it assumes new and complex forms because of the ways the language-based melodic style augments texts in dialect and specific forms of national criticism.[29] The hybridity that accompanies the globalisation of popular music has created the means and the contexts that pull more and more repertoires into the narrative sphere of the national and the nationalist.

Coda: Kyiv 2005 – The Orange Revolution and the Eurovision Song Contest

'Shche ne vmerla Ukraini' – 'Ukraine's Glory Has Not Perished'
National Anthem of Ukraine – Composed 1864; Adopted 1917/18
Text: Pavlo Chubynskyi; Melody: Mykhailo Verbytskyi

Shche ne vmerla Ukraini, ny slava, ny volja,
Shche nam, brattja – ukraincy, usmyzhnetjsja dolja,
Zginutj nashi voryshenjki, jak rosa na soncy,
Zazhivemo y mi, brattja, u svoij storoncy.

> *Chorus:*
> *Dushu j tylo mi polozhim za nashu svobodu*
> *Y pokazhem, shcho mi, brattja, kozacjkogo rodu.*
> *Dushu j tylo mi polozhim za nashu svobodu*
> *Y pokazhem, shcho mi, brattja, kozacjkogo rodu.*

English translation

Ukraine's Glory has not perished, nor her freedom
Upon us, fellow compatriots, fate shall smile once more.
Our enemies will vanish, like dew in the morning sun,
And we too shall rule, brothers, in a free land of our own.

> Chorus:
> We'll lay down our souls and bodies to attain our freedom,
> And we'll show that we, brothers, are of the Cossack nation.
> And we'll lay down our souls and bodies to attain our freedom,
> And we'll show that we, brothers, are of the Cossack nation.

'Razom Nas Bahato, Nas Ne Podolaty!' – 'Together We Are Many, We Cannot Be Defeated'
Greenjolly – Ukrainian Entry in the 2005 Eurovision Song Contest (Kyiv, Ukraine)

We won't stand this – no! Revolution is on![30]
'Cuz lies be the weapon of mass destruction!
All together we're one! All together we're strong!
God be my witness we've waited too long!

Fal'sifikaciyam – ni! mahinaciyam – ni!
Ponyatiyam – ni! Ni brehni!

Virimo – Tak! Mozhemo – Tak!
Znayu peremozhemo – Tak! Tak!

Chorus:
Razom nas bahato – nas ne podolaty!

What you wanna say to your daughters and sons?
You know the battle is not over till the battle is won!
Truth be the weapon! We ain't scared of the guns!
We stay undefeated, 'cuz together we're one!

My – vzhe razom! My – nazavzhdy!
My Ukrainy don'ki i syny!
Zaraz yak nikoly godi chekaty!

Chorus:
Razom nas bahato – nas ne podolaty!

This chapter closes as it began, with two musical images of Ukraine. It would be easy enough to assert that the contrasts between the two images, each claimed by history and performance as a national anthem, parallel the musical images projected by the Cossack bard and Wernyhora that open the chapter. The official anthem is a historical composition from the nineteenth century, with references to borders and geographical markers – 'from the San to the Don' and 'the Black Sea' and 'the Dnieper' bounding the nation in verse two – typical of the age of rising nationalism. The passage from myth to history – the 'brothers' in verse and chorus traverse between a 'Cossack nation' of the mythical past to the 'free land of our own' in modern history – persists, thereby reflecting the historical *longue durée*. A strictly historical parallel, which might connect the references to Ukraine's Cossack heritage and its response to the need for revolution, does not always yield counterpoint with parallel voices, but the interplay of consonant and dissonant images unquestionably underscores the intent to use both songs, in their own historical contexts, as national anthems. Crucially, the counterpoint of the two anthems took shape in 2004–2005, at a historical moment when the national and the nationalist came into conflict during the 'Orange Revolution'. That music – above all, national song on an international musical and political stage – should be mustered to contribute substantially to the articulation and resolution of a conflict, might seem remarkable in 2005. Still, I should argue that it is not the least bit remarkable if one correctly interprets the narrative subtexts in this chapter, which make the case that music intersects with nationalism not simply to narrate the past, but rather to contribute profoundly to the ways we perceive and understand the history of the present.

Ukraine's official anthem, 'Shche ne vmerla Ukraini', could not be more typical of a national anthem conceived in the nineteenth century and adopted in the twentieth century. The text and melody take the Romantic imagery of nationalism as a given.[31] The verse-chorus structure of the text does no more than announce that this song is national in character and that the land it describes is worthy of nationhood. A generalisable geography, the collective 'we' and the universal recognition of freedom as worthy of nationalistic struggle – all these together are the stuff of national anthems. There is little that is Ukrainian about the melody and the form of the song itself. The minor mode might be more likely in Eastern than in Central Europe, and the relative absence of upbeats reflects the similar absence of articles in the Ukrainian language. All of these traits, however, are also stereotypes, and they must be, if 'Shche ne vmerla Ukraini' is to pass from national to nationalist song from the time of its composition in the mid-nineteenth century to the time of its adoption during Ukraine's nascent nationhood at the conclusion of the First World War.

The unofficial Ukrainian anthem of 2005, 'Razom Nas Bahato', depends no less on stereotype for its journey to a nationalist song as the Ukrainian entry in the Eurovision Song Contest, which was held in Kyiv in spring 2005 because the Ukrainian singer, Ruslana, had won the 2004 competition in Istanbul with her 'Diki Tanzi' ('Wild Dances').[32] The myth surrounding 'Razom Nas Bahato' is that its performers, the hip-hop band, Greenjolly, gathered fragments from street music during the winter Orange Revolution that, through a second election, finally brought Viktor Yushchenko to power. Musically, myth and history necessarily overlapped; especially when we realise the extent to which hip-hop creates its textual and melodic hybrid by employing the technologies of sampling and mixing.[33] The Ukrainian hosts of the Fiftieth Eurovision Song Contest, however, misjudged the borders between the national and the nationalist in Greenjolly's hip-hop entry; when the final vote tally had been phoned in from around Europe, Ukraine finished near the end.[34] Greenjolly's assertion that 'we are many' failed to seduce other Europeans to the Orange Revolution, as universal as it was rendered through confusing references to the 'weapon of mass destruction' and winning the 'battle'. Melody and musical form, no less critically, created a nationalism that the voters from the 40 competing nations, members of the European Broadcasting Union, failed to embrace. Hip-hop, the music of African American struggle, had never fared well in the Eurovision Song Contest, and it would not do so in 2005 while in service to Ukrainian nationalism.

The musical images of Ukraine that begin and conclude this chapter deliberately mix genres and draw upon different forms of narrativity. They juxtapose the past and the present by allowing us to draw parallels between them. It would be misleading in conclusion, however, to suggest that these musical narratives about Ukraine – or about any other nation I might have chosen as a case study – are all the same. Alternatively, to suggest that their myriad differences are effectively reduced to a 'changing sameness', in which the national and the nationalist are distinct but always blurring into each other. The musical genres that narrate nationalism do interact with each other, and they form hybrid genres. They do so, however, because music is performative and its narrativity requires agencies at multiple levels of subjectivity. They do so because they locate the nation in time even more than locating it in space. The Ukrainian anthems that open the coda narrate history by promising action in the future. Narrating the nation by drawing upon music's performative passage through time transforms history itself. The Cossack past provides the historical touchstone at the end of the chorus; the war that will make the many one is still ongoing. The narrativity that produces and accrues to multiple nationalisms, nonetheless, is by no means unique to the genres that constitute musical nationalism. Instead, music, as a non-representational and non-narrative art form, enhances narrativity and deepens the meanings of nationalism. Through its counterpoint with history and the nation, music reminds us that nationalism is an ongoing narrative of our own world.

Notes

1. Figure 12.1 hangs in the National Museum of Fine Arts in Kyiv, while Figure 12.2 hangs in the National Museum of Art in Kraków. Both paintings circulate in national spaces outside and beyond the 'national museums' in which they hang. The Cossack bard adorns posters and postcards generated to symbolise the galleries devoted to Ukraine's epoch of early-modern independence, the 'Cossack Rococo', roughly the late sixteenth to the early eighteenth centuries. 'Wernyhora' enjoys a somewhat more ambiguous presence in the mediation of art historical images, taking its place more often among the musical symbols of Poland than in the monumental art of nineteenth-century Ukraine. I gratefully acknowledge permission to include these illustrations here.

2. National bards, reimagined as modern-day King Davids, playing stringed instruments derived from the biblical harp (*kineret*), populate the narratives of early national history. For a brilliant study of national bards, see K. Trumpener, *Bardic Nationalism: The Romantic Novel and the British Empire*, Princeton, 1997.

3. Nations often claim a national instrument during years of nascent nationhood. The *bandura* is unequivocally the instrument of Ukraine, whereas the *lira*, in the form of the hurdy-gurdy, is international. Modern and postmodern imagery strengthen the national symbolism of the *bandura*, through voluminous articles about organology to websites that reveal endless variants of the bandura, for example on postcards (see http://www.ArtUkraine.com).

4. In an earlier lithograph from 1875, Matejko positions the hurdy-gurdy in Wernyhora's lap, but retains the essential gestures of the epic bard that he would use for the oil painting eight years later (1883). Cf. the two images in S. Witkiewicz, *Matejko*, Lwow, 1912: 144, 147.

5. A hurdy-gurdy allows for continuous playing of the strings by turning a crank connected to a band that, like a violin bow, sounds the strings by being drawn over them. The *bandura* is plucked in the manner of a guitar. The two instruments, in these basic technological ways, represent a type of historical continuum as variants of the national instrument of Ukraine.

6. The Wernyhora of Wyspiański's *Wesele* appears at the November 1900 wedding of the poet, Lucjan Rydel, to a peasant woman. He bears a golden horn in the play, which, when

blown, should call the peasants to uprising. Eventually, the horn disappears, and the wedding guests content themselves with wedding music rather than the call to arms. Wernyhora, then, comes from and returns to the mythical world, with the possibility of peace offered to the historical world of early twentieth-century Eastern Europe. See A. Komaromi, 'Wyspiański's *Wesele*: Poised on the Border', *Theatre Journal* 54, 2002: 187–202.

7.   L. Ivshyna et al., *Viyny i myr*, Kyiv, 2004. See also 'Nationalisation of History', *The Day*, online version, 23 Nov. 2004; http://www.day.kiev.ua/127929/

8.   See, for example, K. Askew, *Performing the Nation: Swahili Music and Cultural Politics in Tanzania*, Chicago, 2002, and T. Turino, *Nationalists, Cosmopolitans, and Popular Music in Zimbabwe*, Chicago, 2000.

9.   See, for example, the classic R. Vaughan Williams, *National Music*, London, 1934; and R. Taruskin, 'Nationalism', *The New Grove Dictionary of Music and Musicians*, 2nd ed., London: Macmillan, 17, 2001: 689–706. In my own study of music and nationalism in Europe I treat the national and nationalist in separate chapters; see P.V. Bohlman, *The Music of European Nationalism*, Santa Barbara, 2004: 81–160.

10. At the present stage in the debate, the Beethoven score is used, but Schiller's text may not be sung to it, even though it provided the basis for the choral movement concluding Beethoven's *Ninth Symphony*. See C. Clark, 'Forging Identity: Beethoven's 'Ode' as European Anthem', *Critical Inquiry* 23, 4: 789–807.

11. Special thanks to Stefan Berger for urging me to consider further the ways in which the distinctions between the national and the nationalist in music merge and overlap.

12. J.G. Herder, *'Stimmen der Völker in Liedern'* and *Volkslieder*, Leipzig, 1778/79.

13. The most recent edition of his complete works, volume 3, with 1531 pages from Herder's publications and with commentary, largely contains books and essays devoted to genres we today, in part influenced by Herder, associate with folk song; J.G. Herder, *Johann Gottfried Herder Werke in zehn Bänden*, vol. 3: *Volkslieder, Übertragungen, Dichtungen*, ed. Ulrich Gaier, Frankfurt am Main, 1990.

14. I am currently translating many of Herder's writings on music and nationalism, which will be published in my forthcoming edition *Herder on Music and Nationalism* (Berkeley, forthcoming).

15. J.G. Herder, *Der Cid, Geschichte des Don Ruy Diaz, Grafen von Bivar, nach spanischen Romanzen*, in *Johann Gottfried Herder Werke*, vol. 3: *Volkslieder, Übertragungen, Dichtungen*, Frankfurt am Main, 1990: 545–693. To facilitate his translation and transformation of the *Cid*, Herder wove individual *romances* ('nach Romanzen'), Spanish ballads, into the larger form of the epic, thus suturing the two narrative song forms together. On the Finnish national epic, see E. Lönnrot, *The Kalevala: An Epic Poem after Oral Tradition*, trans. K. Bosley, Oxford, 1989 and T.K. Ramnarine, *Ilmatar's Inspirations: Nationalism, Globalization, and the Changing Soundscapes of Finnish Folk Music*, Chicago, 2003. The secondary literature devoted to the nationalism in Wagner's *Ring* cycle and its impact on German nationalism, from the late nineteenth century until the present, is virtually endless. The musicality of non-Western epics is no less extensive than of European and Judeo-Christian epics. The *Ramayana*, for example, is the basis for canonical musical genres in South and Southeast Asia, from Indonesian *wayang* (theatre) to Indian Bollywood film.

16. The classic work on epic, from Homer to the Balkans in the modern era, is A.B. Lord, *The Singer of Tales*, Cambridge, MA, 1960.

17. See, for example, S.G. Armistead, J.H. Silverman and I.J. Katz, *Judeo-Spanish Ballads from Oral Tradition: Epic Ballads*, Berkeley and Los Angeles, 1986.

18. Discussions of the text and music in ballads are more often than not separated by disciplines, between philological and contextual approaches. One important exception, in the classic anthology of the canonic English-language ballads, is B.H. Bronson, *The Traditional Tunes of the Child Ballads*, 4 vols, Princeton, 1959–1972.

19. See, for example, W.H. McNeill, *Keeping Together in Time: Dance and Drill in Human History*, Cambridge, MA, 1995.

20. In an American parade, for example, the uniforms of local high school bands are reminiscent of a tradition of discipline and collectivity translated from the band of a local military base. Both uniforms and music are meant to inspire patriotism.

21. See, for example, P. Nettl, *National Anthems*, trans. A. Gode, 2nd ed., New York, 1967; U. Ragozat, *Die Nationalhymnen der Welt: Ein kulturgeschichtliches Lexikon*, Freiburg im Bresgau, 1982.

22. Over the course of the past two centuries, Russia, in its various national forms, has claimed five different national anthems, several of them revived variants of an earlier anthem. As of 2008, the question of which anthem will serve the Russian Federation remains unresolved. See J.M. Daughtry, 'Russia's New Anthem and the Negotiation of National Identity', *Ethnomusicology* 47, 1: 42–67.

23. For a thorough philological study of such practices of covering pre-existing anthems in the German language, see H. Kurzke, *Hymnen und Lieder der Deutschen*, Mainz, 1990.

24. The sonic evidence allows one to judge for oneself, for example, in recorded compilations, such as *Complete National Anthems of the World*, a six-volume set recorded by the CD label, Marco Polo.

25. On the question of national myth, see M. Flacke, ed., *Mythen der Nationen: Ein europäisches Panorama*, Munich and Berlin, 1998.

26. For a discussion of 'pioneer' repertoires in the nation-building of Israel, see my introduction and afterword in H. Nathan, ed., *Israeli Folk Music: Songs of the Early Pioneers*, Madison, WI, 1994. For a critical assessment of the Celtic chorus, see M. Chapman, 'Thoughts on Celtic Music', in M. Stokes, ed., *Ethnicity, Identity and Music: The Musical Construction of Place*, Oxford, 1994: 29–44.

27. In Central and Eastern Europe, the synagogue chorus provides the best example of a choral movement reviving history through virtual performance. Many synagogue choruses exist only through performance in the extraordinary volume of CDs with Jewish liturgical music produced each year and available for purchase at Jewish museums and restored synagogues throughout Europe. At the 10 May 2005 dedication ceremony for one of the most controversial Holocaust monuments, the 'Monument for the Murdered Jews of Europe', for example, choral music was performed by an ensemble described as the Chorus of the White Stork Synagogue in Wrocław. In a state of extensive renovation, however, the White Stork Synagogue, with its conservative, male-only liturgical tradition, could not possibly support the chorus bearing its name, a chorus whose members come from various faiths and musical inclinations from throughout southwestern Poland.

28. For an illuminating study of the politicisation of traditional music drama in Indonesia, see A.N. Weintraub, *Power Plays: Wayang Golek Puppet Theater of West Java*, Athens, OH, and Singapore, 2004.

29. For a comparative study of hip-hop's global expansion and local meaning, see T. Mitchell, ed., *Global Noise: Rap and Hip-Hop Outside the USA*, Middletown, CT, 2001.

30. The mixture of English and Ukrainian is found in the version performed at the final competition of the Eurovision Song Contest on May 22, 2005. Widely circulating cover versions sometimes use more Ukrainian, at other times other non-Ukrainian languages, especially those of Eastern and Central Europe. The official Eurovision recording is on *Eurovision Song Contest, Kiew 2005: Alle Songs der Show* (CMC 0162702CMA, 1998), CD 2, tr. 19.

31. The versions of the Ukrainian national anthem available in reference books and on Internet sites contain abundant variations, some slight, others substantive. Such differences usually reflect the ideological functions of the source. For the two relatively neutral variants used in this chapter, see M. Boyd, 'National Anthems', *The New Grove Dictionary of Music and Musicians*, 17, 2nd ed., London, 2002: 685; and the Internet site, http://david.national-anthems.net/ua-m.jpg. Recorded versions do not always find their way to standard CDs of

PART V

NON-EUROPEAN PERSPECTIVES ON NATION AND NARRATION

Chapter 13

'People's History' in North America: Agency, Ideology, Epistemology

PETER SEIXAS

The protean notion of 'people's history' has multiple meanings in North American culture. It can refer to a narrative whose subject is 'the people', i.e. the masses – in contrast to political, economic and social elites – and thus carry a relatively explicit oppositional ideological orientation. It carries this message in Howard Zinn's *A People's History of the United States* as well as in the *Radical History Review* (1981) section entitled 'Towards a People's History' in an issue on 'Presenting the Past: History and the Public'.[1] The *Review* also used 'people's history' as that which could appeal to a broad audience (as opposed to academic elites), and further, whose production involved a 'shared authority' with 'the people'.[2] This 'people's history' might involve attempts to simplify communication and to explore genres beyond the academic monograph and journal article.

A 'people's history' can also refer to the people as a nation. This is the dominant meaning in the recent Canadian Broadcasting Corporation-Radio Canada production, *Canada: A People's History*, but the airing was preceded by saturation advertising to ensure that it would also be a 'people's history' in the sense of mass audience. The term can further imply a methodological orientation, where the larger story is built upon the biographies of individual people. Finally, there are interesting variations of the phrase. In the best-selling Canadian university textbook, *History of the Canadian Peoples*, the plural form pointedly refers to the multiple collectivities that comprise multinational, multicultural Canada.[3] George Bush's $100 million (US) 'We the People' programme aims to promote pride through knowledge of American history. These meanings are sometimes mutually exclusive, sometimes mutually reinforcing, and sometimes contradictory.

This paper explores the state of national histories in North America, drawing questions from the congeries of ideas implicit in the term 'people's history'. First, how are individuals situated within national history: are they portrayed as agents of change *qua* individuals, or alternatively as members of groups, or finally as beings swept up in an inexorable process that just 'happens', to paraphrase Forrest Gump? Second, what is the moral or ideological valence of the narrative? How is it emplotted? Third, to what extent does the history exhibit the narrator's epistemological self-consciousness and methodological transparency in relation to questions of historical truth? I will call these three questions those of agency, ideology and epistemology, respectively. They will provide a way of analysing the limitations, accomplishments and promises of the last decade's efforts to convey national histories to North American audiences.

The relationship among these questions comes to the fore in a fascinating way in Howard Zinn's *A People's History of the United States*, whose fifth edition appeared in 2003, twenty-three years after its first publication. It may well be, speculates Michael Kazin, 'the most popular work of history an American leftist has ever written' (making it 'people's history' in two senses of the term).[4] Yet Kazin, a Georgetown University historian of populism with a leftist orientation himself, calls it 'bad history'. Kazin's objections speak to all of the questions that this paper addresses. Zinn's story is simple: good versus bad: 'Zinn reduces the past to a Manichean fable [...] 'pitting 99% of the people against a conspiratorial elite of 1% – a premise better suited to a conspiracy-monger's Web site than to a work of scholarship'.[5] From the American Revolution, through the Civil War, through the eras of industrialisation and mass immigration, 'the doleful narrative makes one wonder why anyone but the wealthy came to the United States at all and, after working for a spell, why anyone wished to stay'. In this widely read 'people's history', the 'people' have no agency; the narrative involves no significant change in what really counts most (the struggle for democratic power) and questions of historical truth are managed with a heavy hand.

Ironically, during the same period of time that Zinn's book went through five editions and multiple printings, academic historiography was undergoing a major shift in North America, to include diverse subaltern populations: women, workers, and ethnic and national minorities. The new history dealt with 'the people' or 'the peoples' in ways that were more nuanced and more variegated than the consensus history of the 1950s. Ideologically, furthermore, this represented a shift to the left, particularly as the generation of the 1960s completed PhDs and assumed increasingly central academic positions. As Kazin describes it, 'From the 1960s onward, scholars, most of whom lean leftward, have patiently and empathetically [...] explained how progressive movements succeeded as well as why they fell short of their goals.' While there was real accomplishment, there was also trouble. In one characterisation, the 'centre did not hold'.[6] It became difficult if not impossible, with the lively pursuit of such diversity, for academics to frame a large, inclusive narrative.

There has been considerable debate, in both Canada and the United States, over whether a 'narrative synthesis' could or should provide a resolution to this fracturing. Is there a problem? On the occasion of the 100th anniversary of the inception of the *American Historical Review*, Dorothy Ross commented on William M. Sloane's contribution to the 1895 edition: 'the most striking difference between Sloane and ourselves is his assurance that he knows the grand narrative of all history and that it is a narrative of progress'.[7]

In Canada, whose historiography is heavily influenced by that of the United States, Ian McKay observed the absence of 'strategies of integration, whose feasibility seems to recede with each new addition to the sum of historical research'.[8] In response to this 'crisis', McKay proposed examining Canadian history through the 'implantation and expansion' of the 'politico-economic logic of liberalism'.[9] Thus, he proposed, Canada would become 'less a self-evident and obvious unit, and more an arrestingly contradictory, complicated, and yet coherent process of liberal rule'.[10] Among academic historians in both the United States and Canada, the search for coherence continues.

However, the need seems more insistent in the field of 'people's history'. Historians attentive to a broad, subaltern populace, which they treated with increasing complexity, were vulnerable to the charge that academic histories of 'the people' were actually *less* engaging for popular audiences than the old nation-building epics that they replaced.[11] The absence of a satisfying and meaningful narrative synthesis limited the potential of historical study to map a collective trajectory over time and enable a vision for the future that could be communicated to the 'peoples'.

The producers and promoters of people's histories offer implicit (and sometimes explicit) responses to a series of questions of agency, ideology and epistemology. Can the public handle a complex story involving individual and collective agency? Is the only hope for coherence a return to the old narratives of progressive national development, as has been argued by a vocal constituency in both Canada and the United States?[12] Will the people (beyond the historical profession) shy away from a truly historical epistemology (as opposed to mythic stories about the past)?

These questions have been played out most dramatically in two arenas that hold perhaps the greatest promise for interventions in popular historical consciousness: cinema and the schools. These two also have large and intractable pitfalls. With the contemporary turn towards a visual culture, one might make the claim that historical film *is* people's history. School history is very different. It is the least favourite, involves the 'least connection to the past' and is not particularly trusted.[13] Yet, it too has a strong claim to the title of 'people's history'. Universal schooling means that all North Americans are exposed over many years of their lives to the school history curriculum; moreover, unlike market-driven movies, school history is substantially shaped through public policy decisions.

Film and American History

American historians have recently engaged with film as a medium for the discipline. It can be seen in the films that have become a regular part of the annual history meetings, in the film review sections of both the *Journal of American History* and the *American Historical Review*, in the occasional symposia on film published in the same journals, and in the journal *Film and History*. Academic historians might not have taken notice, except for the overwhelming size of the audiences for history on film. Since film history was 'people's history', in this sense, they were prepared with challenging questions about the way the medium opens some possibilities and forecloses others, most insistently around the issue of truth and interpretation.[14]

The most important American in the field of film and history is Ken Burns, whom David Harlan calls 'the most famous historian in the country'.[15] 'Ken Burns', says Gary Edgerton 'has [...] usurped one of the foremost goals of social history, which is to make history meaningful and relevant to the general public'.[16] Over 23 million people watched the first two episodes of his 1990 television documentary mini-series *The Civil War*, and with the subsequent rebroadcasts (twice in 1991 and regularly thereafter) and video rentals and sales, a total of 50 to 100 million viewers may have seen the series. *The Civil War* is, according to Harlan, 'the most popular history ever written or produced'.[17] This mini-series was a watershed event in a career that continued to develop: Burns claims another 50 million for *Baseball* and an average of 15 million during the debut telecasts of each of his other documentaries throughout the 1990s.[18] Among the 15 major films of his career, the epic lengths of *The Civil War* (1990), *Baseball* (1994) and *Jazz* (2001) stand out against a series of shorter (but still substantial) biographies. The entire *oeuvre* is unified, thematically, methodologically and ideologically. Harlan follows Burns, arguing that 'what is at stake [...] is nothing less than "the historical memory of our people"'.[19]

Burns: Biography and Individual Agency as Methodology

Burns's cinematic strategy is fundamentally biographical. Like his other films, *The Civil War* is 'populated by heroes and villains who allegorically personify certain virtues and vices in the national character as understood through the popular mythology of America's collective memory'.[20] The biographical approach brings history to a close-up and personal scale.[21] Burns explained:

> we are brought to our history [...] with story, memory, anecdote, feeling. These emotional connections become a kind of glue which makes the most complex of past events stick in our minds and our hearts, permanently a part of who each of us is now.[22]

This is the stuff of myth. However, Burns himself rejects the charges that he has oversimplified the story, that he has rendered his characters one-dimensional, or that TV and film must do so. 'We found that by lifting up the rug of history and sweeping out the dirt, we did not in any way diminish the force of our narrative [...] Characters like Lincoln and Lee who have been smothered in myths of perfection over the years were now real people.'[23]

The biographical approach allows the audience to imagine a personal, empathetic connection. Lingering pans and zooms of archival photographic portraits – rather than re-enactments and dramatisations – reinforce a sense of an unmediated personal confrontation with people of the past, both well known and anonymous. *The Civil War*'s strength is at this level, where individual hopes and plans are caught in a web of larger circumstances. However, the larger changes in the political, economic and social structures remain much more obscure in Burns's hands. Industrialisation in the North and the political economy of slavery in the South remain sufficiently unarticulated that they do not contribute to explanations of the causes of the war. Jeanie Attie accuses Burns of presenting history 'as nothing more than collective biography'.[24] Indeed, she charges, 'For an audience accustomed to the creation of celebrity, this *People*-magazine technique of making famous people ordinary and ordinary people famous provides merely the illusion of substance, the illusion of social history.'[25]

Ideology and the Civil War

If the method of *The Civil War* is to focus on the individual, what does the entire eleven-hour series add up to? Lyle Dick, who analyses the documentary in terms of its literary elements, summarises the rise and fall – or the fall and rise – of the plot. It began with the 'United States as a divided society in 1861' followed by 'descent into enmity, mayhem and suffering [...] The sequence of actions ended with the reassertion of political unity, necessary in Burns's view but an imperfect unity'.[26]

The theme of national unity is unambiguously central, but how that theme intersects with those of race, slavery and injustice is much disputed, and this is where the question of ideological stance comes to the fore. Those for whom national unity is the central issue can feel a certain sense of upbeat satisfaction at the end of the film: the union is saved. This can coexist with the contrapuntal themes of the unfinished business of racial inequality, and the slaughter and carnage wrought on the battlefield: an intensely bittersweet lens for the entire era. Indeed, as Harlan sees it, 'the enslavement and eventual emancipation of black people is the moral anchor of *The Civil War* and the central act around which the narrative is constructed'.[27] However, it is hard to reconcile this interpretation with the sentiment repeated throughout by the main narrator, Shelby Foote, that the war was unnecessary folly.

Leon Litwack, Burns's most prominent academic critic, charges that *The Civil War* is a notable example of 'safe, risk-free, inoffensive, upbeat, reassuring, comforting, optimistic history, more often than not an exercise in self-congratulation and a celebration of consensus'. The film is about 'how men died and how they responded to the call of battle, not why they fought and died'.[28] The fundamental issue, slavery, remains in the background.

Litwack points out that there are two conflicts in the Civil War: the military engagements between North and South, and the social upheaval between black and white in the South. Even where there were no Union troops, the film concentrates on the former and slights the latter. However 'the most appalling [...] shortcoming' is the way it deals with the aftermath and legacy of the war. In the final episode, the nation was reborn in the unity of the North and South, 'ignoring the brutality, violence, and racial repression on which that reconciliation rested'.[29] It is certainly possible to imagine a film using Burns's techniques of close-up emotion and personal empathy to make the war over slavery more central. Nevertheless, it is an open question as to how the national audience would have responded to the film that Litwack wanted, and here arises the question: 'what can the public handle?'

Myth and History: Burns's Epistemology

In the words of Cripps, scholars have 'abandoned their role as tribal storytellers who craft tales about the past in which the nation can find its identity'.[30] However, can the mythic function of providing national identity be reconciled through the medium of film with the open-ended, critical, and necessarily complex approach of disciplinary history? Burns's response is that it can. To make powerful 'people's history,' he claims, one does not need to simplify, nor has he. Indeed, he claims that he has preserved the openness and complexity that characterise the best of academic historical writing:

> I think that ambivalence and the tolerance of that kind of opposing view is in fact what film is particularly suited for [...] I have no example of a Civil War *book* that actually tolerates as many diverse viewpoints as our film does, that is to say, gives a Southerner life without accepting in any way a Southern point of view

[…] It actually […] shows Lincoln in his complexity […] I believe that the film has the possibility to actually include *more* points of view.[31]

Two key aspects of the film support Burn's argument that *The Civil War* is multivocal and deals with complicated intellectual ideas. The two historical authorities whose voices appear most frequently are the white, male Southern journalist, Shelby Foote, and the black, female historian, Barbara Fields. They have considerably different approaches to the subject. This multivocality is reinforced on a smaller scale with what Burns calls 'editing clusters', consisting of several commentators, responses to an interpretive question. These commentaries, on top of the barrage of primary sources, potentially convey to audiences the idea that historical interpretation is a problem. Their presence undercuts the notion that Burns simply went out and 'found' the stories, or that such 'found' stories have an intrinsic meaning no matter how they are assembled and presented.[32]

In some ways, then, Burns is successful *both* in conveying an emotionally powerful mythic narrative *and* in conveying a more scholarly notion of the problem of all historical knowledge (and thus the tentativeness of any particular interpretation). Lyle Dick sees this achievement even in Burns's cinematic style: 'While not devoid of rhetoric, Burns's treatment afforded viewers the space in which to formulate their own thoughts and emotions regarding what they were seeing'.[33] David Harlan concludes that Burns is a pioneer on the path to what is needed for a 'people's history' in a democratic and media-saturated culture where only a small minority will ever consider reading academic monographs, but where everyone needs to understand a collective past.

Film in Canada: A People's History

If race has been the central conundrum for the United States, French–English relations and the national question constitute the perennial problematic for Canada (along with aboriginal–white relations). In October 1995, a referendum on sovereignty for Quebec came within a percentage point of receiving an affirmative vote. Mark Starowicz, a Canadian Broadcasting Corporation producer who had been contemplating an epic film series on Canadian history, seized the moment to promote it at the CBC, understanding that the time was right for major public investment in a cinematic campaign promoting national unity.[34] Production began in 1997 and lasted four years at an unprecedented cost of $25 million (Cdn.) at a time when the CBC was suffering huge budgetary cutbacks.[35] The process involved both French and English versions, in a co-production between the CBC and its French counterpart, Radio-Canada, under Starowicz as the executive producer. In

2000–2001, nine episodes offered a sweep of Canadian history from the migration to the continent of the first aboriginals, through the Confederation era in the mid-nineteenth century (the traditional dividing line for high school and university courses in Canadian history). In a second season in 2001–2002, eight more episodes brought the story to 1990. In all, there were thirty-two hours of film.

The first episodes attracted an average of 2.6 million viewers per episode – a Canadian audience participation on the same order per capita as Burns's *The Civil War*.[36] It was sold on videotape and DVD. Teaching materials were developed with lesson plans keyed to each of the episodes. A two-volume 'lavishly illustrated' companion book, written by journalists in both French and English, topped the bestseller list through November and December 2000. A website includes video clips from the episodes, episode summaries, commentary by producers and contributors, and bibliographies for each episode in the first season. It also serves as an advertising and sales vehicle for products associated with the series.

Like *The Civil War*, *Canada: A People's History* relied heavily on a biographical approach to history and used the documentary record to supply many of the words spoken by historical characters. Starowicz later wrote admiringly of Burns's production: 'Telling an epic story through the words and actions of individuals who experienced it makes it accessible to the reader or viewer, because all that is required to understand the story is simple humanity.'[37] Then, however, the methodologies diverged radically. Starowicz and his crew relied overwhelmingly on dramatisations. Where Burns had actors reading off-screen to photographic images, the Canadian production had actors dressed in period garb doing the reading in dramatised settings evoking the historical period. As Lyle Dick has observed, the film-makers favoured politicians and military leaders who led the national story towards unification in 1867 or who promoted it in times of crisis thereafter.[38]

The writers and producers understood Canadian history as a series of stories focused on individuals. 'The main thing is, we approached this as journalists,' says CBC senior producer Gordon Henderson. 'We focus on what are the most important stories, the most interesting stories, human stories [...] and then politics don't matter and agendas don't matter'.[39] For Starowicz, however, this does not end up in an apolitical or anarchic stew of individuals each going their own interesting way. He articulated what he saw as the unifying paradigm for Canadian history: 'We (Canadians) are all immigrants; and other than some adventurers, we are all the rejected; and moreover this makes us all equal. The historical legacy of our immigrant status is that Canadian society is, and always has been, egalitarian'.[40]

This is a new twist on Canadian historiography, which must come to terms with a clergy-dominated New France whose social hierarchies were reinforced by the conquering British (in 1763 before the politics of the French Revolution could sweep the transatlantic colony) and with the legacy of the English-speaking Loyalist émigrés escaping the republican Revolution to the south after 1776. The claim that Canadian society 'always has been' egalitarian comes as news to historians! However, *A People's History*, built on people's stories, has no place for historians debating the meaning of the past, nor any reference to the historiographic controversies that preceded its production.

Ironically, then, this lack of historiographic awareness allows not only flights of egalitarian fancy but also the unconscious incorporation of the more traditional structures of Canadian historiography that recent academic work has challenged. Lyle Dick notes this tendency:

> The final, resonating message of the first episode was one of Aboriginal people inviting Europeans to Canada, their histories serving as prologue to the arrival and future dominance of the Western newcomers. Much of the balance of the narrative replayed the familiar history of European trade, occupation, settlement, constitutional and political developments, culminating in Confederation and the establishment of a transcontinental nation.[41]

Unlike *The Civil War*, no historians (or journalists) appear on screen to 'interrupt' the story. Rather, the story unfolds seamlessly and inexorably, much like a school textbook. This is not an interpretation, the film implicitly claims, this is the way it was. Henderson explains:

> We don't have historians that come on and say 'now what you just saw, let me put it into perspective for you.' We don't have that [...] we tell you the stories [...] We keep driving the narrative and don't stop to look at a person in a tweed suit with a bookcase behind, who'll give you his or her analysis. We let you choose what you think, we let you the viewer pull your stories out.[42]

This approach was explicitly based on what the producers and directors thought would appeal to a broad popular audience. Director of Research Gene Allen drew a sharp dichotomy between the analytical history of professional historians (with 'explicit engagement with questions of sources, methods, and interpretation') and narrative history for a television audience.[43] Writers for the latter, he noted 'have to think seriously about *how* to communicate to a non-specialist audience that isn't highly motivated to stick with your subject if they find it confusing or tedious'.[44]

At a moment when national unity hung in the balance, the CBC/Radio-Canada attempted to offer a synthetic national narrative that would provide personal meaning for all Canadians *as* Canadians. They were fearful, too, that a television audience would not have the patience to sit through interpretive controversy. Here, perhaps at its most stark, is the conflict between national myth making for explicit political ends and the critical practices of academic history. In answering the question, 'what can the public handle?' the CBC production opted for the former. In the end, it deliberately hid the interpretative process which is inherent in the activities of constructing historical representations.

It is instructive, then, to examine the responses of an eclectic group of historians who had in common the fact that they were selected by *The National Post*, the conservative Canadian newspaper founded and at the time owned by Conrad Black, to review the first weeks' episodes. Generally known for views that tend towards the more nationalist (and thus likely to be disposed towards the production) and more conservative end of the spectrum of academic history, Jonathan Vance, David Bercuson, Jack Granatstein and Michael Bliss are also among the Canadian historians most regularly published in the popular press. The first three are associated with military and war history and have a strong constituency among veterans' groups.[45] If these historians did not like the series, it would be hard to find any that did. While generally approving of the narrative line and appreciative of the series' educational potential, they nevertheless offered telling criticism.[46] Historian Jonathan Vance remarked on the problem with the decision to use docudrama and not historians: 'Granted, historians are not the most magnetic television personalities, but at least the on-screen expert style of documentary makes it clear to the viewers they are getting one person's interpretation of historical reality. With actor portrayals, things are murkier.' He illustrates his point with the film's dramatisation of sailor John Jewett's captivity by aboriginals in 1803 at Nootka Sound in what later became British Columbia. The film's account is based not on the Jewett diary itself, but on the 'much-embellished 1815 version, probably written by Richard Alsop, a Connecticut millionaire with a taste for adventure'. We learn nothing of the source from the film.[47]

Jack Granatstein concurred, '[W]hat seems clear after just four hours of TV is that the docudrama style doesn't really work. It's too slow, too stately and, unfortunately, much too boring'. Why not, he suggested, 'emulate the style of Ken Burns's hugely successful PBS Civil War series?'[48] After six episodes, Michael Bliss was more positive, 'this is not a startlingly new perspective by any means, but it has never previously been brought to television in such loving splendour and attention to detail'. He thought it was just right for the public, pitched 'at about the intellectual level of a Grade 9 textbook'.[49]

Schools and American History: Towards George Bush's People's History

It is challenging to give a comprehensive and meaningful picture of national history as it is taught in schools in either the United States or Canada. Both countries embody tremendous regional and cultural diversity, and constitutionally education is the responsibility of state and provincial – not federal – jurisdictions. Nevertheless, there have been significant efforts to steer history education in new directions in the countries as a whole. These reform efforts can provide some insight into the priorities and controversies that currently shape this aspect of 'people's history'.

In 1987, the privately funded Bradley Commission on History in the Schools was created to provide a theoretical framework and practical strategy for history education reform in the United States. Its report laid out a series of principles for constructing history curriculum, including 'History's Habits of Mind' as 'the principle aim' of history education.[50] These stressed the open-endedness and complexity that students should understand as the nature of history, by the end of their schooling. The Bradley Commission was a successful collaboration of people from the academic left (e.g., Leon Litwack) and the academic right (e.g., Diane Ravitch) who would engage in intense public verbal warfare over the next five or six years.

The US National Standards for History in the Schools were a direct descendent of the report of the Bradley Commission. In 1992, the National Endowment for the Humanities (under chair Lynne Cheney) and the US Department of Education contracted the National Center for History in the Schools at the University of California at Los Angeles to develop voluntary national standards. Gary Nash, an eminent US historian at UCLA, and Charlotte Crabtree (member of the Bradley Commission), from the School of Education, organised a broad consultative process involving history teachers and historians around the United States. After circulating a number of drafts in co-operation with the Organisation of American Historians, the American Historical Association, and the National Council for Social Studies, the Standards were published in 1994. The ideological orientation of the standards reflected recent American historiography, in bringing forward previously marginalised individuals and groups: African Americans, women and the poor and working class. The Bradley Commission's strengths were tucked into a portion of the document devoted to 'Historical Thinking Standards', but the authors had attempted to show how these could be applied to the topics in teaching suggestions, which made up the bulk of the document.

Just prior to the Standards' release in October, Lynne Cheney led the charge against them from the right with an inflammatory attack in the *Wall Street Journal*.[51] Cheney argued that the Clinton election in 1992 had 'unleashed the forces of political correctness', and that the left-leaning academic historians of the American Historical Association had 'hijacked standards-setting'. 'Imagine an outline for the teaching of American history', she began, 'in which George Washington makes only a fleeting appearance and is never described as our first president'. Indeed, most of Cheney's piece was cast in terms of which historical individuals were included or excluded either as heroes or as villains. She decried both the absence of Paul Revere (a staple of heroic, nation-building school history), and the inclusion of nineteen mentions of Joseph McCarthy (cast as a villain). In Cheney's writing, the ideological valence of the historical narrative was largely shaped by the characters that were included or excluded as heroes. Charges and counter-charges were hurled in the press, but to a remarkable degree, Cheney's opinion piece set the terms of the public debate over history in the schools. In January 1995, the US Senate passed a resolution expressing its disapproval of the Standards by a vote of 99 to 1, noting, following Cheney, the omission of Thomas Edison, Robert E. Lee and George Washington.[52] Nash, Crabtree and their colleague Ross Dunn responded to the criticisms.[53] In the media storm over which individual characters would set the moral and ideological meaning of American history, the public debate entirely missed the Bradley Commission's 'principal aim' of the history curriculum, to develop 'history's habits of mind' and historical thinking.

By 1996, the UCLA Center had revised the Standards and responded sufficiently to the attacks, that the new edition received approval from two independent, bi-partisan, high-level review panels. Public debate at the national level was largely defused, as many states, which had the constitutional mandate to implement curriculum reform, started working with the revised Standards as a template in a wide variety of different ways, with different emphases and radically different interpretations.

One report of the total cost of the History Standards was $2.2 million (US).[54] In 2001, Senator Robert Byrd initiated a 'Teaching American History' Project with a series of 60 grants totalling $50 million, a figure that doubled the next year to more than $100 million, funding 114 programmes during each of the following two years: financially, the scale of this initiative dwarfed the Standards.[55] The programme supports coalitions of local school boards, museums, libraries and other non-profit history organisations, and higher education institutions – many on the order of $1 million – 'to raise student achievement by improving teachers' knowledge, understanding, and appreciation of traditional American history'.[56]

After the second year of the programme, in May 2003, the Bush administration renamed it 'Teaching Traditional American History', perhaps in an attempt to define its ideological thrust explicitly. Yet Michael Ebner, who was involved with the grant programme from its inception, advised potential applicants from the American Historical Association, 'Do not anguish endlessly over the contentious word "traditional" [...] Endlessly debating about what "traditional" does or does not mean will yield a most dissatisfying and pointless chase'.[57]

Guidance from the Department of Education as to the goals of history education is a long way from the thrust of the Bradley Commission: 'The Secretary construes traditional American history to mean the following: Traditional American history teaches the significant issues, episodes, and turning points in the history of the United States, and how the words and deeds of individual Americans have determined the course of our Nation.'[58] Moreover, traditional American history is defined as teaching how the principles of freedom and democracy, articulated in our founding documents, have shaped – and continue to shape – America's struggles and achievements, as well as its social, political, and legal institutions and relations. Traditional history puts its highest priority on making sure students have an understanding of these principles and of the historical events and people that best illustrate them.

If the programme is successful, then US history will be a source of patriotic inspiration.

In fact, the grants awarded by these programmes appear from the abstracts on the Department of Education and National Endowment for the Humanities web pages to encompass a full range of complexity, ideology, geographic location, subject matter and pedagogical approach. For example, New York projects included one designed and run in conjunction with CUNY's American Social History Project (initiated by labour historian Herbert Gutman), a collaboration with Princeton University's James Madison Programme in American Ideals and Institutions and the right-leaning National Association of Scholars, and a project which promised to give 'the Hotinonshonni historical perspective, which enables teachers and students to understand how the Native American cultural traditions complement rather than conflict with traditional views of American history'.[59]

From the Bradley Commission to Teaching Traditional American History, at the level of policy debates and discussions, if not at the level of the classroom, a shift is evident. Historians coming back to interest in schools after a long absence were eager to bring the fruits of a more diverse new history along with history's disciplinary habits of mind. These, rather than a powerful new narrative synthesis, were central in the new proposals. The culture wars of the 1990s largely sidetracked public discussion of the initiatives. The Cheney attack claimed that what was uncertain was whether students would end up being proud or ashamed of the story they learned, not whether they would have the resources to pursue thoughtful and open-ended investigations of American history. When this round was over, the Cheneys were back in office, and unprecedented amounts of money were being provided with the stated aim to use history education to promote knowledge of and pride in American heroes and values. However, the grants were aimed for collaborative efforts between schools and academic historians, who would probably bring to their projects some of the same insights that had been articulated by the Bradley Commission more than a decade earlier.

Schools and Canadian History: Historica and the Dominion Institute

The crisis of unity posed by the withdrawal of Quebec from Confederation is one perceived threat to Canada. A comparable fear is absorption into the sphere of the United States. As the country moves further from the 1995 referendum, and the Bush administration's 'war on terror' takes centre stage on the continent, Canadians watch the border with wary eyes, with a majority of the country supporting the decision not to join the American coalition to invade Iraq. If Canadian unity was English Canada's rallying point for the first threat, Canadian identity is that for the second. Both unity and identity play out quite differently in Quebec, of course. The campaign for history education reform in Canada has been largely supported by the notion that Canadian citizens' knowledge of history will help to ensure both Canadian unity and identity.

The kind of history that most directly supports these aims is a narrative which emphasises a coherent essence of nationhood, exemplary heroes who help to drive the project of nationhood forward (thus political history), the struggles against external enemies to maintain and fully realise the national essence, and the sacrifice of those who participate (thus military history). In other words, the aims of national unity and identity are most directly supported by a mythic history.[60] Canada's linguistic diversity and multinational composition impose complicating factors: in order for history education to contribute to the construction of national unity and identity, individuals, ethnic minorities and peripheral regions have to be able to identify with the national project. To fulfil these objectives, then, history education has to provide the linkages.

As in the US, Canadian education is constitutionally based beneath the federal jurisdiction, in the provinces. There have been no Canadian government initiatives at the federal level comparable to these recent attempts at history education reform in the United States. We need to look rather to the work of two non-profit organisations that have made history education reform their central mission. Both were initiated in the late 1990s; both are closely identified with their corporate donors and sponsors.

The Dominion Institute was founded in 1997 by four young men and quickly achieved a public presence through well-timed surveys that demonstrated how poorly Canadians fared on quizzes about Canadian history facts. The Institute was heavily funded by the Donner Canadian Foundation, whose mission is 'to encourage individual responsibility and private initiative to help Canadians solve their social and economic problems'.[61]

The results of their first poll, released the day before Canada Day (1 July), showed Canadian youth 18–24 answering only one third of the questions correctly. Only slightly more than half, for example, knew that John A.

MacDonald was Canada's first prime minister. Questions covered politics (9 questions), Canada–US relations (4 questions), ethnic and cultural diversity (5 questions), military history (5 questions) and arts and human interests (7 questions). Rudyard Griffiths, the head of the Institute, offered three policy recommendations, purportedly on the basis of the survey: the institution of a uniform national history framework with a 'minimal list of people and events to be worked into provincial history curricula' to be implemented by the Council of Ministers of Education, mandatory history classes in provinces with no history requirements, and 'a Two-Minute Silence on November 11 to promote national awareness of the sacrifices of Canadian war dead and veterans'.[62]

Since the initial survey, the Dominion Institute has followed up with one to three polls each year, all timed around national commemorations for maximum press coverage. Griffiths successfully commanded prominent places in the press for a consistent message about history education reform on the occasion of each one of the surveys. In a 2000 op-ed feature, he used the results of a survey of opinions of the 'most important event in Canadian history' to explain his own sense of why the top choices – Confederation, War of 1812 and Vimy Ridge – were the most significant. '[T]hese events represent [...] the principles and passions of our nationhood. From them emanate hard-won and heartfelt lessons in national survival, political accomplishment and collective heroism'.[63] National identity is built, in this vision, through a common knowledge and recognition of great political and military events and the heroes that made them happen. What is confronted and overcome in the high points of the national narrative are either external enemies, or the problem of divisiveness itself.

Lest the nineteenth and early twentieth century political and military history stand too far away from individuals today, other programmes of the Dominion Institute offer an eclectic mix of educational programmes in the service of nation-building. 'Passages to Canada' deals with stories of immigration as well as the military, with speakers' bureaus, digital archives and articles. Rather than have the immigration stories offer a discordant counterpoint to the stories of politics and war, these serve to bring new groups into a unifying trajectory in which nation-building is still the central theme.[64]

Operating on very much the same front as the Dominion Institute, and using the results of the Institute polls as a rationale for many of its activities, is the Historica Foundation (in operation since 1999). Unlike the Dominion Institute, which gets its operating and programme funding from outside sources, much of the Historica funding comes from an endowment initiated by businessmen Charles R. Bronfman and L.R. Wilson (Chairman of Bell Canada Enterprises, Nortel Networks and CAE). They promised $25 million (Cnd.) in matching donations. The target of a $50 million endowment had been reached by 2004. While far more modest than the Teaching Traditional American History grants, it provides substantial support for programmes and reform efforts in the

Canadian context. Its Board of Directors is composed of a dozen high profile figures from business, politics and law. A much larger advisory Council, which meets once a year, includes professionals from education and history, but the organisation remains highly identified with its major business donors.

Historica has been less focused than the Dominion Institute in defining a direction for reform. Indeed, its folksy mission statement is more remarkable for its global non-specificity than for any particular direction in which it might move Canadian history education: 'Canada has a distinct and identifiable national character that is in large part the result of its unique history. Historica's role is to engage our young people in the fascinating stories that make our country unique.'[65]

Historica inherited several programmes that pre-dated its existence and has developed some new ones. While it has been working to bring them together under a coherent 'branding' strategy, it takes some analysis to detect any underlying orientation towards Canadian history or history education. Historica Fairs is the new name for school-based 'Heritage Fairs' (much like History Day in the United States), where students' history projects from Grades 4 to 9 compete at school, regional and provincial levels, with the winners invited to a national fair. In 2003, 194,000 children participated in 808 schools from across Canada. Historica advises students 'to explore themes or stories they are curious or passionate about'. Beyond that, the suggestions uniformly direct students to investigate local historical issues related to their own families or communities. The nation-building pedagogy arises only insofar as students feel that their project is part of a Canada-wide programme, and thus, by analogy that their family or local history is related to the larger national story. This may indeed be a powerful lesson, particularly as it is conveyed through the hierarchy of competitions leading to the national fair.

A similar dynamic of 'people's history' is evident in the sixty 'Historica Minutes', which the organisation inherited from Bronfman's CRB Foundation. These are widely viewed one-minute vignettes of defining moments in Canadian history, most focused on heroic actions of Canadians overcoming adversity. The heroes are frequently drawn from beyond political and military history, and the contributions they make are not necessarily to a *nationally* defined goal – women's equality, literacy, medical advances and racial equality, for example, are among the dramatic struggles. Yet the uniform format and the logo, 'a part of our heritage,' that appears at the dramatic ending of each one bring the diverse stories into a common project: Canada. On the website, students have instructions on how to 'make your own minute' on a hero of their choice.

Historica also hosts an online version of the *Canadian Encyclopaedia*, an online student forum on global issues (Historica Youthlinks), and a summer institute for about 150 teachers. Only rarely do explicit signs of a historical epistemology make an appearance in any of the Historica materials. The

Minutes are too short; the Encyclopaedia is presented as a source of information, not interpretation. Even in the 'make your own minute' and Heritage Fairs materials, there are no tools to help students to engage in critical history, no guidance for students about the selection, interpretation or presentation of primary source materials and none for teachers to help assess students' learning of these practices. Thus, conveying the meaning of history as a discipline remains for the time being on the sidelines of the pedagogical agenda of the organisation.[66]

What Can They Handle?

In both Canada and the United States, the oppositional ideological stance framed by Zinn, *Radical History Review* and the Left in the 1970s and early 1980s has been largely eclipsed in 'people's history'. Rather, for film producers and history education reformers, the individual hero looms very large, whether it is the politician or military leader on the one hand or the 'everyday' people who exemplify traits of the national character, on the other. 'Hero' is a category from myth, however, not from critical history. Heroes have a place in people's history for one of two reasons, which Nietzsche's scheme of historical consciousness may help us with.[67] Either they are there because of their great deeds and noble values that can inspire those who are taught about them to be good and do well (Nietzsche's 'monumental' use of history), or they are there because they sacrificed and lost for the good of their national progeny and we owe them a debt of memory (Nietzsche's 'memorial' use of history[68]).

Such a focus on the individual supports a grand narrative of the nation, while rendering nuanced discussion of interpretations of the larger historical trends and forces more difficult. As Starowicz argued, all that is required to understand a history told through individuals is 'simple humanity.' Such a method tends to revert to traditional, default periodisations and narrative trajectories. James Wertsch has detected enduring 'narrative templates' that continue to shape people's understandings of the national past, even after such major political upheavals as the end of the Soviet Union.[69] In a similar vein, Jocelyn Letourneau and Sabrina Moisan have found that young people in Quebec continue to hold on to traditional narratives of Quebec history and heroes, even after major revisions in political climate and academic historiography.[70]

In the past decade, a generation or two beyond the path-breaking work of E.P. Thompson, Eugene Genovese and Joan Scott, North American historians have continued to build a more nuanced view of historical agency, with attention to the interplays between the powerful and the subaltern, between individuals and collectives, and between the choices offered and constraints imposed by the past upon the present. Moreover, while the postmodern enthusiasms of a decade ago appear to have had their day, they have left in their wake a new methodological and epistemological self-consciousness among historians. These historiographic trends have rendered historical syntheses based on a narrative of national progress problematic at best. In contrast, the major projects in 'people's history', – historical film and educational reform initiatives (perhaps for different reasons) – continue in both Canada and the United States to promote national mythologies sprinkled with heroes, largely devoid of the open, critical contentiousness that characterises the work of historians.

What would it take to shift the enduring national mythologies that animate these projects? Blockbuster film and television productions may generate large audiences only to the degree that they fit comfortably with what people in their homes already want to believe. Compulsory history courses in the schools, to the extent that they are conceived in terms of the mythic survey of monumental and memorial heroes, may become more inclusive, and may change the cast of characters without dramatically altering the narrative of which they are a part (as Jonathan Zimmerman has argued[71]).

The way to move beyond mythology would be to promote media, public and educational policy that support not an education in mythology at all, but an education in history. If young people were taught 'historical habits of mind', and if the public at large were offered historical narratives that exposed their own construction, then, rather than seeing heroes as transcendent embodiments of national character, these audiences could contemplate and discuss the role of the individual and group in the making of historical change. The seemingly inexorable stories of national development could be subjected to critical scrutiny, not necessarily rejected, but seen in relationship to complex interplays among peoples and forces both within and beyond the national borders. Could the public handle *this*? Contrary to Mark Starowicz and Gene Allen, we really do not know. Despite some initial attempts, we still have much to learn about how North American peoples, young and old, cope with the complex task of understanding history.

Notes

1. H. Zinn, *A People's History of the United States* (1980), New York, 2003.
2. M. Frisch, ed., *A Shared Authority: Essays on the Craft and Meaning of Oral and Public History*, Albany, NY, 1990.
3. M. Conrad and A. Finkel, *History of the Canadian Peoples*, Toronto, 2002.
4. M. Kazin, 'Howard Zinn's Disappointing History of the United States', *History News Network*; http://hnn.us/articles/printfriendly/4370.html
5. Ibid.
6. P. Novick, *That Noble Dream: The 'Objectivity Question' and the American Historical Profession*, Cambridge, MA, 1988.

7. D. Ross, 'Grand Narrative in American Historical Writing: From Romance to Uncertainty', *American Historical Review* 100, 3, 1995: 651; see also T. Bender, 'Strategies of Narrative Synthesis in American History', *American Historical Review* 107, 1, 2002: 129–53.

8. I. McKay, 'The Liberal Order Framework: A Prospectus for a Reconnaissance of Canadian History', *Canadian Historical Review* 81, 4, 2000: 617.

9. Ibid., 621.

10. Ibid., 623; see an extended response to McKay in R. Sandwell, 'The Limits of Liberalism: The Liberal Reconnaissance and the History of the Family in Canada', *Canadian Historical Review* 84, 3, 2003: 423–50.

11. This was true despite the existence of oral historians and others on the left who attempted to negotiate the democratisation of the *content* of history with the democratisation of the *production* and *consumption* of history. This group remained a relatively small minority. See, for example, Frisch, *Shared Authority*; J. Green, *Taking History to Heart: The Power of the Past in Building Social Movements*, Amherst, MA, 2000; B. Levine, *Who Built America*, New York, 1989.

12. See, for example, J. Granatstein, *Who Killed Canadian History?*, Toronto, 1998; A. Schlesinger, Jr, *The Disuniting of America*, New York, 1992.

13. R. Rosenzweig and D. Thelen, *Presence of the Past: Popular Uses of History in American Life*, New York, 1998.

14. See, for example, R.A. Rosenstone, *Visions of the Past: The Challenge of Film to Our Idea of History*, Cambridge, 1995; N.Z. Davis, *Slaves on Screen: Film and Historical Vision*, Toronto, 2000; R.B. Toplin, *Reel History*, Lawrence, Kansas, 2002. On history and film from the other side of the disciplinary divide (i.e., from film studies), see V. Sobchack, *The Persistence of History: Cinema, Television, and the Modern Event*, New York and London, 1996.

15. D. Harlan, 'Ken Burns and the Coming Crisis of Academic History', *Rethinking History* 7, 2, 2003: 169.

16. G.R. Edgerton, *Ken Burns's America*, New York, 2001: 17.

17. Harlan, 'Ken Burns', 169.

18. Quoted in Edgerton, *Burns's America*, 2.

19. Harlan, 'Ken Burns', 170.

20. Edgerton, *Burns's America*, vii.

21. There are many reasons why this works well for 'people's history' in contemporary culture. Mark Phillips has traced this strategy across a number of different historical genres, including academic history (in the form of microhistory), and drawn attention to how the notion of 'appropriate' historical distance varies over time; M.S. Phillips, 'History, Memory and Historical Distance', in *Theorizing Historical Consciousness*, P. Seixas, ed., Toronto, 2004: 86–108.

22. K. Burns, 'Four O'clock in the Morning Courage', in Toplin, ed., *Civil War*, 167.

23. Ibid., 160.

24. J. Attie, 'Illusions of History: A Review of The Civil War', *Radical History Review* 52, 1992: 97.

25. Ibid., 100.

26. L. Dick, 'National History, Epic Form, and Television: Two Examples from Canada and the United States', Paper presented at *Heritage, History, and Historical Consciousness: A Symposium on Public Uses of the Past*, University of New Brunswick, Fredericton, NB, 21–22 October 2003: 9.

27. Harlan, 'Ken Burns', 177.

28. L. Litwack, 'Telling the Story: The Historian, the Filmmaker, and the Civil War', in Toplin, ed., *Civil War*, 127.

29. Ibid., 134–35.

30. T. Cripps, 'Historical Truth: An Interview with Ken Burns', *American Historical Review* 100, 3, 1995: 741.

31. Ibid., 744.

32. Edgerton, *Burns's America*, 13.

33. Dick, 'National History', 18.

34. M. Starowicz, *Making History: The Remarkable Story behind Canada a People's History*, Toronto, 2003. Parts of the following discussion of *Canada: A People's History* will also appear in a chapter entitled, 'Who Needs a Canon?' in M. Grever and S. Stuurman, eds, *Beyond the Canon: History for the 21st Century*, London, 2007.

35. In 2004, the government was gripped by scandals involving charges of profligate spending on advertising national unity in the wake of the referendum.

36. R. Conlogue, 'Our Pick of Canada's Best', *Globe and Mail* (28 December 2000); the text is available online at http://www.carleton.ca/historycollaborative/press_reaction/globe_mail_dec_series/conlogue.html

37. Starowicz, *Making History*, 147.

38. Dick, 'National History', 10–11.

39. CBC, 'Canada: A People's History: Behind the Scenes: About the TV Series: Reconstructing History', http://www.cbc.ca/historys/bs_reenact.html

40. M. Starowicz, 'Keynote Address, Giving the Future a Past', Winnipeg, MB, October 2001; see also P. Clark, 'Conversation with Mark Starowicz', *Canadian Social Studies* 36, 2, 2001.

41. Dick, 'National History', 7.

42. CBS, 'People's History'.

43. G. Allen, 'Canadian History in Film: A Roundtable Discussion', *Canadian Historical Review* 82, 2, 2001: 331–46.

44. Ibid., 333–34.

45. Granatstein's (1998) best selling *Who Killed Canadian History?* had been published two years earlier. His new work is *Who Killed the Canadian Military?*

46. The full text of all of these articles is archived at http://www.carleton.ca/historycollaborative/ (accessed 13 April 2004).

47. J. Vance, 'A Land of Poor Visibility', *National Post* (23 October 2000); the text available online at http://www.carleton.ca/historycollaborative/press_reaction/nationalpost_episode_reviews/episode01_review_vance.html

48. J. Granatstein, 'Slow and Stately', *National Post* (30 October 2000); the text available online at http://www.carleton.ca/historycollaborative/press_reaction/nationalpost_episode_reviews/episode02_review_granatstn.html

49. M. Bliss, 'Canada's History Multiplies', *National Post* (8 January 2001); the text available online at http://www.carleton.ca/historycollaborative/press_reaction/nationalpost_episode_reviews/episode03_review_bliss.html

50. P. Gagnon, ed., *Historical Literacy: The Case for History in American Education*, New York, 1989: 25.

51. L.V. Cheney, 'The End of History', *Wall Street Journal* (20 October 1994).

52. D. Ravitch, 'Revise, but Don't Abandon, the History Standards', *Chronicle of Higher Education*, 1995.

53. G.B. Nash, C. Crabtree and R. Dunn, *History on Trial: Culture Wars and the Teaching of the Past*, New York, 1997.

54. C. Innerst, 'Some Historians See New Standards as Revisionist Coup', *The Washington Times* (27 October 1994), A2.

55. US National Endowment for the Humanities, 'Press Release: Budget FY-2005 REQUEST', https://mail2.cni.org/Lists/NHA-ANNOUNCE/Message/20129-P.txt

56. US Federal Register, 'vol. 68, no. 87, Notices CFDA No. 84.215X', *Department of Education*; http://www.ed.gov/legislation/FedRegister/announcements/2003-2/050603b.html

57. M.H. Ebner, 'Submitting a Proposal for a Teaching American History Grant: An Unofficial Guide', *American Historical Association Perspectives* (October 2003); http://www.historians.org/perspectives/issues/2003/0311/0311not1.cfm

58. US Federal Register.

59. US Department of Education, http://www.ed.gov/programmes/teachinghistory/2003tahabstracts/ny.html. In May 2003, Bush buttressed this programme with the largest ever competitive grants programme administered through the National Endowment for the Humanities, with $100 million (US) over three years for a 'We the People' initiative involving a variety of initiatives aimed primarily at young people in schools. These included an annual lecture on 'Heroes of History', an 'idea of America' history contest for 11th Grade (16- to 17-year-old) students, 'Landmarks of History' for workshops for teachers at historical sites, and seminars and institutes for teachers. It is unclear whether this programme was in addition to the funding for Teaching Traditional American History, or whether it was part of the same pot. http://www.wethepeople.gov/index.html (accessed 19 April 2004).

60. K. Osborne, 'Teaching History in Schools: A Canadian Debate', *Journal of Curriculum Studies* 35, 5, 2003: 585–626; D. Francis, *National Dreams: Myth, Memory and Canadian History*, Vancouver, BC, 1997.

61. Donner Canadian Foundation, http://www.donnerfoundation.org/tocframe.html

62. Ipsos News Centre, 'The Canada Day Youth History Survey, 30 June 1997', http://www.ipsos-na.com/news/pressrelease.cfm?id=871

63. R. Griffiths, 'Mistakes of the Past', *Globe and Mail* (18 September 2000); the text available online at http://www.carleton.ca/historycollaborative/press_reaction/globe_mail_sept_series/griffiths.html

64. Dominion Institute, http://www.dominion.ca/English/home.html

65. Historica, http://www.Histori.ca

66. The author presented these criticisms to the staff, Council and members of the Board, and they were received positively. In 2006, Historica undertook an initiative, 'Benchmarks of Historical Thinking', which will attempt to address them.

67. F. Nietzsche, 'On the Uses and Disadvantages of History for Life', in D. Breazeale ed., *Untimely Meditations*, Cambridge, 59–123.

68. A. Margalit, *The Ethics of Memory*, Cambridge, MA, 2002.

69. J. Wertsch, 'Specific Narratives and Schematic Narrative Templates', in P. Seixas, ed., *Theorizing Historical Consciousness*, Toronto, 2004.

70. J. Létourneau and S. Moisan, 'Young People's Assimilation of a Collective Historical Memory: A Case Study of Quebeckers of French-Canadian Heritage', in *Theorizing Historical Consciousness*, 109–28.

71. J. Zimmerman, *Whose America? Culture Wars in the Public Schools*, Cambridge, 2002.

Chapter 14

The Configuration of Orient and Occident in the Global Chain of National Histories: Writing National Histories in Northeast Asia

JIE-HYUN LIM

Encapsulating National History in Eurocentric 'Tunnel History'

Modern historiography has often been a tool to legitimate the nation-state 'objectively and scientifically'. Despite its proclamation of objectivity and scientific inquiry, modern historiography has promoted the political project of constructing national history. Its underlying logic was to find the course of historical development that led to the nation-state. Thus, national history has made the nation-state both the subject and the object of its own discipline. The 'Prussian school' provides a typical example. Not only was Ranke the official historiographer of the Prussian state, Droysen's distinction between 'History' (*die Geschichte*) and 'private transactions' (*Geschäfte*) also reveals the hidden politics that is inherent in modern historiography. While 'History' referred to the state of the elites and the powerful, 'private transactions' were assigned to the various aspects of the lives of the powerless who did not matter in the narrative of 'History'.[1] The people's history was to be subordinate to the history of the nation-state in this scheme.

Therefore, 'History' became the scientific apologia for the nation-state and the people looked to national history to illuminate the course of human progress culminating in the nation-state.[2] It invoked the desire of the ordinary people to be positioned in the course of national history, and subjected them to the hegemony of state power. When Michelet defined the historian as an Oedipus who teaches the dead how to interpret and decipher the meaning of their own language and deeds not known to themselves, he exposed the historian's professional secret to appropriate the dead for the cause of the nation-state.[3] This explains why the present historical order of national history is 'a curious inversion of conventional genealogy' by starting from the 'originary present'. The nation's biography cannot but be written 'up time' because there is no Originator.[3] The present nation-state became the real ancestor of all historical precedents.

The 'originary present' as the firm footing of national history or a nation's biography justifies Eurocentrism in an intrinsic way, because it reviews the past retroactively from the present world order, which has been overwhelmed by European modernity. The demise of national histories with an increasing Europeanisation of historical writing in Western Europe after 1945 does not mean the end of the national history paradigm. Rather, 'it brings also a danger of new ideological closures, of erecting new borders and building new boundaries' between Europe and non-Europe and constructs 'a homogenised European path' superior to other non-European experiences.[5] What one finds in Richard von Weizsäcker's address that 'Europe itself is a *raison d'etat*' is a broadened scope of the national history paradigm from individual nation-state to the European Union.[6] The national history encapsulated in the Eurocentric tunnel history during the imperialist age remains unshaken in this postcolonial era, leaving the *episteme* of the national history paradigm intact.

The Eurocentric 'tunnel history' within the walls of the spatial boundaries of the EU brings the myth of the European miracle, whose core is the set of arguments about ancient and medieval Europe and the unique historical conditions for its self-generating modernisation in comparison with the 'Rest'.[7] Europe, as a self-contained historical entity, implies European exceptionalism. It asserts that rationalism, science, equality, freedom, human rights and industrialism promulgated by the European Enlightenment are the unique phenomena of European civilisation. The Eurocentric mode of historical thought inherent in this exceptionalism is endorsed by an evolutionary historicism that comprehends both the narrative and the concept of development in a homogenous and unified time of history. Citing Dipesh Chakrabarty, 'historicism is what made modernity or capitalism look not simply global but rather as something that became global *over time*, by originating in one place (Europe) and then spreading outside it. This 'first in Europe, then elsewhere' structure of global historicist time was historicist.[8]

The 'first in Europe, then elsewhere' structure of global historicism time gave rise to Eurocentric diffusionism. It is believed that culture, civilisation and innovations flowed out from the European to the non-European sector.[9] Thus, European history became the hegemonic mirror in which non-Europeans reflect themselves. The Eurocentric mode of historical thought brought an illusion that, if there is progress and development in Europe, there ought to be its equivalent in the peripheries. The historian's task in the peripheries has been to find the symmetrical equivalents to European history. As Sakai Naoki remarked succinctly, 'the attempt to posit the identity of one's own ethnicity or nationality in terms of the gap between it and the putative West, that is, to create the history of one's own nation through the dynamics of attraction to and repulsion from the West, has, almost without exception, been adopted as a historical mission by non-Western intellectuals'.[10]

The Eurocentric national history paradigm consigned the less developed nations to 'an imaginary waiting room of history' in this way. They saw their indigenous history as a history of 'lack' in comparison with Europe.[11] Both the nationalist and Marxist non-European historians have tried to overcome this sense of 'lack' by finding the missing ingredients, such as middle class, cities, political rights, rationalism and, above all, the capitalist mode of production in their own history. They have been very keen to prove that they belong to historical nations by finding European elements, which led them to an endeavour to make their histories intelligible to a Western readership. In order to achieve this goal, the East and West, and the Orient and Occident had to be configured in a way that satisfies the expectation of Western readers in the modern historiography of the peripheries. The result was misery for the East because the configuration of East and West in the Eurocentric historical scheme affirmed once again Occidental superiority and Oriental inferiority.

Neither nationalist nor Marxist historians of the peripheries broke free from the Eurocentric discourse of historicism that projected the 'West' as 'History'.[12] They both have been entangled by the stagist theory of history, which views the European path as the sole universal model. The key concept of modern historiography that European colonialism and third-world nationalism had in common was the universalisation of the nation-state as the most desirable and natural form of political community. This mode of thought forms a global chain that ties together national histories on a worldwide scale, which feeds Eurocentrism and Orientalism. The upshot is that the non-European national histories became the epistemological twins of the Eurocentric national histories of the West by sharing the Orientalist value-code in the form of 'anti-Western Orientalism'.[13] Fernand Braudel's remark that Europe invented historians and then made good use of them to promote their own interests at home and elsewhere in the world demonstrates this phenomenon in a very convenient way.[14]

'Japan': Inventing Orient in an Invented Orient

It was at the request of the Paris international exposition bureau that the first national history of Japan, *A Brief History of Japan* (日本史略), appeared in

1878. Its final revised version of 1888, *View of National History* (國史眼), was adopted as the official history textbook in the newly created history department of Tokyo Imperial University. Thus, the first Japanese national history and official history textbook had 'Western readers' as its primary target.[15] Its main purpose was to present the unbroken imperial line as the chief source of Japan's assumed political sovereignty and legitimacy to the West. It was in tune with the revived interest in ancient history and the growing emphasis on the legitimacy of the imperial lineage at home. Itō Hirobumi, the architect of the modern Japanese constitution, demanded to discover the scattered and forgotten tombs of the emperors and keep them in good order. The imperial house's historical legitimacy invented or rediscovered, he believed, would provide the grounds for his struggle to revise the unequal treaties with the Western powers.[16]

With the establishment of a legitimate imperial genealogy, the Japanese national 'geo-body' took shape as a natural and organically integrated territorial unit that extended back throughout historical time, and its contours were firmly established in the second half of the nineteenth century. A comprehensive effort to 'Japanise' the periphery and construct a Japanese organic geo-body began with the first Japanese national history, which was designed to create the official image of a united and centralised nation-state.[17] A legitimate imperial genealogy and the organic geo-body of the Japanese nation, however, was not enough to construct Japan's national history. The Japanese 'own, indigenous and peculiar' cultural tradition had to be invented to make national history more convincing and appealing to Western readers.

That explains why Kume Kunitake, co-author of *View of National History*, kissed the 'sleeping beauty' of 'No(能)' – a mask dance drama – and made it a national heritage. The old practices of the Japanese imperial rituals had been selected and reinvented too by Iwakura Domomi, who wanted to make use of them for the diplomatic protocols with the Western powers. He left the invented imperial rituals open to any change for diplomatic considerations, if necessary. It is not a coincidence that the trio – Itō Hirobumi, Kume Kunitake and Iwakura Domomi – who contributed to the making of Japan's national history and tradition were members of the forty-eight delegates who visited the United States and several European countries in 1871–73.[18] Based on the models that they saw in the United States and Europe, they invented their own national history and tradition. Thus, Japanese history was intelligible to Western readers.

It is no wonder then that the first book on the history of Japanese art, *Histoire de L'art Japon*, was also published originally in French upon the request of the Paris international exposition bureau in 1900.[19] The motivation to write this book was to glorify the Japanese state by highlighting its national heritage and encouraging 'our own artistic spirit' to keep abreast with the European standard. Around the same year, Okakura Tenshin lectured on the history of Japanese art in the Tokyo Fine Arts Academy. He structured today's Japanese art historiography. He categorised cultural properties into a hierarchical order with national treasure at its top and classified them into sculptures, paintings, crafts, etc., according to the European classifications of art. Suddenly, Buddhist statues shifted from religious objects to objects of artistic appreciation. They then became the equivalents of classic Greek sculptures when Okakura compared Buddhist statues in the Nara period with the classic Greek sculptures.[20]

Moreover, Okakura defined 'Suiko' art as the starting point of Japanese national art history, which was mostly either imported from mainland China and the Korean peninsula or created by migrants from Paikje, the ancient Kingdom that had been located in the southwestern part of the Korean peninsula. Thus, he appropriated the fine arts either created by alien migrants or brought back from neighbours for Japanese national history. He was not reluctant to make a Buddhist statue located in Kyoto's Toji temple, that had been imported from Tang China, into one of Japan's most cherished national treasures. Behind Okakura, however, there stood Ernest Fenollosa, a converted American Buddhist. He helped found the Tokyo Fine Arts Academy and the Imperial Museum by acting as its director in 1888, and he made the first inventory of Japan's national treasures. Later he became the curator of the Oriental arts in the Boston Museum of Fine Arts and founded the Japan Society in Boston.

In a sense, Okakura summarised what Fenollosa had discovered and defined as Japanese art. While the first Japanese national history supposed the Europeans as its readership, the first Japanese art history was formulated by an American Orientalist. It implies that Japan's self-image at its starting point had been confined by either explicit or implicit references to the West. The configuration of East and West, Orient and Occident was inevitable in either case. Once tied to the global chain of national histories by mimetic desire, the historical writings of the peripheries cannot but be discursive prisoners of Eurocentrism and Orientalism. If 'Orientalism is better grasped as a set of constraints upon and limitation of thought then it is simply a positive doctrine',[21] it is not difficult to imagine how this Orientalist set of constraints had influenced the construction of the first Japanese national history and art history. In short, these two books indicate the self-subjection of the Japanese to the putative West because of their desire for Western recognition of their own cultural and national authenticity.

It was a historical event in Japanese modern historiography when Tokyo Imperial University hired 26-year-old Ludwig Riess in 1887, a student of Leopold von Ranke. He taught history and historical methodology in the newly established history department. According to Tsuda's reminiscence, Riess taught a scientific and rationalistic methodology and emphasised the 'objectivity' of Rankean history.[22] It is not clear if he conveyed the Rankean defence of Prussian authority as part of God's design, but Rankean historical methods were not wholly new to some Japanese scholars, trained especially in the tradition of the textual analysis school (*koshogaku*). Their rigorous textual criticism and devotion to gathering facts and compiling chronologies could match well with the Rankean methodology.

However, Rankean history never meant apolitical historiography. Japanese modern historians tried to modernise and renovate Japanese history so that the Japanese nation could be understood in terms of Western history. The political commitment was rampant among them. Kuroita Katsumi, contrary to today's estimation of him as a true founder of the positivist history school in the 1880s and 1890s, was not reluctant to say that if some historical sites can stimulate the people's emotion, then they deserve to be protected as historically important sites regardless of their historical value. It was just as important for him to encourage national sentiments and patriotism as it was to promote objective historical studies. What impressed him most during his visit to Europe was the story and historical sites of Wilhelm Tell, not because it was the historical truth, but because it invoked patriotism among the common people in Switzerland by providing a model patriot.[23] The Japanese positivistic historiography, influenced by Rankean methods, would develop in parallel with the political commitment to the nation-state.

Japanese modern historiography has tried to prove Japan's equivalence with Europe, while simultaneously highlighting its differences from the rest of Asia. It aimed at removing the Japanese image of the invented Orient by capturing European elements in Japanese history and inventing its own Orient of China and Chosŏn (Korea). The more they became familiar with European history, the wider the gap grew between Japan and Europe. The more they tried to find a symmetrical equivalent to the history of the West, the more they had to suffer from the sense of lacking such equivalents. Inventing the Orient of Asian neighbours was designed to make up for that alleged inferiority. When historicism changed the vertical evolutionary time into the horizontal space of an 'imaginative geography', Japan discovered that it lagged behind the unilinear development scheme of world history, and it had to be placed in the Orient in comparison with Europe. By inventing Japan's own Orient, however, Japanese historians could let China and Chosŏn take the place of Japan and allow Japan to join the West in the imaginative geography.

Japanese Orientalism or sub-Orientalism towards its neighbours can be summed up in a new geopolitical entity called 'toyo' (東洋). It means literally 'Eastern Sea', but it was Japan's own formulation of the 'Orient'. The establishment of *toyoshi* (Oriental history) as a separate academic field gave historical and scientific authenticity to the new entity of 'toyo'. It was in 1894 that Naka Michiyo proposed a division of world history into Occidental and Oriental history in the middle school curriculum, and the Ministry of Education accepted his proposal in 1896. Perhaps it is not a coincidence that the establishment of *toyoshi* had the Sino-Japanese war as its historical background, which served to enhance Japanese national pride due to the victory over a Great Power. It was during and after the Russo-Japanese War in 1904 that the position of *toyoshi* was elevated once again. Later Japanese Orientalism was reinforced by acquiring the colonies of Taiwan (1894) and Korea (1910) and thus joining the Western imperialist block.

In the discourse of *toyoshi* the Japanese term for China changed from *chugoku* (literally meaning a central state) to *shina*. Japanese nativist scholars in the nineteenth century used *shina* to separate Japan from the traditional Sino-centric world-view of the barbarian/civilised duality implied in the term of *chugoku*. In early twentieth-century Japan, *shina* emerged as a word to signify China as a troubled place in contrast to Japan – a modernised nation-state.[24] If *chugoku* represents the Sino-centric China, *shina* has the Orientalist implication of making China a periphery nation. It is noteworthy that *shinajin* (China-man), together with *chosenjin* (Korean), has connotations relating to any oppressed or downtrodden people, even if they are Japanese themselves. It is therefore no longer an ethnic term, but serves as an allegory for down-and-out Japanese, e.g. in contemporary popular musicals.

Japanese historians of *toyoshi* borrowed the conceptual tools from the West to make their arguments sound reasonable. For example, Shiratori Kurakichi, the principal architect of *toyoshi*, argued that China reached the most advanced level of fetishism, the first stage in the Comtean framework of the three stages of fetishism, theology and positivism. By arguing that Japan was more highly developed than China, he tried to stop Japan being an object for European Orientalism. He was also keenly aware that 'Occidentals are apt to fall into self-indulgent arrogance and conceit'.[25] *Toyoshi* had an implication not only for Japanese Orientalism but also for Occidentalism in his works. It became increasingly antagonistic towards the West, while retaining the modernist approach to history. Equipped with the Rankean scientific methods, *toyoshi* has been deployed as a disciplinary strategy to distance Japan from both the dark parts of Asia and an atomised Western modernity, and place it in between. It was not only China and Chosŏn but also the West that was stamped as the 'Other' by *toyoshi*.

'Studies of Colonial Policies' represented the vulgar version of Orientalist *toyoshi* discourse. Its main purpose was to draw a line between Japan as the civilised state and China and Chŏsun as barbarian states. If *toyoshi* was focused mainly on China, the main target of 'Studies of Colonial Policies' was Chosŏn-Korea. While historians elaborated on *toyoshi*, social scientists led the 'studies of colonial policies'. Fukuta Tokujo, a pioneer of social policies in Japan, argued that Japan had developed along a historical path formulated by Karl Bücher and had reached the stage of national economy as the final stage of economic progress. In order to make the image of Japanese development more salient, he needed a mirror to reflect Japanese superiority. Chosŏn with its backward economy provided an ideal mirror for reflecting Japanese superiority. Like European Orientalists, Fukuta's 'strategic location' in his text is that of an expert on the economic history of Asia, who resides outside of Asia when he stressed the contrast between East and West with a presupposition that Japan is outside the East.[26]

The Japanese approach to Asian history was simply a copy of the European Orientalist view of Asia. What one finds among the works of Japanese scholars of 'Studies of Colonial Policies' is a representation of Asia spoken in the language of the European Orientalists. The negative images of Chosŏn represented in the works of these Japanese scholars are strikingly similar to the national attributes of Chosŏn that Isabella Bird Bishop enumerated in her account of travel to Chosŏn in the late nineteenth century: obstinate, narrow-minded, suspicious, lazy, shameless, brutal, childish and so on. These studies provided the historical ground which justified the Japanese mission to civilise Korea. It is based on Orientalist generalisations of the role of colonialism to destroy stagnant elements and modernise the colonies by introducing civilisation or the capitalist mode of production in Marxist terms. The discourse on Korea is a typical example of inventing the Orient in an invented Orient.

This Orientalist strategy for writing colonial histories led to the establishment of Japanese exceptionalism. The discursive location of Japanese exceptionalism in the thought of Japanese Orientalists was a convergence point between Orientalism and Occidentalism to conceal an inferiority complex towards the West and exalt a sense of superiority over other Asian neighbours. Japan's non-Asian exceptionalist road to modernisation has been evidenced by the discourse on Japanese feudalism. It asserts that the historical experience of European feudalism is a Japanese peculiarity in comparison with other Asian countries, which made it possible for Japan to succeed in its rapid modernisation. The discourse of Japanese feudalism was constructed just after the Russo-Japanese war as an ideology to support the modern nation-building process.

However, once established, it became regarded as 'normal' and some mainstream historians still adhere to Japanese feudalism as a historical peculiarity. The most widely read East Asian history book among English readers, *East Asia: Tradition and Transformation* dedicates a chapter to this topic under the title of 'Feudal Japan: A Departure from the Chinese Pattern'.[27] This title provides a vivid demonstration of the important role that the discourse of Japanese feudalism played in making Japan a member of the Occident and distancing it from the Orient. This line of historical inquiry expresses the Japanese aspiration to be identified with the West.

The Japanese intellectuals' strategy of inventing their own Orient to escape from the European invention of the Orient is reminiscent of Poles who tried to define their national identity by the invented images of West and East. Polish intellectuals tried to justify their Western aspirations by Orientalising

Russia. When a German soldier, stationed in Poland, wrote in his war diary in 1939 that 'the soul of an Eastern man is mysterious', it suggested that the Polish strategy of becoming incorporated into the West by Orientalising Russia was not so effective.[28] In this sense, it may be a pity for nationalist Japanese intellectuals that Pucchini's 'Madame Butterfly' is more popular among the 'Westerners' than Fairbank and Reischauer's *East Asia*. Perhaps their strategy of inventing the Orient to escape from the European-invented Orient has been most successful among the Japanese, less successful among other Asians and least successful among Western readers.

It is more striking that Marxist historians also deployed the discourse of Japanese feudalism. The famous Marxist controversy over the 'Meiji Restoration' of 1868 between the *Koza-ha* (Lecture's faction) and the *Rono-ha* (Labour–Peasant faction) is based on the assumption that established the existence of Japanese feudalism. While the *Koza-ha* saw the 'Meiji Restoration' as the completion of the absolutist state, the *Rono-ha* interpreted it as a bourgeois revolution. Despite this discord, their arguments were based on the same grounds as the European Marxists' analysis of feudalism, absolutism and the bourgeois revolution and thus tainted with 'red Orientalism'.[29] The Japanese Marxists' primary concern with the 'Asiatic mode of production' can be viewed in the same context. The implicit goal of Marxist Japanese historians was to contrast Japan's normal development in the path of European capitalism with the abnormal development or stagnancy of other Asian nations, which was supposed to be peculiar to the Asiatic mode of production. The Japanese Marxists' argument of the Asiatic mode of production was not a deviation at all, but rather true to Marx's analysis of India and China in the 1850s.[30] Moreover, this Marxist historiographical direction could be resonant with the civilising mission of Japanese colonialism.

It is hard to generalise about post-war Japanese historiography. However, it is not difficult to assert that post-war historiography has maintained a strong continuity with pre-war historiography, especially regarding the discourse of the Orient and the Occident. Little has changed in the production of the historical images of Japan invented by the West and for the West. In critical reviews of the total war system or Japanese fascism in the past, both liberal and Marxist historians continue to blame 'pre-modern' residues and Japan's 'deviated modernity' for the Japanese catastrophe. This approach is premised on the assumption that the Japanese catastrophe could be attributed to 'pathological factors peculiar to Japan, usually interpreted via a theory of pre-modern particularism versus modern universalism'.[31] In a word, it was the Japanese version of the German *Sonderweg* thesis. It signalled a move of Japan's imaginative location in world history from the West to the East, while the West remained the authentic reference.

'Korea': Inventing Nation in an Invented Nation

In the winter of 1999, a Japanese neo-nationalist group published *The History of Nation* as a pilot edition of the forthcoming *A New History Textbook*, which was soon authorised as one of the texts approved for use in Japan's Junior High Schools. This authorisation evoked criticism and furious responses in Japan and abroad because of its historical affirmation of Japanese colonialism, its shameless nationalism and its comfortable negligence of wartime atrocities such as the 1939 Nanjing massacre and Korean 'comfort women' or 'sexual slaves'. In the midst of these tumultuous debates, the *Sankei Shimbun*, a conservative Japanese daily newspaper in full support of *A New History Textbook*, published a series of articles dedicated to the analysis of East Asian history textbooks which urged the Japanese revisionist historians to adopt official Korean history textbooks as a model for Japanese ones. What is worthy of notice in Korean history textbooks, according to the *Sankei Shimbun*, is not their Korean-centric interpretation but rather their narrative strategy that has a firm footing in national history and ethnocentrism.

This farcical episode is highly useful for understanding the topography of competing national histories in Northeast Asia. Leaving aside some of the contemporary issues, the historical controversy over finding a common past in Northeast Asia is not a question of 'right or wrong' concerning historical facts, but the inevitable collision of the conflicting nation-centred interpretations. Behind the conflicting scenes, however, the national histories of Korea and Japan have formed a relationship of 'antagonistic complicity'.[32] It is not hard to find the cultural transfers and antagonistic acculturation in the century-long history of competing historiographies in this region. Indeed the basic concepts that anti-colonial movements have adopted were very often the discursive products of imperialist cultures.[33]

It is in 1895 that one can find a significant paradigm shift in Korean historical writings. The concept of national history and national language appeared for the first time among the reformist government policies of 1895 in the aftermath of the modernist reform of 1894. The reforms emphasised the necessity of teaching national history and national language. Korean history textbooks for primary and junior high school were produced according to government instruction. The most salient point of these history textbooks is the change in the names of neighbouring countries. The name of China was changed from *Hwa* (華: literally meaning 'splendour') to *Jina* (支那: Korean equivalent of *shina*). On the other hand, Koreans changed the name of Japan from *Wae* (倭) with the nuance of contempt to *Ilbon* (日本: Korean equivalent of Nippon that the Japanese prefer).[34] It is noteworthy that this reversal in the signified position of China and Japan occurred in the aftermath of the Sino-Japanese War. It signalled a departure from the traditional Sino-centric world order and indicated a political and discursive realignment of the East.

Soon the repositioning went so far as to Orientalise China in the journalistic writings of Korean reformers. A decentred and provincialised China was described as a barbarous nation full of negative attributes such as laziness, idleness, corruptions and pre-modern obstinacy. Orientalising China was a process of making boundaries of inside/outside and inclusion/exclusion. The Chinese immigrants in Korea were to be blamed, because they had done considerable harm to the Korean people. Even rumours of Chinese cannibalism, that accused the Chinese of kidnapping a Korean baby and eating human flesh, began to spread among the Korean masses. As shown by the claim that China would soon be shamed by even Denmark, contrasts with the West were inherent in these representations of China.[35] Later, this trend developed into an expansionist argument to justify *Drang nach Manchuria*.

The configuration of China and the West in the thought of Korean nationalists led to a new national awakening. It was a way of decentring and provincialising China for Korean Enlightenment intellectuals to adopt the Japanese way of inventing the Orient of China. It satisfied somewhat their burgeoning national aspiration to break away from the traditional Sino-centric world order. This way of inventing the Orient in an invented Orient was a means of appropriating the Western concept of civilisation.[36] A dozen world history books, including general histories like *A History of the Independence Movement in Italy*, *A History of the Fall of Poland*, The *Modern History of Egypt* and biographies of national heroes such as Napoleon Bonaparte, George Washington and Bismarck were published during this period, which were intended to spur a national awakening and encourage the formation of national consciousness.[37]

Except for these books, it was mostly Japan that represented the putative West in Korean historical discourse. Due to the influence of social Darwinism, a form of racial Pan-Asianism emerged as the dominant discourse among the Korean Enlightenment intellectuals by the early twentieth century. It argued that the opposition between the yellow peoples and the white peoples is the true historical struggle. Interpreting the Japanese concept of *toyo* (Orient) in an Occidentalist way, it stressed the ideal of regional solidarity and Japanese leadership. After Japan imposed a protectorate on Korea in 1905, the Pan-Asianism became a weapon of criticism of Japanese colonialism for violating the ideals of Asian solidarity and shirking Japan's leadership responsibilities.[38] Despite such criticism, the strategic position of Japan as the representative of Western civilisation remained unchanged.

The despair with Pan-Asianism led to an increasing emphasis on the national soul, national essence and national spirit, and the ethnic concept of the nation began to prevail in Korean historiography. The ethno-linguistic preoccupation of Korean historians led them to generate images of an authentic Korean culture and pure ethnic identities formed from a unilinear bloodline that purportedly existed for about five thousand years, descending from the mythic figure of Tan'gun. Of course, such insistence on national authenticity was not a unique phenomenon to Korea. Rather, it is found widely in the peripheral historiographies: the nineteenth-century German advocacy of 'culture' against the Anglo–French 'civilisation'; Russian Slavophiles' assertion that 'inner truth' based on religion, culture and moral convictions is much more important than 'external truth' expressed by law and the state; Indian nationalist discourse of the superiority of the spiritual domain over the material domain.[39]

In colonial contexts, such theories of national authenticity imply that the nation is already sovereign and can maintain its own national spirit – the essential domain of the spiritual – even when the state is in the hands of a colonial power. Very often nationalist historians created an organic concept of the nation, which views the nation as eternal reality and collective destiny that constrains every individual. Staying true to the nation-state demands a total subordination of the individual to the national community. Perhaps this collectivist orientation explains the presence of populist or communalist elements in many postcolonial states regardless of their constitutional order. It may be noteworthy also that there is no serious tension between individual and community, individualism and communalism in Polish sociology, where the organic concept of nation has been dominant.[40]

The primordialist view of the nation has prevailed over the constructivist concept of nation in Korean historiography until recently. It tends to essentialise the nation in historical writings and thus reduce all historical events to the development of national history. It presupposes the nation as the major historical subject. The pronouns that appear most frequently in Korean official history textbooks are 'we', 'our nation', and 'our country'. Even in references to ancient history, 'our nation' and 'our country' remains anachronistically the subject of history. National history is described as the history of challenge and response, in which the nation is the supposed subject that overcame national crises even before the era of nation-states. It is a highly effective narrative strategy to make the nation and state an eternal reality in the nationalist imagination. Combined with the discourse of the 'fatherland' and 'national legitimacy', this narrative replaces various historical communities with the imagined nation. Once the imagined nation is established as the major historical agent, an individual's fealty such as loyalty, subjection, contribution and self-sacrifice for national unity becomes the yardstick and the primary focus for historical judgment.[41] It is no wonder that the *Sankei Shinbun* envies Korean history textbooks.

It may be astonishing that the author of *A New History of Korea*',[42] the most widely read Korean history book for university students and general readers both at home and abroad, claimed that 'love for the nation and belief in the truth is the head and tail of the same coin'.[43] Considering that Ki-baik Lee has stressed the Rankean approach to history, which is labelled as 'positivist historiography' in Korea and Japan, it is even more astounding. Such statements are not new, however, if we consider how Ranke could manage an oxymoron of scientific method and Prussian statism. During his studies in colonial Japan, Ki-baik Lee must have recognised how the Japanese Rankean disciples of the 'positivistic historiography' could combine scientificity with the political commitment to the nation-state.

It is not a surprise that Korean self-knowledge in the modernist national form has been influenced by the Japanese production of knowledge about Korea. If Korean national identity was partly a product of a reaction against Japanese aggression, it is also true that it was closely intertwined with Japanese writings about Korean culture and history. 'Inventing the nation' in Korea owes much to the 'invented nation' of the Japanese Orientalists.[44] In particular, the survey of habitual practices in Korea, conducted by the Japanese Government-General just after the annexation of Korea in 1910, was an ideal opportunity to invent Korean traditions by adjusting and deforming realities for the convenience of colonial policies. The details of inventing traditions during this survey are not yet explored because many Korean historians have made use of this survey to find their own traditional practices.

Even before these surveys, Sekino Tadashi, who was an assistant professor in the engineering department of Tokyo Imperial University carried out archaeological and historical research on Korea in 1902 at the request of the Japanese government. In his survey reports, Sekino classified and graded his discoveries of Korean art according to the European model applied to Japanese art history. By evaluating the art of the Unified Silla period (AD 676–918) very highly, he contrasted the remarkable development of art in Silla with the decline of art in the Chosŏn period (AD 1392–1910).[45] A major contrast between the blossoming of Japanese art and the decline of Korean art in contemporary history was implicit in his report on Korean art. This contrast functioned to justify the Japanese annexation of the Korean peninsula and its civilising mission from the viewpoint of art history, because the decline of art signified the degeneration of the Chosŏn dynasty.

Since then, the typical Orientalist image of contrasting 'ancient glory and present misery' has been reiterated in various writings on Korean art history. The image of flourishing art represented at its finest by the pagodas at Pulguk-sa temple and the Buddhist sculptures in the nearby Sŏkkuram grotto, built in the year 751, made a deep impression on postcolonial contemporary Korean historiography, including history textbooks. It is noteworthy that the big archaeological excavation projects of Kyŏngju, the capital of the Silla Kingdom, sponsored by the state in the early 1970s, aimed to discover the glorious indigenous artistic heritage in tune with the *Zeitgeist* of national subjectivity and the 'Korean way of democracy' advocated by the dictatorship. The indigenous style of Korean art invented and discovered by the Japanese colonisers remained a useful tool for inventing national art in postcolonial Korea.

It was Yanagi Muneyoshi who discovered the artistic value of white porcelains in the Chosŏn dynasty. Despite his sympathy for Korean art and criticism of Japanese colonialism, his description of Chosŏn dynasty's white porcelains is full of tropes that feminise Korean culture. It was the coloniser's masculine view of feminised colonies that provides the undercurrents of his definition of Korean traditional colour as the 'innocent white' and of the quintessence of Korean culture as 'her' melancholy of tears and regrets. His discourse was based on the contrast between 'the youthful, dynamic and colourful' Japanese art and 'natural, irrational and monochromatic' Korean art. He posited a masculinised Japan as the subject of estimation and a feminised Korea as the object of observation. It shows the hierarchical relations and construction of gendered cultural forms between the masculinised colonial powers and the feminised powerless colonies. Considering that 'support for a particular kind of gender relations was used as a justification for colonial domination',[46] Yanagi's sympathy towards Korean art cannot be free from the charge of Orientalism.

Amusingly enough, one can find Yanagi's discourse of 'tears and regrets' conjured up by the people involved in contemporary Korean mass culture like cinema whenever it is presented to the Western audience. The practice of discovering the native Korean culture by configuring East and West is also found in folklore and modern literature. Some of the most successful short stories that reflect the nativism of colonial Korea have been produced not by nativist novelists but by modernist novelists. For example, Yi Hyosŏk, who produced the best nativist short story, was a representative 'modern boy'. He could find and describe the beauty of native Korea, not because he was familiar with native culture, but because he was preoccupied with Western culture.[47] Lyrical nativism was possible only in comparison with the West. It fits well with Prasenjit Duara's definition of tradition as 'a reconstructed image that is organised under the new categories and assumptions of the modernist discourse'.[48] Moreover, the tradition reconstructed by the colonisers' modernist discourse was imbued with Orientalism.

Marxist historiography has never been an exception to the practice of configuring East and West in historical thinking and writing. When Marx said that the 'country that is more developed industrially only shows, to the less developed, the image of its own future',[49] he proclaimed the manifesto of Marxist historicism. It changed the spatial difference between East and West into the evolutionary time difference between backwardness and forwardness of the unilinear scheme of human history. It is proven also by his frequent use of the prefix *pre* such as 'pre-capitalist mode of production'. In cases where it is applied to the peripheries, Marxist historical narrative has definitely been inclined to historicism. By way of Marxist historicism, the revolutionary nationalists adopted Marxism as an ideological weapon for the 'follow and catch up' strategy of the peripheries.[50] They looked at Marx as a theorist of modernity.

It is not surprising that the dominant Marxist historical narrative in Korea puts much emphasis on the origins of capitalism and on its endogenous development. Korean Marxist historians tried particularly hard to prove how the emergence of large-scale farming produced class tensions in the countryside and polarised the rural population. They then sought a blueprint for utopia in historical phenomena such as the development of commercial production of specialised crops, development of wholesale commerce, handcraft industries that relied on merchant capital in the putting-out system, mercantilism, and modernist thought. Tracing the emerging capitalist relations of productions, Marxist and Marxisant historians also described slave and feudal societies in ancient and medieval times.

All this provides a familiar landscape and spectacle to those who have read the Marxist economic histories of Europe.[51] However, it is far from any creative application of Marxism, and is more closely associated with the mechanical application of Marxist narratives of European history to Korean history. Those who promoted a discourse that ran contrary to this Eurocentric scheme of Korean history and insisted on a different path, such as arguing that state landownership may have been an obstacle for economic development, were labelled as the theorists of the 'Asiatic mode of production' and, thus, proponents of the stagnation thesis of Korea. It is a vivid example that 'Marx's theory of the modes of production went hand-in-hand with the nation-state's ideology of modernity and progress'.[52]

If one views Marx as a theorist of modernity, one may easily find that 'Marx's account of modernisation was inextricably a description of Westernisation, and therefore that his view of global history was a general history of the West'.[53] The moment Korean Marxists and Japanese Marxists began to stress universal history or the universal laws of world history, they became dependent on the Eurocentric historical narratives and plunged into the discursive pool of 'red Orientalism'. On the other hand, it should be noted that the location of Korean history in Marx's Eurocentric universalist scheme was the result of a desperate effort to deny the stagnancy of the 'Asiatic mode of production'. It is a genuine paradox of Korean Marxist historians to deny Marx's own prognosis of colonialism 'to fulfil a double mission in India: one destructive, the other generating the annihilation of old Asiatic society, and the laying of the material foundations of Western society in Asia'.[54] They preferred the Marxian universalist scheme to the Asiatic mode of production to avoid justifying Japanese colonialism. However, neither the 'Asiatic mode of production' nor the Eurocentric universalist scheme could escape from the charge of 'red Orientalism'.

Towards a Reconfiguration

The configuration of East and West has had an ambiguous effect on historical writings. This ambiguity resulted from different locations of the 'imaginative geography' in the global chain of national histories. Its location in the East used to lead to a history of 'lack' whilst its location in the West would exalt the feeling of national superiority. The Japanese discourse intended to dislocate its past from Asia by inventing the Orient of China and Korea and simultaneously positioning Japan in the West so that it would overcome a sense of lack in its national history. It stood on the modified configuration of China–Korea–Orient and Japan–Occident via Japanese exceptionalism, which dislocated Japan from the East. The idea of an exceptional Japan to Asia presupposed the existence of a Japanese historical peculiarity that was close to European history. Thus, Japanese exceptionalism served as the equivalent of European exceptionalism in world history.

Korean contemporary historiography has also been very keen to discover its own equivalents to European history and thus expressed a strong desire to be located in the putative West. It could escape from the Sino-centric worldview dominating the traditional historiography by riding on the coat-tails of the Japanese discourse of *toyoshi* and constructing its own national history based on the Eurocentric model. But neither the Japanese nor Korean historians could find symmetrical equivalents to European history. It would be an impossible mission. The closer they came to Europe, the deeper their frustration became. The periphery's desire for a stable location in the putative West has never been satisfied. As long as the historians of the peripheries are entangled in the Eurocentric model of history, they must depend on the configuration of East and West that has been outlined by the Orientalist discourse. Combined with the historicist scheme, this trap would necessarily lead them to the recognition of a gap between East and West. The location of the national history in the structure of the 'imaginative geography' has been always in flux, but the gap between East and West can never be closed.

The impossibility of overcoming the East and West binary opposition explains why the global chain of national history that feeds on Eurocentrism must be deconstructed. Without untying that chain, the national history of the peripheries will continue to encourage its own Eurocentric nationalism or anti-Western Orientalism. Most importantly, the configuration of East and West needs to be reconfigured. Yet I am somewhat sceptical that the critical historiography in Europe can contribute to this reconfiguration in a manner that is entirely free from the Eurocentric national history paradigm. The self-criticism of the British 'people's history' by Raphael Samuel deserves to be mentioned: 'people's history or history from below in particular was part of what we were attacking [...] It treats "the common people" as a collective subject, transposing the national epic from the field of high politics to that of everyday life. The "peculiarities of the English" [...] has also helped to foster its own version of "Little Englandism"'.[55] Perhaps the reconfiguration of the world's geo-history demands more radical politics that can articulate the need for deconstructing national histories and the global chain. An alternative narrative to national history should be found not only in the local, but also in the global.

Notes

1. G. Iggers, *Geschichtswissenschaft im 20. Jahrhundert*, Korean trans. S.W. Lim and G.B. Kim, Seoul, 1998: 216.
2. S. Berger, M. Donovan and K. Passmore, 'Apologias for the Nation-state in Western Europe since 1800', in *Writing National Histories: Western Europe since 1800*, eds, Stefan Berger et al., London, 1999: 3–14.
3. B. Anderson, *Imagined Communities*, revised ed., London, 1991: 198.
4. Ibid., 205.
5. Berger et al., 'Apologias', 12.
6. N. Nagao, *Kokuminkokkaron No Satei*, Korean trans. D.Y. Yoon (1998), Seoul, 2002: 56.
7. J.M. Blaut, *The Colonizer's Model of the World: Geographical Diffusionism and Eurocentric History*, New York, 1993: 5–6.
8. D. Chakrabarty, *Provincializing Europe: Postcolonial Thought and Historical Difference*, Princeton, 2000: 7.
9. Blaut, *The Colonizer's Model*, 1.
10. N. Sakai, *Translation and Subjectivity: On 'Japan' and Cultural Nationalism*, Minneapolis, 1997: 50.
11. P. Chatterjee, *The Nation and Its Fragments: Colonial and Postcolonial Histories*, Princeton, 1993: 30.
12. G. Prakash, 'AHR Forum: Subaltern Studies as Postcolonial Criticism', *American Historical Review* 99, 1994: 1475.
13. I. Wallerstein, *The End of the World as We Know It: Social Science for the Twenty-First Century*, Korean trans. S.W. Baik, Seoul, 2001: 248.
14. A.G. Frank, *ReOrient: Global Economy in the Asian Age*, Berkeley, 1998: 2.
15. Sung-si Lee, *Mandlojin Godai* (The Ancient Invented), Korean trans. K.H. Park, Seoul, 2001: 197–98.
16. Ibid., 199.
17. T. Morris-Suzuki, *Reinventing Japan: Time, Space, Nation*, Armonk, NY, 1998: 23.
18. Lee, *Mandlojin*, 199–203.
19. T. Hiroshi, 'Nihon bijutsushi no seiritsu/Shiron' (A sketch of the formation of the Japanese art history), *Nihonshi Kenkyu*, 320, 1989: 74.
20. T. Hiroshi, 'Ilbon Misulsa wa Chosun Misulsa ui Songlip' (Formation of Japanese history of art and Korean history of art), in Jie-Hyun Lim and Sung-si Lee, eds, *Guksa ui Sinhwa rul Nomuseo* (Beyond the myth of national history), Seoul, 2004: 169–70.
21. E. Said, *Orientalism*, New York, 1979, 42.
22. T. Sokochi, 'Shiratori hakushi shoden', cited in S. Tanaka, *Japan's Orient: Rendering Pasts into History*, Berkeley, 1993: 26.
23. Sung-si Lee, 'Shokuminchi bunka seisaku no kachi wo tsuujite mita rekishi ninsiki' (Historical consciousness represented by colonial cultural policies), a paper presented to Kyoto Forum of Public Philosophy, March 13, 2004.
24. Tanaka, *Japan's Orient*, 4.
25. Shiratori, 'Shina jodaishi', in ibid., 60.
26. Kang Sang-jung, *Orientalism No Kanatae* (Beyond Orientalism), Korean trans. S.M. Lim, Seoul, 1997: 94–95.
27. J.K. Fairbank, E.O. Reischauer and A.M. Craig, *East Asia: Tradition and Transformation*, Boston, 1976: 358–91.

28. B. Lagowski, 'Ideologia Polska. Zachodnie aspiracje i wschodnie sklonnosci' (Polish Ideology: Western Aspirations and Eastern Inclinations), in Jie-Hyun Lim and Michal Sliwa, eds, *Polska i Korea: Proces modernizacji w perspektywie historycznej*, Cracow, 1997: 88–97.

29. T. Tibebu, 'On the Question of Feudalism, Absolutism and the Bourgeois Revolution', *Review* 13, 1990: 49–152.

30. See *Karl Marx on Colonialism and Modernization*, ed. S. Avineri, Garden City, NY, 1968. Isn't it wrong to argue that this collection provided some Marxists with the pretext they needed to espouse their own 'red Orientalism'?

31. J.V. Koschmann, 'Introduction to the English Edition', in Y. Yamanouchi et al., eds, *Total War and 'Modernization'*, Ithaca, 1998: xi–xii.

32. For the antagonistic complicity of conflicting nationalisms in Northeast Asia, see Jie-Hyun Lim, 'Chosenhantono Minzokushugido Kenryokuno Gensetsu' (Korean nationalism and the power discourse), Japanese trans. I. Ryuta, in *Gendai Shiso* 28, 2000: 126–44.

33. See A. Nandy, *The Intimate Enemy: Loss and Recovery of Self under Colonialism*, Delhi, 1983.

34. M.H. Do, 'Hanmal yŏksahak ŭi kŭndaesŏng chaeiron' (Reconsidering the modernity in the historiogarphy of the late nineteenth century and early twentieth century)', a paper presented to the 6th Korean-Japanese workshop organised by the 'East Asian History Forum for Criticism and Solidarity, Kyoto, 14–17 May, 2004.

35. A. Schmid, *Korea between Empires 1895–1919*, New York, 2002: 56–59.

36. Ibid., 80.

37. B.C. Kim, 'Han'guk kŭndae pŏnyŏkmunhaksa yŏn'gu' (A study of translations of modern literature in Korea), Seoul, 1975: 171–72.

38. Schmid, *Korea between Empires*, 13.

39. See N. Elias, *Über den Prozess der Zivilisation*, Korean trans. H.S. Yoo, Seoul, 1996: 33–75; A. Walicki, *A History of Russian Thought*, Oxford, 1979: 93–106; P. Chatterjee, *The Nation*, 3–13.

40. J. Kurczewska, 'Nation in Polish Sociology', *The Polish Sociological Bulletin* 15, 1–2, 1976: 62.

41. Su-gul Gee, 'Minjokkwa kŭndae ŭi ijungju' (Duality of nation and modernity), *Contemporary Criticism*, special issue of history report 1, 2002: 58–67.

42. Ki-baik Lee, *A New History of Korea*, Eng. trans. E.W. Wagner and E.J. Shulz, Cambridge, MA, 1984.

43. Ki-baik Lee, 'To readers', in *Han'kuksa simin'gangjwa* (Korean history lecture for citizens), 20, 1997.

44. For the cultural transfer between Japanese imperialist historians and Korean nationalist historians in the colonial period, see H.M. Park, 'Cheguk ilbon'gwa min'kuk han'guk ŭi yŏksahakchŏk kyoch'aro' (Historiographical Crossroads of Imperial Japan and Colonial Korea), a paper presented at the Seminar of Korean committee of the East Asian History Forum for Criticism and Solidarity, 19 May, 2001.

45. Hiroshi, 'Ilbon Misulsa', 180, 187.

46. S. Walby, 'Woman and Nation', in G. Balakrishnan, ed., *Mapping the Nation*, London, 1996: 241.

47. See Hyung-ki Shin, 'Yi Hyosŏk kwa singminji kŭndae' (Yi Hyosŏk and colonial modernity), in Lim and Lee, eds, *Beyond the Myth*, 329–54.

48. P. Duara, 'Knowledge and Power in the Discourse of Modernity', *Journal of Asian Studies* 50, 1991: 68.

49. K. Marx, 'Preface to the First Edition', in *Capital*, vol. 1, trans. B. Fowkes, Harmondsworth, 1990: 91.

50. See Jie-Hyun Lim, 'Befreiung oder Modernisierung? Sozialismus als ein Weg der anti-westlichen Modernisierung in unterentwickelten Ländern', *Beiträge zur Geschichte der Arbeiterbewegung* 43, 2, 2001: 5–23.

51. I have to confess that, in my twenties as a young Marxist historian, I planned to study Korean economic history to find the sprouts of capitalism after reading Marx, Maurice Dobb, Rodney Hilton and especially the controversy over the transition from feudalism to capitalism. Although I no longer agree with this dominant Marxist historical narrative in Korea, the persuading power of Marxist historicism is still vivid in my memory.
52. G. Prakash, 'AHR Forum', 1477.
53. B.S. Turner, *Orientalism, Postmodernism and Globalism*, London, 1994: 140.
54. *Karl Marx on Colonialism and Modernization*, 125.
55. R. Samuel, 'Preface', in *Patriotism: The Making and Unmaking of British National Identity*, vol. 1, London, 1989: xi.

Notes on Contributors

Stefan Berger is Chair of Modern German and Comparative European History in the School of Languages, Literatures and Cultures at the University of Manchester, and Chair of the ESF research programme 'Representations of the Past: The Writing of National Histories in Europe' (NHIST, 2003–2008). His recent publications include: *Writing the Nation: Towards Global Perspectives* (Houndmills, 2007), *Inventing the Nation: Germany* (London, 2004), *Dialog der Schwerhörigen? Geschichte, Mythos und Gedächtnis im deutsch-englischen kulturellen Austausch 1750–2000*, eds P. Lambert and P. Schumann (Göttingen, 2002), *Writing National Histories: Western Europe since 1800*, edited with Mark Donovan and Kevin Passmore (London, 1999), *The Search for Normality: National Identity and Historical Consciousness in Germany since 1800* (Oxford, 1997, 2nd rev. ed., 2003).

Mark Bevir is a Professor in the Department of Political Science, University of California, Berkley. He is author of *The Logic of the History of Ideas* (Cambridge, 1999) and *New Labour: A Critique* (London, 2005), and co-author, with Rod Rhodes, of *Interpreting British Governance* (London, 2003) and *Governance Stories* (London, 2006). He is also co-editor, with Frank Trentmann, of *Critiques of Capital in Modern Britain and America* (Basingstoke, 2002) and *Markets in Historical Contexts: Ideas and Politics in the Modern World* (Cambridge, 2004), and, with Robert Adcock and Shannon Stimson, of *Modern Political Science: Anglo-American Exchanges since 1880* (2007).

Philip V. Bohlman is the Mary Werkman Distinguished Service Professor of the Humanities and of Music, and was Chair of Jewish Studies at the University of Chicago from 2003 to 2006. He has written and published extensively, and among his most recent publications are *World Music: A Very Short Introduction* (Oxford University Press, 2002), *The Music of European Nationalism* (ABC-CLIO, 2004; 2nd rev. ed., Routledge, 2009), *'Jüdische Musik' – eine mitteleuropäische Geistesgeschichte* (Böhlau, 2005) and *Jewish Music and Modernity* (AMS Studies in Music, 2008).

Linas Eriksonas was Project Co-ordinator for the European Science Foundation Programme 'Representations of the Past: The Writing of National Histories in Nineteenth and Twentieth Century Europe'. He is the author of *National Heroes and National Identities: Scotland, Norway and Lithuania* (Brussels, 2004) and co-editor, together with Leos Müller, of *Statehood before and beyond Ethnicity: Minor States in Northern and Eastern Europe, 1600–2000* (Brussels, 2005).

Hugo Frey is Principal Lecturer and Subject Leader in History at the University of Chichester, England. He is the author of *Louis Malle* (Manchester, 2004) and has co-edited (with Benjamin Noys) a special issue of the journal *Rethinking History* (6.3 Winter 2002) that is devoted to popular visual representations of history in 'graphic novels/*bande dessinée*'. Selected publications include: 'Rebuilding France: Gaullist Historiography, the Rise-Fall Myth and French Identity (1945–1958)' in S. Berger, M. Donovan and K. Passmore, eds, *Writing National Histories: Western Europe since 1800* (London, 1999); and 'Pierre Drieu la Rochelle, Louis Malle and the Ambiguous Memory of French Fascism', in William Kidd and Brian Murdoch, eds, *Memory and Memorials: The Commemorative Century* (London, 2004). In 2003, co-authored work written with Professor Christopher Flood regarding the French extreme right-wing was included in the 'Routledge Reader' series title, James D. Le Sueur, *Decolonization: A Reader* (New York, 2003). In 2004, he provided an 'Afterword' to the French colonial fantasy novel, Pierre Benoit, *The Queen of Atlantis* (Lincoln, NE, 2004).

Wulf Kansteiner is Associate Professor of History and Judaic Studies at Binghamton University where he teaches German history, media history and historical theory. He is the author of 'In Pursuit of German Memory: History, Television, and Politics after Auschwitz' and the co-editor of 'The Politics of Memory in Postwar Europe' (both 2006). He is also co-editor of the Sage-journal *Memory Studies*.

Jie-Hyun Lim is Professor of History and Director of the Research Institute of Comparative History and Culture at Hanyang University, Seoul. He had been a visiting scholar at the University of Glamorgan, Harvard-Yenching Institute, Cracow Pedagogical University. He has written extensively on the issues of comparative histories of nationalist movements and the socio-cultural history of socialism in Northeast Asia and Eastern Europe. Among his historiography works in English are: 'The "Good Old Cause" in the New Polish Left Historiography', *Science and Society*, 61 (Winter, 1997); 'The Nationalist Message in Socialist Code: On Court Historiography in People's Poland and North Korea', in Sølvi Sogner, ed., *Making Sense of Global History: The Nineteenth International Congress of the Historical Sciences Oslo 2000 Commemorative Volume* (Oslo, 2001); 'From Hard History to Soft History: Cultural Histories of the Korean Working Class', *International Labor and Working-class History* 61 (2004). Currently, he is leading a comparative research project on mass dictatorships in collaboration with various international institutes.

Chris Lorenz is Professor of Philosophy of History at the VU University Amsterdam. Relevant publications include: *Konstruktion der Vergangenheit. Eine Einführung in die Geschichtstheorie* (Cologne/Weimar/Vienna, 1997); 'Comparative Historiography: Problems and Perspectives', *History and Theory* 39 (1999), pp. 25–39; 'Towards a Theoretical Framework for Comparing Historiographies: Some Preliminary Considerations', ed. Peter Seixas, *Theorizing Historical Consciousness* (Toronto, 2004), pp. 25–48; (co-author Stefan Berger), 'National Narratives and their "Others": Ethnicity, Class, Religion and the Gendering of National Histories', in: *Storia della Storiografia* 50 (2006), pp. 59–98; '"Won't you tell me, where have all the good times gone?" On the advantages and disadvantages of modernization theory for historical study', in: *The Many Faces of Clio: Cross-cultural Approaches to Historiography*, eds. Q. Edward Wang and Franz L. Fillafer, New York and Oxford 2007, pp. 104–127; 'Scientific Historiography', in: Avizer Tucker (ed.), *A Companion to Philosophy and Historiography*, Oxford 2008, pp. 393–404; *Bordercrossings. Explorations between History and Philosophy*, Poznan 2008 (in Polish); (with Stefan Berger, eds), *The Contested Nation. Ethnicity, Religion, Class and Gender in National Histories*, Houndmills 2008.

Allan Megill is Professor of History at the University of Virginia. He specialises in modern European intellectual history and philosophy of history. He wrote *Karl Marx: The Burden of Reason* (Lanham, MD, 2002) and *Prophets of Extremity: Nietzsche, Heidegger, Foucault, Derrida* (Berkeley, 1985); co-edited, with John S. Nelson and Deirdre N. McCloskey, *The Rhetoric of the Human Sciences* (Madison, WI, 1987), and edited *Rethinking Objectivity* (Durham, NC, 1994). His most recent book is *Historical Knowledge, Historical Error: A Contemporary Guide to Practice* (Chicago, 2007). Among his recent essays is "The Rhetorical Dialectic of Hayden White," in *Re-*

Figuring Hayden White, eds. Frank Ankersmit, Ewa Domanska, and Hans Kellner (Stanford, 2008). Currently he is working on the concept of the border as a historical problem.

John Neubauer is Professor Emeritus of Comparative Literature at the University of Amsterdam. His most recent book (co-authored with Marcel Cornis-Pope) is *History of the Literary Cultures of East-Central Europe* (Benjamins, 2004). He has also co-edited several volumes of *Johann Wolfgang Goethe, Sämtliche Werke* (Hanser, 1986). He is the author of *The Emancipation of Music from Language* (New Haven, 1986) and of *The Fin-de-Siècle Culture of Adolescence* (New Haven, 1992).

Ann Rigney holds the Chair of Comparative Literature at Utrecht University. Her research has concentrated mainly on the intersections between literature and historiography, and she has published widely in the fields of narratology, historical theory and cultural memory. She is author of *The Rhetoric of Historical Representation: Three Narrative Histories of the French Revolution* (Cambridge, 1990), *Imperfect Histories: The Elusive Past and the Legacy of Romantic Historicism* (Ithaca, NY, 2001) and 'Plenitude, Scarcity and the Circulation of Cultural Memory', *Journal of European Studies* 35 (March 2005). She was co-editor with Joep Leerssen of *Historians and Social Values* (Amsterdam, 2000). Her current projects include a book on the cultural afterlife of Walter Scott.

Peter Seixas is Professor and Canada Research Chair at the University of British Columbia (Vancouver) and Director of the Centre for the Study of Historical Consciousness (www.cshc.ubc.ca). His research looks at young people's historical consciousness, the relationships among disciplinary and extra-disciplinary approaches to thinking about the past, the education and professional development of history teachers, history curriculum and instruction, and school-university collaboration. He edited *Theorizing Historical Consciousness* (Toronto, 2004) and co-edited, with Peter Stearns and Sam Wineburg, *Knowing, Teaching and Learning History: National and International Perspectives* (New York University Press, 2000). Among his other recent publications are (with Penney Clark) 'Murals as Monuments: Students' Ideas about the Origins of Civilisation in British Columbia', *American Journal of Education* 110 (2004) and 'A School District Develops Historical Thinking Standards', *International Review of History Education* 4 (2001).

Heidemarie Uhl is a senior researcher and lecturer at the Universities of Vienna and Graz. Since 2001 she has been contributing to the research programme on the sites of memory run by the Commission for Culture Studies and History of Theater of the Austrian Academy of Sciences in Vienna. Between 1994 and

2000 she was a researcher for the project 'Moderne – Wien und Zentraleuropa um 1900'. Her major interests are in memory politics, theory of cultural studies and modernity, culture and identity in Central Europe. She is the author of *Zwischen Versöhnung und Verstörung. Eine Kontroverse um Österreichs historische Identität fünfzig Jahre nach dem Anschluß* (Vienna, 1992); the co-editor, with S. Riesenfellne, of *Todeszeichen. Zeitgeschichtliche Denkmalkultur in Graz und in der Steiermark vom Ende des 19. Jahrhunderts bis zur Gegenwart* (Vienna, 1994); editor of *Kultur–Urbanität–Moderne. Differenzierungen der Moderne in Zentraleuropa um 1900* (Vienna, 1999); *Zivilisationsbruch und Gedächtniskultur. Das 20. Jahrhunderts in der Erinnerung des beginnenden 21. Jahrhunderts* (Innsbruck, 2003), author of *Transformationen des österreichischen Gedächtnisses. Zweiter Weltkrieg, Nationalsozialismus und Holocaust in der Erinnerungskultur der Zweiten Republik* (Innsbruck, 2007).

Sigrid Weigel is Director of the Berlin Centre for Literature and Cultural Research (*Zentrum für Literatur- und Kulturforschung Berlin*) and Professor of Literature Studies at the Technical University of Berlin. Previously she was a professor at the Universities of Hamburg and Zürich, a member of the board of the *Kulturwissenschaftliche Institut* in Essen and the director of the Einstein Forum in Postsdam. She has been a visiting professor at the universities in Basel, Berkeley, Cincinnati, Harvard, Princeton and Stanford. Her current research is about secularisation and on the concepts of generation, genealogy and heritage. She is the author of *Genea-Logik: Generation, Tradition und Evolution zwischen Kultur- und Naturwissenschaften* (München, 2006), *Literatur als Voraussetzung der Kulturgeschichte: Schauplätze von Shakespeare bis Benjamin* (München, 2004), *Ingeborg Bachmann. Hinterlassenschaften unter Wahrung des Briefgeheimnisses* (Wien 1999), *Body- and Image Space: Re-reading Walter Benjamin* (London, 1996) and many other books on the varied subjects of cultural history.

Michael Wintle is Professor of European History at the University of Amsterdam, where he directs the degree programmes in European Studies. Before that he held a chair of European History at the University of Hull, UK, where he had taught since 1980. His current research interests are in European identity and especially the visual representation of Europe, cultural aspects of European integration, European industrialisation, and the modern social and economic history of the Low Countries. He has published widely on Dutch and European history, including the following recent books: *An Economic and Social History of the Netherlands* (Cambridge, 2000); *The Idea of a United Europe since the Fall of the Berlin Wall* (Basingstoke, 2000); *Ideas of Europe since 1914* (Basingstoke, 2002); *Image into Identity* (Amsterdam, 2006); and *The Image of Europe* (Cambridge, 2008).

Bibliography

Abraham, N., 'Aufzeichnungen über das Phantom. Ergänzungen zu Freuds Metapsychologie', *Psyche* vol. 8, 1991: 691–98

Adair, G., *Hollywood's Vietnam*, London, 1989

Agulhon, M., *Marianne into Battle: Republican Imagery and Symbolism in France, 1789–1880*, Cambridge, 1981

——— and Bonte, P., *Marianne: les visages de la République*, Paris, 1992

Aitken, I., ed., *Encylopedia of Documentary Film*, New York, 2006

Alpers, S. and Baxendall, M., *Tiepolo and the Pictorial Intelligence*, New Haven, 1994

Andersch, A., *Der Ruf. Unabhängige Blätter für die junge Generation* 1 (15 Aug. 1946), München 1976

Anderson, B., *Imagined Communities: Reflections on the Origin and Spread of Nationalism*, London, 1991

Andrić, I., *The Bridge over the Drina*, trans. L.F. Edwards, New York, 1994

Ankersmit, F.R. and Kellner, H., eds, *A New Philosophy of History*, Chicago, 1995

Arany, J., *Buda halála*, Pest, 1864.

——— , *Összes művei* vol. 10, Budapest, 1962

Armistead, S.G., Silverman, J.H. and Katz, I.J., *Judeo-Spanish Ballads from Oral Tradition: Epic Ballads*, Berkeley and Los Angeles, 1986

Ashby, J. and Higson, A., *British Cinema, Past and Present*, London, 2000

Askew, K., *Performing the Nation: Swahili Music and Cultural Politics in Tanzania*, Chicago, 2002

Assmann, A., *Erinnerungsräume: Formen und Wandlungen des kulturellen Gedächtnisses*, Munich, 1999

——— and Friese, H., eds, *Identitäten. Erinnerung, Geschichte, Identität 3*, 2nd ed., Frankfurt am Main, 1999

———— and Harth, D., eds, *Kultur als Lebenswelt und Monument*, Frankfurt am Main, 1991

Assmann, J., *Das kulturelle Gedächtnis: Schrift, Erinnerung und politische Identität in frühen Hochkulturen*, Munich, 2000

———— and Hölscher, T., eds, *Kultur und Gedächtnis*, Frankfurt am Main, 1988

Attie, J., 'Illusions of History: A Review of The Civil War', *Radical History Review* vol. 52, 1992: 95–104

Austin, G., *Contemporary French Cinema*, Manchester, 1996

Avisar, I., *Screening the Holocaust: Cinema's Image of the Unimaginable*, Bloomington, 1988

Bakhtin, M.M., *The Dialogic Imagination*, ed. M. Holquist, trans. C. Emerson and M. Holquist, Austin, 1981

Balakrishnan, G., ed., *Mapping the Nation*, London, 1996

Balan, A.T., *Bălgarska literatura*, Plovdiv, 1896

Baldwin, P., ed., *Reworking the Past: Hitler, the Holocaust, and the Historians' Debate*, Boston, 1990

de Balzac, H., (1842) *La comédie humaine* vol. 1, ed. P. Citron, Paris, 1965

Banks, M., *Visual Methods in Social Research*, London, 2001

Bann, S., *The Clothing of Clio*, Cambridge, 1984

Barkan, E., *The Guilt of Nations: Restitution and Negotiating Historical Injustices*, New York, 2000

Barnard, M., *Art, Design and Visual Culture: An Introduction*, London, 1998

Bartov, O., *Murder in our Midst: The Holocaust, Industrial Killing, and Representation*, Oxford, 1995

————, *Mirrors of Destruction: War, Genocide, and Modern Identity*, Oxford, 2000

Baxa, J., 'Fr. Schlegels Vorlesungen über die Geschichte der alten und neuen Literatur im Urteile der Wiener Polizeihofstelle', *Der Wächter* vol. 8, 1925–26: 354–59

Beck, U., 'The Cosmopolitan Perspective: Sociology of the Second Age of Modernity', *British Journal of Sociology* vol. 51, 2000: 79–105

Becker, W. and Schöll, N., *In jenen Tagen...: Wie der deutsche Nachkriegsfilm die Vergangenheit bewältigte*, Opladen, 1995

Beckermann, R., *Unzugehörig Juden und Österreicher nach 1945*, Vienna, 1989

Beidler, P., *The Good War's Greatest Hits: World War II and American Remembering*, Athens, 1998

————, *Late Thoughts on an Old War: The Legacy of Vietnam*, London, 2004

Bender, T., 'Strategies of Narrative Synthesis in American History', *American Historical Review* vol. 107, no. 1, 2002: 129–53

Bentley, J., 'Myths, Wagers, and Some Moral Implications of World History', *Journal of World History* vol. 16, no. 1, 2005: 51–82

Berger, S., *Inventing the Nation: Germany*, London, 2004

————, 'A Return to the National Paradigm? National History Writing in Germany, Italy, France and Britain, 1945 to the Present', *The Journal of Modern History* vol. 77, 2005: 629–678

————, ed., *Writing the Nation – Towards Global Perspectives*, Houndmills, 2007

———, Donovan, M. and Passmore, K., eds, *Writing National Histories: Western Europe since 1800*, London, 1999

——— and Lorenz, C., eds, *The Contested Nation: Ethnicity, Class, Religion and Gender in National Histories*, Houndmills, 2008

——— and Mycock, A., eds, *Europe and Its National Histories*, special edition of *Storia della Storiografia* vol. 50, no. 4, 2006

Berghahn, K., Fohrmann, J. and Schneider, H., *Kulturelle Repräsentationen des Holocaust in Deutschland und den Vereinigten Staaten*, New York, 2002

Bernstein, R., *The Restructuring of Social and Political Theory*, Philadelphia, 1976

Bevir, M., *The Logic of the History of Ideas*, Cambridge, 1999

———, 'Historical Explanation, Folk Psychology, and Narrative', *Philosophical Explorations* vol. 3, 2000: 152–68

———, 'On Tradition', *Humanitas* vol. 13, 2000: 28–53

———, 'Political Studies as Narrative and Science, 1880–2000', *Political Studies* vol. 54, 2006: 583–606

Bhaba, H., ed. *Nation and Narration*, London, 1990

Billard, P., *D'or et de palmes*, Paris, 1997

Billig, M., *Banal Nationalism*, London, 1995

Binyon, T.J., *Pushkin: A Biography*, London, 2002

Bischof, G., *Austria and the First Cold War, 1945–55: The Leverage of the Weak*, Basingstoke, 1999

——— and Pelinka, A., eds, *Austrian Historical Memory and National Identity*, Contemporary Austrian Studies 5, New Brunswick, NJ, 1997

Blanning, T.C.W., ed., *The Oxford Illustrated History of Modern Europe*, Oxford, 1996

Blaut, J.M., *The Colonizer's Model of the World: Geographical Diffusionism and Eurocentric History*, New York, 1993

Bohlman, P.V., *The Music of European Nationalism*, Santa Barbara, 2004.

Brewer, J., *The Common People and Politics 1750–1790s*, Cambridge, 1986

Brinks, J.H., Timms, E. and Rock, S., eds, *Nationalist Myths and the Modern Media: Cultural Identity in the Age of Globalisation*, London, 2005

Brobjer, T.H., 'Nietzsche's View of the Value of Historical Studies and Methods', *Journal of the History of Ideas* vol. 65, no. 2, 2004: 301–322

Bronfen, E., Erdle, B.R. and Weigel, S., eds, *Trauma – Zwischen Psychoanalyse und kulturellem Deutungsmuster*, Köln, 1999

Brown, M., ed., *The Uses of Literary History*, Durham, NC, 1995

Bude, H., *Das Altern einer Generation. Die Jahrgänge 1938–1948*, Frankfurt am Main, 1995

———, *Generation Berlin*, Berlin, 2001

Bunzl, M., 'On the Politics and Semantics of Austrian Memory: Vienna's Monument against War and Fascism', *History and Memory* vol. 7, no. 2, 1996: 7–40

Burke, P., *Eyewitnessing: The Use of Images as Historical Evidence*, London, 2001

Burrow, J., *Evolution and Society: A Study in Victorian Social Theory*, Cambridge, 1966

Burrow, J., *Whigs and Liberals: Continuity and Change in English Political Thought*, Oxford, 1988

Carr, D., Flynn, T.R. and Makkreel, R.A., eds, *The Ethics of History*, Evanston, IL, 2004

Chakrabarty, D., *Provincialising Europe: Postcolonial Thought and Historical Difference*, Princeton, 2000

Chatterjee, P., *The Nation and Its Fragments: Colonial and Postcolonial Histories*, Princeton, 1993

Chmielowski, P., *Historya Literatury Polskiej*, 6 vols, Warsaw, 1899–1900

Clark, C., 'Forging Identity: Beethoven's "Ode" as European Anthem', *Critical Inquiry* vol. 23, no. 4: 789–807

Cohen, R., 'History and Genre', *New Literary History* vol. 17, no. 2, 1986: 203–18

———, 'Introduction: Notes toward a Generic Reconstitution of Literary Study', *New Literary History* vol. 34, no. 3, 2003: v–xvi

Colley, L., *Britons: Forging the Nation 1707–1837*, New Haven, 1992

Collingwood, R.G., *The Idea of History*, Oxford, 1976

Collini, S., *Liberalism and Sociology: L.T. Hobhouse and Political Argument in England, 1880–1914*, Cambridge, 1979

———, *English Pasts: Essays in History and Culture*, Oxford, 1999

———, Whatmore, R. and Young, B., eds, *History, Religion, and Culture: British Intellectual History, 1750–1950*, Cambridge, 2000

———, Winch, D. and Burrow, J., *That Noble Science of Politics*, Cambridge, 1983

Collins, R., 'Concealing the Poverty of Traditional Historiography: Myth as Mystification in Historical Discourse', *Rethinking History* vol. 7, no. 3, 2003: 341–65

Colombat, A.P., *The Holocaust in French Film*, Metuchen, 1993

Confino, A., 'Introduction', *Histories and Memories of Twentieth-century Germany*, special edition of *History and Memory* vol. 17, nos. 1–2, 2005: 5–14

Conrad, M. and Finkel, A., *History of the Canadian Peoples*, Toronto, 2002

Cooper, D., *Satyajit Ray: Between Tradition and Modernity*, Cambridge, 2003

Cornelißen, C., Klinkhammer, L. and Schwentker, W., eds, *Erinnerungskulturen. Deutschland, Italien und Japan seit 1945*, Frankfurt am Main, 2003

Cornis-Pope, M. and Neubauer, J., eds, *History of Literary Cultures of East-Central Europe. Junctures and Disjunctures in the 19th and 20th Centuries*, Amsterdam, 2004

Corson, J.C., *A Bibliography of Sir Walter Scott*, Edinburgh, 1943

Cowan, E. and Gifford, D., ed., *The Polar Twins*, Edinburgh, 2001

Croker, J.W., *Stories Selected from the History of England from the Conquest to the Revolution: For children*, London, 1817

Culler, J., 'Anderson and the Novel', *Diacritics* vol. 29, no. 4, 1999: 20–39

Dachs, H., Gerlich, P. and Müller, W.C., eds, *Die Politiker. Karrieren und Wirken bedeutender Repräsentanten der Zweiten Republik*, Vienna, 1995

Danto, A.C., *Narration and Knowledge*, New York, 1985

Daughtry, J.M., 'Russia's New Anthem and the Negotiation of National Identity', *Ethnomusicology* vol. 47, no. 1: 42–67

Davies, N., *The Isles*, Oxford, 1999

Davis, N.Z., *Slaves on Screen: Film and Historical Vision*, Toronto, 2000

Deutsches Film Institut., ed., *Die Vergangenheit in der Gegenwart: Konfrontationen mit den Folgen des Holocaust im deutschen Nachkriegsfilm*, Frankfurt am Main, 2001

Dilthey, W., *Gesammelte Schriften* vol. 5, Stuttgart and Göttingen, 1964

Diner, D., *Beyond the Conceivable: Studies on Germany, Nazism and the Holocaust*, Berkeley, Los Angeles and London, 2000

———, ed., *Zivilisationsbruch: Denken nach Auschwitz*, Frankfurt am Main, 1988

Doneson, J., *The Holocaust in American Film*, Philadelphia, 1987

Douglas, L., *The Memory of Judgment: Making Law and History in the Trials of the Holocaust*, New Haven, CT, 2001

Douglas, R., *'Great Nations still Enchained': the Cartoonists' Vision of Empire 1848–1914*, London, 1993

Drewitz, I., *Gestern war heute. Hundert Jahre Gegenwart*, Düsseldorf, 1978

Duara, P., 'Knowledge and Power in the Discourse of Modernity', *Journal of Asian Studies* vol. 50, 1991: 67–83

Duffy, M., *The Englishman and the Foreigner: The English Satirical Print 1600–1832*, Cambridge, 1986

Duncan, I., *Modern Romance and Transformations of the Novel: The Gothic, Scott, Dickens*, Cambridge, 1992

Dürr, S., *Strategien nationaler Vergangenheitsbewältigung: Die Zeit der Occupation im französichen Film*, Tübingen, 2001

Edgerton, G.R., *Ken Burns's America*, New York, 2001

Einfalt, M., Jurt, J., Mollenhauer, D. and Pelzer, E., eds, *Konstrukte nationaler Identität: Deutschland, Frankreich und Großbritannien (19. und 20. Jahrhundert)*, Würzburg, 2002

Eley, G. and Grigor Suny, R., eds, *Becoming National: A Reader*, Oxford, 1996

Elias, A.J., *Sublime Desire: History and Post-1960s Fiction*, Baltimore, MD, 2001

Elias, N., *Über den Prozess der Zivilisation*, Frankfurt a.M., 1997

Ellwood, D. and Kroes, R., *Hollywood in Europe: Experiences of a Cultural Hegemony*, Amsterdam, 1994

Elsaesser, T., *New German Cinema*, London, 1989

———, Horwath, A. and King, N., eds, *The Last Great American Picture Show*, Amsterdam, 2004.

Engel, C., ed., *Geschichte des sowjetischen und russischen Films*, Stuttgart, 1999

Eriksonas, L., *National Heroes and National Identities: Scotland, Norway and Lithuania*, Brussels, 2004

Erll, A., *Kollektives Gedächtnis und Erinnerungskulturen: Eine Einführung*, Stuttgart, 2005

———, 'Re-writing as Re-visioning: Modes of Representing the "Indian Mutiny" in British Novels, 1857 to 2000', *EJES: European Journal of English Studies* vol. 10, no. 2, 2006: 163–185

Evans, M. and Lunn, K. *War and Memory in the Twentieth Century*, Oxford, 1997

Fairbank, J.K., Reischauer, E.O. and Craig, A.M., *East Asia: Tradition and Transformation*, Boston, 1976

Falkowska, J. and Haltof, M., *The New Polish Cinema*, Trowbridge, 2003

Fay, B., *Contemporary Philosophy of Social Science*, Oxford, 1996

Febvre, L., *A New Kind of History and Other Essays*, trans. K. Folca, New York, 1973

Felman, S. and Laub, D., *Testimony: Crises of Witnessing in Literature, Psychoanalysis, and History*, New York, 1992

Ferenc, T., *A magyar nemzeti irodalom története*, 2 vols, Pest, 1851. Rpt. Budapest, 1987

Ferrari, M. and Sternberg, R., eds, *Self-awareness: Its Nature and Development*, New York, 1998

Ferris, Ina., *The Achievement of Literary Authority: Gender, History, and the Waverley Novels*, Ithaca, NY, 1991

Finley, M., 'Myth, Memory, and History', *History and Theory* vol. 4, no. 3, 1965: 281–302

Flacke, M., ed., *Mythen der Nationen. Ein europäisches Panorama*, Munich, 1998

———, ed., *Mythen der Nationen. 1945: Arena der Erinnerungen*, 2 vols, Mainz, 2004

Flanzbaum, H., ed., *The Americanization of the Holocaust*, Baltimore, 1999

Fludernik, M., *Towards a 'Natural' Narratology*, London, 1996

Fogu, C., Kansteiner W. and Lebow, N., eds, *The Politics of Memory in Postwar Europe*, Durham, NC, 2006

Forbes, D., *Hume's Philosophical Politics*, Cambridge, 1975

Forte, D., *Das Muster*, Frankfurt am Main, 1992

———, *Der Junge mit den blutigen Schuhen*, Frankfurt am Main, 1995

———, *In der Erinnerung*, Frankfurt am Main, 1998

Fournier Lanzoni, R., *French Cinema: From Its Beginnings to the Present*, New York, 2002

Francis, D., *National Dreams: Myth, Memory and Canadian History*, Vancouver, BC, 1997

Francois, E., Siegrist, H. and Vogel, J., *Nation und Emotion: Deutschland und Frankreich im Vergleich 19. und 20. Jahrhundert*, Göttingen, 1995

Frank, A.G., *ReOrient: Global Economy in the Asian Age*, Berkeley, 1998

Franklin, H.B., *Vietnam and Other American Fantasies*, London, 2000

Freeman, J. and Millington, R., eds, *Hitchcock's America*, Oxford, 1999

Frey, H., *Louis Malle*, Manchester, 2004

Friedländer, S., *Reflets sur le Nazisme*, Paris, 1982

Friedrich, S., 'Erinnerung als Auslöschung: Zum Verhältnis zwischen kulturellen Gedächtnisräumen und ihrer medialen Vermittlung in Victor Hugos *Notre-Dame de Paris* und *Les misérables*', *Arcadia: Zeitschrift für vergleichende Literaturwissenschaft* vol. 40, no. 1, 2005: 61–78

Friese, H., ed., *Identities: Time, Difference and Boundaries*, Oxford, 2002

Frisch, M., ed., *A Shared Authority: Essays on the Craft and Meaning of Oral and Public History*, Albany, NY, 1990

Fritzsche, P., *Stranded in the Present: Modern Time and the Melancholy of History*, Cambridge, MA, 2004

Frohnen, B., 'Tradition, Habit, and Social Interaction: A Response to Mark Bevir', *Humanitas* vol. 14, 2001: 108–16

Fukuyama, F., *The End of History and the Last Man*, New York, 1992

Fulda, D., *Wissenschaft aus Kunst. Die Entstehung der modernen deutschen Geschichtsschreibung 1760–1860*, Berlin and New York, 1996

Gagnon, P., ed., *Historical Literacy: The Case for History in American Education*, New York, 1989

Garrity, J., *Step-daughters of England: British Women Novelists and the National Imaginary*, Manchester, 2003

Geary, P., *The Myth of Nations: The Medieval Origins of Europe*, Princeton, NJ, 2002

Geddie, W., *A Bibliography of Middle Scots Poets; with an Introduction on the History of Their Reputation*, Scottish Texts Society, Edinburgh, 1912

Gellner, E., *Nationalism*, New York, 1998

Gervais, M., *Ingmar Bergman: Magician and Prophet*, Montreal, 1999

Gillespie, D., *Russian Cinema*, Harlow and London, 2003

Gilroy, P., *There Ain't No Black in the Union Jack: The Cultural Politics of Race and Nation*, Chicago, 1991

———, *The Black Atlantic: Modernity and Double Consciousness*, London, 1993

Golsan, R., ed., *Fascism's Return: Scandal, Revision, and Ideology since 1980*, Lincoln, 1998

Gorman, J. 'Historians and Their Duties', *History and Theory* vol. 43, no. 4, 2004: 103–17

Gounarridou, K., ed., *Theatre and Nationalism*, New York, 2004

Grafton, A., *The Footnote: Curious History*, Harvard, 1997

Granatstein, J., *Who Killed Canadian History?*, Toronto, 1998

Green, J., *Taking History to Heart: The Power of the Past in Building Social Movements*, Amherst, MA, 2000

Grever, M. and Stuurman, S., eds, *Beyond the Canon: History for the 21ˢᵗ Century*, London, 2007

Habermas, J., *Die Normalität einer Berliner Republik*, Frankfurt am Main, 1995

Hacker, W., ed. *Warnung an Österreich. Neonazismus: Die Vergangenheit bedroht die Zukunft*, Vienna, Frankfurt am Main and Zürich, 1966

Hake, S., *German National Cinema*, London, 2002

Hames, P., *The Czechoslovak New Wave*, Berkeley, 1985

Hanisch, E., *Der lange Schatten des Staates. Österreichische Gesellschaftsgeschichte im 20. Jahrhundert*, Vienna, 1994

Hansen, M., 'Schindler's List is Not Shoah: The Second Commandment, Popular Modernism, and Public Memory', *Critical Inquiry* vol. 22, 1996: 292–312

Harlan, D., 'Ken Burns and the Coming Crisis of Academic History', *Rethinking History* vol. 7, no. 2, 2003: 169–92

Harley, J.B. and Woodward, D., eds, *The History of Cartography* vol. 1: *Cartography in Prehistoric, Ancient and Medieval Europe and the Mediterranean*, Chicago, 1987

Harper, S. and Porter, V., *British Cinema of the 1950s*, Oxford, 2003

Haskell, F., *History and Its Images*, New Haven, 1993

Häupl, M., Swoboda, H. and Pasterk, U., *Zum mahnenden Gedenken, in: Judenplatz Wien 1996. Wettbewerb Mahnmal und Gedenkstätte für die jüdischen Opfer des Naziregimes in Österreich 1938–1945*, Vienna, 1996

Hayward, S., *French National Cinema*, London, 1993

Heehs, P., 'Myth, History and Theory', *History and Theory* vol. 33, no. 1, 1994: 1–19

Heidegger, M., *Sein und Zeit*, Halle/Saale, 1927

Hempel, C., 'The Function of General Laws in History', *Journal of Philosophy* vol. 39, 1942: 35–48

Herder, J.G., *Johann Gottfried Herder Werke in zehn Bänden* vol. 3: *Volkslieder, Übertragungen, Dichtungen*, ed. Ulrich Gaier, Frankfurt am Main, 1990

Herrmann, R., Risse, T. and Brewer, M., eds, *Transnational Identities: Becoming European in the EU*, Lanham, 2004

Hettling, M., ed., *Volksgeschichten im Europa der Zwischenkriegszeit*, Göttingen, 2003

Hewison, R., *The Heritage Industry: Britain in a Climate of Decline*, London, 1987

Higson, A., 'The Concept of National Cinema', *Screen* vol. 30 no. 4, 1989: 39–47

Hilberg, R., *Die Vernichtung der europäischen Juden*, 3 vols, Frankfurt am Main, 1990

Hjort, M. and Mackenzie, S., eds, *Cinema and Nation*, London, 2000

Hobsbawm, E., *Nations and Nationalism since 1780: Programme, Myth, Reality*, Cambridge, 1990

——— and Ranger, T. *The Invention of Tradition*, Cambridge, 1983

Hodson, M.H., *Wallace; or, The Fight of Falkirk*, London, 1809

Hörisch, J., ed., *Mediengenerationen*, Frankfurt am Main, 1997

Horváth, J., *A magyar irodalom fejlődéstörténete*, Budapest, 1980

Hosking, G. and Schöpflin, G., eds, *Myths and Nationhood*, London, 1997

Huntington, S., *The Clash of Civilisations and the Remaking of the World*, New York, 1996

Hutcheon, L., *A Poetics of Postmodernism: History, Theory, Fiction*, New York, 1988

Iggers, G., *Geschichtswissenschaft im 20. Jahrhundert*, Göttingen, 1993

———, 'Historiography between Scholarship and Poetry: Reflections on Hayden White's Approach to Historiography', *Rethinking History* vol. 4, no. 3, 2000: 373–90

——— and von Moltke, K., eds, *The Theory and Practice of History*, Indianapolis and New York, 1973

Illies, F., *Generation Golf*, Berlin, 2000

Insdorf, A., *Indelible Shadows: Film and the Holocaust*, 2nd ed., Cambridge, 1989

Irwin-Zarecka, I., *Frames of Remembrance: The Dynamics of Collective Memory*, New Brunswick, NJ, 1994

Jameson, F., *The Political Unconscious: Narrative as a Socially Symbolic Act*, Ithaca, NY, 1981

———, 'Morus: The Generic Window', *New Literary History* vol. 34, no. 3, 2003: 431–51

Jamieson, J., ed., *The Bruce and Wallace: Published from Two Ancient Manuscripts Preserved in the Library of the Faculty of Advocates* vols 1–2, Edinburgh, 1820

Jeismann, M., *Auf Wiedersehen Gestern: Die deutsche Vergangenheit und die Politik von morgen*, Stuttgart, 2001

Jelínek, H., *Histoire de la Littérature Tchèque: Des origines à 1850* vol. 1, 5th ed., Paris, 1951

Jenkins, B. and Sofos, S.A. *Nation and Identity in Contemporary Europe*, London, 1996

Jenkins, K., ed., *The Postmodern History Reader*, London, 1997

Jones, E., *The English Nation: The Great Myth*, Stroud, UK, 1998

Jordan, S., ed., *Lexikon Geschichtswissenschaft. 100 Grundbegriffe*, Stuttgart, 2002

Juarrero, A., *Dynamics in Action: Intentional Behaviour as a Complex System*, Cambridge, MA, 1990

Judt, T., *Geschichte Europas von 1945 bis zur Gegenwart*, Munich and Vienna, 2006

Kaes, A., *From Hitler to Heimat: The Return of History as Film*, Cambridge, MA, 1989

Kalin, J., *The Films of Ingmar Bergman*, Cambridge, 2003

Kannapin, D., *Antifaschismus im Film der DDR: Defa Spielfilme 1945–1955/56*, Köln, 1997

Kannonier-Finster, W. and Ziegler, M., *Österreichisches Gedächtnis. Über Erinnern und Vergessen der NS-Vergangenheit*, 2nd ed., Vienna, Cologne and Weimar, 1997

Kansteiner, W., 'Entertaining Catastrophe: The Reinvention of the Holocaust in the Television of the Federal Republic of Germany', *New German Critique* vol. 90, 2003: 135–62

Keyserlingk, R.H., *Austria in World War II: An Anglo-American Dilemma*, Kingston, OT and Montreal, 1988

Kiš, D., (1983) *The Encyclopedia of the Dead*, trans. M.H. Heim, Evanston, IL, 1997

Klamper, E., 'Ein einig Volk von Brüdern. Vergessen und Erinnern im Zeichen des Burgfriedens', *Zeitgeschichte* vol. 24, nos. 5–6, 1997: 170–85

Klein, K.L., 'On the Emergence of Memory in Historical Discourse', *Representations* vol. 69, 2000: 127–50

Knigge, V. and Frei, N., eds, *Verbrechen erinnern. Die Auseinandersetzung mit Holocaust und Völkermord*, Munich, 2002

Knoch, H., *Die Tat als Bild: Die Fotografien des Holocaust in der deutschen Erinnerungskultur*, Hamburg, 2001

Koch, G., *Die Einstellung ist die Einstellung: Visuelle Konstruktionen des Judentums*, Frankfurt am Main, 1992

Komaromi, A., 'Wyspiański's *Wesele*: Poised on the Border', *Theatre Journal* vol. 54, 2002: 187–202

Koselleck, R. et al., eds, *Objektivität und Parteilichkeit in der Geschichtswissenschaft*, Munich, 1977

Kramer, L. and Maza, S., eds, *A Companion to Western Historical Thought*, Oxford 2002

Kronish, A., *World Cinema: Israel*, Trowbridge, 1996

Kurzke, H., *Hymnen und Lieder der Deutschen*, Mainz, 1990

Kushner, T., *The Holocaust and the Liberal Imagination: A Social and Cultural History*, Oxford, 1994

LaCapra, D., 'History and Genre: Comment', *New Literary History* vol. 17, no. 2, 1986: 219–21

———, *History and Memory after Auschwitz*, Ithaca, 1998

Landsberg, A., *Prosthetic Memory: The Transformation of American Remembrance in the Age of Mass Culture*, New York, 2004

Langford, P., *Englishness Identified: Manners and Character 1650–1850*, Oxford 2000

Lawton, A., *Before the Fall: Soviet Cinema in the Gorbachev Years*, 2nd ed., Xlibris, 2002

Lee, K-B., *A New History of Korea*. Eng. trans. E.W. Wagner and E.J. Shulz, Cambridge, MA, 1984

Leerssen, J., 'Nationalism and the Cultivation of Culture', *Nations and Nationalism* vol. 12, no. 4, 2006: 559–78

———, *National Thought in Europe: A Cultural History*, Amsterdam, 2006

Lentricchia, F. and McLaughlin, T., eds, *Critical Terms in Literary Study*, Chicago, 1995

Leo, A. and Reif-Spirek, P., eds, *Helden, Täter und Verräter: Studien zum DDR-Antifaschismus*, Berlin, 1999

Levine, B., *Who Built America*, New York, 1989

Levy, D. and Sznaider, N., *Erinnerung im globalen Zeitalter: Der Holocaust*, Frankfurt am Main, 2001

——— and ———, *The Holocaust and Memory in the Global Age*, Philadelphia, 2005

Lim, J-H., 'Chosenhantono Minzokushugido Kenryokuno Gensetsu' (Korean nationalism and the power discourse), Japanese trans. I. Ryuta, *Gendai Shiso* vol. 28, 2000: 126–44

———, 'Befreiung oder Modernisierung? Sozialismus als ein Weg der anti-westlichen Modernisierung in unterwickelten Ländern', *Beiträge zur Geschichte der Arbeiterbewegung* vol. 43, no. 2, 2001: 5–23

——— and Lee, S-S., eds, *Guksa ui Sinhwa rul Nomuseo* (Beyond the myth of national history), Seoul, 2004

——— and Sliwa, M., eds, *Polska i Korea: Proces modernizacji w perspektywie historycznej*, Cracow, 1997

Lord, A.B., *The Singer of Tales*, Cambridge, MA, 1960

Lorenz, C., 'Historical Knowledge and Historical Reality: A Plea for "Internal Realism"', *History and Theory* vol. 33, no. 3, 1994

———, *Konstruktion der Vergangenheit. Eine Einführung in die Geschichtstheorie*, Cologne, 1997

———, 'Can Histories Be True? Narrativism, Positivism and the "Metaphorical Turn"', *History and Theory* vol. 37, no. 3, 1998: 309–29

———, '"You Got Your History, I Got Mine": Some Reflections on the Possibility of Truth and Objectivity in History', *Österreichische Zeitschrift für Geschichtswissenschaften* vol. 10, no. 4, 1999: 563–84

Loshitzky, Y., *Identity Politics on the Israeli Screen*, Austin, 2001

Lukács, G., (1936–37) *The Historical Novel*, trans. H. Mitchell and S. Mitchell, Harmondsworth, 1981

Lyotard, J-F., *The Post-Modern Condition: A Report on Knowledge*, trans. G. Bennington and B. Massumi, Minneapolis, MN, 1984

Macaulay, T.B., *Critical, Historical and Miscellaneous Essays* vol. 1, New York, n.d.

MacDonald, S. and Fyfe, G. *Theorising Museums: Representing Identity and Diversity in a Changing World*, Oxford, 1996

McKay, I., 'The Liberal Order Framework: A Prospectus for a Reconnaissance of Canadian History', *Canadian Historical Review* vol. 81, no. 4, 2000: 620–1

McNeill, W., *Mythistory and Other Essays*, Chicago, 1985

———, *Keeping Together in Time: Dance and Drill in Human History*, Cambridge, MA, 1995

Mali, J., *Mythistory: The Making of a Modern Historiography*, Chicago, 2003

Maltby, R. and Stokes, M., *American Movie Audiences: From the Turn of the Century to the Early Sound Era*, London, 1999

Mandler, P., *Aristocratic Government in the Age of Reform: Whigs and Liberals, 1830–1852*, Oxford, 1990

———, *History and National Life*, London, 2002

———, *The English National Character: The History of an Idea from Edmund Burke to Tony Blair*, New Haven, 2006

Manzoni, A., (1850) *On the Historical Novel*, trans. S. Bermann, Lincoln, NB, 1983

Margalit, A., *The Ethics of Memory*, Cambridge, MA, 2002

Marßolek, I. and von Saldern, A., eds, *Radiozeiten: Herrschaft, Alltag, Gesellschaft (1924–1960)*, Potsdam, 1999

Marx, K., *Surveys from Exile, Political Writings* vol. 2, ed. D. Fernbach, New York, 1973

———, *Capital* vol. 1, trans. B. Fowkes, Harmondsworth, 1990

Matejka, L. and Pomorska, K., eds, *Readings in Russian Poetics*, Cambridge, MA, 1978

Megill, A., 'Fragmentation and the Future of Historiography', *American Historical Review* vol. 96, no. 3, 1991: 693–98

———, *Historical Knowledge, Historical Error: A Contemporary Guide to Practice*, Chicago, 2007

———, ed., *Rethinking Objectivity*, Durham, NC, 1994

Meyerhoff, H., ed., *The Philosophy of History in Our Time*, New York, 1959

Michalek, B. and Turay, F., *The Modern Cinema of Poland*, Bloomington, 1988

Michelet, J., (1872–74) *Histoire du dix-neuvième siècle*, ed. B. Leuillot, Paris, 1982

Millgate, J., *Walter Scott: The Making of the Novelist*, Toronto, 1984

Mitchell, T., ed., *Global Noise: Rap and Hip-Hop Outside the USA*, Middletown, CT, 2001

Mitten, R., *The Politics of Prejudice: The Waldheim Phenomenon in Austria*, San Francisco and Oxford, 1992

Momigliano, A., *The Classical Foundations of Modern Historiography*, Berkeley, 1990

Monk, C. and Sargeant, A., *British Historical Cinema*, London, 2002

Moretti, F., *Atlas of the European Novel 1800–1900*, London, 1999

Morris-Suzuki, T., *Reinventing Japan: Time, Space, Nation*, Armonk, NY, 1998

Murphy, M., 'Explanation, Causes, and Covering Laws', *History and Theory* vol. 25, 1986: 43–57

Murphy, R., ed., *The British Cinema Book*, 2nd ed., London, 2001

Nagao, N., *Kokuminkokkaron No Satei*, Korean trans. D.Y. Yoon, Seoul, 2002

Nandy, A., *The Intimate Enemy: Loss and Recovery of Self under Colonialism*, Delhi, 1983

Nash, G.B., Crabtree, C. and Dunn, R., *History on Trial: Culture Wars and the Teaching of the Past*, New York, 1997

Nathan, H., ed., *Israeli Folk Music: Songs of the Early Pioneers*, Madison, WI, 1994

Neame, R., with Cooper, B.R., *Straight from the Horses Mouth – Ronald Neame an Autobiography*, London, 2003

Nephi Smithson, R., *Augustin Thierry: Social and Political Consciousness in the Evolution of a Historical Method*, Geneva, 1973

Nettl, P., *National Anthems*, trans. A. Gode, 2nd ed., New York, 1967

Neugebauer, W. and Schwarz, P., *Der Wille zum aufrechten Gang. Offenlegung der Rolle des BSA bei der gesellschaftlichen Reintegration ehemaliger Nationalsozialisten*, Vienna, 2005

Niethammer, L., *Kollektive Identität: Heimliche Quellen einer unheimlichen Konjunktur*, Reinbek, 2000

Nietzsche, F., *Untimely Meditations*, trans. R.J. Hollingdale, 1874; Cambridge, 1983

——, *On the Genealogy of Morality: A Polemic*, trans., with notes, M. Clark and A.J. Swensen, 1887; Indianapolis, IN, 1998

Niv, K., *Life Is Beautiful but Not for Jews: Another View of the Film by Benigni*, Lanham, 2003

Niven, B., ed., *Germans as Victims: Remembering the Past in Contemporary Germany*, Houndmills, 2006

Nora, P., ed., *Les Lieux de mémoire*, 7 vols, Paris, 1984–92

——, *Realms of Memory: Rethinking the French Past* vols 1–3, ed. L.D. Kritzman, trans. A. Goldhammer, New York, 1996–1998

——, ed., *Zwischen Geschichte und Gedächtnis*, Berlin, 1990

Novick, P., *That Noble Dream: The 'Objectivity Question' and the American Historical Profession*, Cambridge, 1988

——, *The Holocaust in American Life*, Boston, 1999

Nowell Smith, G. and Ricci, S., eds, *Hollywood and Europe: Economics, Culture, National Identity 1945–1995*, London, 1998

Nünning, A., *Von historischer Fiktion zu historiographischer Metafiktion*, Trier, 1995

Olick, J.K. and Robbins, J. 'Social Memory Studies: From "Collective Memory" to the Historical Sociology of Mnemonic Practices', *Annual Review of Sociology* vol. 24, 1998: 105–40

Osborne, K., 'Teaching History in Schools: A Canadian Debate', *Journal of Curriculum Studies* vol. 35, no. 5, 2003: 585–626

Otáhal, M., 'The Manuscript Controversy in the Czech National Revival', *Cross Currents* vol. 5, 1986: 247–77

Palacký, F. and Šafařík, J., *Počátkové českého básnictví, obzvláště prozodie*, Prague, 1818

Panofsky, E., *Meaning in the Visual Arts: Papers in and on Art History*, Garden City, NY, 1957

Parsons, C., 'Sir Walter Scott: Yesterday and Today', *Proceedings of the American Philosophical Society* vol. 116, no. 6, 1972: 450–57

Paxton, R., *Vichy France: Old Guard and New Order 1940–1944*, New York, 1972

Pelinka, A., *Austria: Out of the Shadow of the Past*, Boulder, CO, 1998

Perkins, D., ed., *Theoretical Issues in Literary History*, Cambridge, MA, 1991

Petersen, J., 'How British Television Inserted the Holocaust into Britain's War Memory in 1995', *Historical Journal of Film, Radio, and Television* vol. 21, 2001: 255–72

Pick, H., *Guilty Victim: Austria from the Holocaust to Haider*, London, 2000

Pittock, M., ed., *The Reception of Sir Walter Scott in Europe*, The Athlone Critical Traditions Series: The Reception of British Authors in Europe, London, 2006

Platt, K. et al., eds, *Generation und Gedächtnis. Erinnerungen und kollektive Identitäten*, Opladen, 1995

Popper, K., *The Poverty of Historicism*, London, 1957

Porter, R.S., 'Seeing the Past', *Past and Present* vol. 118, 1988: 186–205

Prakash, G., 'AHR Forum: Subaltern Studies as Postcolonial Criticism', *American Historical Review* vol. 99, 1994

Ramnarine, T.K., *Ilmatar's Inspirations: Nationalism, Globalization, and the Changing Soundscapes of Finnish Folk Music*, Chicago, 2003

Raphael, L., *Geschichtswissenschaft im Zeitalter der Extreme*, Munich, 2003

Raskin, R., *Nuit et Brouillard: On the Making, Reception and Function of a Major Documentary Film*, Aarhus, 1987

Reichel, P., *Erfundene Erinnerung: Weltkrieg und Judenmord in Film und Theater*, München, 2004

Reulecke, J. and Müller-Luckner, E., eds, *Generationalität und Lebensgeschichte im 20. Jahrhundert*, Munich, 2003

Rice, L., 'The Voice of Silence: Alain Resnais' *Night and Fog* and Collective Memory in Post-Holocaust France, 1944–1974', *Film and History* vol. 32, 2002: 22–29

Rich, P., *Race and Empire in British Politics*, Cambridge, 1986

Richards, J., *Films and British National Identity: From Dickens to 'Dad's Army'*, Manchester, 1997

Ricoeur, P., *Memory, History, Forgetting*, Chicago, 2004

Rigney, A., *Imperfect Histories: The Elusive Past and the Legacy of Romantic Historicism*, Ithaca, NY, 2001

———, 'Portable Monuments: Literature, Cultural Memory, and the Case of Jeanie Deans', *Poetics Today* vol. 25, no. 2, 2004: 361–96

———, 'Scarcity, Plenitude and the Circulation of Cultural Memory', *Journal of European Studies* vol. 35, nos. 1–2, 2005: 209–26

Robertson, F., *Legitimate Histories: Scott, Gothic, and the Authorities of Fiction*, Oxford, 1994

Rosenstone, R.A., *Visions of the Past: The Challenge of Film to Our Idea of History*, Cambridge, 1995

Rosenthal, G., ed., *Die Hitlerjugend-Generation. Biographische Thematisierung als Vergangenheitsbewältigung*, Essen, 1986

Rosenzweig, R. and Thelen, D., *Presence of the Past: Popular Uses of History in American Life*, New York, 1998

Ross, S., ed., *Movies and American Society*, Oxford, 2002

Roth, P., 'Narrative Explanation: The Case of History', *History and Theory* vol. 27, 1988: 1–13

Rousso, H., *The Vichy Syndrome: History and Memory in France since 1944*, Cambridge, MA, 1991

Ryan, M-L., *Narrative as Virtual Reality: Immersion and Interactivity in Literature and Electronic Media*, Baltimore, MD, 2001

Said, E., *Orientalism*, New York, 1979

St Clair, W., *The Reading Nation in the Romantic Period*, Cambridge, 2004

Sakai, N., *Translation and Subjectivity: On 'Japan' and Cultural Nationalism*, Minneapolis, 1997

Samuel, R., *Theatres of Memory*, London, 1994

——, *Theatres of Memory* vol. 2: *Island Stories: Unravelling Britain*, London, 1999

——, ed., *Patriotism: The Making and Unmaking of British National Identity* vol. 1: *History and Politics*, London, 1989

Samuels, M., *The Spectacular Past: Popular History and the Novel in Nineteenth-century France*, New York, 2004

de Sanctis, F., *Storia della letteratura italiana* vol. 2, Bari, 1925

Sandwell, R., 'The Limits of Liberalism: The Liberal Reconnaissance and the History of the Family in Canada', *Canadian Historical Review* vol. 84, no. 3, 2003: 423–45

Sang-jung, K., *Orientalism No Kanatae* (Beyond Orientalism), Korean trans. S.M. Lim, Seoul, 1997

Schlesinger, Jr, A., *The Disuniting of America*, New York, 1992

Schmid, A., *Korea between Empires 1895–1919*, New York, 2002

Schmitz, W., ed., *Erinnerte Shoah: Die Literatur der Überlebenden*, Dresden, 2003

Scholz, G., *Zwischen Wissenschaftsanspruch und Orientierungsbedürfnis. Zu Grundlage und Wandel der Geisteswissenschaften*, Frankfurt am Main, 1991

Schöttler, P., ed., *Geschichtsschreibung als Legitimationswissenschaft 1918–1945*, Frankfurt am Main, 1997

Schwab-Trapp, M., *Kriegsdiskurse: Die politische Kultur des Krieges im Wandel 1991–1999*, Opladen, 2002

Scott, J., 'History in Crisis? The Other Side of History', *American Historical Review* vol. 94, 1989: 680–92

Scott, W., 'Culloden Papers', *The Quarterly Review* vol. 28, art. 1, 1816

——, *The History of Scotland from the Earliest Period to the Close of the Rebellion 1745–46, Contained in Tales of a Grandfather*, Edinburgh, 1836

Segel, H., *Stranger in Our Midst: Images of the Jews in Polish Literature*, Ithaca, 1996

Seixas, P., ed., *Theorizing Historical Consciousness*, Toronto, 2004

Shandler, J., *While America Watches: Televising the Holocaust*, Oxford, 1999

Shelton, D.L., ed., *Encyclopedia of Genocide and Crimes against Humanity* vol. 1, New York, 2004

Shlapentokh, D. and Shlapentokh, V., *Soviet Cinematography 1918–1991: Ideological Conflict and Social Reality*, New York, 1993

Slaveikov, P., *Săbrani săchineniya* vol. 5, Sofia, 1958–59

Smith, A.D., *The Nation in History: Historiographical Debates about Ethnicity and Nationalism*, Cambridge, 2000

Sobchack, V., *The Persistence of History: Cinema, Television, and the Modern Event*, New York and London, 1996

Soila, T., Söderbergh-Widding, A. and Iversen, G., *Nordic National Cinema*, London, 1998

Sorlin, P., *European Cinema, European Societies 1939–1999*, London, 1991

———, *Italian National Cinema*, London, 1996

Stapleton, J., *Englishness and the Study of Politics: The Social and Political Thought of Ernest Barker*, Cambridge, 1994

———, *Political Intellectuals and Public Identities in Britain since 1850*, Manchester, 2001

———, *Sir Arthur Bryant and National History in Twentieth Century Britain*, Lanham, MD, 2005

Starowicz, M., *Making History: The Remarkable Story behind Canada – a People's History*, Toronto, 2003

Stern, F., *The Whitewashing of the Yellow Badge: Antisemitism and Philosemitism in Postwar Germany*, Oxford, 1992

———, ed., *The Varieties of History: From Voltaire to the Present*, 2nd ed., New York, 1972

Stokes, M., ed., *Ethnicity, Identity and Music: The Musical Construction of Place*, Oxford, 1994

——— and Maltby, R., *Identifying Hollywood's Audiences: Cultural Identity and the Movies*, London, 1999

Suleiman, S., *Authoritarian Fictions: The Ideological Novel as a Literary Genre*, New York, 1983

Sultana, D.E., *From Abbotsford to Paris and Back: Sir Walter Scott's Journey*, Stroud, UK, 1993

Szerb, A., *Magyar irodalomtörténet*, 2 vols, Cluj/Kolozsvár, 1934

Tacke, C., *Denkmal im sozialen Raum: Nationale Symbole in Deutschland und Frankreich im 19. Jahrhundert*, Göttingen, 1995

Tajfel, H., *Human Groups and Social Categories*, Cambridge, 1981

Tanaka, S., *Japan's Orient: Rendering Pasts into History*, Berkeley, 1993

Tanner, J. and Weigel, J., eds, *Gedächtnis, Geld und Gesetz. Vom Umgang mit der Vergangenheit des Zweiten Weltkriegs*, Zürich, 2002

Taylor, R., Wood, N., Graffy, J. and Iordanova, D., eds, *The BFI Companion to Eastern European and Russian Cinema*, London, 2000

Thiele, M., *Publizistische Kontroversen über den Holocaust im Film*, Münster, 2001

Tibebu, T., 'On the Question of Feudalism, Absolutism and the Bourgeois Revolution', *Review* vol. 13, 1990: 49–152

Tilly, C., *Coercion, Capital, and European States, 990–1990*, Cambridge, MA, 1992

Torstendahl, R. and Veit-Brause, I., eds, *History-making: The Intellectual and Social Formation of a Discipline*, Stockholm, 1996

Toubiana, S., *Cannes-Cinéma: Cinquante ans de festival vus par Traverso*, Paris, 1997

Trimborn, J., *Der deutsche Heimatfilm der fünfziger Jahre: Motive, Symbole und Handlungsmuster*, Köln, 1998

Trumpener, K., *Bardic Nationalism: The Romantic Novel and the British Empire*, Princeton, 1997

Turan, K., *Sundance to Sarajevo: Film Festivals and the World They Made*, London, 2002

Turino, T., *Nationalists, Cosmopolitans, and Popular Music in Zimbabwe*, Chicago, 2000

Turner, B.S., *Orientalism, Postmodernism and Globalism*, London, 1994

Uhl, H., ed., *Steinernes Bewusstsein. Die öffentliche Repräsentation staatlicher und nationaler Identität Österreichs in seinen Denkmälern* vol. 2, Vienna, Cologne and Weimar, 2006

Ungurianu, D., 'Fact and Fiction in the Romantic Historical Novel', *Russian Review* vol. 57, no. 3, 1998: 380–93

Utgaard, P., *Remembering and Forgetting Nazism: Education, National Identity, and the Victim Myth in Postwar Austria*, New York and Oxford, 2003

Valenti, V. and Willemen, P., eds, *Theorising National Cinema*, London, 2006

Vanvugt, E., *De maagd en de soldaat: koloniale monumenten in Amsterdam en elders*, Amsterdam, 1998

Vaughan Williams, R., *National Music*, London, 1934

Verković, S., *Veda Slovena. Le Veda Slave. Chants populaire des Bulgares de Thrace & de Macédonie de l'époque préhistorique & préchretienne* vol. 1, Belgrade, 1874

———, *Veda Slovena. Le Veda Slave. Chants populaire des Bulgares de Thrace & de Macédonie de l'époque préhistorique & préchretienne* vol. 2, St Petersburg, 1881

Veyne, P., *Comment on écrit l'histoire, suivi de Foucault révolutionne l'histoire*, Paris, 1978

Wackwitz, S., *Ein unsichtbares Land. Ein Familienroman*, Frankfurt am Main, 2003

Walicki, A., *A History of Russian Thought*, Oxford, 1979

Walsh, M., 'National Cinema, National Imaginary', *Film History* vol. 8, 1996: 5–17

Wang, E.Q., ed., *The Many Faces of Clio: Cross-cultural Approaches to Historiography. Festschrift for Georg G. Iggers*, Oxford, 2006

———, Fillafer, F. and Iggers, G., eds, *Turning Points in Historiography: A Cross-cultural Comparison*, Rochester, 2002

Warner, M., *Monuments and Maidens: The Allegory of the Female Form*, London, 1985

Wassermann, H.P., *'Zuviel Vergangenheit tut nicht gut!' Nationalsozialismus im Spiegel der Tagespresse der Zweiten Republik*, Innsbruck, Vienna and Munich, 2000

Wegner, R., ed., *Kunst – die andere Natur*, Göttingen, 2004

Weigel, S., *Genea-Logik. Generation, Tradition und Evolution zwischen Kultur- und Naturwissenschaften*, München, 2006

——— and Erdle, B.R., eds, *50 Jahre danach. Zur Nachgeschichte des Nationalsozialismus*, Zürich, 1995

Weintraub, A.N., *Power Plays: Wayang Golek Puppet Theater of West Java*, Athens, OH and Singapore, 2004

Wende, W., ed., *Geschichte im Film: Mediale Inszenierungen des Holocaust und kulturelles Gedächtnis*, Stuttgart, 2002

Wenzel, E., *Gedächnisraum Film: Die Arbeit an der deutschen Geschichte in Filmen seit den sechziger Jahren*, Stuttgart, 2000

Werbner, P. and Modood, T., eds, *Debating Cultural Hybridity*, London, 1997

Wesseling, E., *Writing History as a Prophet: Postmodernist Innovations of the Historical Novel*, Amsterdam, 1991

White, H., *The Content of the Form: Narrative Discourse and Historical Representation*, Baltimore, MD, 1987

Williams, A., ed., *Film and Nationalism*, New Jersey, 2002

Wilmer, S.E., ed., *Writing and Rewriting National Theatre Histories*, Iowa City, 2004

Wilson, D., *The Life and Times of Vuk Štefanović Karadžić 1787–1864*, Oxford, 1970

Wintle, M.J., 'Renaissance Maps and the Construction of the Idea of Europe', *The Journal of Historical Geography* vol. 25, no. 2, 1999: 137–65

———, *The Image of Europe: The Portrayal of Europe in Cartography and Iconography throughout the Ages*, Cambridge, 2007

Witkiewicz, S., *Matejko*, Lwow, 1912

Wolfgram, M., 'West German and Unified German Cinema's Difficult Encounter with the Holocaust', *Film and History* vol. 32, no. 2, 2002: 24–37

Woolf, D., ed., *A Global Encyclopedia of Historical Writing* vol. 2, New York and London, 1998

Yamanouchi, Y. et al., eds, *Total War and 'Modernization'*, Ithaca, 1998

Zerubavel, E., *Time Maps: Collective Memory and the Social Shape of the Past*, Chicago, 2003

Zerubavel, Y., *Recovered Roots: Collective Memory and the Making of Israeli National Tradition*, Chicago, 1995

Zimmerman, J., *Whose America? Culture Wars in the Public Schools*, Cambridge, 2002

Zinn, H., *A People's History of the United States*, New York, 2003

Index